Cornerstone of the Nation

Harvard East Asian Monographs 467

Cornerstone of the Nation

The Defense Industry and the Building of Modern Korea under Park Chung Hee

Peter Banseok Kwon

Published by the Harvard University Asia Center
Distributed by Harvard University Press
Cambridge (Massachusetts) and London 2024

Published by the Harvard University Asia Center, Cambridge, MA 02138

The Harvard University Asia Center publishes a monograph series and, in coordination with the Fairbank Center for Chinese Studies, the Korea Institute, the Reischauer Institute of Japanese Studies, and other facilities and institutes, administers research projects designed to further scholarly understanding of China, Japan, Korea, Vietnam, and other Asian countries. The Center also sponsors projects addressing multidisciplinary, transnational, and regional issues in Asia.

Library of Congress Cataloging-in-Publication Data

Names: Kwon, Peter Banseok, author.
Title: Cornerstone of the nation : the defense industry and the building of modern Korea under Park Chung Hee / Peter Banseok Kwon.
Other titles: Defense industry and the building of modern Korea under Park Chung Hee | Harvard East Asian monographs ; 467.
Description: Cambridge : Harvard University Asia Center, 2024. | Series: Harvard East Asian monographs ; 467 | Includes bibliographical references and index. |
Identifiers: LCCN 2023042573 | ISBN 9780674293823 (hardcover); 9780674297135 (paperback)
Subjects: LCSH: Park, Chung Hee, 1917–1979. | Defense industries—Korea (South)—History—20th century. | Militarization—Korea (South)—History—20th century. | Korea (South)—Politics and government—1960–1988. | Korea (South)—History—1960–1988. | Korea (South)—Military policy.
Classification: LCC DS922.25 .K97 2023 | DDC 320.9519509/04—dc23/eng/20231107
LC record available at https://lccn.loc.gov/2023042573

Index by Anne Holmes

Printed on acid-free paper
Printed in the United States of America

For Suji

Contents

Figures and Tables

Figures

Tables

Acknowledgments

My journey studying the Korean defense industry began around twelve years ago when I was conducting field research in South Korea as a PhD student from Harvard University. During my visit to the Presidential Archives in Seongnam, for a different research project, I stumbled on a trove of recently declassified documents on South Korea's secret weapons programs in the 1970s. Fascinated by these new archival records, I was immediately drawn to explore the history of South Korea's military modernization. I soon realized that piecing together this history was akin to solving a jigsaw puzzle with a significant portion of the pieces missing, due to the scant documentary evidence available on the Korean defense industry. However, the challenge only made me more curious.

As I mulled over a fitting title to encapsulate the essence of my research, I noted the words of President Park Chung Hee. He had described the Agency for Defense Development (ADD)—an institution he founded for weapons R & D—as "the cornerstone of the national defense" (*kukpang ŭi ch'osŏk*). As I delved deeper into my research, it dawned on me that the defense industry's growth had far-reaching impacts, significantly shaping South Korea's economic, industrial, political, and cultural landscape. This realization led me to modify Park's phrase, and thus I adopted "cornerstone of *the nation*" (*kukka ŭi ch'osŏk*) as the title of this book.

Now, more than a decade after my fateful encounter with those declassified military records, I have documented the fascinating story of the Korean defense industry in the pages of this book. I am filled with humility and gratitude, knowing that this endeavor would not have been possible without divine intervention, boundless grace, and the steadfast support of my colleagues, friends, and family members.

I am thankful for the earliest influences on my academic career. My heartfelt appreciation goes to my PhD adviser at Harvard University, Carter J. Eckert, whose unwavering support and sage advice have been my guiding compass through the twists and turns of this work. I am also deeply indebted to Sun Joo Kim for fostering my intellectual and personal development at Harvard, and for her invaluable insights, which greatly honed the dissertation on which this book is based. My deep thanks extend to Andrew Gordon, whose astute feedback on my dissertation helped me understand the complex interplay between Japan's and South Korea's developmental histories. Moreover, I am immensely grateful to Hyung-A Kim of Australian National University. Her generosity in sharing her extensive knowledge of South Korea's heavy and chemical industrialization, in addition to facilitating introductions through her network, was invaluable in the data-gathering process.

At Harvard, I thank Myong Chandra, Paul Yunsik Chang, Catherine Glover, Nicholas Harkness, Chris Kim, Jina Kim, Susan Laurence, and Si Nae Park of the Korea Institute; Margaret Lindsey of the Regional Studies–East Asia program; and Jim Zigo of the Department of East Asian Languages and Civilizations for their warm support. Gratitude is also due to my undergraduate mentors, Dorothy Solinger, Robert Uriu, and Duncan Williams, for inspiring my early passion for East Asian studies. Additionally, my sincere thanks go to Ruth Barraclough, Ellie Choi, Bruce Cumings, Todd Henry, Ingu Hwang, Kyung Moon Hwang, Immanuel Kim, Jisoo Kim, Michael Kim, Taeyang Kwak, Hyunjoon Park, James Lee, Ji-Eun Lee, Sung-Yoon Lee, Youngju Ryu, Andre Schmid, Clark Sorensen, Maya Stiller, and other scholars in the Korean studies field who played an important role in my growth as an academic.

The following individuals offered me detailed comments on the manuscript: Anthony DeBlasi, Inga Kim Diederich, John DiMoia, Carter Eckert, Susanna Fessler, Dong-Won Kim, Jiyul Kim, Sung Eun Kim, Jong-Dae Shin, Balázs Szalontai, and Will Thomas. The Nam Center for Korean Studies at the University of Michigan hosted a book workshop in May 2022 at which I received valuable in-person feedback from two excellent peer reviewers, Mitchell Lerner and Kongdan Oh-Hassig. In addition, three anonymous readers solicited by the Harvard Asia Center enriched this work with their remarks. Scholars who influenced the shaping of the book through their critiques of my dissertation drafts, articles, conference presentations, and other research work include Gregg Brazinsky, Patrick Chung, John Duncan, Cai Jian, Bee Yun Jo, Katherine Moon, Seungsook Moon, Hwasook Nam, Albert Park, Eugene Park, Tae Gyun Park, Sang-young Rhyu, and Sem Vermeersch. I am also grateful to my former teachers at Harvard, who contributed to my academic and intellectual growth as a scholar, including Deborah Anker, Helen Hardacre, Tomoko Kitagawa, Shigehisa Kuriyama, David McCann, Michael Puett, Anthony Saich, and Hue-Tam Ho Tai.

I spent several years in South Korea doing research for this book. Gaining valuable information on the Korean defense industry would have been impossible without the trust, generosity, and kindness of many people. I am profoundly grateful to the following scholars in South Korea: Chang Wonsuk, Choi Hyungsub, Do Jein, Ha Young-Sun, Han Do Hyun, Hong Doo-Seung, Kang Azariah, Kim Jin Ki, Lee Dongwon, Lee Mi-sook, Lee Sang-ho, Lee Sinjae, Lee Wanbom, Moon Kyounghee, Park Dong Chan, Park Eun Mee, Park Myunglim, Park Young June, Shim Kyongwook, Ueyama Yurika, and Um Jungsik.

I am grateful to Kim Kwangmo and the late Kim Chung-yum, both of whom as former policymakers under President Park Chung Hee offered deep insights and important data that shaped my analysis. I extend sincere thanks to Kim Ch'angsik of the ADD for sharing his remarkable stories and connecting me with his former colleagues in the agency. I am also indebted to the following scientists and former directors of the ADD for agreeing to be interviewed: An Tongman (Ahn Dongmhan), Chŏng Hongyong, Kim Pyŏnggyo, Kim Yŏngsu, Ku Sanghoe, Pak Ch'angkyu, Yi Kyŏngsŏ, and one anonymous interviewee. I would also like to thank Kim Inho of the ADD for sharing the official publications by the ADD with me. My sincerest gratitude also goes to Min Pyŏngman and Yi Ch'anggi of Hanwha for their interviews and for introducing me to former Hanwha colleagues whom I was also able to interview. In addition, I would like to express my deep appreciation to Kim Seungyeon, the chairman of Hanwha Group, as well as Hanwha's Hwang Jin Woo, Kim Jin Song, Kim Young-Jin, and Lee Sang Muk.

I am grateful to former workers at Kia, Daewoo, Poongsan, Samsung, Tongil, and Hyundai who agreed to be interviewed for this research. I owe special thanks to Yu Hansik, a first-generation skilled worker at Kia and former president of EM Korea, for his interviews and for connecting me with others who worked at Korean defense plants in Ch'angwŏn in the 1970s. Hwang Ilhong of the Presidential Archives in Sejong and Chung Okhee of the National Archives of Korea in Taejŏn provided critical help in gathering Korean government documents. I would also like to thank Pak Kwanil, director of the Koreatown Senior and Community Center in Los Angeles, Casper Claussen, Ji-Won Lee, and my parents-in-law, Kim Gwangsu and Park Youngja, for their assistance with my surveys in South Korea and the United States.

To my inestimable colleagues in the Department of East Asian Studies at the University at Albany—Andrew Byon, Dorothy Chauvin, Fan Pen Chen, Anthony DeBlasi, Susanna Fessler, Chamanka Gamage, Jim Hargett, Charles Hartman, Devin Jinadasa, Jinny Kang Mason, John Person, Aaron Proffitt, Fang Wang, and Michiyo Wojnovich—thank you for your encouragement, camaraderie, generosity, and kindness. Additionally, I want to add a special note of thanks to all of my students at the University at Albany, both past and present.

I am deeply grateful to the editors and others who have helped me bring this book to print, particularly the staff of the Harvard Asia Center's Publications Program, its director Kristen Wanner, former director Bob Graham, Daniel Seungchurl Lee (Japan/Korea editor), and the members of the Executive Committee. Their support and assistance have made this book a reality. I am forever indebted to Julie Hagen and Andrea Rupert for their editorial input, keen insights, and support in bringing the story of the South Korean defense industry to life. Kristen Wanner and Angela Piliouras at Westchester Publishing Services oversaw the final copyediting and typesetting for the book. I would also like to thank Sungik Yang and Elisa Sujin Han for their editorial assistance in the romanization of Korean references in the bibliography.

I am grateful for the support I received from the Association for Asian Studies through the 2022–23 AAS Publication Support Grant, as well as from the 2023 Korean Studies Grant Program of the Academy of Korean Studies (AKS-2023-P-002), for the publication of this manuscript. The Academy of Korean Studies in South Korea provided two fellowships that helped fund my field research in 2012 and 2017, for which I am also grateful. The Soon Young Kim Postdoctoral Fellowship in Korean Studies at Harvard afforded me the invaluable opportunity to focus on my writing and field research during the academic year 2017–18. I am sincerely appreciative of support I received from the Foreign Language and Area Studies (FLAS) Fellowships Program of the US Department of Education, the Institute of Korean Studies at Yonsei University, the Kyujanggak Institute for Korean Studies at Seoul National University, and the Korea Institute, Regional Studies–East Asia program, and Department of East Asian Languages and Civilizations at Harvard. I thank the editors and publishers of the *Seoul Journal of Korean Studies* (Kyujanggak Institute), *Journal of Asian Studies* (Duke University Press/Cambridge University Press), *Korea Journal* (Academy of Korean Studies), and *Journal of Korean Studies* (Duke University Press) for granting me permission to use portions of my previously published articles in this book.

The following friends and family members all played a special role in getting me to where I am today: Grace An, Jason Ahn, Jinah Ahn, David Byun, Harrel Carmen, Charlie Cho, Taeho Cho, Gyusam Choi, Andrew Choo, Steven Chow, Elbright Eum, John Fonseca, Joshua Ha, Inhye Han, Jamie Han, Waranon Hanchaiyasri, Shennon Ho, Seungeui Hong, Insoo Hwang, Sam Jin, Grace Jo, Yeonsil Kang, Yungmee Kang, Brian Kim, David Kim, Han Yeup Kim, Israel Kim, Jin-ji Kim, Jungsook Kim, Kevin Kim, Minsu Kim, Moon Kim, Samuel Kim, Soyoon Kim, Su-kyung Kim, Youngseok Kim, Daniel Ko, Ilbum Kwak, Boyoung Kwon, Dongik Kwon, Jayoung Kwon, Fun Lau, Anthony Lee, Jude Lee, Ryan Lee, Mike Lesnick, Isabel Lim, An Linjing, Yanling Liu, Matthew Lynch, Ashley Mann, Myles Mann, Tommy McGrail, Chen Meng, Roberto Miranda, Jinwook Nam, Daniel Oh, Justin O'Neill, Dooyong Pai, James Park, Jessie Park, Joshua Park, Lauren Park, Mike Park, Sonya Park, George Popovac, Gregory Ring, Eliud Sandoval, Casey Shotwell, Yunsik Son, John Suh, Terry Um, Neal Wang, Jude Wolf, Aeon Wood, Onejin Wu, Masutsugu Yamamoto, Jaeduk Yi, Hyoungsik Yim, Jason Yoon, and Minhong Yoon.

I am also grateful to my graduate school colleagues, who were pivotal in my personal and intellectual growth, including Victor Ban, Timothy Benedict, Peter Blair, Wenjiao Cai, Javier Cha, Dongyeon Cho, Ilsoo Cho, Yutin Dong, Philip Gant, Kwan Woo Hahn, Andrew Hong, Jane Hong, Jessica Hong, Sejong Hong, Christie Jeon, Hyeok Hweon Kang, Sara Kang, Gene Kim, Il-hoon Kim, John Kim, Moon

Kim, Lami Kim, Nuri Kim, Amy Lee, Anna Jung-eun Lee, Jessica Lee, John Lee, Josie Lee, SangJae Lee, Katy Matsuzaki, Ian Miller, Yuka Minagawa, Vernie Oliveiro, Alejandro Perdomo, Jia Kai Phua, Graeme Reynolds, Yongwook Ryu, Victor Seow, Aeri Shin, Jae-ho Shin, David Shuster, Keebaik Sim, Caron Suh, Qiaomei Tang, Michael Tworek, Xiyue Wang, Jongsik Christian Yi, Wonwoo Yi, Jamie Yoo, Seungmin Yoo, Jennifer Yum, and Zhang Zhan. There are too many others to name, and some I may have unintentionally failed to mention here, without whom this book would not have been possible.

To my wife, Suji, thank you for bearing with the countless hours I spent writing and revising, for your selfless reading and critical appraisal of early drafts of this book, and for keeping the munchkins away from my computer. To my daughters, Kallah and Serenity, thank you for your munchkin love, laughter, and all the ways you remind me of the most important reasons for my work. To my parents, John and Maria Kwon, thank you for your prayers and support as I try to make good on the principles that you instilled in me. I also thank my extended family members, Andy and Holden Rupert.

The year 2024 holds great historical significance, as it marks the fiftieth anniversary of the inception of the Yulgok Operation in 1974—a key initiative spearheaded by President Park to forge South Korea's path toward arms independence under his policy of self-reliant national defense. To me, it is both fitting and fortuitous that this book comes to fruition in such a momentous year.

PBK
Albany, New York

Abbreviations

ADD	Agency for Defense Development
CIA	Central Intelligence Agency (US)
CIL	Canadian Industries Limited
DAPA	Defense Acquisition Program Administration
DIPC	Defense Industry Promotion Council
DMZ	Demilitarized Zone
DPRK	Democratic People's Republic of Korea
EPB	Economic Planning Board
FIP	Force Improvement Plan
FMS	Foreign Military Sales
FNVM	Factory New Village Movement
FOIA	Freedom of Information Act (US)
FRUS	*Foreign Relations of the United States*, by US Department of State
FYEDP	Five-Year Economic Development Plan
GFRI	government-funded research institute
GNP	gross national product
HCI	heavy and chemical industrialization
HCI Policy	Heavy and Chemical Industrialization Policy
HGKK	*Han'gukhyŏng kyŏngje kŏnsŏl* [The South Korean model of economic development], by O Wŏnch'ŏl
HHI	Hyundai Heavy Industries
HIK	*Hanwha Inch'ŏn Kongjang 50-yŏn* [Fifty years of Hanwha Inch'ŏn factory], by Hanwha Inch'ŏn Kongjang 50-yŏn P'yŏnch'an Wiwŏn

HPPP	History and Public Policy Program, Wilson Center Digital Archive, Woodrow Wilson Center for International Scholars, Washington, DC
HRF	Homeland Reserve Forces
IISS	International Institute for Strategic Studies
JCS	Joint Chiefs of Staff
JUSMAG–K	Joint US Military Affairs Group–Korea
KAERI	Korea Atomic Energy Research Institute
KAIS	Korea Advanced Institute of Science
KIST	Korea Institute of Science and Technology
KKYS	*Kukpang Kwahak Yŏn'gusosa* [The history of the Agency for Defense Development], by Kukpang Kwahak Yŏn'guso
KPA	Korean People's Army
KS	Korean Industrial Standards
KWP	Korean Workers' Party
MAP	Military Assistance Program (US)
MCI	Ministry of Commerce and Industry
MIC	military-industrial complex
MND	Ministry of National Defense
MOFA	Ministry of Foreign Affairs
MPL	Military Procurement Law
MST	Ministry of Science and Technology
NDD	National Defense Donation
NDT	National Defense Tax
NH	Nike Hercules
NIF	National Investment Fund
NPT	Non-Proliferation Treaty
NSC	National Security Council
NSM	National Scientization Movement
NVM	New Village Movement

OPCON	operational control
PA	Presidential Archives
POSCO	Pohang Iron and Steel Company
PPCHS	*Pak Chŏnghŭi Taet'ongnyŏng yŏnsŏl munjip* [President Park Chung Hee's speeches collection], by Taet'ongnyŏng Pisŏsil
PS	Presidential Secretariat
R & D	research and development
ROK	Republic of Korea
S & T	science and technology
SES	Second Economic Secretariat (Office of the Second Senior Presidential Secretary for the Economy in the Blue House)
SIPRI	Stockholm International Peace Research Institute
SNPE	Société nationale des poudres et explosifs
SSM	surface-to-surface missile
T & E	test and evaluation
TDP	technical data package
TNT	trinitrotoluene
UN	United Nations
USFK	United States Forces Korea

Note to the Reader

In this work, I use the McCune-Reischauer system to romanize Korean words and phrases, except for Korean names that have been widely adopted in English, such as Park Chung Hee, Kim Il Sung, Rhee Syngman, Chung Ju-yung, and Chun Doo-hwan. The same exception applies to famous company names like Hanwha, Samsung, Hyundai, and Daewoo, as well as widely known terms and place names, such as *juche*, chaebol, Seoul, and Pyongyang. For the Korean author names, I follow the cultural convention of placing the family name before the given name, except for those who publish under Western conventions using English names. Throughout the manuscript, I use "South Korea" or "ROK (Republic of Korea)" to denote the state and territory of South Korea, while "North Korea" or "DPRK (Democratic People's Republic of Korea)" refers to the state and territory of North Korea. All English translations of Korean documents and other works cited in this book are mine unless otherwise noted.

INTRODUCTION

Korea's Militarized Journey toward Self-Reliance

> Warfare is the greatest affair of state, the basis of life and death, the way to survival or extinction. It must be thoroughly pondered and analyzed.
>
> —Sun Tzu, *The Art of War*

> If God were to ask me, "What is your wish?" I would not hesitate and would reply, "My wish is for the independence of Korea." If asked what my next wish is, I would say, "It is the independence of our country." And for the third question, what my next wish is, I would raise my voice even louder and respond, "My wish is for the complete and self-reliant independence of our country, Korea."
>
> —Kim Koo, "My Wish," *Paekpŏm ilji*

In the late 1960s, the authoritarian regime of President Park Chung Hee faced its most serious crisis yet as escalating tensions with North Korea coincided with the United States' reduction of military aid and plans to withdraw its troops from the Republic of Korea (ROK or South Korea). In response, President Park set his sights on independent national security, launching parallel programs to pursue the twin goals of economic growth and military self-sufficiency. With his guiding slogan of "rich nation, strong army" (*puguk kangbyŏng*), he rallied South Koreans behind his message. As Park vigorously promoted a spirit of self-reliance (*chaju*) in the Korean people, he urged them to embrace patriotic sacrifice in the drive to accelerate defense development and achieve freedom from dependence on foreign aid. Park's speeches and the state-run media, in conjunction with government-led mobilization campaigns and social reforms, ensured that the politically sanctified doctrine of *chaju kukpang*, "self-reliant national defense," permeated South Korea's society and culture throughout the 1970s, leading to the emergence and rapid growth of a powerful new military-industrial complex.[1]

The pursuit of self-reliance during the Park regime (1961–79) strikingly mirrored developments in North Korea (formally the Democratic People's Republic of Korea, or DPRK), despite the fact that the two Koreas had been archrivals and ideological opposites since the division of the Korean peninsula in 1945. Amid the DPRK's falling out with its communist patrons the Soviet Union and China in the 1960s and 1970s, its leader, Kim Il Sung (who ruled North Korea from 1948 to 1994), adopted his *pyŏngjin* (side-by-side) policy, prioritizing the simultaneous advancement of the national economy and the military.[2] By 1972 Kim's own version of self-reliance, *juche*, had replaced Soviet communism as North Korea's official state ideology, signaling an era of autarkic nationalism that still characterizes the country's politics.[3]

North and South Korea thus shared uncanny similarities in the 1970s as they embarked on their respective policies of self-reliance. Both Korean regimes strategically merged industrialization with national armament to create a path to political autonomy, both combined an ideologically mobilized indigenous culture with increased appeals to Korean nationalism, and both systematically transformed themselves into heavily militarized garrison states under totalitarian rule. The concept of self-reliance, which had its origins in anticolonial and nationalistic responses to Korea's experiences under foreign imperialism during the late nineteenth and early twentieth centuries, had by the end of the 1970s crystallized into a sacred ideology for all Korean people.[4]

To this day, the ideological and militarized push for self-reliance guides Korean politics and foreign policy, and in many observable ways the national identities of both Koreas can be traced back to the 1970s. Large swaths of the speeches by the DPRK's chairman Kim Jong Un (2012–present) read as if lifted straight out of his grandfather's speeches in the 1960s and 1970s, when the elder Kim steered the nation toward the military buildup he believed to be crucial for the regime's survival.[5] Despite Kim Jong Un's adopted version of the *pyŏngjin* policy (2013–18), with its emphasis on advancing the economy, and his subsequent reinforcement of economic priorities under the "new strategic line" policy (2018–present), the regime's unabated affirmation of *juche* continues to locate militarization (centered on nuclear missile capability) at the heart of its national political and economic system.[6] It comes as no surprise, then, that despite the crushing poverty facing North Korea's twenty-five million citizens, Pyongyang continues to invest heavily in its nuclear missile program and boasts the world's fourth largest military, with one out of every twenty North Koreans in active service.[7] South Korea, which has emerged as one of the most vibrant democracies and largest exporters in the world, also has self-reliance ingrained in its national policies and ethos.

Even President Moon Jae-in (2017–22), notwithstanding his liberal stance on improving ties with North Korea, maintained as his administration's primary goal the ROK's five-decade commitment to self-reliant national defense and even claimed that his policy of rapprochement with the North rested on South Korea's "strong defense capability."[8] He echoed the message of his northern counterpart, that only an independent national security system can ensure national peace and safety. Unsurprisingly, in spite of the protection extended by the United States in the 1953 Mutual Defense Treaty between the United States and the Republic of Korea (abbreviated as the "US-ROK Mutual Defense Treaty" in subsequent chapters), South Korea's relentless investment in its military has catapulted it to sixth place among the world's military forces in terms of power and eighth in size, with 555,000 active troops in 2023—despite the nation's rapidly shrinking and aging population.[9]

The clearest manifestation of the ROK's self-reliant national defense ideology in the past fifty years has been its focus on domestic arms production.[10] Even with the strategic impracticality and heavy economic cost incurred by this defense pattern, post-Park administrations—conservative or liberal—have continued to prioritize independent defense capability as an inviolable security principle intertwined with national identity and sovereignty.[11] In explaining the ROK's drive toward military modernization as a means to achieving security independence, scholars have stressed the country's indigenous "strategic culture," which grew out of its long cultural and geopolitical discourse, particularly with imperial powers.[12] Yet grasping Korean self-reliance in its current context also requires that we understand the internal processes that led the ROK to develop its own defense industry.

The Fusion of Ideology and Praxis

How did an impoverished country that was fully reliant on US military support until the early 1970s modernize its defense and commercial industries in less than a decade? Examining the roles that government and the citizens played in that transformation reveals the broad influence that defense industry policies wielded in South Korea in the 1970s.[13] What emerges is a vivid portrait of what is arguably the most revolutionary decade in Korean history, one whose influence continues to be felt in the ROK's domestic politics, society, economic policies, industrial technology, and international relations.

As the narrative of the self-reliance movement of the 1970s unfolds, we will see how the Park government steered both the consciousness and the industrial capacity of the Korean populace along a path toward security independence. In accordance with Park's ideology of self-reliant national defense, civilians were treated as the main drivers of the development of independent national security, and state strategies systematically merged national industries, the civilian workforce, and the body politic through the creation of the new indigenous defense industry. The total mobilization effort proceeded through complex mergers, submerged tensions, and negotiations of state goals with civilian material and ideological interests, eventually forging self-reliant national defense into a bona fide national movement. The distinguishing marks of the ROK's military modernization become evident as we appreciate how the Park state led the processes by which civilian citizens became active agents in a radical reformulation of South Korea's national defense system.

The rise of the ROK as an advanced industrial nation cannot be separated from the growth of its national security system, which fundamentally reshaped the country's civilian economy and society and galvanized a new national identity based on self-reliance. Park's self-reliant national defense agenda and his formation of the defense industry not only supported modern arms production but also underpinned South Korea's distinct socioeconomic and cultural transformation. Although the changes were orchestrated from the top down and led by the state, they were ultimately achieved through an all-out citizen-powered effort and a total merging of the public and private sectors.

The development of the ROK's defense industry during this period offers a window into how the citizenry, nationalist ideology, military production, and technology fused to form the foundation on which South Korea now thrives in the global economy. Korea's quest for "modernization" (*kŭndaehwa*)—which under Park meant achieving self-reliance in national defense and the economy—simply cannot be fully understood without a deep appreciation of the role that militarization played in the process.[14] The rise of South Korea's defense industry proved central to the unprecedented growth in industry and exports that is known as the "miracle on the Han River."

Militarism and Modernization

Militarism has been intertwined with Korea's national odyssey for the past century, beginning with the peninsula's encounters with Western imperialism and colonization and throughout its national liberation, division and civil war, and postwar authoritarianism, and it persists as a prevailing force in Korea today. A modern form of militarization took hold in the late nineteenth century with the military reforms initiated by rulers of the Chosŏn dynasty (1392–1897), in response to French and US intrusions as well as interference from Qing China and Meiji Japan.[15] However, amid continuous external interventions and internal divisions, the Chosŏn reform measures failed to modernize the army, and political and economic reforms likewise failed to strengthen the nation, rendering Korea unable to resist annexation by Japan in 1910. Under colonial rule by Japan, the Government General of Korea (1910–45) implemented militaristic policies that transformed Korea into an industrial base for the expanding Japanese Empire. Immediately following the nation's long-awaited liberation in 1945, the world's two emerging superpowers intervened in Korea, with the Soviet Union occupying and arming the North and the United States doing the same in the South. After the devastating Korean War (1950–53) ended in an armistice agreement, the newly established Republic of Korea experienced political and economic instability under the regimes of Rhee Syngman (1948–60) and Chang Myŏn (1960–61). This was followed by the government's takeover by Army Major General Park Chung Hee, whose rule from 1961 to 1979 ushered a new era of military domination in South Korea. After Park's assassination in 1979, another coup was carried out by General Chun Doo-hwan, who extended the country's rule by military dictatorship for nine more years (1980–88).

While North Korea's radical militarization has attracted immense scholarly interest, the military history of South Korea has not received a similar level of attention. This lack of scholarship is surprising, given that South Korea's postwar economic development, a popular topic of study, occurred through a highly organized and deliberate militarization process set in motion under Park—a process that was at the core of his political and economic agenda and determined the course of life for the vast majority of civilians during Park's time. The militaristic designs and patterns that transformed the nation remain conspicuous in the fabric of Korean society and culture. In her study of the politics of membership in modern Korea, the sociologist Seungsook Moon has used the phrase "militarized modernity" to analyze the process through which Korea's military-style (*kundae-sik*) development promoted a rigid, hypermasculine gender identity within its industrial workforce and enforced similarly gendered distinctions in the citizenry as well.[16] Other scholars have also highlighted the lasting influence of militarism in the country's national identity and developmental trajectory, using the terms "martial orientations," "militarized masculinity," "militarized citizenship," "developmental dictatorship," and "anticommunist militarism," and I myself use "militarized industrialization" to characterize South Korea's development under Park.[17] As historical methodology has expanded, recent South Korean scholarship has incorporated oral histories to reveal aspects of the impact of the military on contemporary Korea's sociocultural and political transformation that cannot be demonstrated with documentary sources alone.[18]

Nevertheless, academic inquiry into the connections between Park's militarism and South Korea's modernization in the 1970s remains meager. One explanation for this is Park's legacy. Arguably the most polarizing figure in modern Korean history, Park came to power through a military coup d'état in 1961 and ruled the nation with an iron fist until his assassination in 1979. His implementation of the authoritarian Yusin Constitution in 1972 allowed him to exercise (at a heavy cost to democratic institutions) a militaristic command system to mobilize Koreans for rapid industrialization. In addition, his deep connections to Japanese militarism—he had been an officer in Imperial Japan's Manchukuo Army and had used the Japanese name Takagi Masao (高木 正雄) during the colonial era—further complicate his legacy for many Koreans still embittered by Japan's role in Korea's past. Any discussion of Park runs the risk of becoming ensnared in the political polemics of the two ideological camps that divide South Korea. Conservatives praise him unreservedly as the father of modern South Korea and the architect of its unprecedented economic growth, crediting him with delivering the nation out of poverty. Yet to liberals, Park is the embodiment of tyrannical oppression, a military dictator who sacrificed democratization in the name of economic development. Even four decades after his death, he remains a polarizing figure, making a politically disinterested historical inquiry into his legacy seem unachievable (at least in South Korea).[19]

Militarism itself did not escape becoming politicized. Park's successor, Chun Doo-hwan, continued to suppress democratization, and the resulting three decades of military dictatorship by former generals inextricably linked the military with government suppression and control. A series of scandals involving bribery and financial mismanagement in the ROK military's weapons procurement process in the 1990s and 2000s further blighted the institution in the public eye.[20] And scholars and activists have criticized the ROK military for its historical role as the main accomplice in the government's brutal anticommunist crackdown during the Cold War. This legacy has deeply tainted the military's image among the Korean people and hindered more open dialogue about the variegated impact of Korean militarism.

Only recently have the roots of militarism in Park's developmental strategies been examined historically and empirically. Notably, the historian Carter Eckert traces the origins and structural principles of Korean militarism during the Park regime to Park's training as a colonized soldier in Imperial Japan's Manchurian Military Academy in the early 1940s, an experience that powerfully shaped Park and the postwar generation of South Korean military leaders. Eckert argues that the Japanese ethos of military discipline was internalized by Park and his Korean cohorts in the Japanese army, forging the "martial templates" of centralization and total mobilization that were later used in the Park regime's nation-building efforts.[21] Placing the military at the forefront in the narrative of South Korea's postcolonial modernization, Eckert pithily observes that "the history of the South Korean army is not unlike the history of modern South Korea itself."[22]

The Defense Industry in South Korea

The promotion of militarism under Park worked hand in hand with his development of the defense industry. Understanding the industry's emergence is critical to comprehending the country's internal transformation as well as its relations with the rest of the world in the past half century. While the Park government's buildup of the all-important heavy and chemical industries in the 1970s is largely seen as having kick-started South Korea's economic growth, it can be properly understood only in the context of Park's self-reliant national defense policy, which was centered on the construction of the country's independent weapons industry.

During Park's regime, the defense industry, or *pangwi sanŏp* in Korean, was formally defined as any business involved in the research and development (R & D) or the production of "military products."[23] Yet this official definition fails to adequately capture the scope and sophistication of what quickly became an all-encompassing industrial network operating at the intersection of military and civilian life—essentially, a new military-industrial complex (MIC). The South Korean MIC, established in the 1970s as a distinct segment of the national economy and dominated by state-selected private chaebol (large family-owned conglomerates), grew into a system in which the public and private sectors converged to provide national security while strengthening capitalist enterprise.[24]

Although a good amount of literature exists on the MICs of the United States, European NATO states, and other East Asian neighbors of South Korea, such as Japan, China, and North Korea, very few studies have taken an in-depth look at the history of South Korea's defense industry in connection with the country's economic growth. Those that have tend to rely on secondary analyses, external data, and personal memoirs—in particular, the memoirs of O Wŏnch'ŏl, who from 1971 to 1979 worked in the Blue House (the South Korean equivalent of the White House) as Park's top technocrat in charge of developing the defense industry and heavy and chemical industrialization (HCI).[25] Based on O's testimony, a number of academics—most notably Hyung-A Kim, who was the first scholar to conduct extensive interviews with O—have drawn attention to how Park's HCI initiative was established to support domestic arms production in response to security threats in the late 1960s.[26] The published memoirs by other key officials under Park, such as Kim Kwangmo and Kim Chŏngnyŏm, also provide valuable insider accounts of the growth of the defense industry during the Park regime.[27] But there has been very little empirical analysis of primary materials regarding the direct connections between the development of South Korean heavy and chemical industries and the expeditious appearance of the indigenous defense industry.[28] While the Heavy and Chemical Industrialization Policy (HCI Policy) is widely recognized as Park's central economic policy of the 1970s and the Korean rags-to-riches story has become a well-researched topic, the far-reaching influence of HCI on the intricate connection between national industrialization and militarization has seldom been analyzed—especially with the support of empirical evidence.[29] This is related to the scarcity of available primary sources on HCI and to the secrecy that surrounds the Park state's HCI Policy, specifically, owing to its association with the defense industry.

The relative lack of attention to HCI's broader, multifaceted role in South Korea's modernization also has to do with the widespread, critical view in South Korea of the Park era's authoritarianism, and with the focus in recent scholarship on the negative effects of Park's industrial policies on economic equity and political liberalization. Consequently, these dynamics in the highly politicized environment have led to limited appreciation of HCI's contributions to the nation's scientization, technological transformation, and military modernization.[30]

While there are some official military and government publications devoted to the rise of the defense industry in South Korea, the academic literature has examined the topic only sparingly—especially in the field of historical studies.[31] In addition to the scarcity of HCI-related documents, as previously mentioned, this is largely due to the limited access to South Korean military data from the 1970s. In Park's time, the dual threats of aggression from North Korea and US restrictions on the development of advanced weapons induced a government culture of near-total secrecy. The vast majority of official military records from this period are missing from government publications and remain classified to this day.[32] Furthermore, in defiance of US policies restricting the provision of arms to South Korea, Park created a top secret program for independent military modernization—the Yulgok Operation—that exacerbated tensions in the US-ROK alliance in the late 1970s. All data on Yulgok, including controversial developments in nuclear arms and ballistic missiles, were classified, and much of the information about it was never even entered into written records.[33] Other military files remain inaccessible for security reasons related to the ongoing conflict between the two Koreas. Until now, no work of historiography has deeply investigated how the construction of the defense industry contributed to the institutional and ideological transformation of South Korea under Park.[34]

Access to New Sources

With the strengthening of democracy and corresponding improvements to freedom of information in South Korea, gaining access to Korean primary sources on the defense industry has become increasingly possible.[35] The jewel of this study is the trove of newly available and wide-ranging primary sources, through which I offer the most complete account to date of the history of the South Korean defense industry under Park. My work draws on declassified archival materials and other primary sources, many of which remain largely untapped, as well as in-person interviews with key participants in the nascent defense industry during the Park era. By combining these sources, I have been able to bring new insights into both micro-level technicalities and macro-level state dynamics; along the way, I also reveal the interstitial processes between policymaking and civilian action that enabled South Korea to launch a defense industry in parallel with its programs for rapid socioeconomic transformation.

Specifically, in my research I have explored declassified source materials from South Korea's official archives that are available in the Presidential Archives, the National Archives of Korea, the Ministry of National Defense's Institute for Military History, the Ministry of Foreign Affairs' Diplomatic Archives, the Institute of State Governance Studies at Yonsei University, the Korean Defense Industry Association, and the Agency for Defense Development. These sources illuminate Korean policymaking and the agencies that came to the fore during South Korea's military modernization. From policy records to internal documents from the Blue House, various ministries, the state propaganda apparatus, military bureaus, research institutes, and other national or local government units, the materials evince broad state efforts to integrate and mobilize the military and civilian sectors to build a defense industry. In addition to domestic sources in South Korea, I incorporate information from primary sources in the United States—including documents from presidential libraries, the State Department, the Department of Defense, Congress, the Central Intelligence Agency, and the National Security Archive at George Washington University—to analyze the emergence of South Korea's MIC in the context of the US-ROK alliance and US foreign policy in the 1960s and 1970s. I have also consulted the rich reservoir of declassified foreign policy documents from the United States and other nations, including former communist allies of North Korea, that have been made available by the History and Public Policy Program (HPPP) at the Wilson Center in Washington, DC.

Information from the corporate records of private companies that functioned as first-generation arms manufacturers in South Korea during the 1970s also proved invaluable, because these sources reveal the ways that commercial industry joined with regime policy to achieve the state's military-industrial agenda.[36] Other materials that inform this study include newspaper articles pertaining to the local and national collections of civilian defense donations in the late 1960s and the 1970s.[37]

Given the limited recorded and written data on the Korean defense industry, I sought to fill in the gaps through a series of interviews and surveys. I spoke with former Blue House technocrats, business executives, plant managers, and both skilled and unskilled workers in the weapon factories. The narrative is further substantiated by information gleaned through interviews with researchers who worked under President Park at the Agency for Defense Development (ADD), the research institute that oversaw classified military projects, and former engineers, technicians, and craftsmen for Hanwha, Poongsan, Kia, Hyundai, Daewoo, Samsung, and Tongil who participated in those projects. My interviews offer rare eyewitness accounts of how the ADD and defense contractors embodied and advanced President Park's priorities to achieve greater security independence and, in so doing, exercised their own agency in catalyzing developments in science and technology. Such an in-depth analysis of the ADD and its corporate contractors and their relationship with each other had not been done before this study.

Finally, I also draw from the interviews and surveys I conducted with ordinary civilian participants in the defense donation movement—men and women from varying socioeconomic levels and different regions—all of whom were involved in the Park regime's efforts to develop the defense industry. Popular "strong state" interpretations of South Korea's economic development under Park often portray nonstate actors as faceless stewards of the government, but the recollections gleaned from these personal interviews put a human face on the structural forces that drove defense industrialization. These firsthand accounts offer a valuable "bottom-up" perspective on societal and corporate responses to state mobilization and the transformation of national security that truly deepens the discussion. Together, the diverse sources used in this book bear witness to the distinct national and transnational processes that forged Korea's military modernization and the industrial complex undergirding it.

A Distinctly Korean Model

Taking a critical look at Park's policy of self-reliant national defense and its impact on the new defense industry and the nation as a whole forces one to reassess the history of South Korea and its economic growth. This study uncovers the internal and external forces—and especially the less known indigenous actors and institutions—that enabled the distinct military-civilian convergence in South Korea's defense-centered industrialization. More broadly, it situates the ROK in the global and historical debate about the connections between militarism and capitalism, outlining a narrative of South Korea's socioeconomic transformation that transcends both the Cold War context and US-centered interpretations.

The military modernization that led to South Korea's rapid economic growth was produced by an inharmonious yet complementary relationship between state-initiated militarization and civilian participation. This complicates the view expressed in past scholarship that, following the conventional East Asian model, South Korea's growth resulted exclusively from the muscular actions of a top-down developmental state.[38] That paradigm certainly finds support in the Park state's directives for economic growth, its technocratic policies for concentrated investment in select industries and protections against foreign competition, its regulation of market demand and supply, and the controls the Park regime placed on capital and labor. But the strong-developmental-state argument implies dichotomous categories, and the corresponding assertions of "weak labor" and "weak business" are often susceptible to politicization and overgeneralization.[39] A closer look indicates that a more reciprocal, integrated, and dynamic state-society dialogue shaped South Korea's particular form of defense-focused industrialization during the Park period. The recently accessible information enables us to make a deeper exploration and a richer assessment of the real-life interplay of government, industry, society, and the military that shaped the nation's development. The complex alliances formed among state officials, industrialists, scientists, laborers, and citizens indicate the processes by which Korean civilians and societal structures complied and collaborated with the state.

This more nuanced interpretation transcends dualistic models, which have been challenged by Jie-Hyun Lim (Im Chihyŏn) and his colleagues, who apply the grayer concept of "coercion and consent" to explain the multifaceted realities of state-society relations and state hegemony under Park.[40] Following the theory of what he calls "mass dictatorship" (*taejung tokchae*), Lim has argued that the Park regime, like other fascist regimes in the twentieth century, was able to mobilize popular support for national modernization by first gaining the mass consent and participation that empowered the process from both above and below.[41] Lim analyzes the state-civil society dynamic in the Park period through the theoretical lens of Antonio Gramsci (1891–1937), whose interpretation of state power blurs the line between the state and civil society; as depicted by Gramsci, the two sides are actually deeply intertwined.[42] Rather than looking at government power as the static capacity of an autonomous state (and its apparatus) vis-à-vis civil society, Gramsci suggests that the state's relation and correlation to society are what determine de facto state power, as state hegemony lies in a negotiated space between them. In addition to Lim's work, over time the developmental-state literature has expanded its focus to include the social ties and coalitions between the state and its bases of support.[43]

Building on the coercion and consent approach, my research suggests that Park's system for self-reliant national defense could not have come to fruition through state directives alone. Rather, the South Korean equivalent of a "total war" system—what Park called the "total security" system (explained in detail in chapter 1)—emerged through an institutional and ideological nexus of state actions, entrepreneurship in the private sector, the industriousness of the workforce, and the participation of average citizens, all reinforced by the ROK's collective experience of external threats from North Korea and US troop withdrawals.[44] Accounts of private citizens interacting with the state as agents for security independence have been overshadowed by a disproportionate focus on high politics or polity in the state-centric narratives. In contrast, although this study explores how the state worked to manufacture consensus, it also details the way in which diverse nonstate and external factors, as well as Koreans' prior collective experience of wars and colonialism, contributed to making self-reliant national defense a powerful movement in the 1970s, with legacies that continue today. This analysis adds a corrective nuance to traditional models by revealing how Park's defense industry plans required an active and vibrant business sector, as well as proactive citizens, including scientists, engineers, laborers, and taxpayers. Throughout my examination of defense industrialization, I argue that civilian engagement was an essential ingredient in the state's ability to lead South Korea's modernization under Park, and that the Korean model of economic development should be reconceptualized to place more emphasis on the symbiotic ties between the state and society, in spite of the controlling power of the state under Yusin. Finding that a much more dynamic state-society discourse was at work in the construction of the South Korean MIC under Park, the following chapters focus on how that combination of forces functioned.

Since the 1980s, political scientists and other scholars have predominantly viewed South Korea during the Cold War as a client of the United States—a country that enjoyed a "free rider" status in its expansion as an export economy through a form of dependent capitalism.[45] Accordingly, scholars have treated US policy as the primary catalyst of South Korea's military modernization and technological advancement.[46] Many studies have especially pointed to the US technological aid that South Korea received during the Vietnam War as key to the country's economic and military modernization.[47] The arms policy of the United States and the US-ROK security alliance have likewise dominated Korean scholarship on Park's development of independent weapons, including his nuclear missile program.[48]

Largely missing from consideration has been the role the ROK played in its own military modernization. Newly available materials demonstrate that although US involvement in Korea's military modernization was indeed pervasive, the development of arms production in the ROK in the 1970s paints a much more intricate picture. While aggressively pursuing foreign military technology, the ROK under Park simultaneously conducted an all-out campaign to create its own defense technology, mobilizing industry, labor, science, and the citizenry. Indeed, the comprehensive initiatives for military modernization that Park's government launched through the HCI Policy and the Yulgok Operation even altered the trajectory of US foreign policy on South

Korea.[49] Empirical data from interviews with military scientists, industrialists, and corporate engineers who were involved in the early phases of defense industrialization document South Korea's own agency in the rise of its domestic defense industry and technological modernization, countering the view that primarily attributes the ROK's military modernization to exogenous factors alone. This complicates the conventional portrayal of the US-ROK alliance in the Park era as a narrowly defined patron-client relationship.[50]

If we reframe or reinterpret the Cold War narrative of US-ROK relations in this way, South Korea's defense industrialization demands a more complex explanation in terms of the historical forces and connections that shaped the nation. Recent studies have examined the transnational flow of technology, industry, and skilled labor at the interface of imperialism, colonization, US militarism, and pan-Asianism, and how their confluence affected the development of postwar East Asia.[51] Rather than treating the rise of South Korea as an isolated and unique case, the hybrid origin of the South Korean MIC invites comparison with other advanced, private sector–based MICs, such as those of the United States, the United Kingdom, Germany, Israel, and in particular Japan. The Park regime even revitalized former colonial structures and emulated earlier Japanese military-industrial strategies for merging the public and private sectors in defense production (while domesticating them to fit Korea's own needs and circumstances).[52] This more complete picture of the ROK defense industry will enhance broader discussions of the global rise of total war states, war capitalism, and MICs generally, illuminating topics such as mass mobilization and the eroding divisions between military and civilian spheres of society.

As mentioned above, few systematic studies have investigated the impact of the Park state's defense industry on South Korea's transformation into one of the world's advanced economies. In framing defense industrialization as the key narrative behind Korea's economic miracle, this book stands apart from other works on the nation's development under Park. It is the first detailed study of the civil-military relationship that undergirded the establishment of the South Korean MIC under the Park regime, particularly the first to take a deep look at the inner workings of specific defense enterprises, their workers, and the ADD.[53]

By highlighting the dynamic and enduring interconnectedness of military and economic growth that led to the distinct contours and content of South Korean capitalism, the following chapters delineate the Korean model of economic development, as distinguished from other models of state-led economic development—which in turn elucidates the importance of the South Korean case for comparative studies of capitalism, militarism, and nation building. This more localized and historical approach to South Korea's defense industrialization elucidates Korea's distinct pathway to national development and modernization, in which South Korea varies from other newly industrialized countries in East Asia as well as from other emerging arms producers in different parts of the world.

South Korea's development under Park can be seen as a story of symbiosis between capitalism and militarism, one that challenges both the classic "guns versus butter" trade-off, with its "peace dividend" accruing with butter, and the tendency to dichotomize capitalism and militarism.[54] The rise of South Korea offers an illuminating example of military and capitalist development mirrored in security and technological growth. This comports with the views of Emile Benoit, Jacques Gansler, Stephanie Neuman, and more recently Linda Weiss and Margaret O'Mara, whose studies have shed light on the multifaceted connections for the economy between national defense industries and the development of a national technological base.[55]

My focus on the development of the ROK defense industry and its connection to the country's growth is not an endorsement of the Park government's developmental policies or tactics, which were carried out at great cost to the Korean people. Indeed, this study of the origins of the defense industry sheds additional light on the coercive tools and methods by which Park's authoritarian regime mobilized the nation for rapid development—methods that introduced some of the deep social, cultural, and economic problems South Korea still suffers from today. Clearly, Korea's economic miracle did not get under way during Park's dictatorship without significant pain, conflict, and sacrifice. Under the Yusin system, Park's HCI Policy prioritized accelerated production at the expense of wealth distribution, social welfare, and civil liberties, leading to the concentrated growth of select industries and their power over labor. This approach resulted in a significant socioeconomic gap and the rise of progressive opposition to Park, which contributed to the consolidation of the extreme left-right political division in South Korea, a chasm that continues to persist.[56] It is therefore only by coming to grips with the history of the defense industry under Park that we can fully understand the making of modern-day South Korea.

Outline of the Book

Chapter 1, "Park Chung Hee's Total Security System," details the external threats of the late 1960s and early 1970s that gave Park his rationale for pursuing self-reliant national defense. Central to the context of Park's new policy were the DPRK's actions in the late 1960s, the announcement of the Nixon Doctrine in 1969, and the United States' subsequent reduction of its troops in South Korea in 1971. The Park regime capitalized on these security threats, mobilizing civilian forces to build Korea's independent defense industry and leading civilian industry and culture to embrace the national defense agenda and support defense industry development. By engaging maximum civilian participation, the Park government transformed South Korea into a total war state fully mobilized for defense industrialization. At the intersection of ideology and praxis, and aided by favorable geopolitical winds, Park's policies and reforms reconfigured the nation's military, economy, and educational system, as well as the mentality and culture of the South Korean people, to fit his militaristic vision of a new, self-reliant nation.

Park's implementation of the HCI Policy is the topic of chapter 2, "'Rich Nation, Strong Army.'" It explores the origins and development of the Park government's strategy of integrating HCI with the creation of an independent defense industry. Operating under Park's authoritarian system and backed by the Yusin Constitution, HCI supported the expansion of defense-related civilian industries for Korean arms production. The chapter details the state's planning and execution of HCI, especially its policies for leveraging the civilian industries and their workforces for defense-centered industrialization. The HCI Policy enacted under Park accelerated the growth of the defense industry while simultaneously powering the competitiveness, technological innovation, and productivity of commercial industry.

Chapter 3, "The Militarization of the Chaebol," opens with a discussion of the chaebol in the 1960s and early 1970s (prior to defense industrialization), when the state began to groom them as partners in Park's economic and military plans. To examine their transformation into defense contractors and large conglomerates under the HCI Policy instituted in 1973, the chapter looks closely at the case of Hanwha (Korea Explosives), one of the first major Korean corporations to enter arms production under Park. The narrative of Hanwha's rise provides an example of how the chaebol complied with, adapted to, and even enthusiastically advanced state policies for military production.[57] Supporting materials from Hanwha and other corporations elucidate the extent to which the chaebol were transformed by the HCI Policy and also reveal the role the companies played in developing the defense industry. Through the case of Hanwha, the chapter provides a detailed picture of the business structure, culture, and labor force of the chaebol, as well as of their independent responses and contributions to the state's defense agenda. The combination of mutually proactive state policy and private enterprise fashioned a distinctly Korean, chaebol-led model of military modernization in the 1970s.

Chapter 4, "National Scientization and the Agency for Defense Development," examines the ways and the degree to which defense building under Park shaped Korea's technological landscape. The National Scientization Movement, launched alongside Park's defense-centered HCI Policy, gave rise to a highly skilled workforce and advances in domestic R & D. The government's establishment of the ADD for weapons R & D, along with the creation of new research institutes specializing in HCI technologies—all organizations that collaborated closely with the chaebol—provided a national research infrastructure for the private-sector advancement of weapons-related technology. Overcoming technical challenges at the ground level, individual scientists, engineers, and technicians rigorously adopted and furthered the technologies and the technical skills to develop domestic weapons. New capabilities for weapons production were then "spun off" to modernize commercial industries and the skills of their workers. This chapter analyzes the dynamic interconnectedness of defense industrialization and commercial technological growth, highlighting how defense science and engineering played into South Korea's larger techno-industrial transformation.

In chapter 5, "Mobilizing to Weaponize the Nation," I focus on Park's pursuit of large-scale public support for national defense through civilian financial drives in support of weapons production. The chapter details how the state funded the clandestine Yulgok Operation, Park's signature initiative for South Korea's military modernization in the mid- to late 1970s. South Korean society's total mobilization via the National Defense Donation program and the National Defense Tax was accompanied by a sweeping transformation of the people's attitudes toward national security, which led to a fundamental shift in the discourse on security and the ROK's quest for political autonomy within the US-ROK military alliance. The movement for security independence, as well as Yulgok's defiance of US arms restrictions, led to further shifts in US policy on the ROK, including transfers of previously banned weapon technologies to South Korea and the reversal of the plan to withdraw US troops.

The concluding chapter, "Self-Reliant National Defense—The Cornerstone of Modern Korea," discusses the historical significance of military-civilian engagement, state-capital integration, and the convergence of state and society under Park's policy for self-reliant national defense—what soon became a national ideology that launched the nation on its trajectory toward full economic and military modernization. Regarding the legacy of Park's self-reliant national defense policy and the defense industry it spawned, the conclusion looks at how both factors have influenced South Korea's military, political, technological, and economic growth during the post-Park period. It leaves the door open for dialogue on the broader implications of defense industrialization and invites comparative discussions about the global rise of defense industries and their impact on national modernization, capitalist systems, and democratic governance.

The story of South Korea's rapid transformation during the Park era would be incomplete without the complementary narrative of its simultaneous programs for economic expansion and military modernization and how they drove each other forward. The tandem growth of the economy and defense was propelled by advanced civilian manufacturing and a highly skilled workforce, along with the citizens' commitment to national prosperity and sovereignty. Ultimately, self-reliant national defense became an indelible part of South Korea's national identity, politics, and economy because it was a nationwide project in which both the state and civil society were stakeholders. This book uncovers the defense industry's deep involvement in the overall modernization of South Korea, and what that means for our understanding of militarization and development.

To embrace a new national identity based on Park's concept of self-reliance, South Korea had to change. Under Park, the ROK brought about that change through strategic policies for a civilian-powered defense industry, ideological education, institutional arrangements for weapons-production infrastructure, and systems for mobilizing the private sector and training a skilled workforce, in combination with powerful bottom-up efforts by the citizens themselves to support security. Together these factors created a distinctly Korean brand of economic development, or what can be called militarized industrialization.

CHAPTER ONE

Park Chung Hee's Total Security System

There is neither front line nor rear in national security.
For the battlefront to be healthy, the home
front must be much healthier.
—Park Chung Hee

The rise and fall of a nation depends on whether the people
of a country have the conviction and desire for self-reliance,
independent existence, and development, whether they
have the courage to fight against the enemy at the risk
of death, and whether such conviction and courage
can be made into organized forces.
—Park Chung Hee

Troubling threats to South Korea's security, including mounting incursions from the DPRK, reached a frightening new level in January 1968 when North Korean commandos attacked the Blue House with the aim of assassinating President Park Chung Hee. Just days later, North Korean forces seized the USS *Pueblo*, a US Navy intelligence ship, and took its crew hostage. To Park's dismay, the United States, South Korea's main ally and its protector, took what seemed to be a passive stance in response to these shocking actions. Even worse, in the following year the United States announced the Nixon Doctrine, which declared that all US allies, including the ROK, should assume primary responsibility for their own defense. Then, in 1971, a division of the US forces withdrew from South Korea. For the Park government, these alarming events, together with the fear and sense of vulnerability they created among South Koreans, constituted a state of emergency that highlighted the nation's need for an independent defense industry. Determined to transform South Korea's national security posture, Park seized on domestically driven military modernization and weapons production as the means by which the ROK could withstand the DPRK's aggression while also reducing its military dependence on the United States.

The international tensions, combined with the Park government's efforts to mobilize the Korean populace, ignited a radical national security movement based on Park's vision of self-reliant national defense. Capitalizing on the security crisis, from 1968 to 1972 the Park regime worked to secure full civilian participation in the government's efforts to improve national security, bringing about a political and cultural transformation in the ROK as it took its first major steps toward constructing a domestic military-industrial complex. The threats of the late 1960s thus served as the catalyst not only for the Park government's military modernization project but also for the sociocultural changes through which the state forged a new ideology founded on the urgent need for independent national security.

Park's goal of military modernization can be seen as operating hand in hand with the Korean people's aspirations for national security, especially in the face of their lived and perceived vulnerability. As the government manufactured a new, militarist version of Korean nationalism, it brought the state, industry, labor, and the citizenry together in an unprecedented way, with a new civilian-military relationship cohering around the goal of self-reliant defense. Building on this coalition, Park unveiled his "total security" system that, under the authoritarian Yusin Constitution, laid the political groundwork for the execution of heavy and chemical industrialization (HCI) and the intertwined development of the defense industry. This chapter will delve into how three sets of key factors, both external and internal, led to the formation of Park's total security system under Yusin: the DPRK's provocations in the late 1960s; US foreign policy, including the Nixon Doctrine and the withdrawal of US troops; and South Korea's domestic factors, encompassing its historical experiences of wartime mobilizations and Park's agency in responding to the national security crisis. These factors collectively fostered a conducive environment for Park's development of a robust national security state in South Korea.

North Korean Factors

After the Korean War ended in 1953 with an armistice but no peace agreement, the two Koreas continued to wage political, economic, and ideological war against each other, as they still do today. Yet in spite of their differences, North and South Korea followed similar courses in their quests for political and military autonomy in reaction to the withdrawal of great-power patronage in the late 1960s: both began to pursue military and economic independence through industrialization. To understand the origins of South Korea's self-reliant national defense initiative, it is important to see how its rivalry with North Korea informed the strategies Park chose to pursue.

Cold War superpower conflict between the United States and the Soviet Union shaped the perspective of early scholars of the period, who depicted the Soviet Union, the DPRK's chief patron, as the main impetus behind Pyongyang's increased militancy in the late 1960s and offered only limited analysis of indigenous policymaking in North Korea.[1] However, post–Cold War research based on declassified US, Soviet (or Russian), and Eastern European archival materials has revealed that the DPRK made significant policy choices that were independent of—and even at odds with—both the Soviet Union and the People's Republic of China, North Korea's other major patron.[2] The DPRK's military brinkmanship under Kim Il Sung in the late 1960s should therefore be understood vis-à-vis Kim's own outlook and motives. Rather than being constrained by its patron states, the DPRK operated independently, without necessarily adhering to Soviet and Chinese strategic priorities in the region.

Amid the rising security crisis of the late 1960s, Park came to perceive the DPRK's actions as an authentic threat that warranted immediate military reform in South Korea. Indeed, as Pyongyang's relations with Moscow and Beijing were deteriorating, the DPRK was taking a dangerous path toward military self-reliance and "adventurism," as evidenced by its incursions into the ROK.[3] As a result, South Korea's sense of security suffered a significant blow as an increasingly autonomous and unconstrained North Korea escalated its raids, largely with the political aims of disrupting South Korea's society and government and harming its relationship with the United States during the US-led war in Vietnam, in which ROK troops aided US forces.

Incursions from the North

The Sino-Soviet dispute of the 1960s placed Pyongyang in a perilous diplomatic position between the two economic and military patrons that had supported Kim Il Sung's regime since North Korea's nation building began after World War II. Chinese Communist Party leaders opposed and refused to follow the de-Stalinization campaign of Nikita Khrushchev, first secretary of the Communist Party of the Soviet Union (1953–64), who aimed to liberalize his country's authoritarian political system and pursue a policy of peaceful coexistence with the West. As China remained critical of Khrushchev's reforms into the 1960s, communists worldwide were forced to choose sides, and the DPRK was powerfully affected by the split between the two communist powers.[4] Pyongyang resisted Moscow's reforms, which threatened Kim's totalitarian rule and his Stalinesque cult of personality and conflicted with his vehement opposition to the United States' "imperialist" presence in South Korea.

An additional source of tension between Pyongyang and Moscow was Kim Il Sung's opposition to the international Nuclear Non-Proliferation Treaty endorsed by Khrushchev in 1962.[5] As declassified Soviet sources reveal, Kim was already determined to develop his own nuclear weapons, believing they would significantly aid the DPRK's achievement of greater political and military sovereignty.[6] However, Moscow, wary of Kim's nuclear ambitions, refused to provide the necessary technical aid.

The relationship between North Korea and the Soviet Union had grown more acrimonious through the events of October 1962, when Pyongyang criticized the Soviet role in the Cuban Missile Crisis and also supported China during the Sino-Indian border conflict, in which

Moscow sided with India.[7] During the subsequent Soviet-DPRK arms supplies negotiation that took place from November 29 to December 5, 1962, Moscow demanded immediate payment for the new military supplies requested by Pyongyang (instead of selling them on credit as Moscow had done in the past), which effectively cut off the military aid on which Pyongyang had relied since the Korean War.[8] The failed arms negotiation quickly triggered the DPRK's pursuit of an independent defense system in which the lack of needed weapons would be at least partially offset by other military capabilities. On December 10, the DPRK government declared its goal of "self-reliance in national security" (*kukpang esŏ ŭi chawi*) and introduced four strategic principles intended to transform North Korea into a militarized garrison state independent of foreign military assistance.[9] These principles, which would later become Kim's Four Military Doctrines (Sadae Kunsa Nosŏn), were: (1) the armament of all North Korean people, (2) the fortification of the entire national territory, (3) the training of all troops as Korean Workers' Party (KWP) cadres, and (4) the modernization of military equipment.[10] Thus North Korea declared its own policy of self-reliant national defense ahead of the official initiative President Park undertook in South Korea in 1968.[11]

Although the DPRK initially tried to strengthen its relationship with China for economic and military support, China was dealing with its own internal challenges—especially in the aftermath of its failed economic reforms in the late 1950s—and lacked the means to make up for the Soviet aid that North Korea had lost. In a speech at the Plenary Session of the KWP in October 1966, Kim promulgated his Four Military Doctrines as he promoted military modernization and *juche* (self-reliance), emphasizing North Korea's need for further independence from the "great powers."[12] At this time, the DPRK's Korean People's Army (KPA) began to adopt more guerrilla-style tactics as a way to reduce its reliance on weapons and equipment from the Soviet Union. Even though Soviet military aid resumed in 1966, much of the KPA's military equipment had deteriorated by that point, which further inspired Kim's use of irregular warfare as a cost-effective way to make up for his army's disadvantages in conventional military strength.[13]

Kim Il Sung strengthened his commitment to self-reliance when his relationship with China began to deteriorate during the Cultural

Revolution (1966–76), when the Chinese Red Guards, led by Mao Zedong, attempted to consolidate Maoist-Communist orthodoxy in resistance to new reformist leaders in China.[14] As the Red Guards targeted and expelled Chinese "revisionists" and "capitalists" from the People's Republic of China, they similarly criticized Kim and his regime for straying from party orthodoxy and pursuing their own path through reforms.[15] In March 1967 the Soviet embassy in North Korea reported, "Events in China associated with the so-called 'Cultural Revolution' have seriously alarmed the Korean leadership, which has reason to fear its negative influence on the DPRK."[16] The Red Guards' hostility toward Kim and his regime endured through the late 1960s, at times bringing the two neighboring countries to the brink of military conflict.[17] This dramatic falling-out with Beijing led Pyongyang to turn back to Moscow for support. Even so, the DPRK's rift with China and the ongoing Sino-Soviet disputes solidified Kim's goal of greater political and military independence, with a result that led North Korea to begin distancing itself from both patrons. Less restrained than before by his traditional patrons, Kim increasingly resorted to military measures against the United States and South Korea to advance his regime's goals. Beginning in late 1966, the DPRK launched a series of special military operations across the Demilitarized Zone (DMZ) that clashed with both US and ROK forces.[18]

Clearly North Korea's mounting aggressions toward the South from 1966 to 1969 were driven by Kim's own interests.[19] Different interpretations of Kim's motives have been put forth to explain his belligerency during this period.[20] First, according to the Central Intelligence Agency (CIA) and many scholars, the impetus for Kim's shift to aggressive tactics was likely the Vietnam War.[21] There is certainly ample evidence that Kim saw the war and the US-ROK alliance in Vietnam as an expansion of the American war on communism, which he feared could spread to North Korea.[22] While Park dispatched tens of thousands of ROK troops to Vietnam in the mid-1960s to fight in support of the United States, the DPRK saw "the struggle of the Vietnamese people against the American imperialism as its own."[23] From 1966 onward, it is likely that Kim waged a war of disruption against US-backed South Korea to distract both the United States and South Korea from Vietnam.[24]

Second, some experts have interpreted the DPRK's frequent infiltrations across the border as attempts to weaken Park's domestic support by creating instability in South Korea and sparking an indigenous uprising against the Park government.[25] This is substantiated by Kim's own speeches. In his speech to the KWP in October 1966, for example, Kim said that "to vanquish counter-revolution and win victory for the revolution in [S]outh Korea, powerful revolutionary forces must be prepared," and he called for action by revolutionaries in South Korea to help bring down the Park regime and reunify the peninsula.[26] Because Park had taken power through a coup in 1961 and initially lacked popular support, one can surmise that Kim's special-forces incursions were designed to provoke internal resistance to Park's government that would lead to its overthrow and the subsequent unification of the two Koreas under Kim's communist regime. As the Vietnam War diverted South Korea's attention and, more importantly, reduced its military capacity (the ROK deployed three of its premier units to Vietnam), Kim may have seen the war as his opportunity to topple Park's government.

A third view is that Kim's provocations were efforts to stall the ROK's economic progress under Park's Five-Year Economic Development Plans, which were boosting domestic approval for Park and drawing negative attention to the failure of Kim's own first Seven-Year Plan (originally set from 1961 to 1967).[27] For instance, O Wŏnch'ŏl, Park's top aide in the Blue House (see chapter 2), wrote in his memoir that Kim had escalated his military threats to disrupt the ROK economy in response to the widening economic gap between the two Koreas.[28] A fourth interpretation suggests that Kim's provocations were driven by changing international circumstances in the Cold War, such as the US-Soviet rapprochement and China's Cultural Revolution (discussed earlier).[29] Scholars who hold this view claim that these worldwide events encouraged North Korea to increase its military activities against the South and pushed Kim to pursue Pyongyang's own interests and maintain an independent policy line despite concerns from its communist patrons. Overall, these scholars believe that external circumstances played a dominant role in shaping the DPRK's policies.

Finally, the historian Mitchell Lerner has pointed to Kim's genuine adherence to his nationalist ideology of *juche* and its principle of self-reliance as the chief motive behind his independent and militant policymaking.[30] I believe each of these arguments offers valuable insights into our understanding of the contextual factors that influenced Kim's mindset. When considered together, they provide a comprehensive rationale for Kim's decision-making in the late 1960s.

Kim's sporadic but increasing offensives against South Korea involved small, highly agile attacks—raids, ambushes, and rural combat. These tactics were inspired by his own experience as a former anti-Japanese guerrilla fighter in Manchuria and by the successes of the Vietnamese in their battles against superior US military forces.[31] The number of armed infiltrations into South Korea rose from 13 in 1966 to 121 in 1967, and then nearly doubled to 217 in 1968, with the Park government taking countermeasures in response.[32] However, the string of especially bold provocations by the North in 1968 raised tensions to new heights and brought the two Koreas to the brink of war more than at any other time since the Korean War. North Korean aggressions that year included the commando raid on the Blue House on January 21, the taking of the USS *Pueblo* on January 23, and the landing of North Korean special forces near Ulchin and the city of Samch'ŏk on October 30. These stepped-up attacks were pivotal, as they prompted the Park government's decisions to reorganize South Korea's security forces through the enlistment of civilian reserves, initiate a plan for domestic arms production, and mobilize an all-out effort for reforms that would establish what President Park called "total security" in South Korea.

The Blue House Raid

Of all the incursions from the North in 1968, the raid on the Blue House proved the most decisive for Park's initiation of self-reliant national defense policy. On the night of January 21, a band of North Korean officers from the elite Unit 124 of the KPA attempted to infiltrate the Blue House, the presidential residence in the heart of Seoul, in a plot to assassinate Park. The commandos had made it to within a mere three hundred yards of the Blue House before a police chief stopped them, leading to a shoot-out between South Korean security forces and the North Koreans. Of the thirty-one commandos who took part in the failed operation, twenty-nine were killed in action that night and over the following days, one eventually made it back to North Korea, and one, Lieutenant Kim Sinjo, was captured and taken prisoner. On the South Korean side, twenty-three soldiers and seven civilians were killed and fifty-two were injured.[33] In a highly publicized press conference broadcast on national radio and television stations on January 22, the night after the attack, the captured officer testified to a shocked South Korean audience that the North Korean commandos had infiltrated Seoul "to cut off the head of Park Chung Hee."[34]

The now famous Blue House Raid set off a security emergency throughout South Korea. The minister of national defense at the time, Kim Sŏngŭn, recalled the seriousness of the incident in his memoir: "When I think about it, I am deeply appalled, because the attempt to assassinate the president through their attack on the Blue House came so close to succeeding. . . . [T]hey could have invaded the Blue House and killed the president."[35] The impact of the incident that night and the ensuing violence perpetrated on civilians by the fleeing North Koreans instantly united the government, national security forces, the media, and the rest of the Korean population in a massive effort to find and eliminate the surviving commandos.[36] During confrontations the first night, the streets of Seoul were filled with gunfire in what amounted to the most serious national security situation since the Korean War.[37] One resident's testimony conveys the threat of danger felt throughout the city on the dreadful night of the raid: "A little past 10:00 p.m., I heard a strange sound like an explosion and began to wonder if it was an earthquake. After ten seconds, I heard the same sound of an explosion so I went out to the front yard. . . . Afterward it got quiet, and then, thirty, forty minutes later, there was the same sound of an explosion. The sound of shooting was ringing out all night around the Ch'angŭimun Gate [a historic gate in Seoul], and the atmosphere was like a war; everyone in town stayed up all night in fear."[38] In other testimonies, citizens expressed outrage over the North Korean intrusion and demanded stronger national security.[39]

In the days and weeks following the attack, citizens actively cooperated with the police by not only reporting sightings of the remaining commandos but also fighting them off and denying them aid. South Korea's mass media played a major role in mobilizing citizens to collectively thwart the commandos' attempts to obtain food and assistance from local people; as a result, almost all of the North Koreans who had escaped on the night of the raid were quickly tracked down and killed. Kim Sinjo's widely aired confession was sensationalized to stir up national sentiment and rally support for President Park. Newspapers aided in the nationwide hunt for the fugitives by publicizing civilian casualties and reporting on armed attacks carried out by escaping commandos against civilians.[40]

From Pyongyang, the embassy of the Czech Republic, a socialist ally of the DPRK, reported in a telegram to Prague on the Park government's measures against commandos: "The last ones killed from the group of thirty one were physically weak and hungry, which among other things showed that by the very first appeals, South Korean propaganda was able to deter civilians from helping the armed group in any way. These propaganda efforts of South Korean ruling circles were also accompanied by internal measures that were aimed at practically every South Korean and strictly limited possibilities to provide meaningful assistance to members of the armed group."[41] The Czech embassy's report also notes that "South Korean propaganda was able to sustain the wave of anti-Communism" by fully exploiting the deaths and funeral ceremonies of civilians and police officers who were killed by the North Korean commandos. It describes the raid's political impact as well: apparently, even disagreements between Park's ruling party and the opposition party were immediately set aside after the raid. The report states: "The opposition party showed maximum willingness to cooperate with the ruling party 'in the light of serious danger to security of the South Korean state from North Korean infiltrators[,]' in the sense that it was not just an isolated action of thirty one armed men, but a systematic and planned activity of the DPRK with the final objective of 'armed aggression against South Korea.'" The Park regime made considerable political gains as a result of the Blue House Raid, the Czech embassy's report added, stating that the South Korean government had made "a complete success" out of the event by "[turning] public attention from criticizing the government, army and police to a more acceptable matter—[rising up] against the DPRK."[42]

Of course, the anticommunist and anti–North Korea propaganda that South Korean citizens had been indoctrinated with since the 1950s had also prepared the ground for their quick rise in support of national security. The South Korean people were primed to respond against the North, and the state quickly used the Blue House Raid to mobilize them. Im Tongwŏn, former head of strategic planning for the ROK's Joint Chiefs of Staff (1973–76), who helped devise the ROK military's implementation of the self-reliant national defense policy, points to the Blue House Raid as the decisive event that triggered the policy.[43] Overall, the raid not only influenced the security measures taken by the government but also galvanized South Koreans' commitment to stronger national defense.

The Pueblo *Incident*

Concern over the DPRK's threat escalated to a heightened, international level just two days after the Blue House attack, when North Korean patrol boats and a fighter jet seized the USS *Pueblo* (henceforth referred to as "the *Pueblo*"), a US Navy ship conducting intelligence-gathering operations, and its crew of eighty-three, off the coast of North Korea near Wŏnsan. One member of the crew was killed and three others were wounded; the remaining crew members were captured and imprisoned in North Korea. Creating a further complication, the DPRK framed its seizure of the *Pueblo* as an act of self-defense against a hostile ship that had trespassed into its coastal waters.[44]

The DPRK's daring action exposed the asymmetry and fragility of the US-ROK relationship. Although Park and his officials urged the US government to respond swiftly and firmly, the United States refrained from retaliation, both out of concern over deepening its military involvement in the Korean peninsula and because there was little chance that a special military operation into North Korea would succeed.[45] Furthermore, President Lyndon Johnson (1963–69), who was campaigning for reelection, viewed the release of the *Pueblo*'s crew as his top priority, whereas Park demanded that the United States first mount a strong military response to the Blue House Raid.[46] Their disagreement over the appropriate response to the DPRK initiated a rift in the otherwise amicable relationship the allies had enjoyed since 1965, when Park agreed to send troops to Vietnam.

Another reason for Washington's reluctance to punish the DPRK was the fact that American policymakers initially believed the Soviet

Union had instigated the ship's capture to distract the United States from the Vietnam War.[47] In fact, however, declassified Russian documents show that Moscow was equally caught off guard by the action and was worried that Kim Il Sung was trying to drag the Soviet Union into a war with the United States.[48] The DPRK's relations with the Soviet Union had improved in the late 1960s, with the resumption of Soviet military aid, but the two governments differed in their approaches to the United States. Kim emphasized the imminent US threat to North Korea, whereas the Soviets remained vigilant about avoiding conflict with the Americans. On January 24, S. Golosov, second secretary of the Soviet embassy in Pyongyang, told the Romanian ambassador to North Korea, Aurelian Lazar, that "Soviet diplomats were extremely worried with respect to the unrestrained actions undertaken by the DPRK against the ROK (the January 21 attack in Seoul) and against the USA, manifested in the capturing of the military vessel AGER-2 [the USS *Pueblo*]."[49]

Declassified diplomatic sources confirm that the North Korean leadership acted completely on its own in taking the *Pueblo*.[50] Unlike the Johnson administration, which had assumed Soviet involvement in the affair and sought their cooperation in resolving the matter, Park was convinced that Kim Il Sung had directed the taking of the ship, and he urged the United States to punish North Korea directly to prevent future intrusive acts.[51] The Americans' refusal to retaliate signaled to Park a clear unwillingness to engage in the existential conflict on the Korean peninsula.

Creation of the Homeland Reserve Forces

His confidence in US protection badly shaken, two weeks after the *Pueblo* Incident, at the opening ceremony for the new Pusan-Kwangju rail line on February 7, 1968, Park announced his plan to create the Homeland Reserve Forces (HRF; Hyangt'o Yebigun).[52] The idea of a reserve force had been on Park's mind since the beginning of his rule. His military junta had passed the Homeland Reserve Forces Act in December 1961 to organize local reserves, but owing to a lack of funding and other problems, that initiative was not realized.[53] Since then, the DPRK's infiltrations had exposed the ROK's weak counter-infiltration capabilities, including the limited ability of local police forces to confront well-trained North Korean commandos, and the inefficiency of relying on the military to conduct massive sweeps against a small number of invaders from the North.[54] The 1968 incidents served as the last straw for Park in his decision to launch the reserves.

When he announced the creation of the HRF, Park also spoke publicly about the nation's need to develop domestic arms manufacturing.[55] South Korea had to "fundamentally alter its national defense posture," Park said, to "defend through our own strength as the first line of defense."[56] The structure of the HRF as he described it demonstrated his intention to spread the responsibility for national security across the entire South Korean population. He proposed that citizen reserve units would guard their own villages, towns, and cities, and would also participate in the ROK military's counter-infiltration, counterinsurgency, and counterespionage operations. In addition, Park spoke of "spiritually fortifying" the people to fight the communists, and he criticized the nation's tendency to depend on its military and United Nations forces (and the United States) for South Korea's defense.[57]

The HRF represented a total reconfiguration of the civilian role in national defense. At the ceremony formally launching the HRF on April 1, Park declared, "The primary responsibility for our national defense lies with our nation, and it is also each individual citizen's sacred and absolute duty. Our allies' aid and the collective security system are only to assist us; they are certainly not to bear any of our own responsibility."[58] In a new capacity, South Korea's citizens were to share national security duties through their participation in the HRF, which would serve to both bridge the military and civilian worlds and deeply integrate them.

The HRF was organized into a regional unit, consisting of the groups established in local communities, and a workplace unit, called the workplace reserve troops (*chikchang yebigun*), that was made up of worksite-based cohorts (including company employees, factory workers, public sector and education employees, and college students). This organizational structure allowed for the quick and efficient mobilization and deployment of reserve forces in case of national security threats. In 1969 the Kapho Unit (young troops mostly under the age of thirty in local towns and villages) was added to reinforce regional security in case of war or a national emergency.[59] Civilians nationwide, from the urban centers and populous coastal areas to the most remote villages in the countryside, were tasked with maintaining vigilance and defending their communities against North Korean invaders.[60]

The HRF became one of the most important components in Park's plan to mobilize the civilian population for self-reliant defense.[61] The reserve troops included both men and women, although most were men who had completed their compulsory military service and then been redrafted to serve in HRF divisions near their home or work.[62] In its first several years the reserve forces also included a large number of experienced veterans returning home from the Vietnam War. Ordered by Park to serve as "the eyes and ears" of national security, this paramilitary organization would become "the most comprehensive anti-Communist intelligence network in [South] Korea."[63]

The HRF was called into action just six months after its establishment, following a large-scale infiltration by the DPRK. Around midnight on October 30, 120 elite soldiers of Unit 124 of the KPA landed at eight separate locations on the eastern coast of South Korea between Ulchin and Samch'ŏk. As part of Kim Il Sung's special operation to foment local revolts against the Park government from outlying areas of South Korea, the invading troops set up bases in the nearby T'aebaek Mountains, where they planned to train South Korean guerrilla fighters to carry out long-term insurgencies.[64] The KPA unit began by recruiting and conducting ideological education sessions among the locals, sometimes killing villagers who resisted their efforts. On November 3, after a local civilian reported the presence of the North Koreans, the ROK military launched a counteroperation in the mountains, where it spent the next two months eliminating the infiltrators.[65] North Koreans' operation in the region aided Park by helping him to mobilize the newly created HRF in a powerful way, as its civilian reserves were called on to support the military's campaign against the invaders. Local HRF units in Ulchin and Samch'ŏk, familiar with the region's terrain and the mountains, provided valuable surveillance and guidance to assist the military in swiftly locating and defeating the North Koreans.[66]

National Responses to the Security Crisis

In addition to prompting Park to establish and then expand the HRF, the 1968 security crisis also helped him drive forward the nationwide reforms that would support his self-reliant national defense initiative. He was able to achieve a general consensus among high-level state officials and military leaders to improve security measures against North Korean infiltrations and expedite indigenous arms production.[67] Although some scholars debate the authenticity of the DPRK's threats in 1968 and interpret them as political fabrications by Park to prolong his rule, studies based on diplomatic correspondence between the United States and South Korea at the time, as well as declassified Russian and Eastern European reports of the DPRK's allied governments, make it clear that the DPRK provoked the vast majority of the military confrontations in the late 1960s.[68] Consequently, the threats posed by the DPRK—at least as they were felt in the ROK—were real. Civilians' testimonies, military reports, newspaper headlines, and public surveys also indicate that the sense of insecurity felt in South Korea was not limited to those in government but was shared by most of the population.[69]

The security crisis undoubtedly proved advantageous for Park politically in his efforts to unify South Koreans.[70] Faced with the DPRK's threatening actions, South Koreans increasingly sided with Park's stance on prioritizing national security and the economic development he insisted was essential for an independent national defense system. With widespread public support for his security measures, Park was able to overcome opposition leaders and the pro-democracy movement that resisted his heavy-handed leadership. Military objectives were prioritized over socially progressive agendas, such as social welfare programs, advocated by progressive intellectuals and labor activists. In fact, in a highly charged atmosphere of fear and anticommunist fervor, it became nearly impossible to oppose the Park government's march toward security independence. The security climate would also supply political justification for Park's amendments to the constitution in 1969 that allowed him a third presidential term and, in 1972, for his implementation of the Yusin Constitution, which cemented his authoritarian rule.

The events in 1968 also catalyzed military reforms that supported and complemented the newly established HRF. Although the public generally accepted the HRF as a necessary security measure, some of Park's political opponents protested the involvement of civilians in armed conflict. Opposition groups such as the New Democratic Party (Sinmindang) were concerned that civilian reserves would be ill-prepared to fight, in spite of the compulsory HRF military training (which consisted of just twenty days each year) and most reserves' prior military experience.[71] Chang Chunha, a member of the New Democratic Party and one of the leading critics of Park's authoritarian regime, advocated for more rigorous training of existing soldiers in the army instead of deploying civilian reserves.[72] And because the core leadership of the HRF came from members of Park's ruling Democratic Republican Party (Minju Konghwadang), Park's opponents accused him of using the HRF to elevate his own party's power and expand state control over people's lives.[73] Despite such protests, the security threats in 1968 enabled Park to override all opposition and expand the HRF as the cornerstone of his national security program.[74]

The creation of the HRF opened the door to broader national militarization. Because Park sought to equip the HRF, which consisted of twenty divisions of a projected 2.5 million troops, with domestically produced weapons, he began pushing government agencies and civilian enterprises to develop the infrastructure for arms production (see chapter 2). The nation's sense of urgency also gave Park leverage with the populace, allowing him to establish national donation campaigns that would help finance the state's new defense industry (see chapter 5). In effect, the precarious situation with North Korea was extremely valuable for Park's regime: it sparked a collective militarization of the population and helped Park promote a sense of common purpose with respect to independent national defense.

US Factors

The DPRK's provocations reverberated through the US-ROK relationship, a bilateral dynamic that had its own complexities. When the United States decided not to retaliate militarily against the DPRK after the Blue House Raid, and again after the *Pueblo* Incident when its own ship was seized, Park and his aides were embittered, especially because the incident at the presidential mansion could have ended Park's life. During a Ministry of National Defense (MND; Kukpangbu) briefing with leaders of the US Forces Korea (USFK) and the United Nations Command on the day the *Pueblo* was captured, Minister of National Defense Kim Sŏngŭn—described by the USFK commander Charles H. Bonesteel as "emotionally irate"—expressed his frustration over the Americans' lack of response to the attempted assassination of President Park two days earlier.[75]

The subdued US response damaged South Korea's trust in its ally. Since the signing of the US-ROK Mutual Defense Treaty on October 1, 1953, the ROK had seen US protection as the main deterrent to a North Korean invasion. Now the Park government was skeptical of the Americans' commitment to South Korea's security and was gravely concerned about what might follow from North Korea. Furthermore, notwithstanding the ROK's insistence on being included in negotiations with the DPRK over the release of the *Pueblo* crew, US delegates left the South Koreans out of those talks and met exclusively with North Korean representatives, leaving Park feeling alienated and dismayed.[76] It also represented a loss of face for Park in the eyes of the Korean people, and for the nation as a whole, that the United States would not even respond to the attempt on the president's life.[77] Over subsequent meetings, and in letters and telegrams sent to US military officials, the US embassy in Seoul, and government officials in Washington, South Korean leaders openly expressed their frustration over a US approach that offered only diplomatic solutions to the *Pueblo* Incident and dismissed military countermeasures against North Korea.

What South Koreans saw as passivity reflected the Johnson administration's policy to limit US military actions in Asia where possible in order to avoid escalating conflicts into full-scale wars. The evolving situation in Vietnam was a major factor in Johnson's decision not to retaliate against the DPRK in January 1968.[78] North Vietnam's Tet Offensive took place only a week after the *Pueblo* Incident, casting doubt on the prospect of a swift resolution to the war in Vietnam.[79] With antiwar protests escalating throughout the United States, Johnson could not risk another war in Asia. In addition, in spite of the recent provocations, the US intelligence community did not believe that a full invasion of South Korea by the DPRK was imminent.[80] Nevertheless, Park's officials continued to object to the Americans' lack of assertiveness and to threaten the ROK's own action against the DPRK. They complained that Johnson was more concerned with his own reelection and with avoiding conflict in the Korean peninsula than he was with supporting South Korea as an ally.[81]

In response, Johnson sent a special envoy, Cyrus R. Vance, to Seoul on February 11 to reaffirm the US commitment to South Korea and to secure Park's promise not to take independent military actions against North Korea.[82] The intense negotiations that ensued between Vance and an irate Park resulted in rewards and costs for both parties. Vance was able to deter Park from launching an immediate attack on North Korea, although Park did not promise long-term restraint.[83] Park, in turn, secured an additional $100 million in military aid from the US and separate financial support for the construction of an M16 rifle plant in South Korea, but Vance refused to guarantee US retaliation against future North Korean provocations. In the end, Park was not reassured.

As his negotiations with Vance had failed to mend South Korea's relationship with the Johnson administration, Park persisted in his demand for military measures against North Korea, driving a deeper wedge in the US-ROK alliance. When Johnson asked Vance why Park and his ministers were so angry with the United States, Vance replied: "Because we did not permit any retaliatory action on the attack on [the] Blue House. The depth of feeling over that is very deep. . . . They considered it very serious that the raiders got within 300 yards of [the] Blue House[,] bent upon killing the President and his family." Vance warned that "there is a very strong danger of unilateral action by [Park]."[84]

A year later, on April 14, 1969, Park's fears about the Americans' waning security commitment were exacerbated when North Korea shot down a US Navy EC-121 reconnaissance plane in international airspace about eighty miles from the North Korean border, and once again the United States did not retaliate. Despite Park's advice to newly elected president Richard Nixon (1969–74) that "this incident will be followed by others [by the DPRK] unless some strong reply is made," Nixon, like Johnson before him, decided to forgo a military response against North Korea for fear of getting involved in another war.[85] Amid another wave of antiwar protests against US involvement in Vietnam, Nixon's interest in politics at home far outweighed his concern for South Korea's security.

The Nixon Doctrine

In retrospect, Nixon's lack of response to the EC-121 incident was a prelude to his historic announcement a few months later of what came to be known as the Nixon Doctrine, a new foreign policy that entailed the deliberate stepping down of Cold War tensions between the United States and the communist regimes of China and the Soviet Union. Nixon first spoke of the policy change at an informal gathering with reporters on July 25, 1969, during an international trip that included visits to countries in Asia and Eastern Europe.[86] Nixon stated, "We must avoid the kind of policy that will make countries in Asia so dependent upon us that we are dragged into conflicts such as the one we have in Vietnam."[87] In response to a reporter's question, Nixon affirmed that the United States would "honor its treaty commitments," but he added that "as far as the problems of internal security are concerned, as far as the problems of military defense, except for the threat of a major power involving nuclear weapons, . . . the United States is going to encourage and has a right to expect that this [type of] problem will be increasingly handled by . . . the Asian nations themselves."[88]

During his stop in Bangkok a few days later, at a meeting with the US ambassadors serving in Southeast Asia, Nixon reiterated the policy, stating more specifically: "Where [the] problem is internal subversion, countries must deal with [the] problem themselves. We will help—but not [with] American ground forces."[89] From the beginning of Park's military rule in 1962, the presence of US troops in South Korea had guaranteed his regime's stability as well as South Korea's national security, allowing the country to focus on its economic development. Nixon's announcement and his subsequent remarks confirmed Park's long-held concern that the United States would renege on its security commitments.

On August 21, during a meeting with Nixon in San Francisco, Park attempted to convince him of the urgency of South Korea's security situation, telling him that withdrawing US forces would be just what Kim Il Sung wanted. At the same time, Park was fairly realistic about the public pressure on Nixon to disengage the United States from foreign conflicts. In making his case for keeping US troops in South Korea while also acknowledging the ROK's need to develop its own military capabilities, Park sought to convince Nixon that increasing US military aid to modernize the ROK Armed Forces would help reduce US security involvement in Korea: "A way to achieve [that] objective is to strengthen the equipment and combat capability of the ROK forces . . . to the extent that the ROK can single-handedly resist North Korean invasion."[90]

Nixon agreed with Park that "military and economic self-reliance [were] the correct road to take."[91] In supporting South Korea's military modernization, Nixon broke with previous US actions that had deterred the South Koreans from developing their own weapons and rendered the ROK military totally dependent on US arms imports for most of the 1960s.[92] He also assured Park that "We will honor the U.S.–ROK Defense Treaty" and that the United States would "not retreat from the Pacific area" and would maintain its security commitment to its allies in the region.[93]

Withdrawal of US Troops

The Nixon Doctrine dramatically transformed US foreign policy through the withdrawal of US forces from Indochina and the establishment of détente with the Soviet Union and China. And although Nixon had promised Park that the United States would keep its defense commitment to the ROK, just seven months after their meeting in San Francisco the United States announced troop withdrawals from South Korea as well. On March 20, 1970, Nixon decided to reduce the US military presence in South Korea by almost a third (about 20,000 of the 64,000 USFK troops) by the end of fiscal year 1971.[94] Less than a week later, the US ambassador in Seoul informed Park of the plan to withdraw the US Army's Seventh Infantry Division (part of USFK), which numbered around 20,000. The announcement stunned Park, who had been led to believe the United States would not begin downsizing its military presence until South Korea had acquired the economic capability and resources to support its own military modernization—which he did not expect to achieve for at least five years.[95] Although Nixon remained firm, ROK officials continued to press the United States for more time, insisting that military modernization goals had to be met before US troops were pulled back.[96]

Vice President Spiro Agnew traveled to South Korea in August to discuss the Nixon administration's withdrawal policy and negotiate the terms of the plan. In his meetings with Park on August 25 and 26, Agnew sought to explain the administration's rationale. As Kim Chŏng-nyŏm, Park's chief of staff, recalled, Agnew explained that the Nixon Doctrine was a response to Americans' opposition to US military intervention abroad and that, consequently, the size of the US military, including its bases and troops stationed in foreign countries like South Korea, would be reduced.[97] Agnew added that it was necessary to decrease military spending because of the US government's fiscal circumstances. He reaffirmed that, as a part of the plan, the Seventh Infantry Division in South Korea would be withdrawn by the end of June 1971.[98]

Agnew promised increased military aid in exchange for the withdrawal of US ground troops. However, although Park asked for approximately $3 billion over the following five years for modernizing South Korea's military equipment, Agnew would agree to only $1.5 billion, to be distributed over the same five-year period (1971–76). Park and Agnew and their teams engaged in long and heated debates over the United States' commitment to South Korea's long-term security, US military aid, and troop withdrawals. In the end the two sides agreed to hold further discussions to resolve their remaining issues, including Park's request for assurance that the United States would not remove more than 20,000 troops from South Korea, before they finalized an agenda for the implementation of the withdrawal.[99] But Agnew broke that agreement almost immediately, telling American reporters on his way to board the plane for his departure from South Korea that the United States would withdraw all USFK troops—not just the Seventh Infantry Division—within five years.[100]

From the perspective of Park and his policymakers, therefore, South Korea had only until 1976 to modernize its military and establish its security independence.[101] When the Seventh Infantry Division pulled out the next year, in March 1971, the ROK military took charge of defending the 155-mile-long DMZ for the first time since the end of the Korean War.[102] For Park, the US withdrawal in the face of escalating threats from the DPRK necessitated the quickest possible upgrade of South Korea's defense capabilities.

Declassified documents from the Nixon administration help explain the deeper logic behind the decision to withdraw USFK troops. In addition to the political and fiscal demands in the United States at the time for reduced military involvement in Asia, Nixon had also considered the military preparedness of South Korea. His policy advisers had determined that the ROK Armed Forces, aided by existing US and UN forces in South Korea, were already sufficiently armed and positioned to defend against a North Korean attack, especially if the North lacked Soviet or Chinese support. For example, a memorandum to then-National Security Advisor Henry Kissinger from Laurence E. Lynn Jr., a staff member of the National Security Council (NSC), reveals that the NSC had concluded that "a decision to withdraw a U.S. division and to maintain an 18 or 19 division ROK force structure involve[d] no military risks of any significance" to South Korea, and that the United States "need not 'modernize' the entire ROK 18 or 19 division force structure to enable them to defend themselves against the present or likely future North Korea force structure."[103] This memorandum and other documents show that Nixon and his advisers disagreed with Park's assessment of the North Korean threat, and some even believed the ROK government was intentionally exaggerating the dangers of its security situation to win a stronger US commitment to South Korea.[104] Nixon's decision also reflected his administration's general belief that the Soviet Union and China would not support Kim Il Sung in an invasion of South Korea and risk another Korean War.[105]

Notwithstanding the assessment by the Nixon administration, Park's view of South Korea's security situation merits further consideration from a domestic and psychological standpoint. Although the ROK military, backed by a reduced number of US troops, might have been able to defend South Korea in the event of a conventional assault, Kim Il Sung's use of special operations and small-scale infiltrations, such as the Blue House Raid, had a disproportionately powerful effect on South Korea's political and social stability.[106] In the context of the ideological warfare between the two Koreas, with each regime seeking to portray the other as illegitimate and weak, the "shock value" of North Korea's incursions was powerful. The KPA commandos had undermined South Korea's sense of security, leaving people feeling deeply vulnerable and reinforcing a public image of the Park government as unprepared to meet Kim's tactics.[107]

Adding to Park's perception of threat from his rival, the DPRK had already begun to carry out its own rapid industrialization and military modernization under its slogan "parallel economic construction and defense building."[108] Thanks to the massive amounts of Soviet military aid it received in the late 1950s and early 1960s, followed by the Soviet Union's provision of military equipment and industrial resources from 1966 to 1969, the DPRK had by the late 1960s developed the ability to equip its military with domestically produced conventional infantry weapons.[109] Meanwhile, largely owing to US policies designed to keep the ROK dependent on US weapons and military aid, South Korea did not even have a defense industry in the late 1960s.[110] The ROK relied entirely on US military aid for gun and ammunition purchases, and it was still using outdated, US-supplied M1 rifles, which the MND complained were "heavier, longer, and slower" than the firearms produced in North Korea.[111] Pressured by South Korea's aggressive negotiations with other foreign suppliers to acquire a domestic gun factory, both the US Department of State and the Department of Defense agreed in June 1969 to the construction of an M16 rifle manufacturing plant in South Korea; however, production negotiations would drag on for another three years.[112]

Park's Response to the Nixon Doctrine

When the Nixon administration offered only $1.5 billion in military aid to help soften the blow of its troop withdrawal, Park knew that amount would not be adequate to modernize the entire ROK military, with its glaringly obsolete equipment. Frustrated once again by what he felt was lackluster support from the Americans, including their unwillingness to transfer advanced weapons-manufacturing technology to South Korea, Park became determined to develop the required military technology domestically, independent of US constraints.

As a first step, on August 6, 1970, Park established the Agency for Defense Development (ADD), a special institute charged with advancing research and development for Korean-made weapons (for more on the ADD, see chapter 4). The US State Department and the American embassy in Seoul questioned Park's motives for establishing a separate institute specializing in weapons development when the ROK's Korea Institute of Science and Technology, a multidisciplinary agency founded in 1966 through US foreign aid, already had the capacity for basic weapons research.[113] Americans' suspicion that Park intended to develop advanced weapons that could disrupt regional stability was also raised by his Weapons Exploitation Committee, which the US House of Representatives' Committee on International Relations described as "a covert, ad hoc governmental committee responsible to the Blue House for weapons procurement and production," and which worked in close coordination with the ADD on procuring weapons from abroad.[114] In the early 1970s the Weapons Exploitation Committee—whose members included Park's senior secretaries, the minister of national defense, and the director of the ADD, as well as a handful of top military advisers and scientists—made secret expeditions to weapons plants in Taiwan, Norway, France, Switzerland, England, and Israel to study the work of advanced defense manufacturers.[115] As the United States suspected, the committee's primary objective was to obtain weapons technologies that the United States had banned from South Korea. These included technologies related to the nuclear arms and guided missiles that Park considered indispensable for South Korea's self-defense, especially in light of the United States' decision to withdraw its troops.

Park took further steps toward the development of a self-reliant national defense system with the launch of his Five-Year Military Modernization Plan (1971–76). In February 1971 the ROK finalized the agreement with the United States on its withdrawal of the Seventh Infantry Division, including the promised $1.5 billion in US military assistance that would kick-start Park's new military program.[116] And in the next month, after three years of negotiation, the MND finally signed a manufacturing contract with US defense manufacturer Colt Industries to produce M16 rifles in South Korea.[117]

Although the upgraded US military aid package under the Nixon Doctrine opened South Korea's access to American weapons technology via approved technical data packages, which included technical blueprints to enable South Korea to manufacture basic US-model weapons, the United States never offered a "blanket endorsement of Korean defense production."[118] The US government was primarily concerned, especially after the Blue House Raid, that South Korea's militarization might encourage Park to launch an attack on North Korea, whether in retaliation or as an effort to pursue reunification.[119] Washington also feared that South Korea's ability to manufacture advanced weapons could spark an arms race in East Asia.[120] Maintaining the balance of power between the Soviet Union and the United States and their allies in the region was the Americans' first priority, and the Nixon administration was also eager to preserve the climate of East-West détente it had just established with China in 1971. Park's aggressive pursuit of weapons played directly into US fears.[121] Although the Nixon Doctrine encouraged "self-defense abilities" among its allies, the United States continued to enforce its interests in the region and in many cases interfered with South Korea's weapons initiatives.[122] As the House Committee on International Relations noted in 1978, "The United States [in the 1970s] followed an ambiguous policy with respect to Korean self-sufficiency that both left the door open to Korea to pursue its own goals, and probably created uncertainty as to the exact intentions of the United States."[123] The contradictions in US policy and actions increased Park's distrust of the United States and its security commitments.

The shift in US foreign policy to push South Korea to defend itself had an important effect on Park's new self-reliant national defense strategy. In practice, the Nixon Doctrine superseded the North Korean threat as the primary concern driving Park's campaign for self-reliant defense. With regard to the ROK, the doctrine set two basic principles for US policy: (1) to promote the "total forces concept" put forth by Secretary of Defense Melvin Laird and encourage the ROK to employ all its resources, including the expanded civilian reserve forces, as integral components in the nation's defensive military strength; and (2) to limit security assistance to technical and financial aid, without the support of US ground troops.[124] The basic tenets of Laird's total forces concept became part of what Park would officially put forward in 1972 as his total security system (*ch'ongnyŏk anbo ch'eje*); both versions stressed that large-scale civilian participation was crucial to the nation's military strength. The Nixon Doctrine's deadline and its reinforcement of the ROK's use of its own defensive power thus created a political and security environment that would justify Park's totalitarian, total security approach to developing an independent defense industry.

The geopolitical context and events as recorded in available government documents support the argument that the DPRK's actions and US policies in the late 1960s triggered Park's decision to build an arms industry that would bolster self-reliant national defense. Given the rise of the democracy movement in South Korea, it would have been politically unfeasible for Park to institute his aggressive strategies for military modernization if North Korea's threats had not escalated public concern about security. The shock of the Nixon Doctrine, combined with US arms restrictions and troop withdrawals, also presented the ROK leadership with a situation that justified and necessitated a fundamental restructuring of its national defense system, both practically and conceptually.

Domestic Factors

Alongside the external drivers of policy coming from North Korea and the United States, South Korea's own history and the influence of Park himself were strong internal forces behind the Park regime's total security system and its policy of self-reliant national defense. In January 1972, when Park announced his plan for a nationwide total security system, he explained that it would prepare citizens to respond as a unified force to a North Korean attack at any time or place (fig. 1.1).[125] In essence, under the total security system the government and the Korean people would fight as "a harmonious whole" (*honyŏn ilch'e*), or "one body," to defend the nation.[126] This notion was similar to the concept of "total war states" that first arose in World War I, when warring nations systematically erased the distinctions between the military and civilian spheres and between the battlefront and the home front.[127] Total war states, such as Japan and Germany during World War II, completely mobilized their populations and imposed their authority over their citizens to reconfigure society into a function-based system dedicated to carrying out a total war.[128] Fortunately for Park, Koreans of his generation had been groomed for war mobilization over the preceding forty years, through the Asia-Pacific War (1931–45), the Korean War (1950–53), and the Vietnam War (1964–73).[129] This historical context provided a strong foundation for Park's total security system and self-reliant national defense policy.

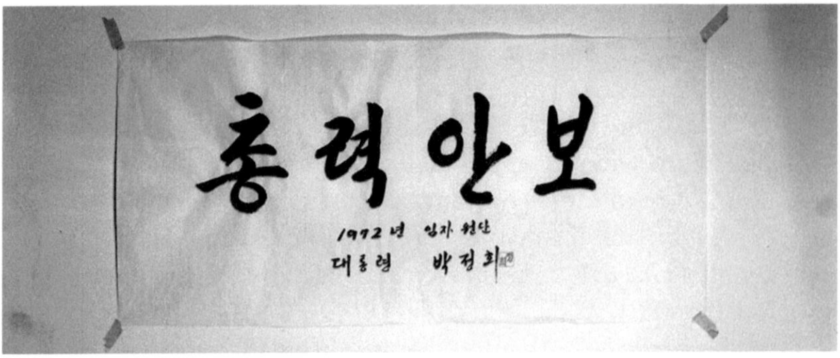

FIG. 1.1. "Total security" (*ch'ongnyŏk anbo*), calligraphy by Park Chung Hee in 1972. *Source:* National Archives of Korea; file no. CET0023198.

Historical Foundations

Koreans had their first exposure to modern wartime mobilization in the 1930s and 1940s, when Korea was transformed into a military-industrial supply base for Imperial Japan's campaigns in Manchuria and China, and later when Japan fought against the US-led Allies in the Pacific theater of World War II (1941–45).[130] Under Japan's highly centralized colonial rule, Koreans had been marshaled and mobilized for rapid industrial production in order to supply Japanese war efforts. Park's key strategies for national development in the 1970s under the total security system—HCI, the merging of the private and public sectors, the mass mobilization of industrial labor, the implementation of modernization campaigns such as the New Village Movement (NVM; Saemaŭl Undong), and the state's use of mass culture and media for patriotic propaganda—were reminiscent of what Park and his fellow Koreans had experienced under Japanese rule.

In fact, Park had been formally trained in the concept of total war during his education for service in the Imperial Japanese Army in the early 1940s. At the Japanese Military Academy he had studied "the idea and 'necessity' in 'modern warfare' of supporting the nation's military campaign with an all-embracing 'systematic control' (*soshiki tōsei*) of politics, economics, thought, and culture."[131] Park and his fellow students came to envision total war as "a war of [the] populations (*jin'insen*), requiring improvement in the physical and mental capacities of the people," and the academy also focused on the psychological or "spiritual" aspect of total war (*seishinsen*).[132] Japan's teachings would be reflected in the Park regime's strategies for achieving material and ideological change.

Another major catalyst for the regime's rapid manifestation of a total security system was the experience of the Korean War, which directly exposed the Korean people to a modern war that affected their day-to-day lives and demolished the physical and psychological boundaries around warfare. The Korean War involved massive propaganda battles between the communist and capitalist states that intensified anticommunism in South Korea, demanded the complete unity of government and civilian forces, and rallied the nation ideologically. A study of Korean War prisoners of war by Monica Kim provides details about some of the highly sophisticated methods of the Cold War–driven state propaganda machines and how they penetrated the minds of ordinary people during the Korean War.[133] Amid the total war between the North and South Korean states, people on both sides were thoroughly exposed to the ideological and organizational mechanisms that their respective governments employed to justify military actions and mobilize the populace for war efforts. Koreans' direct experiences of war, both in the Korean War and through Japan's fifteen-year war in the Pacific, had shaped their understanding of the urgent need for and value of defense industrialization, for which the Park state's total security system would serve as the backbone in South Korea. In North Korea after the Korean War, these shared values and experiences would play out in the making of Kim Il Sung's own variant of a total security state that mobilized the North Koreans for a similar military-style industrialization.

South Korea's more recent history with the Vietnam War also contributed to its citizens' ability to mobilize as if for war. The ROK government had depicted the war in Vietnam as an international battle against communism that all South Koreans, as a nation, had to join, whether they fought on the front line or the home front.[134] As "national citizens" (*kungmin*), they had been required to integrate the war abroad into their daily lives, to fight along with the troops in Vietnam through their active material (financial) and moral support at home.[135]

Although historical context provided a foundation for the Park regime's mobilization of Korean society, it was Park Chung Hee who inspired (and coerced) the populace to adopt his national defense policy. To grasp how he did this, it is essential to understand his ideology and how he conveyed it to the nation. Park saw that he needed to change people's collective perspective so they would work to transform South Korea into a nation with a strong and self-reliant national defense.

Park's Self-Reliant National Defense Ideology

Park began actively promoting self-reliant national defense as his main political and military slogan after announcing the creation of the HRF in February 1968. On February 26, at the Seoul National University's graduation ceremony, Park mentioned "self-reliant national defense" in a public speech for the first time, stating, "We must fully utilize the knowledge we have acquired to build a self-reliant economy and self-reliant national defense. To advance towards self-reliance, prosperity, and unification, there should be no distinction between you and me; all citizens must unite and cooperate wholeheartedly."[136] On March 6, at a commission ceremony for student reserve officers, Park again used the phrase when he declared, "Self-reliant national defense is none other than the power of the young generation in this country."[137] He emphasized self-reliant national defense once more at a meeting of public officials the next day.[138] During the official ceremony on April 1 that celebrated the launch of the HRF, Park declared, "The time has come for us to rally for the construction of self-reliant national defense," once more emphasizing that the South Korean people should no longer depend exclusively on their ally (United States), or even on their own military, for their defense.[139] According to Park, the military power for self-reliant defense could be acquired through modernization, better training of troops, mobilization of the HRF, and the development of the defense industry; however, those military efforts had to be backed up by civilians, through their economic strength as well as their will to protect the nation.[140] Along with establishing indigenous arms production to equip South Korea's military and reserve troops with Korean-made weapons, Park determined that he had to cultivate a sense of ownership among civilians regarding the goal of security development. A strong national drive to "protect one's own country with one's own power" would be critical to the success of his agenda.[141]

As one model for self-reliant national defense, Park looked to Israel—which, like the ROK, had been established in 1948. Similar to the ROK, Israel was a small state surrounded by larger neighbors. It had developed the ability to defend itself through strong civilian participation in national defense and a vibrant domestic defense industry that supplied advanced weapons (including nuclear arms) to its own defense forces—achievements that Park admired and praised.[142] When Park established the ADD in 1970, he ordered the new agency to set goals for South Korea that would put its independent weapons system on a par with Israel's.[143] A team of scientists, technocrats, and military advisers was dispatched to Israel for a month (April 1–May 5, 1970) to study its "fountain of strength," including its military strategies and organization, training, arms procurement policies, and reserve army, as well as its experience in the Six-Day War.[144]

A second model was Meiji-era Japan (1868–1912). Park often referred to Japan's successful modernization of the economy and military during this period as a model for South Korea's development.[145] Indeed, his promotion of both a "self-reliant national economy" (*charip kyŏngje*) and self-reliant national defense harked back to the motto of the modernization movement in Meiji Japan, *fukoku kyōhei*, or "rich nation, strong army," which Park adopted for South Korea (see chapter 2).

Although he looked abroad to other nations that could serve as good models, Park's defense agenda must nevertheless be understood as a product of his own political vision for Korea, based on his historical and cultural understanding of the nation.[146] In his writings, Park describes Korea's past as "a history of suffering and foreign invasion," and he decries his country's past lack of will for self-development, noting the "absence of [a] spirit of national independence" and Korea's historical reliance on foreign powers.[147] He believed these conditions had rendered Korea perennially vulnerable to both internal disorder and external subjugation. Park wrote, "That ours has been a history of suffering is not just a dogmatic assumption. In view of our national character and geopolitical position, ours has been a history of internal pauperization, and internal and external oppression."[148] Given this protracted history of interference from powerful neighbors, the concept of national independence from foreign intrusions was central to Park's vision for the nation.

Park honed his nationalist message of self-reliance to resonate with the post–Korean War populace, which had collectively endured the trials and violence of the foreign struggle for control of the Korean peninsula. This generation saw Korea as perpetually victimized and had a deep distrust of the larger powers. In addition, especially since the North Korean invasion that had provoked the Korean War, the vast majority of South Koreans were strongly anticommunist, which they expressed through their growing support for stronger defenses to protect against threats from the North.[149] The phrases Park used, such as "self-reliant national defense" and "modernization of the fatherland," as well as his militarized rhetoric—his "can-do-ism" and talk of "rich nation, strong army"—echoed their own sentiments. His ideals matched their collective hunger for national independence and prosperity. In this regard, as Chung-in Moon and Byung-joon Jun have proposed, "Park's ideational structure was by and large a reflection of the South Korean people. . . . [His] modernization can be seen as the crystallization of the aspirations of the South Korean populace, who struggled to overcome backwardness, poverty, and military vulnerability."[150]

The Second Economy Movement

To convince the South Korean people to work together to build a defense industry, Park focused on instilling in them a sense of collective responsibility for the nation's security. Although South Koreans had long aspired to national independence, aside from compulsory military service for Korean men, the ROK had not established strong cultural or social structures to engage citizens directly with national security, which was widely perceived as the domain of the military and government. After the 1968 security crisis, however, Park began to criticize this view and advocate for a fundamental change in the people's "mental (or spiritual) attitude" (*chŏngsinjŏk chase*).[151] In his speeches, Park increasingly stressed the need to transform the mentality and culture of both the people and the government by setting forth a new philosophy on national defense.[152]

Even prior to the 1968 security crisis, Park had preached the need for a change in attitude, chiefly when he introduced the concept of the "second economy" (*che-2 kyŏngje*) in a speech celebrating the fourth annual Export Day, on November 3, 1967.[153] But his focus at the time had been on inspiring people's participation in national economic development. Park described the second economy as the "moral economy" on which the real economy—the "first economy" (*che-1 kyŏngje*)—was built.[154] Based on this idea, he proposed a nationwide moral revitalization campaign that would secure South Koreans' support for his economic development plan.[155]

The idea of the second economy received more attention at Park's annual New Year's press conference, on January 15, 1968.[156] In response to a reporter's question about the term, Park explained: "The 'second economy' is not an academic term. . . . It is a term that I came up with. . . . It means that while we are building our economy, which requires our efforts in the visible physical and material realm, at the same time our *mental attitude* must be correct, in order for us to more efficiently pursue 'economic development' or the 'modernization movement.'"[157] Park argued that this immaterial, mental aspect—the people's collective mindset, or the second economy—had to be transformed to complement the development of the material economy, or the first economy.[158] To accomplish such a revolution in national character, Park sought to inculcate in Korean citizens a new ideology that would alter historical and cultural discourse from the inside out and would even outlast the nation's material development. With this aim, he announced the Second Economy Movement, which was designed to impart—through discipline, economic frugality, and hard work—the spiritual or mental outlook Koreans needed to build up the economy, increase productivity, and raise the nation's per capita income.[159] Kim Yonghwan, a former senior presidential secretary for economic affairs, elaborates on Park's vision and rationale: "President Park Chung Hee believed that economic development would be impossible without the active energy of the citizens through their participation and agreement. To achieve this Park believed, first, that the underlying defeatist mentality in people's consciousness had to be eradicated, and that a spiritual revolution was necessary to transform [that] defeatism into confidence. Park thought that the people's confidence was so important that it should even be specifically labeled; hence the term 'second economy.'"[160]

Park's concept was akin to the theory of national transformation (*minjok kaejoron*) put forward in 1922 by the Korean nationalist Yi

Kwangsu (1892–1950). Yi had prioritized educating the Korean people to foster their cultural development and enlightenment, and to cultivate an attitude of independence while Korea was under Japanese colonial rule.[161] The idea of the second economy was also connected to Park's long-held goal of "social reconstruction," which he wrote about in his book, *Our Nation's Path: Ideology of Social Reconstruction*, published in 1962 (and also published in English).[162] The Second Economy Movement signaled that, for Park, the spiritual and moral reconstruction of the Korean people was of utmost importance to the nation's economic development.[163]

The ideological emphasis of the Second Economy Movement led Park's critics and political opponents (as well as later scholars) to accuse him of bundling noneconomic factors into his economic developmental model in an effort to subvert democracy and impose his ideology in all areas of society and politics.[164] While Park denied this, the movement portended his regime's drastic, wholesale indoctrination of the citizenry to support the state's plans for independent national defense. After the Blue House Raid, which occurred on the heels of Park's announcement of the Second Economy Movement, the concept of spiritual and psychological reconstruction was immediately reframed as part of a new security campaign—promoting self-reliant national defense—to transform the people through military and educational programs promoting patriotism, anticommunism, and loyalty to the state. Park quickly redirected the Second Economy Movement's ideological energy toward this self-reliant defense initiative, a strategy he also tied to industrialization and economic development. The official Second Economy Movement lasted barely a year; the government ceased referring to it after 1968, owing to ongoing public confusion over the concept and its poor reception in the media.[165] Nonetheless, the idea of moral and spiritual transformation was preserved in the sociocultural campaign promoting self-reliant national defense.

Park's ideological reform effort, initiated with the Second Economy Movement, sought to transform the people's thinking at an even deeper level as he began building his total security system. To achieve total security, he knew it was critical that he motivate the citizenry to work for national defense. Park presented his plan for a radically new national security system as a broad movement in which all Korean citizens had a stake, and his campaign for self-reliant national defense aimed to foster their willing and earnest participation. The state apparatus, working at the grassroots level through educational and cultural reforms, enlisted all people to make personal sacrifices in their total commitment to national security.[166] Along with physical conscription through the HRF, the state called upon the people to contribute to the strengthening of national defense by donating financial resources, engaging in rigorous labor for state-led military-industrial projects, and supporting propaganda campaigns, which will be further explored in the subsequent chapters.

In 1968, the same year that Park established the HRF and announced self-reliant national defense, the Ministry of Education (Mun'gyobu) announced its new National Charter on Education, created to incorporate the teaching of anticommunist, nationalist values in primary and secondary school curricula. Designed to indoctrinate Korean youth in the government's vision for security independence, the educational initiative appealed to younger students through their understanding of Korea's history and its place in the world, a fundamental piece of which was the idea that Korea was in dire need of national strengthening.[167] As Park stated in the opening of the charter:

> We were born into this land to carry out the historical mission of national restoration. It is time to revive the shining spirit of our ancestors, to establish a self-reliant inner attitude and, outside [our borders], to contribute to the welfare of humanity. . . . [This is] the goal of our education. . . . Realizing that the country develops through our creativity and cooperation, and that the nation's prosperity lies in our individual growth, we will fulfill the responsibilities and duties that are required for freedom and rights and raise the national spirit of every citizen participating in the building of the nation. With patriotic love, which is fully committed to an anticommunist democratic spirit, is the way we live our lives; this is the basis for realizing the ideals of the free world.[168]

Park appropriated long-standing ancestral values to encourage a sense of unity and to foment a patriotic fervor for modernization, all the while emphasizing education and individual growth as key to South Korea's advancement.

In 1969, the government also instituted a mandatory military education and training curriculum (*kyoryŏn*) for students in high school and college.[169] All male students were required to participate in weekly military drills and lectures, and male high school students wore special uniforms on their training days and carried replicas of carbines or M16 rifles for combat training. Female students had to attend training in first aid and nursing. High school students received this military education for two hours each week during the academic year, for a total of sixty-eight hours per year. College students also trained for two hours each week, for a total of sixty hours per year. In addition to teaching practical military skills, the *kyoryŏn* curriculum, like the National Charter on Education, inculcated strong anticommunist values in these students. With the National Charter on Education mobilizing primary and secondary schools and *kyoryŏn* providing battle training in the high schools and universities, the government's educational reforms systematically instilled in the nation's youth an intense militaristic loyalty to the state.[170]

Another transformative sociocultural program that evolved out of the Second Economy Movement was the New Village Movement (NVM). The NVM would become one of the state's most useful and comprehensive tools for integrating national security and economic development into civilians' daily lives. Initiated in 1970 as Park's signature program for rural modernization, the movement began as a campaign to carry the "spirit of *chaju*" (self-reliance) to the local people in underdeveloped regions. Through state-established NVM training centers, the government promoted the virtues of an independent Korean spirit, a strong work ethic, and loyalty to the state, underscoring the idea that these concepts were based on traditional Korean values that needed to be reawakened to drive Korea's modernization.[171] By strategically framing the NVM to focus on developing rural regions and aligning its messages with the indigenous values of Korea's largely rural populace, Park made it easier for the people to embrace his policy of modernization for self-reliant national defense. In 1974, the government followed the rural NVM with the Factory New Village Movement (Kongjang Saemaŭl Undong) to inculcate discipline and nationalistic values among urban factory workers (see chapter 3). Imbuing workers with the state's militarist-nationalist ethos, the Factory New Village Movement mobilized the labor force to push forward various government-led industrial and defense projects. Through this movement, a vibrant Korean form of industrialism built on anticommunism and militant nationalism would emerge.

Yusin Manifests Total Security

After the United States withdrew its Seventh Infantry Division in March 1971, the Park regime began limiting freedoms in South Korea under the pretext of protecting national security. On December 6, 1971, Park declared a national state of emergency, stating, "At the present time . . . the threat from outside is extremely urgent."[172] One month later, in his New Year's press conference on January 11, Park officially announced his plan to establish a total security system to prepare the nation for a potential North Korean attack. (However, as earlier discussions in the chapter have shown, Park had been in the process of creating such a system since 1968, albeit unofficially.) Total security, he said, meant that national security would be maintained through the combined strength of the state and the people: "We need to mobilize and organize our entire nation's strength so that we can build the total security system, first and foremost."[173] Given North Korea's superior military strength, he said, it was imperative that the government and the people of South Korea unite and bring all their power to bear on building up national security.[174] Total security could be achieved, Park insisted, only with the sacrifice, devotion, and hard work of every Korean citizen.[175]

Park publicly promoted total security throughout 1972. In a March 24 speech at the National Conference for Educators, for example, he reflected on the important role of education and educators in fostering participation in the new defense posture.[176] The government also spread the goal of total security through the NVM, which worked to expand both ideological and financial support (donations) for Park's campaign for self-reliant national defense.[177] Through their use of anticommunist propaganda and educational materials, civilian-based military organizations such as the South Korea Veterans Association, as well as the local divisions of the HRF, facilitated the promotion of self-reliant national defense at the grassroots level.[178]

On October 17, Park announced what became known as the Yusin (or "revitalization") system, launching a more draconian form of authoritarian rule by declaring martial law and suspending the 1963 constitution. On December 27, a new Yusin Constitution, which dismantled checks on executive power by giving the president complete control over state affairs and removing term limits, was passed by the National Assembly. With this authoritarian constitution in effect, the Park government completed the comprehensive political, social, and economic reforms it had designed to shape Korea into a total war state. Yusin produced a totalitarian and militarist system similar to wartime Japan's in the early Shōwa era.

Through the creation of the HRF and the implementation of the NVM and other mass ideological and educational reforms leading up to adoption of the Yusin Constitution, Park had fostered cultural nationalism as a prerequisite for self-reliant national defense. With the constitution's adoption, the regime succeeded in installing its total security system—which, in turn, would lay the groundwork for defense industrialization. Yusin gave the Park government the power to fully conscript domestic society, including civilian businesses and their workforce, into this effort.

Park's promulgation of Yusin and its authoritarian policies stirred strong democratic protests among opposition-party members, intellectuals, students, and workers. His opponents accused him of once again piggybacking on the security threat posed by North Korea to implement his domestic policies, as he had done with the establishment of the HRF and the National Charter on Education—which critics said had also been instituted as part of a methodical plan to strengthen his control over the populace and pave the way for Park's totalitarian rule.[179] Prior to Yusin, Kim Dae-jung, a liberal opposition leader who would become South Korea's eighth president, had demanded the cancellation of the HRF and even accused Park of escalating tensions with North Korea to rationalize his iron grip on the government.[180] Kim had used "Abolish the reserve forces" as a campaign slogan during his run for president in 1971, when he nearly defeated Park, and Kim continued to be one of the most outspoken critics of Park's dictatorship into the 1970s after the adoption of the Yusin Constitution. Indeed, the clash between the democratic movement and Park's Yusin politics was a significant driver of Park's consolidation of power under the total security system, and it would continue to play a role in the way that industrialization was carried out.

Notwithstanding this existential challenge to Park's political and social policies, his self-reliant national defense ideology resonated with large segments of the populace. The message of self-reliance he crafted appealed to Koreans through their history of oppression and sense of national grievance, striking a chord with their longing for autonomy and national security. His emphasis on external threats and South Korea's need to protect its sovereignty also connected with people's intense alertness to national security issues at the time. In the end, the Yusin state's mobilization and co-optation of society constituted a complete conscription of the citizenry; all Koreans were to take part in the national security structure. Throughout his efforts to build his total security system, Park endeavored to transform the people's collective consciousness, to make them willing, patriotic, and self-sacrificing agents of national security independence. In this way, they would execute his defense plans fully and expeditiously.

Conclusion

When the DPRK's provocations in 1968 and the Nixon Doctrine of 1969 led Park to question the ROK's national security, his regime formulated a radical response that would transform South Korea within a decade. The security crisis that arose in the late 1960s gave Park an ideal opportunity to bring together the government, military, citizenry, and means of production for constructing a new total security system. The year 1968 was an especially critical turning point for South Korea's new defense posture, as it was when Park created the HRF and initiated his plan for domestic arms production to pursue Korea's self-reliant national defense. However, while the North Korean threat set the stage for the HRF and other policies that supported self-reliant national defense, including HCI and Yusin, it was the Nixon Doctrine that ensured and expedited their implementation.

Seizing on the perceived state of emergency to ignite people's patriotic fervor for sovereignty and security, Park expanded the state's power for building Korea's national defense. Employing a combination of military and civilian forces, the government formed a broad national coalition under the ideology of self-reliant national defense to achieve Park's total security system and build the infrastructure for a South Korean defense industry. Through the NVM, the National Charter on Education, and other programs for reeducation and ideological reform, Park constructed a new militarist, nationalist identity that eventually complemented his Yusin state and other repressive policies. Reaching far beyond the military arena, Park's total security system came to represent an ideology as much as a policy for economic development and defense.

Park's total security system was the key to a new national culture and a new attitude toward national security.[181] It facilitated the widespread participation that would be vital to defense industrialization under the state's HCI Policy in the 1970s. The system also instilled a wartime sense of urgency in all aspects of production, altering the trajectory of South Korean defense. Total security was the starting point for a reconceptualization of military-civilian relations—one that caused a paradigm shift as South Korea's quest for independent security became a push for self-reliance as part of its broader national identity.

CHAPTER TWO

"Rich Nation, Strong Army"

"Rich nation, strong army" is the only path to our survival
in the current international environment.
—Park Chung Hee

Do you not understand that the plans elaborated in
a little chamber decide success over thousands of miles?
—Liu Bei, *The Romance of Three Kingdoms*

The ROK's heavy and chemical industrialization (HCI; *chunghwahak kongŏphwa*) gave rise to a distinctive military-industrial complex (MIC) in South Korea, where civilian industries became deeply intertwined with a national system for arms production. Newly established heavy and chemical industries, intended to serve both military and commercial purposes, forged unprecedented links between the public and private sectors that drove the joint development of the defense industry and the economy. In fact, the Heavy and Chemical Industrialization Policy (HCI Policy; Chunghwahak Kongŏphwa Chŏngch'aek) of Park Chung Hee's administration, implemented in 1973 to support weapons production, ignited the remarkably rapid industrial transformation South Korea experienced during the last decade of Park's rule.

An array of recently declassified Korean sources illuminates Park's coeval policies for industrialization and national security independence, most notably his master plan for HCI and its consequences for South Korean weapons production. These sources reveal the ideological and policy origins of HCI alongside Park's planned defense industry development, and also give us a clear view of how the national priority of self-reliant defense wove civilian participation into the state's economic and defense industrialization—what I refer to as its "militarized industrialization."

Foundations of Heavy and Chemical Industrialization

From the earliest days of his rule, Park preached that the people's freedom and safety—as well as the security of the nation as a whole—were inextricably linked to economic development.[1] "Economic construction is the foundation for national strength," Park frequently declared, a conviction he underscored with his government's signature slogan promoting defense and economic development: "Let us fight and build!" (fig. 2.1).[2]

Amid South Korea's precarious security environment from the late 1960s through the 1970s, Park also used the catchphrase "rich nation, strong army" to emphasize his goal of simultaneously advancing the economy and the military.[3] Spurred by the DPRK's provocations and the US plan to reduce its forces in South Korea in accordance with the Nixon Doctrine, Park called for large-scale domestic arms production, to be achieved through rapid industrialization. He asserted that self-

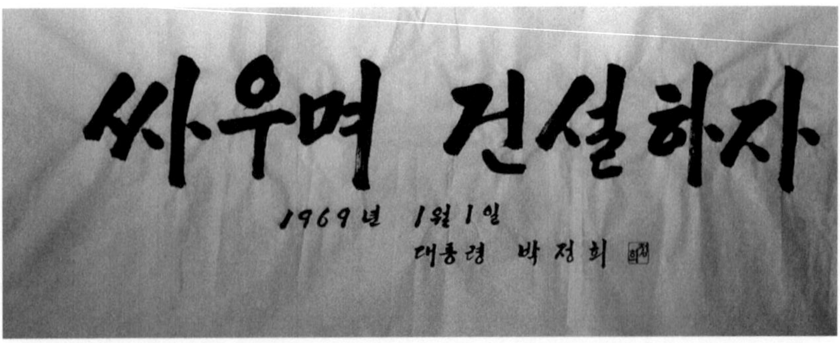

FIG. 2.1. "Let us fight and build," calligraphy by Park Chung Hee in 1969. *Source:* National Archives of Korea; file no. CET0026091.

reliance, *chaju*, was of primary importance as he urged the South Korean populace to build the self-reliant economy that would form the foundation for a self-reliant national defense (fig. 2.2).[4]

The president's agenda required the full engagement of commercial industry and the civilian workforce. To build support for that agenda, Park described in many speeches the symbiotic relationship between civilians' economic contributions and a strengthened military,

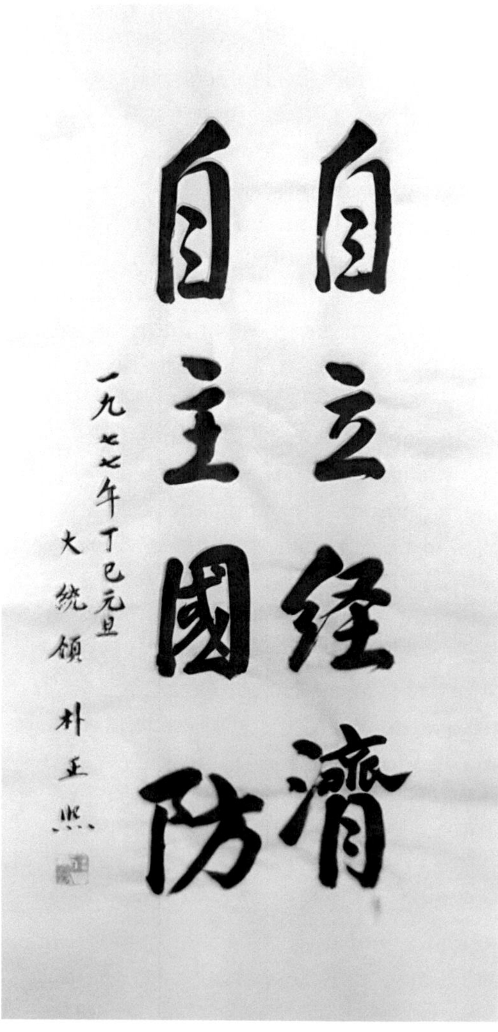

FIG. 2.2. "Self-reliant national defense, self-reliant national economy," calligraphy by Park Chung Hee in Chinese characters in 1977. *Source:* National Archives of Korea; file no. CET0023403.

promising that a strong military would, in turn, provide the stability and security needed for economic productivity.[5] South Korea would achieve "national restoration" (*minjok chunghŭng*), Park declared, only with an independent national defense and an equally strong and independent economy, both to be built by Koreans themselves.[6]

Early Arms Production

Although HCI did not become an official state priority until the promulgation of the administration's formal HCI Policy in January 1973, establishing domestic heavy and chemical industries had long been a goal in South Korea. The three-year economic development plan (1960–62) devised by the Committee for Industrial Development in 1959 under President Rhee Syngman included policies for developing some of these industries.[7] However, before his plan could be executed, Rhee's government was overthrown in April 1960 by student-led democratic protests against his authoritarian rule and electoral corruption—what came to be known as the April 19 Revolution. In the early 1960s, Park followed through with some of Rhee's plans, initiating shipbuilding as well as steel and chemical production in an effort to transition Korea away from its focus on light industry. Like Rhee, Park recognized that HCI was the necessary next stage in South Korea's development. As steelmaking was essential for any major industrialization plan, including those for weapons production, a domestic steel industry was at the top of Park's list of key industries to be established in his first Five-Year Economic Development Plan (FYEDP), for 1962–66.[8] However, South Korea's lack of capital and resources, and its failed attempts to obtain US endorsement and the loans needed for a new integrated steel mill, delayed the founding of its first steel company until the late 1960s.[9]

Park's plans for domestic arms manufacturing began to take shape in response to a series of cuts and delays in the US military aid package that was promised in 1966 in return for South Korea's help in Vietnam.[10] Determined to move forward, especially after the DPRK's 1968 threats, Park's government formed a plan to leverage private domestic firms, using their manufacturing facilities and labor force to produce arms cost-effectively and more independently of US aid. In 1968, under Park's order to arm the new Homeland Reserve Forces (HRF) troops with Korean-made weapons, the government drafted a three-year plan (1968–71) called the Three-Year Defense Industry Development Plan (Pangwi Sanŏp Chŏngbi 3-kaenyŏn Kyehoek), and ordered the Ministry of National Defense (MND) to incorporate the civilian manufacturing infrastructure into its strategy for basic weapons production.[11] To support the plan, the government promoted the expansion and improvement of local commercial factories in defense-related industries such as machinery, shipbuilding, and chemicals.[12]

By the late 1960s, officers at South Korea's Army Staff College were studying the US MIC through their coursework and familiarizing themselves with the concept of *kyŏngje kunsahwa*, or "economic militarization," a notion inspired by the American defense industry and its approach of contracting and integrating civilian manufacturers into arms production.[13] The US system provided a key example for the Park regime's conceptualization of private enterprise as the foundation for defense production. This new "national defense economy" (*kukpang kyŏngje*) model, which combined modern capitalism with the MIC, blurred distinctions between commercial and military production—and peacetime and wartime industries—by equipping civilian plants to manufacture defense products full-time in the event of war.[14]

Park wrote in his diary about using civilian factories for arms production, announced the strategy in his speeches, and closely involved himself in the MND's execution of the policy. In his diary entry for April 25, 1970, Park noted that he planned to equip local civilian-owned plants with additional facilities to support their weapons production, the alternative he preferred to financing separate, government-owned arms factories.[15] Without state resources to fund new military infrastructure from the ground up, and especially given the cuts in US military aid, Park recognized that upgrading existing commercial plants would save time and resources in the rush to arm the HRF and supply the ROK's military. Speaking at a ceremony celebrating the completion of the T'aech'ang Textile Corporation's factory in Okch'ŏn on July 4, 1970, for example, Park pointed out that the factory could convert to producing firearms in the event of a national emergency, serving as a model for all manufacturing facilities.[16]

In the same year, Minister of National Defense Chŏng Raehyŏk declared that military equipment, including land vehicles, communications devices, and small watercraft, would also be produced by civilian manufacturers, in parallel with corporate advancements under Park's current FYEDP.[17] In keeping with the aforementioned Three-Year Defense Industry Development Plan, the ministry increasingly assigned defense-related production to civilian factories and shipyards.[18] On June 12, 1970, the Secretariat of National Security (Kukka Anbo Samuguk) reported to Park on the status of work by the National Security Council's Emergency Planning Committee, discussing ongoing efforts by the committee to install an emergency planning officer (with the military rank of at least colonel) in each of seventy-seven selected enterprises.[19] These officers were to ensure the companies' readiness to serve defense needs in a national emergency. In April 1971 Sin Wŏnsik, assistant secretary of weapons supplies in the MND, announced that the state would increase technical support to civilian manufacturers to help expand their arms production.[20]

Overall, the Park administration's strategy for civilian-centered defense industrialization, the basis for what would later constitute the 1973 HCI Policy, was instituted in 1968 and fully in play by 1971. This important early period in the state's policymaking for a domestic defense industry, prior to the so-called technocratic state of the 1970s, has not been thoroughly examined.[21] Most studies of Park's program for independent military modernization have focused on the policies of O Wŏnch'ŏl, the technocrat whose long tenure as Park's head of defense industry development began in 1971 and lasted until Park's death in 1979.[22] However, recently accessible records have revealed that specific government actions were directed toward merging civilian and defense production as early as 1968, and that this laid the conceptual and strategic groundwork for HCI in South Korea.

Pohang Iron and Steel Company and the Four Core Factories

As part of his second FYEDP (1967–71), Park sought to advance integrated steel production, smelting, shipbuilding, and machinery manufacturing, in keeping with his goal to develop defense-related heavy and chemical industries.[23] Then in February 1968, following the Blue

House Raid, the Ministry of Science and Technology's (MST; Kwahak Kisulch'ŏ) Economy and Science Council proposed to include the goal of achieving a national defense economy (which, as mentioned earlier, entailed a deeper integration between the military and commercial industry) as one of the government's objectives in the second FYEDP. The council recommended that the government "strengthen the foundation of the national defense economy by systematically linking the economy and national defense."[24]

In response to the DPRK's military threats in 1968, Park redoubled his efforts toward HCI, with a particular focus on domestic steel production, as steel was essential to both the defense industry and other civilian heavy industries.[25] Two of Park's earliest and most significant projects were the Pohang Iron and Steel Company (P'ohang Chonghap Chech'ŏl Chusik Hoesa, or POSCO, as it came to be known in the 1990s) and the Four Core Factories (Sa Taehaek Kongjang). With Park's full support, POSCO, South Korea's first steel manufacturing corporation, was founded in April 1968 as a joint venture between the ROK government and the Korea Tungsten Company, a state enterprise.[26] Park personally appointed Pak T'aejun, the CEO of Korea Tungsten Company and a former military officer under Park's command, to head POSCO.[27] Kim Hangyŏl, deputy prime minister and head of the Economic Planning Board (EPB), and one of Park's most trusted aides, successfully secured Japanese funds to finance construction of the POSCO mill, which took place from 1971 to 1973 under Pak's supervision.[28]

The second early project, the Four Core Factories, came out of a 1970 proposal by Harry Yongwha Choi of the US-based Battelle Memorial Institute, which worked with the Korea Institute of Science and Technology (KIST) to help advance South Korea's industrialization.[29] Following Park's priorities, Four Core Factories was essentially a plan for developing an industrial base for a domestic defense industry.[30] In May 1970, KIST and the Battelle team completed a report titled *Plan for Development of Korean Mechanical Engineering Industry*, which detailed strategies for developing export-oriented industrial sectors such as heavy machinery, foundry pig iron, special steels, shipbuilding, automobiles, and electrical machinery.[31] The report concluded by narrowing the candidates for development down to four industries: heavy machinery, foundry pig iron, special steel, and shipbuilding—all of which were essential to the defense industry.[32]

In a briefing for President Park in June 1970, Choi stated that South Korea would be able to build the foundation for industrialization by constructing four key factories: a special-steels plant, a large shipyard, a foundry, and an integrated machinery factory.[33] South Korea would also require an integrated steel mill, a project that the ROK government had already embarked upon with the POSCO mill. Choi's suggestion that South Korea could build its own modern defense industry once these five factories were operational sparked Park's interest. At the conclusion of the briefing, Park committed to the establishment of the four needed factories. He again tapped Kim Hangnyŏl of the EPB to oversee the project, which Kim named the Four Core Factories.

In July, as part of an EPB briefing for Park on the Four Core Factories project, Yi Kyŏngsŏ, a head engineer from the KIST team that collaborated with Battelle, reported to Park about their progress on the plan. When Yi emphasized, "heavy industries are equal to the defense industry," Park beamed.[34] As Yi recalled, "I told President Park that we can develop tanks if we develop the heavy industries, just as gunpowder can be made at a fertilizer plant. Immediately [Park] said 'OK,' on the spot."[35] Significantly, Yi claimed that KIST's proposals for the Four Core Factories project, based on the *Plan for Development of Korean Mechanical Engineering Industry*, planted the seeds for the heavy and chemical industrialization South Korea would eventually pursue in the 1970s.[36] In the interview I conducted with Yi, he was critical of O Wŏnch'ŏl, widely known today as the architect of HCI, for taking all the credit for HCI in his published memoirs.[37] "O Wŏnch'ŏl came up with the HCI Policy by adding a bit of coating on the [KIST] *Plan for Development of Korean Mechanical Engineering Industry*," Yi said.[38] Indeed, as a prelude to the HCI Policy, KIST's strategy for the Four Core Factories planned the use of large private firms as dual-purpose manufacturers, an approach that imitated Japan's investment in select civilian industries that could be converted to military production. Under KIST's guidance, the government selected four companies to execute the Four Core Factories project: Hyundai Construction Company to develop a shipyard, Kangwon Coal Company to build a foundry, Daehan Heavy Machinery Industry to produce special steels, and Shinjin

Motors to make heavy machinery.[39] According to Yi, the design for the Four Core Factories set an important precedent for O's later planning for large private firms that would serve as multipurpose manufacturers under the HCI Policy.

Despite its ambitious beginning and Park's full support, the Four Core Factories project stalled because it was dependent on external aid from Japan. Kim Hangnyŏl had counted on his previously successful strategy of securing funding through Japanese loan assistance, as he had done for POSCO. However, this time Japan denied his repeated requests, suspecting that the new factories would be used to develop a South Korean defense industry, in spite of Kim's assurances to the contrary.[40] Aside from its own concerns about South Korea's armament, Japan's reluctance to support its ally's military buildup was influenced by the United States, which had imposed strict controls on the ROK's military development.[41] The US-Japan alliance was central to US security policy in Northeast Asia, and Japan, which depended on the alliance for its defense during the Cold War, aligned its policies with Washington's interests in the region.[42] Beyond a certain level of military-technical collaboration, the Japanese government proved unwilling to commit any major aid that might be used for a Korean defense industry. After Japan's final refusal to fund the Four Core Factories project at a Korea-Japan ministerial meeting in Tokyo in August 1971, Kim turned to the United States and European nations for loans, but to no avail.

On November 10, a year and a half after Park's order to build the core factories, the EPB briefed him on the breakdown in financing. According to Kim Chŏngnyŏm, who was present, the president deeply lamented this setback, especially because his Five-Year Military Modernization Plan (1971–76) hinged on the success of the Four Core Factories.[43] Park's sense of urgency was heightened by President Richard Nixon's plan for the withdrawal of US ground troops by 1976—a schedule to which Park had reluctantly agreed, anticipating that the factories would be completed by then, at the end of his third FYEDP (1972–76).[44] Now South Korea had less than five years to find another way to establish independent weapons production before most of the US forces were removed.

Park's progress toward military modernization was certainly slowed by US restrictions on sharing weapons technology with South

Korea. As discussed in chapter 1, even after the announcement of the Nixon Doctrine and the US promise of more military aid to compensate for planned troop withdrawals, Washington had intentionally limited the sharing of data for advanced weapons to keep ROK offensive capabilities in check. However, the refusal to help South Korea acquire new weapons technology only fueled Park's drive to develop an independent defense industry. Although the Four Core Factories project was not realized, the basic principles behind it, such as focusing on critical industrial sectors and mobilizing private industry for arms manufacturing, became fundamental elements of the HCI Policy that emerged in the 1970s.

Planning for Weapons Production

The EPB's failure to fund the Four Core Factories project led to the rise of new technocratic leadership in the Blue House. Central to this shift was O Wŏnch'ŏl, whom Park appointed in 1971 as the second senior presidential secretary for the economy, or the head of the Office of the Second Senior Presidential Secretary for the Economy in the Blue House (hereafter referred to as the Second Economic Secretariat, or SES; Kyŏngje Che-2 Pisŏsil). In this new role, O was charged with spearheading the development of a new domestic weapons industry. A graduate of Seoul National University with a degree in chemical engineering, O had previously worked as the assistant secretary for mining, industry, and electronics in the Ministry of Commerce and Industry (MCI; Sanggongbu) before being promoted to the role of senior secretary to the president. His extraordinary rise came about after a four-hour meeting with Park and his chief of staff, Kim Chŏngnyŏm, on November 10, 1971. O, who had attended the EPB's briefing for Park that same day, shared with the president an alternative plan for developing a defense industry, outlining the basic principles for an indigenous arms production system that he believed could meet Park's goal of equipping HRF troops with Korean-made arms in the shortest time possible.[45] Both Park and Kim were particularly intrigued by O's strategies for maximizing domestic resources, having just witnessed the failure of the EPB's plan that had relied exclusively on foreign loans.[46] Following that meeting with Park, O emerged as chief policymaker for South Korea's defense industry within the framework of what would become the Park government's HCI Policy.

Among the key strategies in O's plan for weapons production, five basic principles stand out. The first was that weapons parts should be manufactured separately, then assembled into complete weapons.[47] Given that South Korea lacked complete blueprints for basic US-model weapons because the United States refused to share them, O argued that Korean engineers could figure out how to reproduce the weapons on their own through reverse engineering, disassembling US-made weapons and precisely replicating each part. The parts could be mass-produced domestically and then assembled into exact copies of the original weapons. Japanese manufacturers in the electronics, software, and semiconductor industries had successfully employed a similar reverse-engineering strategy since the 1960s.

The second basic principle in O's plan was that domestic manufacturers had to be trained for highly precise work—specifically, they had to be capable of accuracy in precision steel cutting to within one one-hundredth of a millimeter.[48] At the time, South Korean manufacturers could perform precision work only to within one-tenth of a millimeter. The goal of training a modern skilled workforce was not new. In the previous year, the Economy and Science Council had pointed out South Korea's critical lack of skilled workers and recommended overhauling workforce training to meet the technical demands of industrialization.[49] Park, whose government had already been promoting technical training as part of his second FYEDP, had good reasons to embrace this principle of O's plan.[50]

The third basic principle was to designate existing civilian manufacturers to produce the different weapons parts, instead of establishing stand-alone weapons plants (with the exception of the M16 factory that was already under construction). Localizing the production of weapons parts in existing factories would be a cost-saving alternative to centralized production in independent military facilities. The MND had been utilizing civilian facilities for basic weapons production since the late 1960s, but O's approach would expand this method to a new scale for the mass production of arms, which Park strongly supported.[51] Using civilian facilities would also promote competition between companies vying for government contracts, which could encourage innovation and lead to higher product quality.

O's fourth principle was that the defense industry should be developed within a broader effort for HCI, because the mass production of modern weapons required high-level heavy and chemical industries. With this, O proposed expediting development by investing in strategic industries, promoting the mass production and exportation of advanced products, and increasing the influx of foreign capital.[52] O's emphasis on HCI resonated with Park's pursuit of heavy and chemical industries going back to his first FYEDP, which had included early efforts to establish steelmaking and shipbuilding.[53] Likewise, with his second FYEDP Park had promoted both the development of key industries and the training of the technical workforce needed to support export-oriented industrialization and national defense development.[54] According to Kim Chŏngnyŏm, in his role as minister of commerce and industry from 1967 to 1969 he had also promoted heavy and chemical industries under the second FYEDP, when South Korea began to actively expand its exports.[55] And the Four Core Factories project undertaken by KIST and the EPB had targeted specific industries for development (heavy machinery, special steel, pig iron, shipbuilding), which set a strategic precedent for sector-based development. O can be credited, however, with proposing practical, comprehensive policies that strengthened the Park regime's industrialization model and synchronized it with the mass production of arms.

The fifth basic principle in O's plan was that weapons parts and hardware produced by civilian companies should be subject to verification by the Agency for Defense Development (ADD), and that only parts that passed inspection would be sent to the military arsenals (*kunch'ang*) for assembly. This requirement would consolidate the ADD's central management of weapons research and development (R & D) and establish a close relationship between the agency and local producers of weapons parts. O's promotion of the ADD reinforced the critical role envisioned by Park when he founded the agency in 1970 as part of his initiative for independent military modernization (for more on the ADD, see chapter 4).

O assured Park that with the plan and principles he described, basic infantry weapons—such as rifles, machine guns, mortars, grenades, and mines—could be manufactured in South Korea in a mere six months, without foreign loans.[56] Park agreed to O's proposal and ordered him to work from inside the Blue House from the next day forward, so that his design for HCI and weapons production could be executed under Park's direct watch. With Park's approval of O's plan, the Four Core Factories project was immediately canceled.

Notwithstanding the persuasiveness of O Wŏnch'ŏl's plan, Park embraced O's ideas so quickly because they comported with his own vision and what various agencies in his government were already doing. While the convergence of the military and private sectors had not reached the scale O envisioned, the government's previous experiments with civilian manufacturers for basic arms production undoubtedly disposed Park to accept O's approach; in many ways, O presented an upgraded version of the government's earlier plan for building a national defense economy.[57] Nevertheless, O was indispensable in pushing forward a concrete agenda for HCI, especially for the development of a commercial-military mass production system. Viewed within a broader historical context, a combination of internal and external factors contributed to O's rise with his plan for HCI: the government's previous experience with civilian arms manufacturing, lessons learned from American and Japanese models, the lack of foreign aid, and Park's willingness to take huge political and economic risks to achieve self-reliant national defense for South Korea through domestic arms production.

The Second Economic Secretariat

O Wŏnch'ŏl's overnight promotion to head the SES elevated his authority to a level unmatched by that of any other government official except Park or his chief of staff, Kim Chŏngnyŏm. With O in charge and working out of the Blue House, the SES became the president's personal task force for developing the defense industry and HCI. For security purposes, because US surveillance was so intense, the SES disguised its efforts toward arms production as general industrial reforms under HCI.[58] The term "defense industry" was not used in any HCI-related official communications outside the Blue House, and the SES was deliberately described in public and in the media as overseeing HCI, without any reference to arms manufacturing.[59]

The SES was different from other government agencies in that it reported only to Park. With the president's complete support, it had the power to send out direct orders from the Blue House to other ministries, bypassing formal procedures, political opposition, and bureaucratic restrictions. In this way it could advance HCI without impediment. As Kim Kwangmo, O's top assistant in the SES, stated in an interview, "Having such support from the president was the only way the SES could have pushed through its measures for HCI development."[60] In addition to functioning as the "control tower" and overseeing defense industry planning, purchases, and weapons procurement, the SES would later carry out Park's covert order for developing nuclear missiles.[61] Furthermore, the SES mediated between defense industrialization goals and national economic development, as its policies reformed military and economic structures. With O at the head of the SES, Park had in place what Hyung-A Kim has called the "HCI Triumvirate": O, who managed the policies for HCI and defense industrialization; Kim Chŏngnyŏm, Park's chief of staff, who oversaw general economic policy to fund HCI development; and Park, who provided political reinforcement as the ultimate authority.[62]

The elevation of O and the SES signaled an important shift in the power structure that unsettled the boundaries between military and civilian positions at the top levels of government decision-making. Under Park's drive to advance domestic science and technology for HCI, a new group of civilian experts with technical training, like O, rose to prominence in governmental policymaking on industry and military-related research, taking over roles previously held by traditional bureaucrats and military officers. O himself recruited four technocrats from the MCI to work with him in the SES (Kim Kwangmo, Yi Sŏkp'yo, Kwŏn Kwangwŏn, and Ch'oe T'aech'ang), and he later added Kim Pyŏngwŏn, who served as a secretary in the Blue House protocol office—bringing the total number of staff members in the SES to six.[63]

O's rise also signified a shift in Park's administration of the economy, as decisions previously made by EPB bureaucrats were handed over to O's MCI-affiliated technocrats.[64] Even before O's promotion there had been strife between the EPB's US-educated economists, who advocated macroeconomic policies, and the ministry's technocrats, who preferred more hands-on, state-led, microeconomic reforms for national economic development.[65] Since his appointment of Kim Chŏn-gnyŏm (former minister of commerce and industry, as previously mentioned) as chief of staff in the Blue House in 1969, Park relied increasingly on the MCI. The EPB, which had been in charge of Park's first and second Five-Year Economic Development Plans, originally did not include HCI in the third FYEDP (1972–76), but when Park promoted O, his plan for HCI became the centerpiece of a revised FYEDP.[66] And although Park had commissioned the SES specifically to develop the defense industry, its role quickly expanded into broader areas of the economy, since defense industry development under HCI eventually required an overhaul of Korea's entire industrial base. Over time, the SES replaced the EPB as the main agency in charge of national economic policy.

The Lightning Operation Exhibits Basic Weapons

When he first met with Park in November 1970, O assured the president that reverse engineering would lead to the domestic production of basic infantry weapons within six months.[67] Just three days later, on November 13, O ordered the ADD to produce prototypes of eight basic weapons for a secret project code-named the Lightning Operation (Pŏn'gae Saŏp).[68] However, the ADD, the administration's research arm, was only little over a year old and was still underequipped for weapons R & D.[69] When the agency's director at the time, former general Sin Ŭnggyun, responded that "the task would be impossible to carry out with our current level of skill," Park called Sin to the Blue House and rebuked him. "Director Sin," Park asked, "did we not create the Agency for Defense Development to develop domestic weapons in preparation for the withdrawal of US forces in Korea? The US military has already begun to withdraw. If there's a war, we are all dead. In this national security situation, there is no room to say 'yes' or 'no.' Make the weapons, no matter what."[70] Dissatisfied with Sin, Park soon put O in full charge of the Lightning Operation.[71] O gave the ADD until the end of the year to complete the initial eight prototypes, to be reverse engineered from US models (table 2.1).[72]

Table 2.1.
Weapons Prototypes in the Lightning Operation, 1971

Weapon type	Model × number produced
Carbine guns	M2 × 10
Automatic pistols	M1 × 2
Machine guns	M1919 A4 × 5
	M1919 A6 × 5
Mortars	60 mm M19 × 4
	81 mm M29 × 6
	60 mm (lighter version) × 2
Rocket launchers	M20 A1 (3.5-inch) × 2
	M20 B1 × 2
Grenades	MK2 × 300
Antipersonnel mines	M18 A1 × 20
Antitank mines	M15 × 20

SOURCE: Data from O W., *Han'gukhyŏng kyŏngje kŏnsŏl*, 5:38.

Ku Sanghoe, the ADD scientist in charge of developing rocket launcher prototypes for the Lightning Operation, recalled the painstaking work he and his colleagues carried out under pressure in this extremely condensed time frame.[73] To reverse engineer the weapons, they began by borrowing a US-made rocket launcher from the ROK Army and dismantling it, then precisely measuring and sketching each part by hand to create a blueprint. However, according to Ku, "The rocket launchers borrowed from the military were at least twenty years old, so it was impossible to find out the exact size of each part due to severe wear and tear. Parts were loose. When I finished drawing the blueprint for each part and then the blueprint for the assembly, they did not match."[74]

Ku was often called to the Blue House to report to O on his team's progress, even as O frequently visited Ku's laboratory at the ADD for in-person inspections. Their meetings sometimes turned into heated arguments, with Ku resenting the pressure O placed on the ADD scientists for the Lightning Operation. Despite this, Ku noted that he and O grew to respect each other through the rigor of the work and their mutual determination to develop the weapons at any cost.[75] The ADD facility operated a twenty-four-hour heating system, so researchers could work around the clock. The scientists would stop only for quick naps, taken with their heads on their desks. After countless attempts and failures, they completed the blueprints and coordinated with Korean factories to produce prototypes of each part. Finally, they assembled the parts into complete weapons.

A little more than a month after O's order, ADD scientists achieved what had seemed impossible, even completing the weapon prototypes ahead of the deadline. On December 16, O exhibited the first batch of domestically produced basic infantry weapons to President Park, who declared, "This is the best Christmas gift I have received this year!"[76] Tests of the weapons from the Lightning Operation were successful in spite of the rush, much to the relief of the ADD teams. With Park's instant approval, O ordered the ADD to develop a second round of weapons, including upgrades of the models that had just been shown and tested. Impressed by the demonstration of South Korea's new arms-producing potential and the Lightning Operation's efficiency and output, Park also secretly ordered O to begin developing guided missiles—advanced weapons that would be capable of hitting Pyongyang, 160 kilometers into North Korea—as a deterrent to invasion by Kim Il Sung.[77]

The Defense Industry Promotion Council

In his New Year's address on January 1, 1972, President Park reiterated his primary security goal: "We must develop weapons with our own hands and modernize our military's weapons."[78] Increasingly confident about South Korea's capabilities, he pushed through policies in 1972 to expand defense industry development to a national scale. To that end, the Defense Industry Promotion Council (DIPC; Pangwi Sanŏp Yuksŏng Hoeŭi), a formal council led directly by the president and tasked with planning the development of the defense industry, held two important meetings with government, military, and science leaders in February and October.[79] Through discussions at those meetings, the council officially adopted O's plan to build up the defense industry within the framework of HCI and formulated policies for weapons

R & D, weapons production, and the training of a skilled workforce to enable such production.[80]

As its principal strategy, the DIPC endorsed the "total empowerment of the trinity of military, business, and science" to advance South Korea's defense industrialization.[81] The three sectors, the council concluded, had to be fully mobilized to acquire the state-of-the-art technologies necessary for defense production.[82] The ADD and MND took immediate measures to ensure active cooperation among the military, industry, and research institutes to improve Korean-made military products.[83]

At its first meeting, on February 21, 1972, the DIPC set O's reverse-engineering principle as state policy and formalized a six-point strategy to achieve domestic weapons production:

1. Develop weapons production in parallel with peacetime industry. As a cooperative system between the military and civilian industrial sectors, weapons production must be founded on civilian industry.
2. Designate civilian companies as defense contractors for the production of individual weapons parts.[84]
3. Make the civilian defense contractors responsible for manufacturing weapons parts and the individual military arsenals [of the army, navy, and air force] responsible for assembling those parts [into complete weapons].[85]
4. Assess the safety of the locations of defense [contractors'] factories and enforce security measures from the start.
5. Develop the highly skilled technical workforce required for precision manufacturing and weapons production.
6. Align military and civilian product standards as closely as possible, so the peacetime industrial base could be turned quickly toward defense industrialization.[86]

Because South Korea's fledgling industrial base was unprepared for defense production, the DIPC's plan focused on first developing the "peacetime industry" of civilian-owned companies. The state would strengthen the companies' commercial manufacturing operations while also developing their capacity to produce weapons parts.[87] The

SES technocrats had set a 30/70 production ratio for defense contractors: factories would devote 30 percent of their production to arms and 70 percent to commercial goods, but in a national emergency they would shift to 100 percent arms production.[88] In peacetime, manufacturers would maintain assembly lines for defense products while continuing to profit from commercial production. With this scheme, the DIPC sought to minimize the economic impact of future fluctuations in weapons demand.

As the sixth point in the strategy indicates, the council foresaw the possibility of a complete convergence of military and peacetime (civilian) industries for military production. In contrast, most of South Korea's neighbors—North Korea, Taiwan, China, and the Soviet Union—had at this time invested a large proportion of their state funding in separate munitions plants for weapons manufacturing. They had built what were basically state-run defense industries, with their defense ministries overseeing all aspects of arms production, from designing prototypes to manufacturing final products. Given the ROK government's limited resources and the imminent deadline imposed by the Nixon Doctrine, O was convinced it would be too costly and time-consuming to build factories dedicated solely to making weapons. To maximize efficiency and speed, South Korea would focus on supporting private-sector manufacturers that could produce weapons parts as needed.[89]

At its February meeting the council also established criteria for selecting the companies that would serve as defense contractors. Approved manufacturers would exhibit the following qualities: healthy management practices and financial stability, the ability to perform precision manufacturing, suitable facilities for prototype manufacturing and assembly-line production, self-monitoring systems to promote product quality, and strong research capability.[90] By selecting and investing in only the most qualified and capable companies, the state hoped to minimize its development costs.

A declassified SES report titled "Weapons Production System," prepared for Park prior to the DIPC meeting, contains additional strategic guidelines that were adopted by the council in February.[91] The report proposed applying the concept of "system[s] engineering" to integrate the efforts of all units (private companies, military arsenals, and research institutes) toward the goal of mass-producing weapons parts in the shortest possible time.[92] The SES report identified the machinery industry as the central locus of indigenized weapons production, and specified that multiple companies should be selected to manufacture each weapon part, to promote higher quality through competition and offer greater security with diversified production. In principle, the SES technocrats' systems-engineering approach envisioned the HCI program as synchronizing the work of government, industry, and private manufacturers in a single well-oiled process.

New Lightning Exhibits and a Second Defense Industry Promotion Council Meeting

After the Lightning Operation's initial success in producing basic weapons, ADD scientists struggled to replicate the more sophisticated US weapons that O had ordered for a second exhibition. Fortunately, the Lightning Operation's first exhibit and its display of South Korea's determination to develop its own capabilities persuaded the United States to soften its arms restrictions, at least temporarily, and to offer additional technical aid. The exhibition had given credence to the argument by the US Department of Defense that increasing US technical aid to support the ROK's independent weapons production would help the United States accelerate its withdrawal of troops in accordance with the Nixon Doctrine.[93] In addition, South Korea's demonstrated capabilities supported the US Army's position that the older US weapons could be manufactured by Koreans and sold to other allied nations that still relied on the same US-model weapons.[94] Persuaded, the Nixon administration dispatched an Advanced Research Projects Agency technical assistance team, headed by Clyde D. Hardin, to work with the ADD.[95]

Hardin's team arrived in South Korea on January 7, 1972, bringing critical aid in the form of American technical knowledge and field training for making US-model weapons. However, according to Ku Sanghoe of the ADD, Hardin's assistance exceeded what the US government had intended to offer. Crucially, Hardin and his team helped ADD scientists gain access to classified data and blueprints for US-model weapons, which proved key to their production of weapons for the second exhibit of the Lightning Operation.[96] The Advanced Research Projects Agency also introduced ADD researchers to a weapons-research management system called Life Cycle Management, which was used by the US Department of Defense. The ADD's adoption of this system helped the agency upgrade its handling of every stage of development, from R & D to the test and evaluation (T & E) of weapons products.[97] Meanwhile, the ADD also expanded its collaboration with South Korea's other allies, seeking assistance from Japan's Special Technical Research Laboratory to advance R & D for developing Korean-model guns, and working with Taiwan for weapon sample exchanges, joint research activities, and technical support.[98]

On April 3, less than five months after O and Park's first meeting, the ADD's second Lightning Operation exhibit showcased domestically produced carbine guns, machine guns, grenade launchers, antitank rocket launchers, antipersonnel mines, and antitank mines (figs. 2.3a and 2.3b).[99] O had fulfilled his promise to develop modern, Korean-made basic weapons within six months and had demonstrated the ROK's ability to produce them. Originally, O and his SES team had been tasked only with replacing the outdated firearms available to the Homeland Reserve Forces. Now Park was so impressed by the weapons in the second exhibit that he immediately expanded his armament plans to equipping the ROK Armed Forces with domestically produced weapons, including Korean-made howitzers, tanks, aircraft, naval vessels, and even submarines.[100]

From April to October 1972 the ADD proceeded with its work for a third round of the Lightning Operation, this one aimed at upgrading existing prototypes and developing new ones, including military communication devices and personal military equipment, to the point that they could be mass-produced.[101] The success of the Lightning Operation and its three rounds of exhibits enabled South Korea to quickly develop prototypes of conventional US infantry weapons and equipment. However, their mass production necessitated large factories and new manufacturing technologies, requirements that added impetus to fully expanding HCI. Blue House reports from 1972 contain evidence that the Park government's development of industries such as special metals and machinery, which could mass-produce both commercial items and military products, was already under way.[102]

Following the Lightning Operation, Park's confidence in O and his HCI strategy continued to grow. In October 1972 the DIPC held

FIGS. 2.3A AND 2.3B. Park Chung Hee at the Lightning Operation's second exhibition of Korean-made weapons on April 3, 1972. *Source:* National Archives of Korea; file nos. CET0023045 1-1 and CET0023045 3-3.

a second meeting, at which the council confirmed its commitment to O's plan for boosting the civilian industrial capacity for weapons production and adopted his HCI agenda. As O recalls, the policy agenda items for HCI and defense industry development were reported on together at this meeting, a claim that supports his assertion that HCI was set in motion to support the defense industry.[103] Guided by the basic principles it set forth in February, the DIPC now established measures to commence HCI-based defense industrialization. The council officially designated twenty-nine civilian businesses to serve as the first government contractors for weapons parts.[104] To attain the highly skilled workers necessary for weapons production, the DIPC also deliberated policies for workforce training, including plans for state-subsidized technical high schools and vocational training.[105]

From O's first meeting with Park in November 1971 to the DIPC's official adoption of the HCI plan in October 1972, HCI and defense industry policies were inextricably linked. After the successful Lightning Operation and the DIPC's meetings, Park's top policymakers and military leaders began translating O's ideas into state policies for defense industrialization.[106] In the background, despite Nixon's agreement to finance Park's Five-Year Military Modernization Plan, the United States had already begun cutting its military aid to South Korea by this time, leaving the MND little choice but to turn to domestic production to meet the military's needs.[107] Then, in the same month that the DIPC reached its consensus on HCI, Park announced his Yusin reforms, creating a new government that gave him unlimited political authority to carry out his militarized industrialization plan. The stage was set for Park's official declaration of HCI as a national policy.

Heavy and Chemical Industrialization and the Defense Industry

Park publicly proclaimed his administration's new HCI Policy at his New Year's press conference on January 12, 1973, declaring that South Korea had entered the "age of heavy and chemical industrialization" and that the nation's industry and economy would now be built around that priority.[108] The HCI Policy set forth sector-specific development goals, directing concentrated state investment in heavy and chemical industries and their export products, including steel, ships, heavy machinery, and petrochemicals. The goal, Park explained, was to increase South Korea's export income to $10 billion a year and the nation's annual per capita income to $1,000 by the next decade. In addition, Park announced his initiation of "the movement to scientize all citizens" (*chŏn kungmin ŭi kwahakhwa undong*), referred to here as the National Scientization Movement (NSM), to support the scientific and technical training needed to produce a highly skilled domestic workforce.[109]

This speech by Park, which officially promulgated both the HCI and NSM without ever mentioning the defense industry, could seem to be entirely about the economy if viewed apart from his defense industry planning up to this point. However, Park's turn toward civilian-based defense industrialization after the national security crisis of 1968, and his government's steadfast advancement of this approach since then, point to the main motive behind the formal HCI Policy: to establish an independent defense industry based on civilian infrastructure. HCI embodied and realized the catchphrase "rich nation, strong army" in that it tied the knot between the processes of civilian industrialization and militarization. For Park and his advisers, the term "HCI," although it carried the economic objective of shifting Korea to export-oriented industrialization, served as a strategic cover to conceal the ROK's independent defense industry plans from US scrutiny.[110] The SES, the governing agency behind the HCI Policy, continued to work toward its primary goal of developing South Korea's defense industry by restructuring the domestic industrial base for arms production.[111]

A Tangled Relationship

The degree to which Park's HCI Policy was enmeshed with the defense industry is evident in various government actions, policy measures, and memos written to the president shortly after his promulgation of the policy. Less than two weeks later, O sent Park a memo, titled "Report on South Korea's Weapon Production Abilities," on the status of domestic arms production.[112] In the memo, O charted the number of defense contractors designated to produce parts for each of seven types of weapons, along with their combined production capacity (table 2.2).

Table 2.2.
South Korea's Arms Production Capacity, 1973

Weapon type	No. of contractors for production	Total production capacity (units)
Grenades (M61, M67)	8	420,000
Antipersonnel mines (M18, A1)	5	36,000
Antitank mine	3	30,000
Mortar (60 mm)	8	900
Mortar (81 mm)	8	600
Rocket launcher (3.5 inch)	4	1,200
Grenade launcher	6	2,400

SOURCE: Data from PS, "Pyŏnggi saengsan nŭngnyŏk pogo," Jan. 23, 1973, EA0004651, PA (Seongnam).
NOTE: The total number of contractors in the table is forty-two; this number exceeds the twenty-nine individual contractors in the first state-selected group, as some contractors worked on multiple types of weapons.

The information he presented indicates that South Korea's weapons-production system had achieved considerable progress even before Park's public announcement of the HCI Policy. Evidently, the seven types of weapons listed had already passed the experimental stage, thanks to the Lightning Operation, and were ready for large-scale production. Clearly the government had both a well-developed plan and the basic infrastructure in place to begin mass-producing weapons by the time the official policy was promulgated in January 1973.

During the year leading up to that promulgation, from the end of 1971 to late 1972, SES technocrats O Wŏnch'ŏl and Kim Kwangmo had drafted a course for HCI in a document they titled *Chunghwahak kongŏphwa chŏngch'aek sŏnŏn e ttarŭn kongŏp kujo kaep'yŏnnon* (Theory on the restructuring of industrial organization in accordance with the HCI promulgation; hereafter *Kaep'yŏnnon*).[113] When Park put forward the state's new HCI Policy publicly, not all government officials were convinced of its merit, prompting Park and O to hold a briefing for ministerial heads and other principal policymakers on January 31.[114] At that meeting O presented plans for both reorganizing the nation's industrial structures for HCI and developing the defense industry, goals he identified as "one overarching project."[115] With the Korean-made weapons from the Lightning Operation proudly on display, O gave Park and his policymakers the final version of the *Kaep'yŏnnon* document he and Kim Kwangmo had prepared.[116] O elaborated on how the interdependent development of heavy and chemical industries and the defense industry would serve economic and defense purposes simultaneously by advancing South Korea's precision manufacturing, increasing the supply of skilled labor, improving mass production, and expanding exports. Most significant for Park, HCI as O outlined it would allow for a national expansion of defense manufacturing that would make it possible to arm the ROK military with Korean-made weapons. At the end of his briefing, O projected that the plan would require a financial commitment of $10 billion in combined domestic and foreign capital. Park told Prime Minister Kim Chongp'il to launch the plan right away (figs. 2.4 and 2.5).

FIG. 2.4. Prime Minister Kim Chongp'il (seated at the table) attends O Wŏnch'ŏl's presentation on the progress of the HCI Policy, March 1973. *Source:* National Archives of Korea; file no. CET0042545.

FIG. 2.5. O Wŏnch'ŏl (with the pointer) explains the HCI development to Kim Chongp'il (in the light suit) at the March 1973 presentation. *Source:* National Archives of Korea; file no. CET0042545.

Two days later, on February 2, Park established the Heavy and Chemical Industry Promotion Council (Chunghwahak Kongŏp Ch'ujin Wiwŏnhoe) to serve as a governing body for HCI. The council was ostensibly chaired by the prime minister, but O was actually in charge, under Park's authority. The council formed a task force of its own, the Heavy and Chemical Industry Promotion Council Planning Corps (Chunghwahak Ch'ujin Wiwŏnhoe Kyehwoektan; hereafter, HCI Planning Corps), to manage and advance the policies supporting the HCI.[117] To ensure concurrent development of the HCI and defense industry, Park appointed O as director of the HCI Planning Corps. (Kim Kwangmo, O's main assistant, became its deputy director.) O's dual position as chief policymaker for HCI and head of the SES in the Blue House further signifies the convergence of industrialization and defense development under Park.

O's first task as director of the HCI Planning Corps was to secure capital for the industrialization effort. A move by the government in 1972 to bail out indebted corporations in exchange for their engagement and investment in state-led HCI sectors—the August Third Measure—had helped the administration obtain domestic capital investments in heavy and chemical industries.[118] O now began a campaign to acquire foreign capital for HCI by inviting US and other international corporations to invest in new joint ventures with Korean companies, placing a priority on investments in machinery manufacturing.[119] In addition, as a source of domestic capital for HCI the Park government established the National Investment Fund (NIF) in December 1973. The fund drew from the savings deposits and pension-fund reserves of banks and insurance companies to provide loans for private manufacturers.[120] Officially intended to finance development projects in all of South Korea's heavy and chemical industries, a significant portion of NIF funding (33.7 percent in 1974 and 43.2 by 1975) went to the machinery industry, the HCI sector with the closest ties to defense. The NIF automatically funded loans for HCI projects under the authority of O's HCI Planning Corps.[121]

Earlier, in February 1973, the government had also enacted new legislation that specifically supported defense-business development. Called the Law on Special Measures for Military Procurement (Kunsu Chodal e kwanhan T'ŭkpyŏl Choch'ibŏp), or the Military Procurement Law, it facilitated the acquisition of state grants, loans, and tax deductions for defense businesses.[122] This incentivized companies to compete for government defense contracts, thereby encouraging further domestic investment in weapons manufacturing. Because the companies that qualified as defense contractors were in the heavy and chemical industries, the law essentially served both defense- and HCI-related manufacturing. Passage of the Military Procurement Law just one month after Park introduced the HCI Policy is another strong indication that HCI and the defense industry were linked.

The Master Plan

At the heart of South Korea's plans for defense development through HCI was the policy laid out in O Wŏnch'ŏl and Kim Kwangmo's *Kaep'yŏnnon*. The SES technocrats' plan was specifically designed to achieve Park's "rich nation, strong army" agenda by establishing an independent economy as a prerequisite for self-reliant national defense. Even though it was intended to support Park's tight security deadline for his Five-Year Military Modernization Plan, *Kaep'yŏnnon* proposed a longer ten-year plan for HCI that would build a permanent economic foundation for arms production. Notably, the actual texts of *Kaep'yŏnnon* make no reference to the defense industry. Kim has confirmed that this omission was intentional, as part of the effort to hide South Korea's plan to build its own MIC.[123] He explained that he and O disguised most written records pertaining to the defense industry as HCI records in order to guard against outside surveillance. Strategies for developing the defense industry were subtly woven into the policies for HCI that would support civilian-led production of basic weapons and a system for mobilizing and training the workforce. To achieve its hidden goal of installing an HCI-based weapons-production system, *Kaep'yŏnnon* promoted public-private sector cooperation, targeted specific industries, prioritized exports, and called for investments in human resources.[124]

In *Kaep'yŏnnon*, O and Kim described how the convergence of the public and private sectors could create a "system of total power" (*ch'ongnyŏk ch'eje*), which the SES secretly intended to use to fully mobilize South Korea for military modernization.[125] They proposed to promote cooperation between private businesses and the government by offering economic, legal, and material support to businesses as well as public funding for their work on the state's industrial projects.[126] Companies selected for HCI contracts would receive state subsidies, tax cuts, and low-interest loans to help build facilities and improve production. Although this point was not openly made in *Kaep'yŏnnon*, the contract-based system was designed to create a mutually beneficial relationship: the defense industry would gain from the entrepreneurial skills, resources, technological innovation, and production capacity of civilian enterprises, and those enterprises would learn to meet the modern international standards for business management, precision, efficiency, and quality control required by the defense industry.

Kaep'yŏnnon outlined the development of five key industries (later expanded to six when nonferrous metals split off from steelmaking)—heavy (or industrial) machinery, shipbuilding, chemicals/petrochemicals, electronics, and steel—and the construction of five distinct industrial complexes to support them.[127] The sectors specified in the report reveal South Korea's shift to heavy and chemical industries, and point toward a focus on expanding exports with the intermediate and manufactured goods they produced. In terms of their relevance to the defense industry, Kim Chŏngnyŏm explains: "Indeed, the steel industry . . . [including] the nonferrous metal industry[,] needed to be developed to produce steel, specialized steel, copper, and zinc, all of which are basic materials of the defense industry. Also, the machinery industry needed to be developed to facilitate precise high-tech processing, along with the electronic industry to produce electronic weapons and components. Also, the scale had to [be] big enough[,] considering the massive demand of having to arm 600,000 soldiers in the standing army and 2.5 million reserve soldiers."[128] In essence, these heavy and chemical industries were designed as dual-purpose industries that would serve as the foundation for localized arms production (fig. 2.6). *Kaep'yŏnnon*, like the SES policy recommendation to Park for the DIPC policies in February 1972, identifies the heavy machinery sector as the pillar of South Korea's heavy and chemical industries, while also acknowledging it as the most underdeveloped sector within these planned industries.[129] To strengthen the sector, *Kaep'yŏnnon* proposed to focus on the mass production of machine (and weapons) parts by civilian plants as the most critical component of South Korea's HCI.[130]

Along with identifying specific industries for development, the SES technocrats' plan was designed to complement South Korea's economic growth with export-oriented industrialization. This strategy aligned with the Blue House's vision of fostering an export-friendly defense industry that could increase Korea's profitability and the inflow of foreign capital through exported goods.[131] Given their concentrated production of exportable parts and essential manufactured items, the heavy and chemical industries were inherently global export sectors.[132] In keeping with *Kaep'yŏnnon*'s plan for the exportation of HCI products, advanced manufacturers in these industries that exported commercial goods would bring their competitiveness and adherence to international quality standards to bear on the military products they produced.[133] This would, in turn, help raise the quality of domestically produced military products to meet global export standards. Moreover, global demand for affordable weapons was high, and the capital South Korea obtained through weapons sales abroad would contribute to

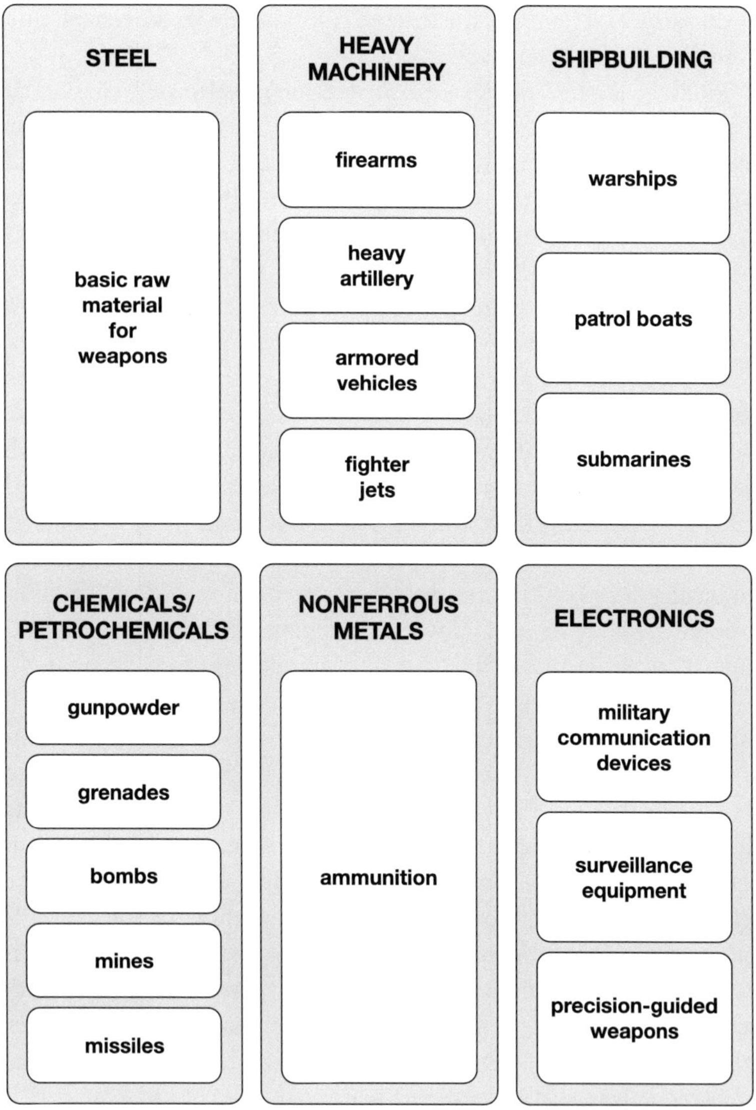

FIG. 2.6. South Korea's dual-purpose heavy and chemical industries in the 1970s. *Source:* Based on Kwon, "Mars and Manna," 22, figure 2.

its economy and increase the foreign funds available for reinvestment in industrial development.[134]

Finally, as part of the administration's National Scientization Movement, *Kaep'yŏnnon* emphasized the need to advance South Korea's human resources in critical fields such as precision manufacturing, engineering, the sciences, and technology—areas that were important to the defense industry.[135] *Kaep'yŏnnon* proposed a national ten-year technical training plan to transform South Korea's workers from predominantly simple laborers into a force of highly skilled, knowledge-based employees.[136]

Overall, *Kaep'yŏnnon*'s far-reaching plan proposed to "restructure" South Korea's industries (as the document's title indicates) to create a new industrial ecosystem conducive to weapons production. It also provided an important impetus for Park's decision to implement the Yusin Constitution, which would give him total control of the state and the economy. Of course, the government under Park had been directing economic policy—with Park deeply involved—long before the advent of the HCI Policy in 1973. However, supporting the new HCI sectors would require significantly deeper and more extensive government intervention in comparison to the state's administration of general industries in the 1960s, when Park's industrial policies were largely aimed at regulating and broadening companies' participation in state projects and foreign trade.[137] Critically, the Park government's new HCI plan called for the Blue House to exercise unilateral control over which industries would receive concentrated infusions of state resources and capital, and to decide which companies were most fit for expedited dual-purpose development. The government had to quickly establish new industries and nurture and expand the capabilities of a handful of corporations that would operate within them, so they could meet Park's urgent goal of defense industrialization. For Park and his policymakers, this would necessitate an authoritarian approach.

Korean-Style Militarized Industrialization

Since the 1990s, Asia's newly industrialized economies have often been grouped together by scholars who view their models of development as similar.[138] In particular, South Korea's HCI Policy in the 1970s has been compared with Japan's heavy and chemical industrialization from 1957 to 1967. Both countries employed strong, state-directed mobilization and technocratic policymaking, both promoted export-oriented industrialization, and both advanced technologies for combined commercial and military purposes during the Cold War.[139] In fact, in drafting *Kaep'yŏnnon*, Kim Kwangmo affirmed that Japan served as the SES's paramount model for writing the policies for HCI.[140] The Korean plan reflects many aspects of Japan's precedent-setting industrialization, including its ten-year development plan, promotion of export-oriented industrialization, development of technology-intensive industries, investment in private manufacturing firms, and training of skilled workers.[141] Postwar Japan's HCI, which was based on large Japanese business conglomerates known as *keiretsu*, also provided a significant reference for South Korea's mobilization of the chaebol to advance civil and military industries.[142]

South Korea, however, incorporated the defense industry into its HCI Policy in a distinct way, as its primary objective differed from Japan's.[143] With its national security fully guaranteed by the US military, Japan could focus its resources and HCI initiatives on economic development rather than national defense. South Korea's HCI, in contrast, was triggered by dire security challenges and shaped by Park's commitment to arming ROK troops with domestically produced weapons. Even though security independence motivated postwar Japan's development of technology to some degree, military concerns weighed far more heavily on the ROK, and it launched its HCI primarily to develop independent arms manufacturing. Likewise, South Korea's economic development differed from that of other developmental states in East Asia, such as Taiwan, Singapore, and Hong Kong, in the extent to which it immediately and completely combined defense and economic sectors for its militarized industrialization.[144]

South Korea's approach can also be distinguished from that of its patron, the United States, even though its HCI plan partly espoused the US-model MIC built on private enterprise. South Korea could not possibly replicate the US market-driven system because it lacked modernized industries and was operating on a very short timeline with limited resources.[145] A highly advanced industrial base was already in place in the United States when it converted private companies into arms producers during World War II, but the ROK government had to develop its private-sector industries first and then quickly guide their transition into defense production.[146] Even when compared with the MICs that have advanced public-private sector partnerships in other countries, such as Japan, France, Germany, and Israel—all of which developed over longer time spans—South Korea's defense industrialization stands out for its rapid pace and the tightly unified participation of the private and public sectors.

Presidential Directives and Military Authority

South Korea's all-out effort to develop its defense industry was enabled by the most defining aspect of the Park government's leadership structure: the presidential directives (*taet'ongnyŏng chisi*) system, which institutionalized Park's absolute authority. The president was exceptionally involved in all aspects of HCI in his effort to achieve weapons production in the shortest possible time. Backed by the Yusin Constitution, Park operated much like a military commander as he determined the structure and culture of HCI.[147] Declassified Blue House documents attest to his active and direct influence on policies related to weapons projects, technology procurement, R & D, and the establishment of facilities for developing the defense industry.[148]

Park's highly centralized, military-style policymaking came out of his background as an officer, first in the Imperial Japanese Army during the 1940s and then as a major general in the ROK Army until the coup d'état he led in 1961. In Park's chain of command for HCI, SES technocrats served as his generals, the HCI Planning Corps was his task force, the ADD was his military think tank, and chaebol leaders and workers were his deputies and soldiers on the ground. This level of direct supervision by a president was unusual; in other countries, ministries of national defense and military leaders tended to oversee efforts to develop the defense industry and the military. Under Park's presidential directives system, all planning and decision-making related to the defense industry had to pass through him and the SES at the Blue House—not the Ministry of National Defense or the Joint Chiefs of Staff—before being handed down to the ADD and select businesses for implementation.[149]

With his militaristic management of HCI, Park put his personal imprint on the entire process. South Korea's militarized industrialization not only reflected Park's administrative style but was also deeply imbued with his ideals and beliefs—more so than any other national project, as it was the only initiative run directly by the president. In Park's campaign to drive defense industrialization, government officials and others executing his orders took up his core principles, such as self-reliant national defense and "rich nation, strong army," and were driven to fulfill them as a national mission.[150]

Park's militarism also pervaded the nation's factories (see chapter 3). The mobilization of companies and workers to advance HCI was heavily influenced by Park's militant anticommunist stance and his fierce personal battle against Kim Il Sung for military and economic superiority.[151] Many workers in HCI factories at the time saw themselves as patriotic "industrial soldiers" rather than ordinary civilians and took pride in their contributions to industrialization and national security.[152]

By stirring up a sense of economic nationalism and competition with the industrialized West and Japan, Park effectively launched a patriotic national drive for HCI and his goal of increased exports.[153] And in declaring that South Korea had to free itself from US interventionist policies as well as its reliance on US aid, he primed Blue House technocrats to defy the United States and its free-market approach to economic development. Asserting South Korea's autonomy, they created an HCI program guided by authoritarian policymaking.

South Korea's administration of HCI under the presidential directive system was characterized by its small, tightly knit leadership team comprising elite SES technocrats who worked directly under Park in the Blue House.[154] To meet Park's priorities of absolute efficiency, secrecy, and minimal delays, O Wŏnch'ŏl and his team followed the "principle of a select few," or *sosu chŏngyejuŭi*, a phrase that came to reflect Park's general operational style.[155] The six members of the SES (but primarily O and Kim Kwangmo) planned and executed government policies to support the HCI, including skilled-labor development, educational reforms, land development for industrial complexes, and the establishment of research institutes.[156] In addition, they oversaw the state's top secret missile and nuclear arms programs, reporting their progress to Park. Compared with the technocratic agencies that guided other Asian developmental states, such as the Ministry of International Trade and Industry in Japan and the Industrial Development Bureau in Taiwan, power over industrial policymaking in South Korea was concentrated among far fewer policymakers in the SES and the HCI Planning Corps (especially owing to their association with secret defense industry plans).[157]

O's adherence to *sosu chŏngyejuŭi* as director of the HCI Planning Corps was mirrored in the corps' dominance over industrial policy. His elite task force had the power to set and implement policies to overhaul the national industrial base and build defense infrastructure. "There was no stronger apparatus" than the HCI Planning Corps, according to Kim Kwangmo, and its decisions were equivalent to orders from the president.[158] Members of the corps designed and executed policies by directly coordinating with heads of the relevant ministries, businesses, and research centers in a streamlined process that accelerated HCI's development.[159] However, O's extraordinary prerogative made him many rivals.[160] Even before the launch of the HCI Policy in 1973, O's unlimited oversight of industrial policy and the influence he wielded in selecting businesses for weapons production had caused frustration among officials in the MND, the MCI, and other agencies.[161] Many of them disagreed with O's policies and presented their concerns, but Park remained firm in his support of O.

The Blue House–centered approach ensured that the SES was virtually unhindered by objections to Park's arms development plan. In 1971 the MND, for example, was opposed to developing an independent weapons industry, favoring continued reliance on US military imports.[162] Even though the MND had followed Park's order to initiate arms production in the late 1960s, the military still preferred importing the majority of its weapons from the United States over producing them domestically. The MND and the ROK Armed Forces, which had close ties to the command of United States Forces Korea (USFK) and had received arms and training with the support of US military aid since the end of the Korean War, preferred US-made weapons—partly for strategic reasons, because they enhanced interoperability with the USFK in case of war.[163] Even more important, ROK Army officials expressed skepticism about the reliability of weapons developed by the newly established ADD, which they regarded as technically underqualified.[164] By continuing to rely on US-made weapons, the MND and the military could also keep South Korea's lucrative weapons procurement deals within their control. Additionally, EPB officials opposed O's HCI plan because of the interventionist policies that it would require, endorsing instead an American-style free-market system. Furthermore, they were concerned about the projected cost of executing the HCI Policy ($10 billion), believing that South Korea's limited financial resources made O's proposal too risky.

Beyond such domestic opposition, the biggest challenge came via US arms regulations, as Washington continued to hold South Korea's military development in check.[165] Because the MND and EPB had close relationships with the United States, which Park no longer trusted, he used the SES as his primary instrument as well as intermediary between himself and the other government agencies for implementing his defense industry plans. Park's distrust of his own military leaders (particularly those in the MND) also influenced his decision to choose private companies, rather than the military's arsenals, to serve as the bases for defense production.[166] In the end, the SES, backed by Park's authority, was able to push his plans forward.

Although Park's presidential directives system under Yusin succeeded in accelerating the course of defense industry development, in the long run his authoritarian approach to HCI would have a negative impact on the defense sector and the corporations involved in it. The companies groomed under the HCI Policy came to depend on the strong state management and support that enabled their initial rapid growth, and this was particularly the case in the defense industry. The true impact of Park's policies on the chaebol and defense production would be demonstrated later, with the sudden end of his regime in 1979—after which South Korea's defense industry lost its direction and fell into a slump, experiencing an immediate drop in production followed by a decade of stalled growth.[167]

Yusin's Ties to Heavy and Chemical Industrialization

The connections between the Yusin reforms and HCI are intricate and far-reaching. Park's imposition of the Yusin Constitution in 1972 gave him unconstrained presidential power, under martial law, to enact comprehensive political and economic reforms in the context of what

Park declared was a national emergency. Park's defense industrialization goals were swiftly achieved, but the nation paid a heavy price in other areas.

With his heavy-handed use of power sanctioned by the Yusin Constitution, Park bypassed governmental checks and balances to achieve defense industrialization at all costs; all operations of the bureaucracy, industry, and society were brought under Blue House control. Park firmly believed South Korea could achieve national security—and even reunification and democracy—only with an independent national economy.[168] However, his "rich nation, strong army" principle prioritized the economy and security over all else, resulting in a neglect of political and social progress. State resources for modernization were largely allocated to the few elite corporations driving HCI, exacerbating economic and social inequities and regional divisions, and leaving a large segment of the populace behind. Civil rights were strictly limited, especially among workers in the crucial heavy and chemical industries, where factories were closely monitored by the state to prevent work disruptions. Workers suffered from draconian working hours and unsafe labor conditions.[169] A growing number of progressive activists and workers united in protesting human rights abuses, and the absence of civil rights—exacerbated under Yusin—would fuel prodemocracy movements long after Park's demise. Because of this legacy, the relationship between Yusin's authoritarianism and HCI remains controversial.

In rancorous public and academic debates, many have argued over whether the Yusin system (*Yusin ch'eje*), in place from 1972 to 1979, was actually essential to—and enacted for—HCI and defense industry development. Some scholars and pundits, as well as former policymakers under Park, have argued that Park established Yusin specifically to develop the ROK's independent defense in response to the threats posed by the DPRK and the Nixon Doctrine.[170] They claim that the Yusin Constitution equipped Park's technocrats with the unchallenged authority that enabled the Blue House to make its "big push" for HCI by immediately mobilizing businesses and the workforce. As O Wŏnch'ŏl himself asserted, "Authoritarianism was prerequisite to HCI," meaning that Yusin and HCI were inseparable: "These days, many say that President Park succeeded in economy but failed in democracy. Even former ministers under the President openly separate HCI from Yusin reform. I tell you: the bitter truth is that *HCI was Yusin and Yusin was HCI*. One did not exist without the other. Korea succeeded in HCI because the President disciplined the state to implement HCI precisely as planned. And the President could not have disciplined the state if there had been no Yusin. It is unconscionable to ignore this fact."[171]

O saw Yusin as necessary for HCI and for enabling the nation's total mobilization for defense industrialization. Additionally, Kim Chŏngnyŏm has remarked that South Korea's dire national security circumstances, especially the DPRK's provocations and the withdrawal of US troops, prompted Park to pursue HCI and build the defense industry.[172] Thus both Kim and O, the officials most familiar with Park's thinking about HCI, claim that the HCI Policy was designed to build the defense industry, in accordance with Park's priority on national security.[173] Park's top two technocrats treated his policy agenda and the consolidation of his power as means to the same end: self-reliant national defense.[174] According to this analysis, Park's implementation of Yusin, like the subsequent launch of HCI and the modernization of the defense industry, were reactions to the perceived security emergency of the late 1960s and early 1970s.

Other scholars and Park's political critics challenge this assessment and view the Yusin reforms as politically motivated.[175] They see Park's installment of Yusin—as well as his policy for self-reliant national defense, the HCI Policy, and defense industry development—as part of a concerted effort to perpetuate his regime.[176] Even Kim Kwangmo, O's closest assistant in the SES and the deputy director of the HCI Planning Corps, disagreed with O on the connection between HCI and Yusin. While acknowledging that Yusin certainly made the HCI Policy operable, Kim argued against O's justification of Yusin as part of the HCI plan.[177] Kim passionately exclaimed in an interview, "You cannot realistically believe that Yusin was started merely to build factories!"[178] He went so far as to declare that if O said Yusin was set up for HCI, then "O Wŏnch'ŏl has, in fact, lied."[179] Kim insisted that it was actually the successful development of HCI and the defense industry that had benefited Park's Yusin politics, not the other way around.[180] Kim further claimed that he had developed the ideas for the HCI Policy independently through his own research on other developed countries, separate from Yusin and defense industry planning. He stated that these ideas were later incorporated into *Kaep'yŏnnon*, the HCI plan he coauthored with O for the government's defense industry agenda, after Park had already adopted the Yusin Constitution.[181]

Kim Kwangmo's emphasis on the independent origins of HCI contrasts with both O's and Kim Chŏngnyŏm's portrayal of HCI and defense building as "one overarching project" launched together as a result of the HCI plan that O presented to Park in November 1971.[182] According to Kim Kwangmo, it was after the institution of Yusin, when Park realized HCI was necessary for his political stability as well as for economic growth and defense industrialization, that he decided to push the technocrats' plan.[183] He noted that Park would not have had a "political justification for Yusin without the [long-term] economic plans offered by HCI."[184] Kim also said Park was motivated to implement Yusin (and thus cement his power) by his extremely narrow victory in the 1971 presidential election, when he ran against the popular democratic activist Kim Dae-jung. Kim Chongp'il, prime minister from 1971 to 1975 under Park and one of his longest-serving political aides, as well as a relative by marriage, shared this view, writing in his memoir that the 1971 election threatened the stability of Park's regime and planted the idea of Yusin in his mind.[185]

But the belief that HCI was a prerequisite for independent defense had been on Park's mind since the early 1960s, beginning with his 1962 plan to develop domestic steelmaking as the foundation for a defense industry. Indeed, Kim Kwangmo's claim about the origins of HCI and Yusin are countered by Park's first and second FYEDPs, his government's Three-Year Defense Industry Development Plan (1968–71) for civilian arms production, and the Four Core Factories project, all of which were connected to, and directed toward, Park's goal of building a domestic weapons-production system on a civilian industrial base. In addition, Park's efforts from 1968 to 1972 to create the total security system—including extensive military reforms and mobilization for domestic arms production to supply the HRF—had blazed the trail for his militarized industrialization under Yusin (see chapter 1). It is therefore likely that Park first envisioned his Yusin-backed HCI program around the time of the 1968 security crisis, when he began initiating major military and ideological reforms for South Korea's militarization in reaction to threats from North Korea. If that is the case, serious Blue House planning for a domestic defense industry and the concept of the Yusin system arose simultaneously in response to the DPRK's provocations and then were sped up by South Korea's unraveling relations with the United States.

Declassified presidential documents show that the mass production of arms by domestic manufacturers officially commenced with Park's HCI Policy in January 1973, shortly after the ratification of the Yusin Constitution in December 1972.[186] This chronology and the documentary evidence back the idea that Yusin was put in place primarily to support a new defense industry, a priority that had by then matured into a concrete plan under the SES. If Yusin had been conceived by Park solely as a way to preserve his own political power, there would have been little reason for his government to immediately launch a defense industry venture that posed a huge political and financial risk for him, given both US and internal opposition to South Korea's independent weapons production. Despite his disagreement with O on the origins of Yusin, Kim Kwangmo fully concurred with him that South Korea's HCI and its defense buildup would not have been possible without the political stability and control provided by the Yusin system.[187] In other words, there would have been no defense industrialization without Yusin.[188]

At the same time—even though the Yusin system was enacted with the goal of achieving self-reliant national defense—Park's decision to implement this system should be examined from multiple perspectives, beyond his aspiration to reinforce national security. His personal experience as a colonial soldier in Manchuria, where he witnessed the industrialization led by the Imperial Japanese Army, may have long before planted the idea of a Yusin-style mobilization in Park's mind as an effective model for industrializing South Korea.[189] His political motives cannot be overlooked either, particularly given his near electoral defeat in 1971 amid a wave of anti-state, pro-democracy protests by dissident intellectuals (*chaeya*) and labor unions. His Cold War rivalry with Kim Il Sung also must have goaded him to fortify his own control: to surpass the North, Park needed a powerful government to push and mobilize the nation for rapid industrialization and economic growth. The evolution in US policy toward Korea—signaled by the

Nixon Doctrine and the US-China détente—undoubtedly had an impact; Park's decision to centralize authority was largely driven by his efforts to reduce the ROK's dependence on the United States.[190] Finally, the ten-year timeline for HCI proposed in *Kaep'yŏnnon* would have further strengthened Park's resolve to hold on to power so that he could realize his goals for the "modernization of the fatherland." Park believed that to carry out his HCI Policy for economic and military modernization, he needed to secure his position of power.

Domestic Weapons Production

The Yusin regime reshaped South Korea by driving the entire nation toward rapid industrialization, fully conscripting civilian manufacturers, as well as the nation's workforce and resources, to support the state-led program for defense production. In its extent, intensity, and pace, South Korea's industrial transformation under HCI in the 1970s was similar to Japan's wartime mobilization of Korea for defense production in the 1930s and early 1940s.[191] Indeed, like Imperial Japan, South Korea strove for self-reliance through its efforts to build up its military technology and industrial capacity while turning away from its dependence on US resources. Under Yusin, the ROK pushed military modernization and the rapid production of arms as if it were a nation preparing for war.

Building Industrial Foundations

Backed by the Yusin Constitution, the HCI Planning Corps mobilized the private sector and reorganized the industrial infrastructure for mass-producing weapons.[192] From 1973 to the end of the decade, the state constructed large industrial complexes to support strategic heavy and chemical industries. Aside from the steel complex run by the state-owned POSCO, all the new industrial complexes were occupied by factories from private companies. These new corporate and manufacturing hubs followed the plan for mass production outlined in *Kaep'yŏnnon*.[193]

In July 1973, after the completion of POSCO's integrated mill, South Korea began to produce steel, fulfilling the first prerequisite for building

FIG. 2.7. POSCO's integrated mill in Pohang, South Korea, 1976. *Source:* HCI Promotion Council, *Heavy and Chemical Industry*, 29.

its defense industry (fig 2.7). The nonferrous-metals industry, which started in 1977 when the Onsan Industrial Complex was completed, initiated the domestic production of special steel and other basic materials.[194] In the nation's new metals factories—which included steel production, iron making and rolling operations, as well as copper and zinc smelting plants—the South Korean workforce gained valuable technical skills that could be applied to both industrial development and defense production.[195] The materials produced by these factories allowed South Korean companies to branch out into industries such as shipbuilding, automobile manufacturing, electronics, and heavy machinery.

With the government's provision of domestic and foreign capital as well as technical support, Hyundai Heavy Industries constructed a new shipyard at Ulsan in June 1974, and by 1976 South Korea had become one of the world's leading shipbuilding contractors and exporters of ships (fig. 2.8).[196] More new shipyards, such as the Samsung Dockyard and Daewoo's Okp'o Dockyard, were built near the South Korean naval base in Chinhae to provide battleships in the event of war.[197] South Korea also established three electronics manufacturing complexes in Kumi, which enabled the production of electronic weapons, communications

FIG. 2.8. Large tankers under construction in a dry dock of the Hyundai Shipyard in Ulsan, South Korea, 1976. *Source:* HCI Promotion Council, *Heavy and Chemical Industry*, 43.

devices, and surveillance equipment for the ROK military.[198] As these new industries matured, they advanced the nation's skilled labor force, R & D, technology, mass production, and quality control, all of which were essential to modernizing the defense industry.

For the all-important machinery sector, the MCI began constructing the Ch'angwŏn Industrial Complex in April 1974, a key industrial hub that would serve as the base for producers of commercial and

FIG. 2.9. Park examines a Korean-made armored vehicle at the Ch'angwŏn Industrial Complex in 1977. *Source:* National Archives of Korea; file no. CET0023910.

weapons-related machinery (fig. 2.9).[199] The machinery sector was central to the HCI Policy's plan to expand civilian machinery manufacturing into a system for the mass production of weapons parts.[200] SES technocrats looked particularly to the example of Hitachi, a Japanese machinery manufacturer that produced both commercial and military products, from electronics to large engines used in commercial vehicles and trains as well as military vehicles and warships.[201]

The government's third and fourth FYEDPs (collectively covering 1972–81) pushed businesses to expand into the defense-related production of engines, electronic equipment, automobile parts, and heavy machinery.[202] Select defense contractors, including manufacturers such as the Kia Machine Tools (later Kia Heavy Industries), Korea Heavy Machinery, and Tongil Heavy Industries, received occupancy approval at the new hub in Ch'angwŏn and, with state funding, began building new plants there in the mid-1970s (figs. 2.10, 2.11, and 2.12).[203] By 1977 there were eighty-eight firms registered at the Ch'angwŏn Industrial Complex.[204] With its new civilian machinery plants, Ch'angwŏn became the largest industrial base in South Korea, and it served the HCI Policy's highest priority: the mass production of weapons.

Security considerations played an important part in determining where the industrial complexes were established. Aside from the Kumi and Yŏch'ŏn complexes, which specialized in the electronics and chemical industries, respectively, all of the HCI complexes and shipyards were built in Kyŏngsang Province in the southeastern region of the Korean peninsula, a location chosen for its security advantages and access to major seaports.[205] Owing to the government's deep investment in Kyŏngsang Province under Park, even today machinery, ship,

FIG. 2.10. Kia's new plant in Ch'angwŏn Industrial Complex, 1976. *Source:* HCI Promotion Council, *Heavy and Chemical Industry*, 72.

FIG. 2.11. Korea Heavy Machinery's new plant in Ch'angwŏn, 1976. *Source:* HCI Promotion Council, *Heavy and Chemical Industry*, 72.

FIG. 2.12. Tongil Heavy Industries' new plant in Ch'angwŏn, 1976. *Source:* HCI Promotion Council, *Heavy and Chemical Industry*, 74.

steel, and nonferrous metal manufacturers are chiefly concentrated in the region.

The Park government made sure that the Ch'angwŏn complex, the epicenter of South Korea's MIC, was the most secure both geographically and militarily. Ch'angwŏn is surrounded by mountains and near the sea—an ideal site for protection against a North Korean attack (fig. 2.13). The mountains provided a natural barrier against incursions, and Ch'angwŏn's easy access to the sea meant that, in the case of an attack, all military products could easily be shipped to Japan, where the United States had a military base.[206] Ch'angwŏn's proximity to the ROK naval base in Chinhae further assured its protection.

FIG. 2.13. An illustration of the government's design for the Ch'angwŏn Industrial Complex in 1976. *Source:* HCI Promotion Council, *Heavy and Chemical Industry*, 61.

Today, the physical layout of Ch'angwŏn, which became South Korea's first planned city, still exhibits vestiges of the Park state's authoritarian efficiency, with its orderly arrangement of buildings laid out on a grid of parallel and perpendicular roads. Ch'angwŏn Boulevard (Ch'angwŏn Taero), around 9.25 miles long, runs across the middle of the city, dividing residential areas from business and factory buildings. As designed, the concentration of massive factory buildings in proximity to one another facilitates efficient collaboration among businesses, allowing them to operate almost like a giant assembly line. Not fancy or beautiful, Ch'angwŏn is certainly modern and practical, well suited to serving as the heart of the nation's military-industrial infrastructure.

Weapons Production Matures

Soon after the HCI Policy was enacted, South Korea was producing an array of new weapons in civilian manufacturing facilities.[207] The ADD successfully displayed the first piece of Korean-made heavy artillery, an experimental 105 mm howitzer produced by Kia, in March 1973, and just three months later, on June 25, South Korea officially exhibited all of its new heavy artillery, including the howitzer, a 106 mm recoilless cannon, and a 4.2-inch mortar.[208] The exhibition demonstrated the defense industry's rapid expansion into a wider range of weapons and its improvements in precision technology, as well as the speed at which domestic contractors, such as Kia, were gaining experience.

The SES mentioned the advances made by local defense manufacturers in a December 4, 1974, report for President Park titled "Establishment of the Mass Production System for Defense Businesses," in which it also introduced the thirty-nine businesses that by then had been selected to mass-produce parts for forty-four different weapons.[209] The SES ranked the contractors according to their developmental stage as weapons manufacturers, from those producing both weapons parts and commercial products in their original commercial facilities to companies manufacturing military products in plants that specialized in them. At the time of the report, there were twelve stage-one companies, which used their existing (commercial) facilities for both commercial and military production; nine stage-two companies, which had weapons-production facilities operating within commercial plants; and eighteen stage-three companies, which had separate plant buildings dedicated solely to weapons production. The report also noted that the SES planned to upgrade stage-one companies to stage two or three by the end of 1975.

Another SES report written for Park that December, titled simply "Defense Industry," confirmed that rapid progress was being made, stating that the domestic defense industry had reached "the stage of mass production" after just two years of developing and producing basic weapons.[210] It attributed the swift pace of progress to the cooperative efforts of businesses, the military, and research institutes. The report also noted that South Korea's approach to arms production—through the localized manufacturing of parts for assembly—had not only indigenized weapons production but had also improved South Korea's ability to maintain its existing older weapons. This detail suggests that reverse engineering had been applied throughout the weapons-production program. According to the same report, the manufacturing of weapons parts had expedited the growth of precision manufacturing in general, benefiting commercial industry as well. Goals outlined for the future of the defense industry included transitioning the Korean contractors from basic weapons to more sophisticated weapons and military vehicles, acquiring new skills and technology by expanding Korean firms' joint production with foreign defense businesses (by "connecting these ventures with the HCI Policy"), and exporting Korean arms and weapons parts to the Southeast Asian market.[211]

Even the United States, which had opposed Park's independent armament agenda, was impressed by the pace of South Korea's industrialization and its independent manufacturing of US-model weapons.[212] South Korea's rapidly expanding MIC could no longer remain concealed within Park's HCI Policy. In fact, its quick progress persuaded the United States to make greater concessions for military technology transfers, as it saw that South Korea would continue to develop weapons with or without US support.[213]

This new capability opened the way for South Korea to transition from its dependency on expensive licensed production (buying the rights to produce another firm's product) to the more profitable coproduction of weapons with US licensors.[214] Korean companies' quick advances in manufacturing also allowed them to subcontract with US defense firms as parts suppliers, which expanded technological collaborations between Korea and the United States.[215] With US-approved technology transfers, Korean defense manufacturers were able to acquire new technical skills and blueprints for US weapons. By the mid-1970s, Korean manufacturers were mass-producing a surplus of ammunition and infantry weapons, and South Korea began to export weapons to other developing nations.[216] Between 1974 and 1976, South Korea was transformed from a nation completely dependent on US military imports into an arms producer and exporter.

All evidence suggests that by 1976 South Korea had achieved the SES's goal of establishing a homegrown system for producing basic weapons, which meant it had also met Park's deadline for having a domestic defense industry in place.[217] Park had originally set 1976 as his goal, with the expectation that most US ground troops would exit South Korea by then.[218] However, Nixon's plan to withdraw American troops would later be scaled back under the new administration of President Gerald Ford (1974–77).[219] Even though Nixon had not openly called for a total withdrawal of US troops, his planned reduction of forces had long been interpreted by ROK officials as "a detachment of the U.S. commitment to support Korea."[220] The recent withdrawal of US troops from Vietnam had hit too close to home for South Koreans, who feared they could be next, abandoned by the United States at any moment. In accord with Nixon's original schedule for the pullback of US troops, Park had devised his Five-Year Military Modernization Plan to coincide with improvements in the domestic economy outlined in his third FYEDP (1972–76). Park's HCI-based militarized industrialization achieved its objectives in both defense and economic development within five years of when the SES technocrats took over development of the defense industry, in November 1971.

By design, the fledgling South Korean defense industry had relied almost completely on copying weapons parts from US models. Reverse engineering had proved effective for setting up a parts manufacturing system and quickly reproducing the basic weapons required for the HRF, but it was not applicable for the advanced weapons and equipment Park turned to next. Without the necessary technology, the ROK's military modernization would remain in its early stages, and South

Korea would still depend on the United States for high-tech weapons such as modern military vehicles, fighter jets, missiles, maritime surveillance systems, and air defense systems. South Korea would not make significant advances in R & D and indigenous technologies until the late 1970s, when the government began aggressively pursuing advanced weapons and technology under Park's new military modernization initiative called the Yulgok Operation.[221] Nonetheless, from 1973 to 1976 the HCI program for mass-producing basic weapons built the infrastructure and technical foundations for later progress in advanced weaponry.

Although the HCI Policy was originally intended to undergird the defense industry, HCI and defense manufacturing reinforced each other. In the late 1970s, Park's support for the defense industry increasingly became a major driving force behind the modernization of technical and technological infrastructure for civilian industries, as well as their export-led industrialization. The HCI Policy set up a system in which military and commercial production goals converged, enabling a greater flow of technology between the public and private sectors and diffusing new technologies and skills throughout civilian companies. The integration of military production, civilian industry, science, and technology forged by the HCI Policy would prove essential for the development of modern industrial Korea.

As HCI opened Korean enterprises to new markets and international competition in the late 1970s, non–defense-related commercial production also increased, leading to a more diverse range of exportable domestic products. With HCI, the Park government sought to scale up exports of such items as commercial ships, fertilizers, television sets and other electronic devices, and agricultural machinery, among others.[222] And manufacturers were increasingly able to meet the ROK's broad economic goals, as evidenced by the fact that exports under the HCI Policy hit Park's original target of $10 billion by 1977, well ahead of his initial deadline of the 1980s. Although some scholars of HCI, such as the economist Pak Yŏnggu, argue that Park's original defense industry objectives in the 1973 HCI Policy were supplanted by his growing economic goals in the mid- to late 1970s, the Blue House actually drastically expanded its efforts for independent arms development during this period.[223] This expansion was largely hidden, however, because

South Korea's weapons programs became even more secretive after Park launched the development of ballistic missiles and nuclear arms as part of the Yulgok Operation, which necessitated increased concealment against US surveillance in the late 1970s. To support Yulgok's banned-weapons programs, Park substantially increased spending for defense R & D and the procurement of new military technologies and diversified the ROK's foreign weapons suppliers to reduce its reliance on the United States.[224] In sum, while the expansion of HCI and South Korea's market exposure greatly broadened the scope of economic production, Park never wavered in his commitment to the defense industry. This is consistent with his speeches and writings throughout the 1960s and 1970s, in which Park treated economic and defense development as mutual, interdependent pursuits, understanding economic strength as essential for a strong national defense.

Conclusion

The Park regime's HCI Policy was fundamentally defense oriented from its official launch in 1973, in keeping with Park's aim to establish national security independence through rapid economic development and military modernization. At the same time, the policy was integral to the creation of the ROK's civil-military production system, which catalyzed South Korea's industrial revolution and the stunning economic success that followed in the 1970s and after. Korea's system of militarized industrialization under the HCI Policy reconfigured private industries to serve both the newly developed national system for weapons production and an export-oriented economy.

Early events during Park's rule indicate that HCI was a goal from the start of his military regime, although North Korea's aggressions in the late 1960s and the US plans to withdraw USFK troops expedited the program's launch as an all-out defense measure. In 1971, O Wŏnch'ŏl's proposal for HCI gave Park an effective blueprint for building a defense industry on civilian foundations. The HCI Policy rapidly fostered the growth of weapons manufacturing within commercial industries, promoted infrastructural support for mass production by domestic firms, and facilitated the training of a skilled technical workforce. The strategy of incorporating the chaebol and their existing manufacturing plants into the state's agenda for defense industrialization also launched South Korea's own MIC.

The controversial Yusin system that Park imposed in 1972 provided critical support for his regime's mobilization for HCI. To implement its HCI Policy, the government had to synchronize the development of the military, business, research institutes, and labor to meet its highly accelerated timetable for weapons production in tandem with economic growth. Transforming the nation's underdeveloped economy into an export-driven system supported by heavy and chemical industries and with a skilled workforce required strong state direction and indoctrination. Yusin equipped Park's government with total political and economic control, allowing it to push its HCI Policy forward without concern for internal politics or external opposition—an important reason why Yusin was critical for HCI, at least from the perspective of Park and his policymakers.

The evidence presented in this chapter on Park's closely aligned military and industrial policies from 1968 to 1972 provides strong support for the argument that defense building in response to the national security crisis prompted Park to effectuate the Yusin system. Prior to Yusin, Park's efforts to build a total security system in reaction to the 1968 security crisis had brought sweeping domestic reforms designed to transform civilian industry and society for the purpose of achieving self-reliant national defense, including independent arms production. But Park still needed a practical, concrete, and affordable strategy to actualize weapons production on a national scale. O delivered that to him in 1971 with the HCI proposal (which evolved into *Kaep'yŏnnon*). Park then enacted the Yusin system to enforce his plan for HCI. Granting Park total authority and cementing his hold on the presidency, the system gave him the power, time, and control he needed to execute his HCI Policy and construct an independent defense industry. Although HCI, the defense industry, and Yusin had separate origins, they worked together as components of a single interwoven program for achieving self-reliant national defense.

The radically deep connection between the public and private sectors (state and chaebol) in the effort to strengthen national defense represents the most distinctive feature of the ROK's development, setting it apart from the United States and other capitalist countries characterized by advanced public-private sector partnerships. The Blue House's push for its HCI Policy facilitated the convergence of military and civilian production, creating channels across industries and sectors that fed both defense and commercial development and establishing powerful ties between the state and private enterprise. The resulting defense industry—rooted in robust public-private sector collaboration—drove the nation's technological and industrial transformation.

HCI also built the foundation for South Korea's eventual economic prosperity, propelling the nation toward Park's goal of "rich nation, strong army." Defense industrialization created a state-secured demand for military products that was crucial for the growth of large private defense contractors. As the defense-related civilian corporations—many of which emerged as chaebol—made rapid advances, their efforts for military modernization benefited commercial production and their defense-related products became export products. Through this process, the state leveraged the strengths of the private sector to serve national defense, and the defense industry became deeply and systematically involved in Korea's economic growth.

In mobilizing the business sector for defense industrialization, the Park government not only created a new industrial system but also propagated Park's ideology, engaging entrepreneurs and workers in a quest to achieve self-reliant national defense through the establishment of a modern defense industry. In this respect, the HCI Policy instigated unprecedented synchronization between civilian commerce and state-led defense manufacturing. An example of their joint achievement is the subject of the next chapter.

CHAPTER THREE

The Militarization of the Chaebol

Our country has lost at least a century . . . compared with other countries. There is no time to lose any more. When others do one thing, we should do ten things, and when others rest, we should act and put into practice.
—Park Chung Hee

An explosives expert must be honest and precise, just like the explosives that must explode exactly at the promised time and place.
—Kim Chonghŭi, founder and former chairman of Hanwha Group

Hey, have you even tried? Don't waste time and money thinking about it without even trying it: just try it!
—Chung Ju-yung, founder and former chairman of Hyundai Group

The Park Chung Hee government strategically reconfigured private enterprise in South Korea by developing and turning large domestic companies into partners in and drivers of national modernization. Groomed in the 1960s as part of Park's first and second Five-Year Economic Development Plans (FYEDPs, collectively 1962–71), many of these companies were chosen to work with the government as defense manufacturers in the 1970s. One such company, Han'guk Hwayak

(Korea Explosives; known as Hanwha since 1993), a commercial explosives manufacturer, contracted with the Park regime to supply explosives for the military. As a case study, Hanwha's story reveals how changes in policy and law designed to accommodate defense industrialization radically transformed large family-owned business conglomerates, the chaebol, such as Hanwha, into state partners in realizing Park's vision of a self-reliant national defense industry.

The quid pro quo that developed between business and the military, combined with mutually proactive state policy and private enterprise, fashioned a form of chaebol-led military modernization within the framework of Park's Heavy and Chemical Industrialization Policy (HCI Policy) that determined the distinct course and character of South Korea's capitalist development. Hanwha's expansion as a dual-purpose manufacturer for the military and commercial sectors highlights the ways in which defense industry policies under Park, in concert with the actions of industrialists and workers, were instrumental in creating an industrialized South Korean economy centered around the chaebol.

Big Businesses Become Conglomerates

South Korea's chaebol—megacorporations involved in multiple industries—did not exist as such before Park's rule.[1] The word "chaebol" itself, the transliteration of the Japanese term for such companies, *zaibatsu* (財閥), was carried over from Japan to colonized Korea in the early 1930s and had been used by Koreans to refer to corporate elites since then.[2] Big companies such as Samsung and Goldstar (now LG), among those that took the lead in Park's first two FYEDPs, were already referred to as chaebol by the 1960s. However, it was not until corporate restructuring in the private sector under Park's heavy and chemical industrialization (HCI) drive in the 1970s that companies began to diversify and conglomerate their multiple entities. This process also gave rise to a new group of HCI-centered chaebol, such as Hyundai, Hanwha, Kia, and Daewoo. Together, along with Samsung and Goldstar, these companies became the core members of the business conglomerates known today as chaebol, as they would go on to dominate South Korea's industries from the 1970s onward. The chaebol were characterized by their horizontal diversification into sectors unrelated to their original business, in contrast to the largest companies during the administrations of Rhee Syngman and Chang Myŏn (1948–61, collectively), which had specialized in only one or two industries.[3] The Park state's economic policy and US foreign aid are often credited with the rise of the chaebol; few empirical studies have investigated the role of defense industry policies in their rapid growth.[4]

When Park's highly centralized HCI Policy was adopted in the early 1970s, the foundation had already been laid for cooperation between big business and the state. Under Japanese rule (1910–45), Korean businesses had participated in the colonial state's push to advance industrialization and commercial trade in Korea. During the Second Sino-Japanese War (1937–45) and World War II, the merging of public and private sectors in Japan's total war effort drove the expansion of war-related heavy industries as well as the growth of a skilled workforce. These wars also offered rare opportunities for Korean entrepreneurs to take part in Japan's mobilization of businesses for the rapid industrialization of its Manchurian colony.[5]

Following Japan's defeat in World War II and the subsequent division of the Korean peninsula, South Korea's newly elected president, Rhee Syngman, relied heavily on US foreign aid to build up domestic industries. Additionally, his government sought the support of Korean business elites, many of whom had collaborated with the former colonial regime. Later, with the influx of US economic aid after the destruction caused by the Korean War, the Rhee government provided various financial incentives to businesses in order to bolster their efforts to rebuild the economy.[6] However, incompetence and bribery plagued both the government and the private sector, as officials colluded with business elites by illicitly handing out production rights, special grants, and low-interest loans. By 1960, the ensuing economic failures and ongoing political instability—combined with national outrage over a rigged vice presidential election and mounting dissent against Rhee's authoritarian rule—culminated in the student-led April 19 Revolution and Rhee's abrupt exile. Even though the brief successor administration headed by Prime Minister Chang Myŏn (1960–61) sought to eliminate illicit government-business collusion by bringing charges against those involved, it could not effectively follow through with prosecution and punishment.[7] Chang ultimately failed to resolve the political and economic turmoil left behind by Rhee.

Soon after Park seized power in May 1961, he undertook to completely overhaul both government and private business sectors. He was determined that South Korea's economic development would be managed through strong government leadership with tight controls on powerful corporations. Twelve days into his rule, Park's Supreme Council for National Reconstruction took up Chang's cleanup efforts by aggressively leveling criminal charges against—and now prosecuting—"illicit profiteers," including public officials, military personnel, and the heads of major corporations.[8] Even influential corporate leaders who had previously been regarded as "untouchable," such as Hong Chaesŏn of Kŭmsŏng Textiles (later, Ssangyong Group) and Yi Pyŏngch'ŏl of Samsung, were arrested or forced to pledge their wealth for national reconstruction.[9] Through such public condemnations and criminal prosecutions, Park sought to legitimize his regime in the public's view as one that would vanquish the forces of past corruption.

While these examples of discipline (or the threat of discipline) to its leaders may have been politically motivated, Park also aimed to enlist the support of big business for his economic development plans. Like Rhee, Park saw little alternative to working with existing business elites, as they alone possessed the expertise, capital, and workforce necessary to spearhead the nation's industrialization and increase exports within the shortest amount of time.[10] Although establishing state-owned enterprises might have been an option for Park, the junta he led with his military colleagues—all graduates of the Korean Military Academy—lacked experience in business operations. Setting up state-run businesses to lead the economy also would have undermined Park's public campaign to reform the past illicit ties between the government and business sector.[11]

In exchange for pardons and not having their assets confiscated, business leaders were obliged to take part in the state's industrialization program and were ordered to build plants for state-selected industries. By these means, they were conscripted as participants in Park's first FYEDP (1962–66), under which corporations were assigned to develop the new light industries needed to kick-start economic development.

By the mid-1960s, Park saw the ongoing Vietnam War as both an economic opportunity to expedite South Korea's growth under his FYEDP and a political opportunity to strengthen the US commitment to South Korean security. When the United States requested support in its fight against communists in Vietnam, Park dispatched noncombatant medical and engineering troops in 1964, followed by a division of ROK combat troops in 1965.[12] He then promised a second combat division in exchange for President Lyndon Johnson's pledge to provide both economic assistance for Park's second FYEDP and a concurrent five-year US military aid package to help modernize the ROK Armed Forces.[13] With the Brown Memorandum of 1966 (signed by US ambassador to South Korea Winthrop Brown) which formalized the agreement between Johnson and Park, Korean companies obtained licenses to supply goods for American and South Vietnamese forces fighting in Vietnam.[14] Companies like Hyundai, Hanjin, and Daewoo benefited from infusions of US capital and low-interest development loans, as well as technical aid for manufacturing US-licensed military supplies, and were drawn into modern weapons production for the first time.[15]

Through numerous offshore procurement contracts for war-related production and construction in Southeast Asia, the engagement of Korean corporations with the United States sparked growth in heavy industries such as machinery, construction, and transportation, while also helping to train the new workforce required to run them.[16] The ROK's participation in the Vietnam War also created opportunities for South Korea's new export industries, as Vietnam became a market for Korean industrial goods.[17] Altogether, the war in Vietnam was pivotal in securing South Korea's transformation into an exporting nation, one of Park's chief goals for his second FYEDP. Nonetheless, significant cuts in US military aid and support for the ROK in the late 1960s (see chapters 1 and 5) meant that US-driven business development was short-lived.

The August Third Measure

By 1968, following an initial five-year period of rapid economic growth, many Korean companies involved in Park's development plans had accumulated substantial debt. To meet the state's increasing export quotas, they had relied on short-term loans to finance their high production rates and then found themselves insolvent because of decreasing net profits. In addition, their concentrated investment in a few export-oriented industries had resulted in an oversupply of certain products, along with limited business diversification and entrepreneurship. Korean exports were also hit by rising trade protectionism in the United States and a global recession that contributed to a slump in the ROK's economy.[18] The resulting financial crisis in South Korea, which would last into 1972, left businesses even more heavily debt-ridden and led to deep government interventions and market regulation. As companies became dependent on the state for help, they handed over the concessions the Park administration needed to engineer the large-scale industrial and defense programs in its HCI plan.

In a drastic attempt to resuscitate insolvent companies, the government issued a national emergency imperative in August 1972 that became known as the August Third Measure. The state minimized domestic banks' interest rates for corporate loans and allowed businesses extended repayment periods, as well as permitting lenders to accept company stock in lieu of cash payments on loans.[19] In exchange for their deliverance from bankruptcy, businesses were expected to join the state's program for HCI and self-reliant national defense. Companies selected to participate in the manufacture of military-related heavy and chemical products (such as ships, steel, automobiles, coal, and petrochemicals) were granted unprecedented aid to expand into multiple industries under the Park administration's HCI Policy—and thus the chaebol, in their signature form as conglomerates with diversified product lines—were born.[20]

Just two months later, the Park administration announced the Yusin reforms, which led to the imposition of eventual state control over all financial resources (including domestic capital and loans) by nationalizing the banks.[21] In this new economic environment, business leaders who refused any government order assumed a huge risk, since losing favor with Park meant losing access to capital and thereby severely limiting their company's prospects. With the Yusin system in place, businesses were enlisted as de facto mercenaries in Park's development programs—a relationship best described as compelled compliance.

Despite these newfound powers, the government often had to go beyond financial compulsion to mobilize the support of businesses for defense building. When the Second Economic Secretariat (SES) launched its plan to build an independent defense industry under the 1973 HCI Policy, most corporate executives were reluctant to join the nascent program, largely owing to its newness and the risks involved.[22] They also felt that their businesses and South Korea's overall technical infrastructure were not ready to meet the high-tech demands of weapons manufacturing. Nonetheless, the HCI Policy committed the nation to establishing a strong private sector at the core of the new military-industrial complex (MIC). In early efforts to recruit contractors, Blue House technocrats and even the president himself often had to exert direct pressure when business leaders refused the government's initial "invitation" to participate.[23]

The Military Procurement Law

On February 17, 1973, the government passed legislation codifying private-public sector cooperation and heavy private-sector investment in the defense industry.[24] The enactment of the Law on Special Measures for Military Procurement (or the Military Procurement Law; MPL) provided the legal basis on which the state would integrate top firms into the defense industry (see chapter 2).[25] And since the businesses selected as military suppliers were in the heavy and chemical industries, the MPL would in effect support manufacturing related simultaneously to defense and HCI. Ultimately the law both induced and compelled leading private manufacturers to join the defense industry while promoting fierce competition for lucrative government contracts among them. This would determine the course of their future development as weapons producers.

For the contracted firms, the MPL authorized government financial support for weapons production and otherwise incentivized their full participation.[26] Businesses received rebates, stipends, low-interest loans, and various tax cuts and exemptions, as well as funding for the procurement of facilities and raw resources.[27] The law allowed the state to tap into large sources of public financing, including the National Investment Fund, for concentrated investment in defense-related businesses. Revisions to the MPL in 1977 established additional sources of capital for the industry, including the Arms Industry Support Fund (Kunsu Sanŏp Chiwŏn Kŭmyung), which collected state and nonstate funds under the jurisdiction of the Ministry of National Defense (MND) to grant loans to help businesses procure, install, maintain, or expand weapons facilities, as well as to acquire raw materials and cover operating costs.[28] The 1977 revisions also expanded businesses' access to foreign currency loans.[29] In addition to financial assistance, the law offered contractors technical assistance for research and development (R & D) through the Agency for Defense Development (ADD) and Korea Institute of Science and Technology, as well as foreign weapons technology transfers.[30]

Although it granted defense businesses generous state assistance, the MPL subjected them to harsher state disciplinary measures than other industries faced.[31] Based on the SES's plan for promoting competition within the defense industry, contractors were rewarded or penalized according to their compliance with strict performance guidelines and their management of state resources. Businesses that met their production quotas, export targets, and quality standards were awarded additional support to increase their output, as well as exclusive licensing rights to produce new military products. But those privileges and supports could be jeopardized by poor performance or failure to comply with product standards and security regulations.

The MPL authorized state surveillance and protection of all aspects of defense factory operations to safeguard them from hazards, outside threats, or information leaks.[32] In addition, the law banned internal labor disputes in defense factories. A disruption in defense production was treated as a threat to national security, and union activity or any other collective action in a defense plant was subject to immediate state intervention.[33] The Yusin reforms empowered the Korean Central Intelligence Agency and the local police to suppress labor unions in defense-related plants.[34] By clamping down on workers, the Park regime was able to keep labor costs low, further helping the chaebol meet or exceed their production and export quotas.

As a result of revisions to the MPL in 1977 and again in 1979, most commercial and contractual responsibilities in the defense industry were transferred from military officials in the MND to civilian technocrats in the Ministry of Commerce and Industry (MCI).[35] Consequently, the newly expanded MCI, which functioned as the SES's right arm in implementing Park's HCI Policy, further increased civilian technocrats' responsibilities for defense products (in addition to the rise of civilian technocrats in the SES).[36] With the 1979 revisions, the government reinforced the MND's concessions by elevating the status of the Korea Defense Industry Association (Han'guk Pangwi Sanŏp Chinhŭnghoe)—a private group that facilitated cooperation between the military and civilians for the promotion of the defense industry—to a government-sponsored association working with the state to further the defense industry's growth and exports.[37] The rising influence of the MCI and the companies signified a decline in the military's control over weapons procurement. Park, notwithstanding his own military background, increasingly depended on civilian technocrats and private businesses to manage defense-building projects.

But the most significant effect of the MPL was the unlimited authority it granted the president over all areas related to defense businesses. In the name of national security, the law secured Park's central control over the entire defense industry. In this respect, the MPL gave the SES—which served as the president's proxy—direct jurisdiction over weapons deals, replacing the MND, which had functioned with full authority in that role prior to the 1970s. And by threatening to impose legal and financial penalties for noncompliance, the law ensured that any manufacturers resisting defense contracts would change course and join Park's weapons-production program.[38] Because the elite corporations already dominating most industries all became defense contractors, Park and his technocrats (through the MPL) now controlled almost the entire private manufacturing sector—a fact that concerned National Assembly members enough for some to publicly criticize Park's unrestrained authority over business.[39]

As coercive as they were, the policies of the MPL led to heavy investments in private companies, which fostered growth and expanded productivity and technological capacity. Although a conventional developmental-state interpretation of South Korea's rapid industrialization would treat the chaebol as loyal—if unwitting—stewards of Park's policy or as mere cogs in the state's machinery, evidence suggests that they were far from passive actors. In fact, the government's elaborate and interlocking strategies facilitated their shift from strictly conscripted agents to active partners in the nation's military modernization, and the chaebol began to make their own contributions to indigenous weapons production, even independently of state directives. The story of Hanwha—one of the first arms producers contracted through the MPL—reveals how the chaebol arose, were transformed through their militarization, and emerged as the commercially and militarily driven forces that built the South Korean defense industry.

From Conscription to Cooperation: The Case of Hanwha

The story of Hanwha's development illustrates the policies, corporate culture, and work environment that shaped the first generation of Korean defense corporations under Park.[40] Though it had already worked closely with the state as a commercial explosives manufacturer, when Hanwha became a defense contractor in 1972, the company adopted the state's goal of indigenized weapons production as its corporate mission. Hanwha's business structure and work culture were transformed through its compliance with the MPL, and it fully internalized the state's principles of anticommunism, extensive security, and labor control—all carried out with strict military order and discipline. In transitioning to defense production, Hanwha encountered numerous challenges and failures, such as the loss of contracts to competitors, financial setbacks, insufficient state funding, and technical limitations. Yet the company survived and ultimately thrived, becoming a dynamic contributor to the state's military modernization. Certainly each corporation's reaction to the state's program was unique, but Hanwha's story shows how, under the defense-oriented HCI Policy, Hanwha and other chaebol became the corporate giants they are today.[41]

Founded by Kim Chonghŭi (1922–81) in 1952, during the Korean War, Hanwha was the first manufacturer of explosives in South Korea. At a time when Korea's infrastructure was being destroyed by the war, Kim anticipated that domestically produced explosives would be vital to postwar reconstruction. In 1958 Hanwha pioneered the domestic production of dynamite, which indeed proved critical in South Korea's rebuilding effort.[42] The product instantly elevated the company's reputation and earned Kim the moniker "Dynamite Kim."

Kim expressed his dedication to national economic recovery and development through his personal motto, "Serve the nation through the explosives industry" (*Hwayak sanŏp ŭl t'onghan saŏp poguk*).[43] His economic nationalism reflected the general mindset of business leaders at the time, who had experienced Japanese colonization, the devastation of the Korean War, and extreme poverty on a national scale. Korea's past struggles led many of these entrepreneurs to seek opportunities, through the development of new industrial skills and products, that would be useful for the country.[44] When Park came to power in 1961, these business leaders were already disposed toward the nationalistic ideals that he would champion (fig. 3.1).[45]

Hanwha became part of Park's first FYEDP when the state chose the company to take on at least one project to aid in the development of light industry. Because of Hanwha's expertise with chemical materials,

FIG. 3.1. Kim Chonghŭi (left) conducts a tour of Hanwha's Inch'ŏn factory for President Rhee Syngman (center) in 1959. *Source:* National Archives of Korea; file no. CET0083890.

Park ordered Kim Chonghŭi to begin a new venture that would support the state's plan to build up a domestic chemical industry. In 1965 Hanwha began constructing a polyvinyl chloride (PVC) factory to manufacture synthetic plastics.[46]

Hanwha joined in the state's early military modernization efforts in 1968, when Park initiated domestic arms production in response to the Blue House Raid. For the newly established Homeland Reserve Forces (HRF), which were to be equipped with Korean-made arms, the government needed the best companies in the machinery, explosives, and special metals industries to begin producing basic weapons immediately. Hanwha was assigned to work with the ADD to develop basic military-grade explosives. With technical assistance from the ADD, Hanwha became the first South Korean producer of grenades, in 1969.[47] In the same year, with the state's support in securing foreign technical aid, Kim Chonghŭi also founded the oil refining company Kyŏngin Energy Corporation, which contributed to launching the domestic petrochemical industry, a signature achievement of Park's second FYEDP.[48]

In the early 1970s, as Park prioritized gun and ammunition manufacturing for his Five-Year Military Modernization Plan (1971–76), which developed in parallel with the third FYEDP, the SES drew Hanwha into the domestic ammunitions business. A report presented to Park by O Wŏnch'ŏl in January 1972 laid out a plan for producing M1 rifles and carbines in commercial factories. The M1 rifle was the main gun used by HRF troops at the time, but since its original US manufacturer had discontinued production, South Korea also needed to produce ammunition for both its existing guns and any newly produced M1s. O assigned Hanwha to manufacture the gunpowder used in M1 and carbine ammunition.[49]

In October 1972, three months before Park's promulgation of the HCI Policy, Hanwha was among the first twenty-nine firms formally selected as defense contractors by the Defense Industry Promotion Council.[50] As mentioned above, Park's declaration of the Yusin reforms that same month, and the resulting nationalization of banks and capital, made it risky for any of the selected corporations to consider opting out. By this time most of Korea's top companies had been enlisted in state service for years under Park's first and second FYEDPs, and their business interests and ventures were already closely tied to government contracts. Additionally, after the passage of the MPL in 1973, businesses that declined contracts could be penalized with heavy fines.

As the sole domestic maker of explosives, Hanwha, which naturally stood to profit from an expansion into the military sector, did not resist joining the defense industry. In fact, early on, in an interview in the newspaper *Kyŏnghyang Sinmun* on July 15, 1968, Kim Chonghŭi had spoken of the business potential of the defense industry:

> The defense industry can basically be divided into the [two] fields: the one that meets only specialized military needs, and the other that can develop in parallel with general civilian industries. . . . [I]f the general [civilian] industries give a little more interest to the defense industry and engage in research and development, there are many areas where they can provide fairly extensive and important military production capacity. Rather than distinguishing between the general industry and the defense industry, if there is a defense industry that can be developed within general industries, that should be fostered with great focus. I believe there is a lot of potential to connect each industry with the defense industry.[51]

Kim's interest in and ready compliance with defense production set Hanwha apart from the corporations that were not enthusiastic about the idea of pivoting to weapons manufacturing. But even the companies that were initially opposed or reluctant to participate, such as Samsung and Kia Motors, eventually bowed to Blue House pressure.[52]

Initially the state closely supervised Hanwha's transition into defense production, intervening directly to mandate the weapons to be produced and the R & D it undertook. Despite the experience Hanwha had gained in the production of grenades, the company still specialized in commercial explosives and possessed only a limited ability to produce the high explosives required for military use. Although the state did not provide sufficient funds to meet all of Hanwha's needs, the Park regime began to invest in the company's R & D and infrastructural expansion while also pushing Hanwha to procure independent technologies, thus laying the groundwork for its development into an independent arms producer.[53]

With the promulgation of the HCI Policy and passage of the MPL, Park strengthened his pressure on the private sector to advance domestic R & D and technology, underscoring the importance of "indigenized production" (*kuksanhwa*) and "specialization of skills" (*chŏnmunhwa*) as the highest goals and the responsibility of manufacturers nationwide.[54] Park directly challenged Korean corporate executives and technicians to give their full attention to the independent "advancement of technical skills" (*kisul kaebal*) for defense manufacturing, instilling in them the conviction that their work was vital to achieving a self-reliant defense industry.[55] In response, Kim took on the indigenization of military explosives as his company's patriotic duty. For Kim, who had long identified himself as a nationalist, his patriotic mindset resonated with Park's ideology of self-reliant national defense in support of South Korea's independent weapons production.

Of course, the opportunity for huge profits in the emerging defense industry further enticed businessmen like Kim to adopt Park's nationalistic ideals and goals. The industry presented Hanwha with endless possibilities for multiplying its advantages in explosives manufacturing as a government contractor. In addition, the vulnerable security environment amid the impending withdrawal of US forces from Korea meant that Hanwha and other chaebol in the group of elite "defense corporations" (*pangsanŏp*) were recognized by the state and society for working to strengthen national security.[56] Their participation was regarded as good business as well as a patriotic duty. Proud of Hanwha's crucial role in both industrializing Korea (through supplying commercial explosives) and arming ROK soldiers, its employees spoke of their own drive to answer the nation's call.[57] Imbued with the nationalist ethos of the day, Kim and other corporate leaders—even those who were initially hesitant to join the defense sector—adopted self-reliant national defense as their corporate mission and were rewarded with social prestige and Park's praise for their patriotism.[58] Ryu Ch'anu of Poongsan Metal Corporation (later renamed to Poongsang Corporation in 1989) used the phrase "self-reliant national defense" in his company's vision statement and as his personal mantra.[59] Even today, in the main entrance of Poongsan's original factory in the town of An'gang, a framed wooden facsimile of the phrase in Park's handwriting hangs on the wall (fig. 3.2). Indeed, nationalistic slogans promoted by the government, such as "self-reliant national defense" and "through business, repay

FIG. 3.2. Facsimile in wood of Park's calligraphy reading "*chaju kukpang*" (self-reliant national defense), displayed inside the main entrance of Poongsan's factory in An'gang, North Kyŏngsang Province. *Source:* Photo by the author.

the nation" (*saŏp poguk*), were often uttered by business leaders and became ingrained in the minds of their workers, signifying the close relationship between the state and the chaebol.[60] At Hanwha, as Kim Chonghŭi embraced Park's national defense agenda, the company expanded operations and shifted its primary focus to serving the state's security needs by producing military explosives and gunpowder.

Indigenizing Explosives

The state's plan for domestic arms production called for Hanwha and other defense contractors to instill Park's ideology as well as his manufacturing goals in both corporate management and the workforce. Kim and his employees fully implemented Park's priorities at Hanwha's flagship factory in Inch'ŏn, which in 1956 became the first South Korean factory to manufacture explosives.[61] When it became a manufacturer of both HCI and defense products after 1973, the factory's management and workers even more relentlessly pursued "self-sufficiency in explosives" (*hwayak chagŭp chajok*), the company slogan, as their highest goal.[62] The state's militaristic approach to developing the domestic arms industry had a militarizing effect on corporate culture as well, as the chaebol became dedicated to the total effort for arms production, both ideologically and industrially. Min Pyŏngman, a chemist who began his career at the Hanwha factory in Inch'ŏn in the 1970s, recalled that the drive to indigenize explosives was like "second nature" to employees at the plant. Hanwha's workers, according to Min, labored under the conviction that "if we don't produce explosives, nobody else [in Korea] can do it."[63]

Because the Inch'ŏn factory was indeed the only domestic manufacturer of explosives at the time, the state relied on it to produce a continuous supply for use in the construction of industrial plants and related infrastructure. Strict international regulations on the transportation of explosives meant imports were limited, which only strengthened the resolve of Hanwha's technicians to produce everything from the most basic ingredients to finished products in-house.[64] And Hanwha engineers were often forced to devise new products on their own since the United States—concerned that advanced explosives technologies could be spun off to develop strategic materials for banned weapons (i.e., missile propellants)—withheld full technical aid from South Korea for developing military explosives.[65] Hanwha's selection as a defense contractor intensified the company's commitment to developing the advanced technology and skills necessary to create new explosives for the military. As it began mass-producing different types of commercial high explosives in June 1973, the company actively expanded its efforts to develop military explosives as well.[66]

The design and manufacture of military explosives did not come easily, as they were more powerful and technically more complex than typical commercial explosives. The Inch'ŏn factory's chemical engineers lacked expertise and formal training in military production, and the factory itself, which had been built for manufacturing commercial explosives, was not equipped for the research required to produce advanced military-grade products. Hence, when Hanwha set out to produce military explosives, it first had to develop the necessary technology. This was an expensive venture, and despite the state subsidies and technical assistance provided by the MPL, the government's aid was not enough to cover the entire cost of Hanwha's R & D.[67] Nevertheless, Hanwha executives knew that if they succeeded, the profits from government contracts would more than offset the initial outlay.

Accepting the risks, Hanwha began pouring its own capital into building new facilities for the experimental production and testing of military explosives, as well as for automation (for mass production) and the refining of essential materials like trinitrotoluene (TNT), an explosive compound commonly used for both military and industrial purposes.[68] Technical support from the state came mostly in the form of joint research with the ADD.[69] Like many private factories experimenting with the development of military products, the Inch'ŏn plant became in effect a government research laboratory and production facility—in no small part because the state lacked the capital and resources to build its own facilities (and in accordance with the HCI Policy, which designated civilian plants—not military arsenals—as producers of the nation's weapons, as discussed in chapter 2).[70]

Yi Ch'anggi, a former chemical engineer who in the 1970s oversaw the Special Defense Development Department in Production Division 2—the Inch'ŏn factory's division in charge of developing military explosives—described the extensive technical collaboration between Hanwha and the ADD during that period.[71] Because the division's activities were classified, projects with the ADD were conducted under state surveillance, with strict regulations to prevent researchers from leaking information. Typically, an ADD research team would approach Hanwha to jointly develop select US-model weapons. Hanwha engineers initially relied heavily on technical aid transfers that the ADD received from the United States. However, that technical support was confined only to what the US government was willing to offer the ROK for defensive weapons.[72] According to former Hanwha workers, US surveillance of Korean weapons production was so tight that agents from the Joint US Military Affairs Group–Korea (JUSMAG-K) and the CIA came to observe the tests of new defense products that Hanwha and the ADD developed.[73] Attempts by ADD scientists and Hanwha engineers to develop a broader range of weapons through reverse engineering often failed because they did not possess the original technical blueprints from the United States.[74] To gain the information and technology it needed, Hanwha expanded its foreign network of technology transfers to countries including Canada, Japan, France, and Israel, in the hope that they would provide the necessary technical skills and data that the United States would not.[75]

Notwithstanding the challenges posed by defense production, the new defense industry benefited Hanwha's commercial business in a variety of ways. According to Yi Ch'anggi, "The integrated and advanced technical skills and technology required to develop military explosives contributed to the advancement of [Hanwha's] commercial products" and led to significant upgrades in areas such as product quality control, equipment inspection, safety procedures, welding and precision technologies, and testing.[76] The indigenization of military explosives also drove the modernization of the Inch'ŏn factory, as it was converted for more scientific and research-oriented operations.[77]

Prior to Hanwha's joining the defense industry, Yi described its quality control as "very poor."[78] Yi and his colleague Kim Ch'angsik, a former physical chemist at Hanwha who later worked for the ADD, both attested that defense manufacturing introduced state-of-the-art quality management methods, as the company had to adopt US standards for producing military explosives.[79] Likewise, Hong Kwangung, a former chemical engineer who oversaw quality control for military explosives at Hanwha in the 1970s, said that the Inch'ŏn factory's adoption of the weapons quality assurance system was critical to the improvement of the factory's quality-control management overall.[80] Hong stated, "With the introduction of defense technology, total quality control was passed down to the Inch'ŏn factory's entire system, for managing raw materials and manufacturing processes as well as for making the intermediate goods into finished products."[81] Hong, who specialized in various compounds for military explosives, such as TNT, Royal Demolition Explosive (RDX), and Compositions B and C4, also recalled, "In the early days [of Hanwha's efforts to develop these explosives], I had to work so hard to make products that could pass [the tests based on] the MIL-SPEC [US military specifications]. Unlike commercial explosives, which were required to meet only the standards set within the company, military explosives had to meet US military standards. And it was more challenging to make these [military] explosives [compared with commercial explosives] because they used the highest quality gunpowder."[82]

In addition to meeting US standards, Kim Chonghŭi and executives at other chaebol operated under the president's direct order to certify the quality of all domestically produced weapons in order to protect the "safety of the soldiers" who would use them.[83] Park regularly convened meetings with leading business executives about their defense products, at first using existing venues such as Defense Industry Promotion Council meetings, but then convening regular biannual council meetings hosted by the Korea Defense Industry Association from 1977 onward (fig. 3.3).[84] Military products and equipment were tied directly to national security, which required their safe and precise operation; there was no margin for error in their production. Corporations had to adopt advanced manufacturing processes that demanded precision, upgraded safety standards, modernized equipment, and the highest-quality raw materials. And as noted, defense manufacturers that failed to meet contracted standards risked serious legal penalties as well as revoked contracts and the loss of government privileges.[85]

For quality assurance in producing its new high explosives, Hanwha had to conduct rigorous tests and countless experiments. These included indoor and outdoor tests, humidity tests, physical and chemical tests, mechanical tests (to determine the correct pressure and speed for ammunition launch), along with weathering and seasoning tests.[86] Its efforts to meet the highest standards in producing military explosives intensified as Hanwha matured as a defense manufacturer. The Inch'ŏn factory's records show that by 1979 a formal quality-control department—the first in the factory—had been created in Production Division 2 (which, as previously mentioned, specialized in defense projects).[87] Similar to that division, the weapons-production divisions in

FIG. 3.3. Park Chung Hee (on the dais at the left) speaks to corporate executives and government officials at a Korea Defense Industry Association council meeting in 1979. *Source:* National Archives of Korea; file no. CET0024979.

other companies were typically the first units to implement formal quality inspections under the guidance of the ADD.[88] Hanwha's modernized approach to weapons production, encompassing stringent testing and inspection regulations, was also adopted for its commercial products.[89]

With the expansion of indigenous weapons production under the Yulgok Operation, Hanwha was also selected to produce smokeless powder, the gunpowder used in ammunition for modern guns and heavy artillery, such as M1 rifles, carbines, and 105 mm and 155 mm artillery.[90] More advanced than the traditional black powder used in older firearms, smokeless powder was essential for Park's plan to supply the ROK Armed Forces and Homeland Reserve Forces with modern, Korean-made weapons.[91] Hanwha quickly began producing nitrocellulose, the basic chemical ingredient in smokeless powder, and continued to research the manufacturing process for the complete product.

Producing specialized military gunpowder was not a cost-effective venture for Hanwha. Even prior to the launch of Yulgok, by 1973, the company had been negotiating with foreign suppliers in Israel, Norway, France, and West Germany for the loan-purchase of facilities and the technology needed to produce smokeless powder domestically.[92] Israel offered the most affordable agreement (at a cost of $2.28 million), but Hanwha could not close the deal because the ROK government was concerned about causing diplomatic tensions with Arab nations.[93] The company was eventually forced to use its own capital to begin developing smokeless powder, but even with heavy investments in R & D, Hanwha encountered technical limitations, and its efforts to produce the powder remained unsuccessful throughout 1974.[94]

The company met with additional challenges from the mid-1970s onward as the government fanned the flames of competition. The SES had purposely weaved competition into its plans for HCI and the development of the defense industry (see chapter 2). The strategy was tied to the state's "subsidies as contracts" system, which drove private firms to improve their production to meet the required specifications for South Korea's desired industries.[95] With the maturation of the defense industry, firms had to compete for contracts by constantly innovating with the latest technologies while also building and improving facilities suited to developing the weapons sought by the state. This was also true for Hanwha: despite its status as the nation's first explosives manufacturer, the government did not favor it over other qualified producers when awarding contracts. Rather, the Park administration saw to it that when Hanwha went after a new contract, the company still had to prove its ability to produce a superior prototype—even when the contract was for gunpowder, its signature product.

Hanwha faced its stiffest competition in 1974 and 1975, when both Hanwha and Poongsan Metal Corporation applied for the exclusive license to produce ball powder, the type of gunpowder used in ammunition for M16 rifles.[96] After South Korea completed its construction of an M16 factory in 1973, the government pursued the indigenous production of ball powder, which would enable South Korea to procure ammunition for its M16s without US aid. Despite Hanwha's previous track record and clear production advantages, the government allowed Poongsan to bid for the contract. The winner of the contract would receive the transfer of facilities and technical aid from the US gunpowder manufacturer Olin Corporation to build South Korea's inaugural ball-powder factory. Recognizing the extraordinary economic opportunities that such a contract would bring, Hanwha and Poongsan competed aggressively.[97]

Although Hanwha invested heavily in pursuing the contract, Poongsan won, based on its all-out efforts, including the acquisition of a used ball-powder manufacturing facility from abroad to demonstrate its production readiness.[98] In late 1975, the government proceeded to build a new ball-powder factory in An'gang, North Kyŏngsang Province—where Poongsan's original factory was, and still is, located—arranging with Olin for the licensed transfer of its facilities and technical aid to Poongsan. In the case of the ball-powder contract, as with other defense contracts, the government did not hesitate to award a major project to the best prepared over the more established competitor. This setback was particularly demoralizing for Hanwha, as it was the first time the company had lost a bidding war for a gunpowder contract.

Determined not to lose more ground in the industry, Hanwha abandoned its ongoing attempt to develop smokeless powder independently and sought technical aid from overseas companies. Hanwha's vice president, Sin Hyŏn'gi, Kim Chonghŭi's most trusted executive, led the company's negotiations with foreign firms to purchase facilities and technological assistance for the domestic production of smokeless powder. As the United States continued to withhold full technical assistance for the development of advanced gunpowder, Hanwha had to piece its production together with technologies from multiple international suppliers. Sin negotiated deals with France and Canada to collect the additional technology his company needed. With the state's approval of domestic and foreign capital loans, Sin finalized deals for transfers of technology and equipment from France in 1975 and the United States and Canada in 1976.[99] Through collaboration with these diverse suppliers, Hanwha aimed to construct a second plant in Yŏsu, South Chŏlla Province, that would specialize in manufacturing military gunpowder, including smokeless powder.

However, manufacturing smokeless powder—as well as developing the advanced propellant technologies newly assigned by the government for missile and rocket launchers—required more than just equipment and data from abroad. Hanwha's engineers also needed hands-on guidance and field training to learn the subtle techniques involved in manufacturing propellants and synthesizing complex chemicals that engineers elsewhere had mastered only with years of experience. These were the types of off-the-books procedures that companies protected as trade secrets.[100] One way Hanwha procured the necessary training was by sending chemists and engineers from its Inch'ŏn factory abroad on "apprenticeship" (*kyŏnsŭp*) tours, to learn directly from foreign technicians.[101] In 1976, for example, Hanwha dispatched a research team to France to visit the explosives producer Société nationale des poudres et explosifs (SNPE) and learn its methods for producing single-base propellant. Hanwha's chemical engineers later combined what they had observed at the French company with what they had learned from the United States to develop the double- and triple-base propellants used for small arms ammunition, cannons, mortars, and rockets.[102] Hanwha's rapid mastery of such techniques was facilitated by the knowledge sharing and hands-on instruction its technicians received from their French and American counterparts.

Yi Ch'anggi—who was part of a Hanwha team sent in 1976 to a US factory in New Jersey that built Nike Hercules missiles—recalled how American engineers welcomed the Korean visitors to observe production sites and shared information, sometimes beyond what was formally allowed.[103] On occasion their generosity extended to giving members of the Hanwha team access to classified company data and files and even permitting them to take samples of products, which afforded Hanwha the chance to reproduce technologies that the US government had officially held back from South Korea.[104] According to Yi, he and his team gained far more information than what was authorized by the United States, largely thanks to the American engineers' unguarded attitude toward sharing technical information with their Korean counterparts and their general underestimation of the Koreans' abilities.

According to Yi, "Because there was such a huge gap between American and Korean technologies, Americans were not on guard against [about sharing knowledge and parts samples with us]. . . . We even became personally close while hanging out and drinking together at bars. . . . My English was poor, but because I understood technical terms and had a clear goal, I could understand the words of American engineers [on technical matters]."[105]

Despite such outside help, mastering the production of military propellants remained a rocky process for Hanwha. Yi noted that "even when we were able to bring the technical skills from the United States, it was still extremely difficult to actually apply these techniques in Korea. The United States was equipped with everything, including the perfect environment [the desert] and facilities for making explosives, whereas Korea's natural environment and work conditions were unsuitable and posed many challenges."[106] Nevertheless, by combining the technical assistance it procured from different suppliers and through joint efforts with the ADD, Hanwha was eventually able to develop composite propellants for rocket launchers and missiles. The company's aggressive accumulation of American and French technologies, combined with the ADD's technical input and purchase of a US propellant plant in 1975 (see chapter 4), contributed to South Korea's development of its own ballistic missile by 1978.[107]

Meanwhile, Hanwha struggled to complete the construction of its new military gunpowder factory in Yŏsu. One of the problems was that its engineers had difficulty integrating the licensed technologies and equipment purchased from Canadian Industries Limited (CIL), an overseas contractor providing Hanwha with technical aid for their military explosives plant. Hong Kwangung was part of a team that Hanwha sent to CIL in April 1976 in accordance with an agreement between the two companies. Hong said learning and adapting CIL's technology for use in Hanwha's new plant was exceptionally challenging due to general differences in manufacturing methods between the Korean and Canadian firms. Even with CIL's assistance, there were technical issues Hanwha engineers had to overcome, and tensions flared up with the Canadian engineers who later came to the Yŏsu plant to offer assistance. Hong, who supervised the construction of the Yŏsu factory after his return from Canada, even recalled getting into a physical altercation with a Canadian technician over a malfunctioning piece of equipment in the TNT manufacturing facility; and after Hanwha finally received clearance and completed construction of the factory in 1978, other technical problems immediately arose. According to Hong:

> After the explosives factory was constructed in Yŏsu and a test run was completed with Canadian engineers, they withdrew. Ten days later, during the night shift, there was a sudden power outage in the RDX [cyclonite, a high explosive] stabilization process, and the emergency generator also went off power, causing emergency sirens in the middle of night. And the gas continued to erupt, and the temperature was not controlled, which made us worry about an explosion. I was distressed by the thought that the factory would be destroyed [under my watch]. I evacuated all employees to save them. After waiting thirty minutes for the explosion, I decided to manually discharge the reactants in the stabilization vessel. I took one other staff person with me, ready to die, wearing a gas mask, and went into the operating room and opened the valve manually to discharge [the unstable] substances. My back still shivers at the thought of it.[108]

After overcoming many such complications, Hanwha was able to commence operations at its second Yŏsu plant, which would soon take over the Inch'ŏn factory's role in producing military gunpowder. The Yŏsu site in South Chŏlla Province—situated much farther south of the DMZ than Inch'ŏn—was chosen by the government for security reasons.[109] Yŏsu was also designated as the location for a new industrial complex—the second one specifically dedicated to the petrochemical sector—under the HCI plan.[110] With the latest production facilities and equipment procured from foreign manufacturers, and employing the skills and training Hanwha technicians had brought back from all over the world, the Yŏsu plant finally began producing smokeless powder and other advanced forms of military gunpowder in 1978.[111]

Notwithstanding substantial state support, the establishment of South Korea's new gunpowder factory in Yŏsu was primarily the fruit of Hanwha's own actions: the management's efforts to thrive in a competitive new industry, the company's initiative in forming international joint ventures, its engineers' acquisition and integration of new skills, and, as I show below, the commitment and sacrifice of its workers, who put their lives on the line in testing new prototypes and manufacturing the final products. These efforts enabled Hanwha to successfully produce South Korea's own high-grade military explosives, a huge step toward realizing a self-reliant national defense.

Militarizing the Work Culture

As Hanwha transformed itself into a modern manufacturer of military explosives, its work culture also underwent a transformation through the militarized system that helped speed defense production among all the chaebol. Under the MPL, military-style corporate management became the norm for HCI firms. Hanwha, as a designated defense manufacturer, was required to operate its Inch'ŏn factory accordingly. The factory's safety regulations had already demanded extreme caution, regularity, and alertness from workers who were handling explosives experiments, equipment, and materials that, with the slightest error, could maim or kill. As former employees recalled, given their factory's dangerous environment, workers readily adopted the "completely militaristic" (*wanjŏn kundaesik*) customs and rules in their daily routines—even going so far as to exchange military salutes.[112] Asked to describe the work culture of the Inch'ŏn factory at this time, Ch'oe Pyŏngyun, a former chemist in the plant, said that it "was more militaristic than the military."[113]

In fact, Park's militarization of industrial plants had begun as early as 1968 with the creation of the workplace reserve troops that were part of the HRF. Since then, workers at Hanwha's Inch'ŏn plant and other major factories were tasked with guarding their own work sites as members of the new civilian reserve force.[114] Employees, motivated by Park-inspired slogans like "protect your workplace with your own hands," conducted military drills to practice defending their factories against North Korean infiltration.[115] Park urged contractors to take more responsibility for "self-defense" at their plants, encouraging them to use their workplace reserve troops for security instead of solely relying on the military or the local police.[116] With the HRF, companies operated in effect as ideological and military training grounds for their workers, and defense manufacturing facilities began to resemble miniature fortresses.

Militarism at Hanwha's Inch'ŏn factory intensified after the HCI Policy began in 1973 and as the MPL granted the MND full authority to impose rigorous security measures at defense plants. Munitions factories were considered essential to national defense, and the Inch'ŏn factory was listed as a "grade A" target facility, requiring the highest level of protection.[117] Strong security measures were to operate at all times to prevent intrusions and to ensure that production technology or the explosives themselves did not fall into the wrong hands, especially after an increase in reported incidents of North Korean espionage targeting major HCI corporations.[118] In November 1973, for instance, a high-level executive at Hanwha was imprisoned for sharing information about the status of the company's defense production with a North Korean intelligence officer in Japan.[119]

In response, the government toughened counterespionage measures at the headquarters and manufacturing plants of HCI companies. According to former Hanwha employees, regulations at the Inch'ŏn factory were ramped up to address concerns about "corporate spies."[120] Employees had no access to phones while at work, and movement was severely restricted during operating hours, both inside and outside the facilities. Workers were kept from entering one another's offices without permission, and even bathroom usage was strictly controlled. At Kia Machine Tools, where Yu Hansik worked as a leading craftsman in manufacturing howitzers, mortars, and recoilless guns in the 1970s, "everything was classified during this period." Information control was so tight within the company, Yu recalled, that coworkers within the same plant "didn't even know what the others were making."[121] Hanwha security guards conducted full body searches as employees exited the factory to ensure that no explosive material, equipment, or technical data left the facility. As former employee Cho Pyŏngch'ŏl said, "We couldn't even carry a rock out."[122]

In addition to the company's private security guards, it was common to see ROK soldiers and police officers patrolling the factory grounds in Inch'ŏn.[123] Security sensors were installed at entrances and along the barbed wire fencing surrounding the property. O Chaedŏk, a former vice president of Hanwha, described the work environment in the following manner: "It was a factory that involved many dangers, and since enemies could easily target it, we were regularly and extensively trained to prepare against their intrusions. Even policemen [those without permits] and media personnel were not allowed access [inside] the factory. The guards barred their entry, and they had to turn back and leave. At the time, therefore, many thought that the Inch'ŏn factory was operated directly by the government."[124] Indeed, due to Inch'ŏn's proximity to the Yellow Sea, even Korea's maritime defense force was involved in security measures; and because it was a weapons factory, all job applicants were required to pass government background checks. According to former employees, this was standard procedure at all Korean defense firms to ensure that no one with a record of communist ties or of disloyalty to the government (e.g., participation in anti-government demonstrations) would be hired.[125]

Regulations were enforced through security provisions in the MPL and justified through the government's anticommunist policies for defense-related industries; these practices were also driven within Hanwha by factory management, including Kim Chonghŭi himself. Procedures were designed not only to prevent outside intrusions but also to enforce security measures within the Inch'ŏn factory.[126] As the national-level military apparatus worked to subvert North Korean espionage and punish DPRK informants, Hanwha's own militarization of its production site worked internally to secure its own factory and workers.

Company records, as well as testimonies from former workers, reveal that in almost every year since the 1960s, various experiments with explosives and related chemicals at the Inch'ŏn factory had caused accidents in which workers were injured or killed, and this continued throughout the 1970s with Hanwha's production of the new military explosives.[127] Kim Chongbong, a chemist who trialed explosives at the Inch'ŏn factory, said he personally witnessed the deaths of more than fifty workers during his tenure there from 1965 to 1979.[128] The development of military explosives, particularly in the absence of complete blueprints from the original foreign manufacturers, forced Hanwha technicians to increasingly rely on dangerous trial-and-error methods to test their prototypes.[129]

According to company records, Hanwha did make substantial efforts to address worker safety.[130] Kim Chonghŭi also provided generous compensatory payments to the families of those injured or killed on the job, including covering the full educational expenses (even college tuition) for the children of deceased employees.[131] In spite of these efforts, the perilous environment caused many workers to become superstitious and resort to traditional rituals at work to ward off bad luck.[132] Ordinarily unexceptional occurrences—such as a spouse's nightmare or an encounter with a certain type of fish—were taken ominously and believed to portend disaster.

In such hazardous conditions, military discipline led to near-universal compliance with the exacting codes necessary to minimize risk and maximize efficiency. In labs conducting experiments with new explosive prototypes—where a tiny technical mishap or even a slight variation in temperature or humidity could cause a catastrophic incident—the lives of the workers depended on their strict adherence to precise rules and regulations.[133] Work sites and labs were plastered with safety rules and warnings to bolster employee vigilance. Slogans such as "absolute safety" (*chŏltae anjŏn*), "safety check" (*anjŏn hwagin*), and "safety first" (*anjŏn cheil*) were ubiquitous, appearing on uniforms, helmets, equipment, walls, and entryways.[134] Each day before starting work, factory workers were required to recite the company's official safety oath in unison, which ended with the following declaration: "As I recognize that safety is my life, and my family's happiness, and the foundation of our company's success, I declare that I devote myself completely to upholding safety."[135] Motivational company songs (*saga*) set to military cadences also extolled job safety–oriented themes.[136]

To ensure that safety codes were followed, factory management deployed its own "safety guards" (*anjŏn yowŏn*), who wore military-style uniforms and oversaw adherence to workplace rules and procedures.[137] Company officials awarded safety medals to production and R & D teams that were able to avoid accidents for long periods.[138] It is no wonder that Yi Kyubyŏng, another worker at the Inch'ŏn factory in the 1970s, reflected that "being employed at the Inch'ŏn factory was like entering the military service all over again."[139]

The militarizing of industrial workplaces also led to unbending hierarchies that affected all interactions, including those between superiors and subordinates, between senior and junior employees, and between male and female workers. Orders and rules were followed from top to bottom, based on a clearly defined chain of command.

Such hierarchies were especially conspicuous in defense factories like Hanwha's Inch'ŏn plant, where Park's military ethos and command system became embedded in the corporate culture. As Yi Ch'anggi reminisced about his days managing the factory's Special Defense Development Department, he commented that Hanwha's militarized corporate culture gave those in charge full authority within their respective divisions. This approach expedited the decision-making process but also risked jeopardizing the entire unit if a project failed.[140]

Such a rigid power structure inevitably created tensions at the Inch'ŏn factory. For Kim Yunsik, who served as chair of the workers' union in the 1970s, the division between white- and blue-collar employees was extreme.[141] The two classes of workers were clearly demarcated by contrasting factory uniforms, and blue-collar workers (laborers) were housed in dormitories that were separated from white-collar employee (office workers) housing. Only white-collar workers had access to the factory's dining hall, whereas blue-collar workers brought food from home and usually ate where they worked. Bonuses were often awarded only to those in white-collar positions, though an enormous wage gap already separated the two groups.

According to Kim Chongbong and Cho Pyŏngch'ŏl, two blue-collar employees who worked at the Inch'ŏn factory from the 1960s through the 1970s, the factory became even more hierarchical and oriented toward highly skilled technical positions after 1974 with the arrival of newly trained and licensed skilled workers (see chapter 4 for further details on these skilled workers). As part of the elite workforce trained specifically to meet Park's goals for HCI, these new skilled workers received far greater prestige and better treatment, pay (including bonuses), and benefits than their blue-collar colleagues.[142]

In many ways, developments at Hanwha's Inch'ŏn factory exemplify the militarism that took root in major HCI corporations during this period. Rigid hierarchies and safety protocols were not limited to Hanwha: military-style measures were applied in all weapons-producing factories. Skilled workers employed by other defense manufacturers in the 1970s—such as Samsung, Daewoo, Hyundai, Tongil, Poongsan, and Kia—recalled working under similar conditions: highly militarized hierarchies, strict rules, and uncompromising security regulations.[143] Because of the precarious national-security context and undeniably high-risk environment, these draconian regulations and practices were generally accepted by employees as necessary precautions.

According to Kim Hujin, a former skilled worker at Daewoo Heavy Industries, which produced 20 mm Vulcan rotary cannons in the late 1970s, the company had a completely "vertical culture" because "orders from above had to be followed in the defense industry."[144] Each team of technicians worked independently on their assigned part of the Vulcan, with minimal interaction between different teams (fig. 3.4).

Kim said that he worked through weekends, on average spending sixty or more hours per week on the job. Products were tested repeatedly and obsessively for quality assurance even when "there was nothing wrong with the product."[145] Nonetheless, as at Hanwha, dangerous incidents occurred frequently in Daewoo's factory because the company lacked experience and the proper equipment for weapons production. Also similar to Hanwha, designated security teams at Daewoo and

FIG. 3.4. Daewoo factory workers assembling a domestically produced Vulcan cannon in 1977. *Source:* National Archives of Korea; file no. CET0030698.

other HCI factories monitored the factory floor and laboratories for safety and provided security for the technical drawings, blueprints, and other sensitive materials critical to the HCI effort.[146]

According to an electrical engineer who, in 1979, took a managerial position at the Hyundai Heavy Industries' (HHI) factory in Ulsan—commonly known as Hyundai Shipyard due to its association with shipbuilding, another of the HCI sectors—militaristic protocols were deeply ingrained throughout the factory.[147] He recalled that even as a white-collar employee assigned to manage transformers in a non–defense-related department, the military mindset was inescapable. HHI imposed a strict regimen on its workers: routine morning group exercises, extensive training sessions, employee uniforms, and military salutations were obligatory. Security clearance measures were also enforced for anyone entering the factory. Culturally, HHI upheld a hierarchical order with clearly defined ranks. This was conspicuous in the company's militarized after-work dining culture (*hoesik munhwa*), where seating arrangements, as well as the order for eating and drinking, were dictated by rank within the company.[148] (In fact, all these practices continue in the Hyundai Shipyard in Ulsan to this day.) Just as in war, though strict safety regulations were in place, fatalities were not uncommon at the Hyundai Shipyard as well as in the factories of its subcontracting firms.[149] Now a proud retiree, this engineer—who had risen to become a high-level executive (*imwŏn*) at HHI—still has his license plate number registered with the factory; and when he visits the Hyundai Shipyard with his still-valid security clearance, donning his old Hyundai employee uniform like "a general wearing his star," current HHI workers continue to greet him with deference and a military salute.

This militarized factory culture in South Korea was buoyed by government propaganda, which created an environment of constant, warlike urgency at industrial sites.[150] In 1974, for example, the government launched the Factory New Village Movement (FNVM; Kongjang Saemaŭl Undong), which was instrumental in invigorating workers' collective efforts toward the HCI. An outgrowth of Park's broader New Village Movement, the FNVM mobilized workers for South Korea's rapid industrialization through training and ideological indoctrination, particularly at HCI plants such as Hanwha's Inch'ŏn factory. To foster anticommunist sentiment and a military mentality, the campaign promoted "total unity" (*ch'onghwa*) between workers and management.[151] Through its "company-as-family" propaganda, the initiative aimed to offset employee-employer tensions by cultivating a sense of shared commitment to national modernization.[152] The FNVM shaped workers' attitudes by inculcating the values of patriotism, discipline, loyalty, and respect for hierarchy, ensuring their allegiance to the company and the state. It also spread regimented work practices, such as arriving at the factory early to clean one's work site before starting, keeping hair at a standard length, not talking during work, and following cost-cutting measures to improve company output.[153] The movement relentlessly promoted the message that it was the workers who, through their sacrifices, would ultimately industrialize the country, increase exports, and thereby secure the nation's self-reliance.[154] These ideals were further shaped by Park's and the FNVM's glorification of skilled workers as "industrial warriors" (*sanŏp chŏnsa*) and by images of the workplace as the front in the nation's economic battle against North Korea. The Park regime's lauding of "industrial warriors" as part of its campaign to inspire the country's workforce echoed Japan's militarized reimagining of industrial workers as *sangyō senshi* (industrial warriors) during the expansion of the Pacific theater in World War II from 1941 to 1945.[155] As Park tapped into propaganda from the Japanese wartime state, industrial militarism—another colonial legacy—became woven into the fabric of everyday working life. The attitude found its way into the Inch'ŏn factory's official anthem, which referred to Hanwha employees as "worker-troops of industrialization" (*sanŏp ŭi yŏkkun*).[156] Even unskilled laborers were proud of being employed by a corporation like Hanwha, as holding any position within the company was deemed highly respectable.[157]

In keeping with government propaganda promoting South Korea's "industrial war" against the communist North, Hanwha's Inch'ŏn factory exhibited a fierce anticommunist stance, reinforcing the government's message of self-reliant defense to inspire the dedication and sacrifice of its workers.[158] Popular slogans, such as "marching forward to the North for reunification" (*pukchin t'ongil*), "reunification through the destruction of communism" (*myŏlgong t'ongil*), and "reunification through complete victory over the communists" (*sŭnggong t'ongil*), epitomized populist hostility toward the government in the North.[159] These messages were prominently displayed throughout the Inch'ŏn factory as well as on posters, signs, and billboards in the surrounding area.[160] A banner above the Inch'ŏn factory's gate in 1977 declared "production in one hand, battle in the other" (*han son ŭro saengsan han son ŭro chŏnt'u*; fig. 3.5). And an iconic wooden sign at the factory entrance served as a fixed reminder of the company's mantra: "explosives for marching to the North; explosives for [economic] construction" (*pukchin edo hwayak; kŏnsŏl edo hwayak*; fig. 3.6). Min Pyŏngman recalled how this sign—together with other heavy-handed methods factory management used to drive pace and enforce discipline—intimidated him as a new worker in the late 1970s.[161] Nationalistic messages were circulated in company publications and promoted during awards ceremonies, sports tournaments, and other community events.[162] Taken together, these propaganda efforts were meant to instill within the worker a deep sense of identification with the state's existential fight against the DPRK.

As the chaebol aligned themselves ever more closely in the mid- to late 1970s with Park's push to increase HCI exports, they prioritized maximum output at minimal cost. Accordingly, wages remained low

FIG. 3.5. A banner (the top one) at Hanwha's Inch'ŏn factory gate in 1977 reads: "Production in one hand, battle in the other." *Source:* Photograph courtesy of Min Pyŏngman.

FIG. 3.6. A sign in front of Hanwha's Inch'ŏn factory reads: "Explosives for marching to the North; explosives for [economic] construction." *Source:* Photograph courtesy of Min Pyŏngman.

for factory workers even as corporate profits increased. The draconian working conditions and long hours instituted to meet ambitious state quotas for exportable products continued to push workers to their limit. According to Ch'oe Pyŏngyun, Inch'ŏn factory employees (like their Daewoo Heavy Industry counterparts mentioned above) typically worked sixty hours and seven days per week—and these hours could increase at any time to meet pressing production deadlines.[163] In order to cope with the long hours, most employees resided in on-site dorms. "I seldom went home," observed Kim Chongbong. "We just continuously worked: there was no room for 'humanism' in that setting."[164]

Although working conditions were repressive, management avoided major conflicts with labor in the 1970s because the MPL put defense corporations under military supervision. The Inch'ŏn factory's status as a defense manufacturing plant meant that any disruption to production, including any hint of labor agitation, would be immediately quelled through controls sanctioned by the MPL. The Yusin system further ensured that any pro-labor action would be suppressed. By the mid-1970s, unions were for the most part collaborating with factory management in their negotiations with corporate ownership.[165] Fortunately for Hanwha, management at its Inch'ŏn factory had developed a relatively good relationship with the well-established workers' union at the plant, one of the oldest in South Korea.[166]

Hanwha's active embrace of the government's plans for defense industrialization and mobilization did have some ancillary benefit for its workers. Former Hanwha employees recalled that some of the "special protections" bestowed by the government to defense corporations included significant leniency from prosecution granted to workers in the aftermath of serious explosives-related accidents. Although culpable workers would be held responsible—especially in any accident involving casualties—they would often be released without serving jail time.[167] According to Yi Ch'anggi: "The government knew that we [the defense contractors] were trying to create something out of nothing, so they protected us in the event of accidents, which were inevitable."[168]

Indeed, government assistance would prove vital for Hanwha after a devastating accident nearly brought the entire company down. In November 1977, a train carrying Hanwha explosives blew up at Iri Station in North Chŏlla Province, killing fifty-six people and injuring more than a thousand others.[169] Hanwha faced public outrage, with numerous calls for the company to cease operations altogether. Some members of the National Assembly proposed confiscation of its explosives business, invoking the long-standing criticism that Hanwha operated as a "monopoly."[170] Yet Hanwha's crucial role in HCI and the defense industry protected it from both shutdown and government takeover. The company was fined nine billion won ($18.6 million) over a three-year period, a sum equal to Kim Chonghŭi's entire personal assets and representing 70 percent of the total thirteen billion won in damages from the Iri Station incident.[171] Despite demands by opposition party members that Hanwha pay for all damages, the Park government used state funds to offset part of the cost, as well as to compensate the injured.[172] Aside from the Hanwha employee deemed directly responsible for the incident (who received a ten-year prison sentence), all other

Hanwha workers and executives involved in the incident received light jail sentences of only eight to ten months, with fines and probation.[173]

The accident dealt Hanwha's reputation a huge blow, but government protection allowed the company to rebound, sparing it and Kim irreversible damage. Indeed, with continued government support Hanwha flourished over time, developing new products and ventures for both the commercial market and the defense industry. The company expanded its production of explosives as well as growing other key defense products and technologies. During the course of its transformation into a weapons manufacturer under Park's HCI Policy, Hanwha had been able to acquire advanced R & D, automation, quality control, and mass-production capabilities, along with a highly skilled workforce, and the state-of-the-art technology and facilities required for the mass production of military-grade weapons—all of which contributed to the company's expansion into other industrial products and exports. As Hanwha went on to win more defense contracts, the company simultaneously advanced its expertise in commercial petrochemical and chemical products. State subsidies and financial rewards were reinvested to expand into business ventures in diverse industries such as construction, manufacturing, transportation, service, finance, and shipping. Overall, Hanwha thrived as an explosives and chemical products exporter under the HCI Policy.[174] Company earnings from exports jumped from $2.19 million in 1977 to $18.27 million by 1980.[175]

The Defense Industry and the Chaebol

As Hanwha's story illustrates, the development of the South Korean defense industry was integral to the growth of the chaebol. Hanwha's transformation under the Park administration's HCI Policy reveals three significant ways that defense building shaped the emergence of these corporations as industrial conglomerates.

The Merger of the Chaebol with State Policy

First, through their connection to national security as arms producers in the 1970s, the chaebol fully merged their activities with the state's policymaking, influenced by the intertwining of industrial and military policy and the convergence of the public and private sectors. Although these large corporations had collaborated with the government prior to the 1970s, and even before the Park administration, the state's involvement in their operations deepened significantly once they became defense contractors under Park's HCI Policy and the MPL. The MPL thoroughly tied the chaebol to Park's military programs and national security measures, and their corporate activities came under constant government surveillance as well as protection. Furthermore, the state's control of the arms industry guaranteed a market for its products, thereby supporting the success of its contractors. The tight interweaving of public and private sectors under the HCI Policy also meant that state and corporate decision-making converged with banking and other public financing sources. At the intersection of state-directed military production and the private market, defense corporations operated in many respects more like quasi-state wartime enterprises than commercial businesses, especially given the Blue House's direct oversight of their management and development.

At the same time, the chaebol were able to leverage their strengths as private enterprises. In the case of Hanwha, although the company was initially conscripted to join Park's new security framework, it developed its own mechanisms for staying competitive while contributing to the push for military modernization. Taking advantage of the MPL's rewards for defense contractors, Hanwha strove to acquire and develop the technical skills and even the raw materials required to manufacture explosives for the military. Facing competition in the new defense industry, Hanwha quickly amped up its efforts to make independent, long-term investments in R & D, beyond the funding available through the state. It incurred large deficits in its development of new prototypes, and it risked steep losses through its product trials and failures. In the end, the most enterprising and competitive companies found ways to manage the heavy cost of meeting the state's demands, and they were the most richly rewarded. Eventually, Hanwha and other successful chaebol were granted increased responsibility and autonomy to implement new industrial and weapons projects. As Hanwha's outcome suggests, corporate participation in defense manufacturing was not only coerced; it also involved consent and compliance, as well as an entrepreneurial drive to succeed. The result was neither a purely state-run defense industry nor purely market-driven one, but a total merging of the public and private sectors through which a distinctive, chaebol-led military-industrial complex emerged in South Korea.[176]

Growth and Diversification

Second, the defense industry shaped the chaebol by facilitating their growth and diversification. The integrated government-chaebol effort to establish weapons manufacturing provided powerful ingredients for the expansion of the chaebol and their diversification into new business sectors. To meet the technological demands of the defense industry, companies were pushed to engage in ADD-supported research, through which they developed new science-based research practices and evaluation methods. The Park regime sought to offset the limits on US technical support by relying on individual chaebol to initiate negotiations with alternative suppliers for new technologies. By the late 1970s, Korean corporations, including Hanwha, were actively procuring technology from abroad, especially through co-production agreements and licensed technology. Through these arrangements, companies adopted modern industrial technologies that spread throughout the defense industry and thus the Korean heavy and chemical industries.

HHI offers a case in point. Tasked by President Park with establishing a shipbuilding industry, Hyundai Group's founder and chairman, Chung Ju-yung (Chŏng Chuyŏng), independently solicited foreign loans to fund the operation and negotiated with foreign shipbuilders for direct licensing agreements that would maximize technology transfers. Starting in the early 1970s, he contracted with companies in England and Scotland for technical assistance in the design and engineering of a shipyard in South Korea, while also reaching out to multiple international suppliers to obtain technical skills training for the Hyundai workforce.[177] Chung also recruited foreign managers to train workers for the Hyundai Shipyard, and he dispatched Hyundai engineers to gain field experience at shipyards in Scotland and Japan. His proactive efforts paid off: by the mid-1970s, HHI was benefiting from diversified shipbuilding technologies, and the company was staffed with skilled workers who then constructed the world's largest shipyard. In 1975 HHI began work on the first Korean-made battleship, the *Ulsan*, a two-thousand-ton vessel that was completed in 1980.[178]

In another case, under Park's 1976 order to indigenize the production of armored vehicles, CEO Kim Sŏnhong of Kia Motors traveled to Germany, Italy, France, and the United States to negotiate with defense manufacturers and procure needed technologies.[179] During his tour of the automaker Fiat's factory in Italy, Kim carefully observed the production methods and facilities for manufacturing armored vehicles, and then recorded the details when he returned to his hotel. He also pocketed welding rods for armored vehicles and smuggled them out of the factory. Later, these rods served as important samples that guided Kia in its selection of raw materials for welding its own armored vehicles. In July 1976 Kia Motors secured a contract with Fiat to coproduce Fiat's armored personnel carrier 6614CM, which became the model for Kia's planned Korean-made armored vehicle.[180] Using Fiat's technology, Kia Motors and its subcontractors also began producing specialized parts for armored vehicles.[181] The most difficult task was steel-welding the armored plates, a highly technical and delicate process that required careful planning and execution.[182] Kia trained its welders and technicians during a six-month welding "boot camp" and also negotiated with the US company General Electric for upgraded equipment for drilling into armored plates. Through these efforts Kia managed to teach its skilled workers highly valuable steel-welding techniques, indigenizing skills that would aid Kia's commercial automobile production as well. By the end of 1977 the company's workers had mastered production of the armored hull, and in collaboration with the subcontractors that supplied other key components, Kia successfully developed a prototype for a Korean-model armored personnel carrier.[183]

When Tongil Heavy Industries, the business arm of the Unification Church (T'ongil Kyohoe) founded by Moon Sun Myung (Mun Sŏnmyŏng) in South Korea, was subcontracted to produce the gun barrel for the 20 mm Vulcan rotary cannon (which Daewoo, the primary contractor, assembled), Tongil leveraged its religious connections with Japanese corporate executives and technicians who were members of the Unification Church to obtain technical assistance with components it could not manufacture domestically. Even though the Japanese government opposed Korea's militarization, Tongil was able to collaborate secretly with a Japanese machine tool company that helped it manufacture the barrel. Cho Kilsu, a former Tongil engineer who was charged with designing the barrel of the US-model Vulcan, was part of Tongil's team sent to the Japanese company (which Cho did not name) in 1978, in accordance with their technical agreement. He stated: "Instead of taking a full US weapon blueprint, I took only the product specs to Japan [to maintain secrecy], so that I could design and manufacture the needed parts with the Japanese engineers."[184] Cho revealed that the Japanese company's officials and engineers were actually aware that they were assisting his team in developing weapon parts. Nevertheless, they signed a secret nondisclosure agreement to ensure the confidentiality of this information. With the help of the Japanese engineers, Cho and his team were able to manufacture in Japan the necessary Vulcan barrel parts and even the broach tools required for making those parts, all of which were then brought to Korea. Similarly, other former skilled workers who were sent to Japan, as well as to the United States, Canada, Europe and elsewhere, have said they brought back (not always legally) product samples and copies of documents to help their companies overcome technical limitations and kick-start weapons production.[185]

The examples of Hyundai, Kia, and Tongil show that South Korea's rapid defense industrialization increasingly pushed companies to exercise their own agency to procure new technologies, and that successful innovation for weapons production depended to a large degree on the efforts of individual business leaders and their workers. Without the impetus of domestic weapons production, however, the companies would not have been as motivated to actively seek and acquire advanced technologies from around the globe. As Alice Amsden observes, the means by which South Korea acquired technology from abroad at this time was not a passive process of simply copying foreign methods and technologies, but rather a highly creative and active one.[186]

As they mastered the domestic production of weapons, the chaebol became scientific and technological pioneers, which had huge ramifications for the growth of technology-intensive private-sector industries in South Korea (see the discussion on "spin-off" in chapter 4). Companies transferred many of the technologies and techniques they acquired in weapons production to civilian manufacturing in such industries as electronics, shipbuilding, heavy machinery, and special metals. In addition, the technical skills acquired by the chaebol workforce as they developed weapons and military equipment enhanced production in civilian industries and improved precision manufacturing, technology, quality control, and product durability across the board.[187] Corporations that developed precision manufacturing for weapons parts and hardware—Kia, Hyundai, Ssangyong, and Daewoo, for example—would emerge as South Korea's top automobile manufacturers.[188] New technologies acquired by manufacturers of engines for military vehicles, tanks, and aircraft, such as STX Engine and Samsung Precision (now Hanwha Vision), would advance commercial engine production as well.[189] Likewise, Park's push to produce helicopters and military jets in the late 1970s would lead to technological breakthroughs for Korean Air, South Korea's signature commercial airline.

Defense-centered industrialization certainly had a significant impact on major corporations overall, but it should be noted that the effects of defense production also varied among chaebol, depending on their products, the proportion of their business devoted to defense production, and the timing of their government contracts.[190] For instance Hanwha, which already specialized in explosives and had prior experience in grenade development in 1968, was able to adapt more swiftly to the requirements of arms production compared with other chaebol that entered the defense industry after 1973. The extent of the defense industry's impact on each chaebol was also closely related to how thoroughly a firm was integrated into the state's HCI program.[191] Large electronics manufacturers like Samsung and Goldstar, for example, maintained more independence because they relied less on state subsidies than companies in other HCI sectors. In general, companies in the electronics industry were not offered the same level of state aid as manufacturers in the other HCI sectors.[192] Nonetheless, the HCI Policy pushed Samsung and Goldstar to expand into new industries—such as shipbuilding, construction, chemicals, and precision machinery—and expedited their reorganization for mass production and diversification.[193] It was after they contracted with the government for advanced weapons projects in the late 1970s that Samsung and Goldstar expanded into the new high-tech sectors of aerospace and telecommunications, respectively.[194] In one way or another, by the late 1970s the proactive chaebol (such as Hanwha) and even initially resistant companies (like Samsung and Kia Motors) were not just participating in but proactively driving HCI and the defense industry, which in turn contributed to their growth. At Samsung, for example, the company witnessed advancements in technology, production capabilities, and quality control because its defense-related subsidiaries Samsung Precision and Samsung Heavy Industries were required to meet the government's high standards for quality control and production capacity under the HCI Policy.[195] As a result, Samsung as a whole benefited from the improvements made by its defense-related subsidiaries. Overall, largely aided by the skills, processes, and technologies gained in order to manufacture advanced weapons, the defense contractors groomed under the Park regime emerged from the 1970s as megaconglomerates with especially deep ties to the defense infrastructure.[196]

Corporate Militarism

The third and final way the defense industry shaped the chaebol was in their radical militarization, through which they became the powerful centerpiece of the ROK's industrial economy. Under defense industry policies backed by the state's centralized system for HCI, all chaebol were profoundly affected by the disciplined military ethos that filtered down from Park Chung Hee in the Blue House. Accordingly, the Hanwha case study captures the militarized experience of many of the chaebol, all of which were molded as defense producers by Park's authoritarian policymaking under the Yusin system, which functioned at its peak in the development of the defense industry.

All corporations engaged in defense production were deeply influenced by Park's military-style management, ideology, and discipline, more so than businesses in other sectors. As the defense industry's commander in chief, Park not only micromanaged the defense contractors (via his Blue House technocrats) but also exerted constant pressure at the structural level, where his policy decisions and their enforcement guaranteed a homogenized weapons-production system. Park demanded immediate, coordinated results from the corporate rank and file, and the heads of the chaebol responded in kind, especially in their initial transition into weapons production under the MPL. Through their participation in the defense industry, most of the companies developed a similar aggressive style and pace, influenced by Park's extremely hands-on involvement and surveillance. As a former officer in an ROK Army artillery unit, Park also had a strong personal interest in arms manufacturing (fig. 3.7).[197] He was a frequent visitor to arms factories, where he inspected their work and followed their progress intently (figs. 3.8 and 3.9).

Requirements imposed by the MPL further boosted the regimentation of South Korean industries and their workers. In the interests of national security, HCI factories militaristically followed government orders and instituted the required security protocols and regulations of operation, following strict technical standards and specifications for production quotas, quality control, R & D, and exports, all as required

FIG. 3.7. Park inspects a defense industry plant in 1977. *Source:* National Archives of Korea; file no. CET0019714.

FIG. 3.8. Park and Park Geun-hye, his daughter, tour the Daewoo Heavy Industries factory in Ch'angwŏn in 1979. On the back of the domestically produced Vulcan cannon is a sticker that reads, "Defense equipment [made] with our deepest care." *Source:* National Archives of Korea; file no. CET0024021.

by special legislation for the defense industry. Companies followed these government directives as closely as possible to receive state privileges and avoid penalties for noncompliance. As the Hanwha story reveals, a corporation's involvement in the arms industry had a profound impact on the transformation of its administration, industrial structure, and corporate culture and ideology. Hanwha's Inch'ŏn factory in the 1970s exemplified how companies and their workers operated in the disciplined and warlike environment created by the countrywide mobilization for national security.

Even chaebol that focused less on arms manufacturing, such as Samsung, were significantly influenced by the state's defense industry regulations. Due to Samsung's integration with the subsidiaries involved in its defense product manufacturing, as well as its collaborations with other firms and subcontractors in the HCI sectors, the company had to adhere to the same military standards and regulations as

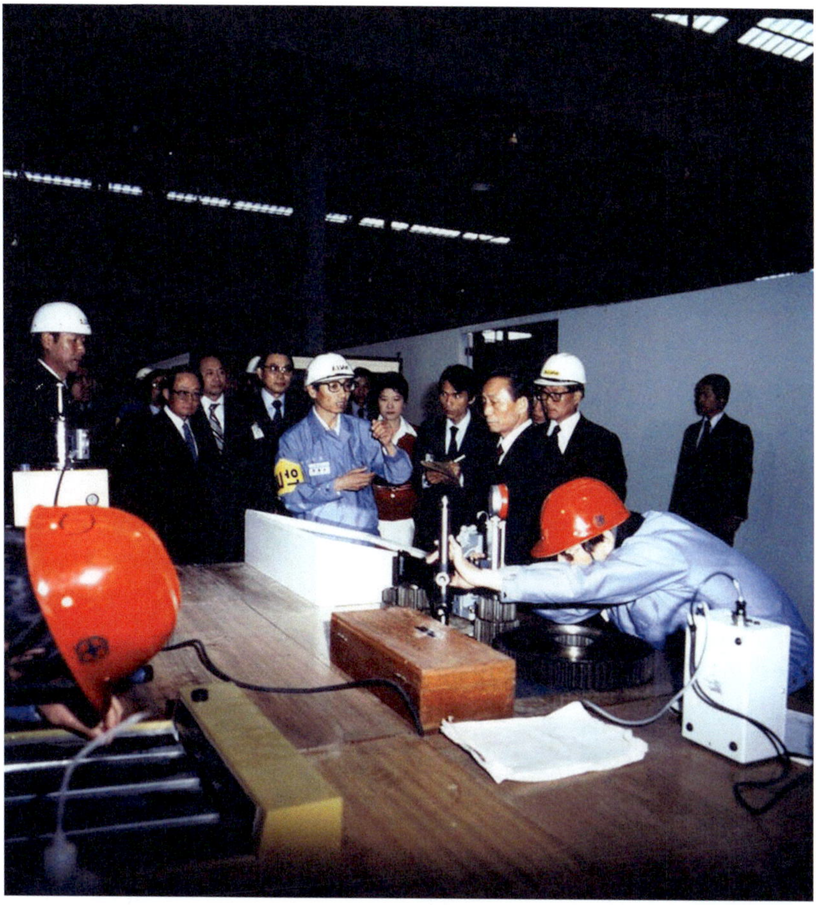

FIG. 3.9. Park tours the Hyundai Heavy Industries factory in 1979 (Park Geun-hye and O Wŏnch'ŏl are in the background, center). *Source:* National Archives of Korea; file no. CET0019788.

other defense (or HCI) corporations. According to Kim Kwŏnjung, a former skilled worker and production manager at the Samsung Heavy Industries factory in Ch'angwŏn in the late 1970s, the strict procedures that governed Samsung's factory were the same as those followed in the military, ranging from policies on entering and exiting the facility to those covering how to handle corporate documents. Whenever employees transferred or shared any product blueprint with another company, they had to follow rigid government guidelines. The government also conducted annual factory-wide security checks and audits during which workers were not even allowed to leave any documents on their desks. As Kim stated, "The culture was pretty much the same among all HCI factories: it was a militarized atmosphere. Aside from not carrying guns, every action we took, from the way we handled the security-related documents, [to] saluting, to getting haircuts [hair could not cover the ears], was essentially the same as in the military. In all ways, we worked with a military mentality."[198] According to Kim, "Samsung's recent image as a manufacturer of cell phones and other commercial items has diminished its militaristic image. . . . But at the time [in the 1970s], the workers in this [HCI] sector had to operate strictly within the special law and system for the defense industry, under tight control and secrecy. . . . Samsung's [conservative] corporate culture as a basic frame, plus the regulations required for the defense industry, formed the 'plus alpha' for militarization." As all HCI companies were redesigned to fit the model created by Park and his technocrats, weapons contractors became homogenized in many aspects, much like soldiers in an army unit, because a common militarized system operated across all HCI sectors.

The militarism undergirding Park's push for economic and defense development became deeply ingrained in the chaebol, and many customs remain a part of Korean workplace culture to this day. Corporate values heavily promoted for HCI under Park—such as aggression, competitiveness, discipline, order, unity, sacrifice, and duty—remain embedded in the organizational culture of South Korea's business, engineering, and science sectors.[199] The culture within these sectors still reflects Park's mobilization of workers as "industrial warriors" and reveals vestiges of industrial militarism in their rigid hierarchies. Conglomerates such as Hanwha, Hyundai, Daewoo, Kia, Goldstar, and Samsung expanded rapidly in the 1970s and after by maintaining these militaristic organizational principles and attitudes. Employing top-down leadership, highly results- and team-based operations, and intensive worker training to cultivate cohesiveness, loyalty, and a strong collective identity, the chaebol promoted a mission-oriented and expansionist mindset that accelerated project progress.[200]

Conclusion

During the Park era, South Korean businesses were quickly transformed in response to state policies for industrialization and defense. With Park's introduction of the Yusin Constitution in 1972 and the promulgation of his HCI Policy in 1973, the government broadened and intensified its conscription of civilian businesses to expand the nation's defense industry. As the MPL locked down the Blue House's control over the chaebol, Park and his technocrats pressed for business development at all levels, and the competition for government licenses and contracts encouraged new research and technological innovation. In addition, at a deeper level than statutory and economic processes, the government and the chaebol worked together to change corporate culture and worker consciousness to reflect Park's defense ideology. The new defense corporations thus transformed themselves physically and ideologically, in sync with Park's self-reliant national defense policy, and in doing so they advanced both domestic arms production and national exportation rates.

Hanwha offers a prime example. Over the course of the company's militarization under Park, Hanwha displayed the dynamic interplay of compliance and initiative exhibited by the chaebol generally, as they first followed state orders and then proactively contributed to the buildup of the defense industry. The company expanded through its furtherance of state policies and prospered as it adopted a newly militarized work culture as well as new business priorities and structures to indigenize weapons production. Like other dual-purpose producers enlisted in HCI in the 1970s—Hyundai, Kia, Doosan, and Daewoo, for example—Hanwha grew by both following and promoting defense industry policies, becoming one of the leading chaebol by supporting South Korea's independent arms production and propelling economic growth. These corporations also worked to realize Park's goal of self-reliance by increasing civilian engagement through workplace education and training.

Although the Park regime initially orchestrated the policies, set the tempo, and directed many aspects of business expansion for military modernization, it counted on motivated companies to respond creatively and vigorously to help strengthen national defense. This chapter reveals that Hanwha was an active and resourceful player and gives us a more nuanced picture of state-chaebol relations than the conventional "strong state, weak business" interpretation of the ROK economy under Park Chung Hee. Building on and deepening the sociologist Eun Mee Kim's depiction of the chaebol as strong, dynamic economic actors working alongside a strong state, this examination of Hanwha's experience highlights the distinct ways that Park's defense industry shaped corporate contractors into megaconglomerates.[201]

Within the expansive scope of South Korea's defense-centered industrialization and the influence it had over private-sector advancement, Hanwha's story encapsulates the growth of the chaebol during the Park regime. Under Park, the chaebol were mobilized, militarized, and modernized for the most daunting national task of their generation: developing a self-sufficient defense industry. While the state proved to be a highly active and powerful partner, and certainly the dominant one when necessary, the chaebol played an equally dynamic and complementary role. It was through the joint actions of state policymakers and the chaebol that South Korea rapidly built its defense industry and emerged as the economic power known today as "Korea, Inc."

CHAPTER FOUR

National Scientization and the Agency for Defense Development

Build the nation with science; achieve self-reliance in technology.
—Park Chung Hee

Defending our nation with the strength of our own science and technology!
—Vision statement of the Agency for Defense Development

"Technological self-reliance" was the fundamental philosophy that drove our efforts for defense R & D.
—An Tongman, former researcher and director, Agency for Defense Development

In January 1973 President Park Chung Hee announced the National Scientization Movement (NSM), an initiative aimed at integrating the country's scientific and technological advancements with his Heavy and Chemical Industrialization Policy (HCI Policy). In alignment with the core objective of the HCI Policy, the key goal of the NSM was to support the development of a national defense industry. Park's early efforts to "scientize" the nation had begun with the establishment of the Korea Institute of Science and Technology (KIST; Han'guk Kwahak Kisul Yŏn'guwŏn) in 1966 and the solicitation of technical aid from the United States and Japan. Then, in response to the security crisis of the late 1960s and the pressing need for a robust, independent defense system that surpassed what KIST and US military aid could offer, Park founded the Agency for Defense Development (ADD; Kukpang Kwahak Yŏn'guso) in 1970. The ADD emerged as South Korea's central institute for weapons research and development (R & D).

Once the HCI Policy began to synchronize ADD weapons research with private-sector production, the Park government moved national scientization to the fore as a means of developing the skilled labor and business R & D infrastructure critical to supporting domestic arms manufacturing. While the ADD fostered major advances in private-sector innovation by localizing R & D, facilitating technological collaborations, and establishing corporate quality control and standardization methods, the NSM, working hand in glove with Park's grand plan for defense industrialization, combined state-sponsored militarization with the promotion of civilian science and technology (S & T).

Few studies have examined the extent to which the military-industrial infrastructure built during the NSM (1973–79) gave rise to South Korea's remarkable rate of technological growth and innovation. Even less research exists on the ADD and its connections to the growth in S & T, partly because of the scarcity of available data on the agency, which, from its inception, operated as a highly secretive institution.[1] When explaining postwar South Korea's rapid advances in S & T sectors, studies often focus on external influences—that is, technological aid that came from the United States and Japan between the 1950s and the 1970s.[2] Works that do discuss domestic factors have mainly looked at the top-down policymaking of elite technocrats, such as O Wŏnch'ŏl and Ch'oe Hyŏngsŏp, in analyzing the growth of Korea's S & T infrastructure.[3] Although the latest literature on South Korea's S & T development has broadened its focus to highlight the domestic contributions of diverse individuals, civic groups, corporations, and research institutes, some crucial indigenous factors—including state militarization efforts and the agency of Korean scientists and engineers themselves—that enabled South Korea's technological modernization have yet to be fully examined.[4] In fact, an in-depth analysis of South Korea's defense industrialization points to militarization as a primary force behind Korea's transformation into a science-oriented, technologically innovative state under Park, a result that earned him the moniker "Science President." In this chapter I examine these less-acknowledged indigenous factors, from both a structural (or policy) view and through the lens of personal testimony, revealing how the defense industry was completely enmeshed with the nation's scientific and technological development.

Early Scientization Efforts

The NSM must be placed within the larger historical context of Park's vision for national industrialization and his earliest efforts to overcome South Korea's reliance on foreign powers for both security and technology. Park's priority on developing domestic S & T to achieve self-reliance in many ways reflected the techno-nationalistic fervor common among postcolonial developing nations after World War II—including North Korea, China, and Japan—many of which pursued scientific and technological prowess as the means to attain economic and military sovereignty.[5] Although efforts had been made toward scientization during the regime of Rhee Syngman—such as the creation of Atomic Energy Research Institute and the adoption of the US-sponsored Minnesota Plan in the 1950s—policies for comprehensive scientific advancement at the national level were not implemented until Park's rule.[6] When Park came to power in 1961, South Korea was still severely lacking in technology and skilled workers, with its economy running on cheap domestic labor and labor-intensive light industries. In 1962 Park launched the first of three successive Five-Year Science and Technology Promotion Plans, which were intended to operate alongside the Economic Planning Board's (EPB) Five-Year Economic Development Plans (FYEDPs).[7] In May 1966 at the first National Science and Technology Conference, Park used the twin expressions "scientific Korea" (*kwahak Han'guk*) and "technological Korea" (*kisul Han'guk*) as he encouraged the nation's scientists and engineers to throw their weight behind the promotion of S & T, saying: "Science and technology are the mother of productivity and the source of power that promotes economic development. In short, [science] is the prerequisite for the modernization of the fatherland."[8] The "modernization of the fatherland" (*choguk kŭndaehwa*) became both Park's rallying cry and his political vision, as he pushed the rapid development of S & T as the foundation for economic development.

Foreign Assistance and the Birth of the Korea Institute of Science and Technology

To kick-start the effort to develop S & T, the Park government sought financial and technical aid from the United States and even from Korea's archrival, Japan. In 1965, against strong domestic opposition, Park signed the Treaty on Basic Relations between Japan and the Republic of Korea (also known as the 1965 Japan-Korea Normalization Treaty) because he deemed Japan's aid necessary for his second Five-Year Economic Development Plan, which included the goal of export-led industrialization.[9] Besides receiving technical aid, South Korea sent workers on training expeditions to study industrial operations and facilities in Japan, which by this time was becoming a world-class manufacturer, and it imported Japanese machine technology and products to make up for technologies the United States had not shared.[10]

Meanwhile, developmental loans and technological aid granted by the Lyndon Johnson administration in return for Park's dispatching troops to Vietnam made it possible for South Korea to establish KIST.[11] Founded in 1966, KIST was Korea's first comprehensive research institute. It was modeled on the Battelle Memorial Institute in the United States, a contract-based research organization under civilian management.[12] Battelle provided essential assistance in establishing KIST's research programs, training researchers, and forming a joint US-ROK study team. Researchers at KIST aimed to develop domestic technologies in strategic manufacturing sectors that were vital to industrialization, including machinery, special metals, electronics, and shipbuilding. KIST later engaged in basic weapons research and participated in the Four Core Factories project (discussed in chapter 2) to build defense-related civilian industries.

As Park's think tank for domestic industrial technology, KIST operated with the financial support of the government on state-mandated research projects. However, as a nonprofit civilian-run foundation (*min'gan chaedan pŏbin*), it enjoyed autonomy in its management and operations.[13] The institute ran a government contracting system with the private sector in which KIST procured advanced foreign technologies and then transferred them to private contractors. This process assisted the contractors in developing industrial products required by the government.[14] In 1967, one year after the founding of KIST, Park established the Ministry of Science and Technology (MST; Kwahak Kisulch'ŏ), which together with KIST began to build up S & T in South Korea.

KIST's earliest efforts for scientization, however, ran up against the limits of South Korea's research infrastructure, which was still too primitive to realize Park's industrial and military goals.[15] In the late 1960s, although KIST pursued the development of domestic science and technology, the institute remained entirely reliant on imported technology and lacked the capacity for R & D.[16] As the historian John DiMoia says, KIST at this time served primarily as "a learning tool" for importing foreign technologies and lacked the ability to devise technologies on its own.[17] Even for its most crucial project, the Four Core Factories, KIST (along with the EPB, responsible for financing the project) was overly dependent both technologically and financially on Japan and other foreign sources.[18] As discussed in the previous chapters, the US government refused to share most of its technical data on weapons with South Korea, and what it did share initially applied to strictly defensive weapons or outdated arms scheduled for retirement.[19]

Due to the restrictions imposed by the United States, which served as KIST's primary source of technological aid, the institute was only able to provide the state with limited assistance in developing arms technology or advancing R & D for the purpose of building a modern defense industry. The ROK Armed Forces used US imports for everything from ammunition to basic weapons, and although the United States supplied the weapons, it largely withheld the technology that would enable Korea to build them itself. South Korea's defense industry development thus remained stunted by an industrial and technological backwardness that persisted in the relatively stable but dependent security environment of the 1960s—that is, up until 1968.[20]

The turn in South Korea's quest for independence in science and technology at that point was sharp, occurring when Park was abruptly confronted with the sudden weakening of the US security commitment and the escalation of threats from the DPRK. In response he became determined to launch an all-out national effort for independent defense industrialization. The 1968 security crisis and the announcement of the Nixon Doctrine in the following year underscored the nation's longstanding need for independent weapons R & D as well as production.

According to statements by Yi Kyŏngsŏ, the former KIST engineer who later joined the ADD (see chapter 2), KIST received a secret order in 1969—the same year the Nixon Doctrine was announced—to establish a lab for conducting research on rocket models for guided missiles.[21] (Although the exact date of the order was not revealed by Yi, it is estimated to be around October 1969, when he joined KIST.[22]) Former ADD researcher Ku Sanghoe and O Wŏnch'ŏl explain that Park's rush to acquire guided-weapons capability was also influenced by the ROK's general unpreparedness for what he saw as a new type of scientific war—one in which quick victories were achieved through preemptive strikes with high-tech airpower, mechanized infantry units, and guided missiles, as first demonstrated to Park by the 1967 Arab-Israeli War.[23] Park's concern that the DPRK, with its superior arms technology, could launch a similar attack against South Korea necessitated the swift acquisition of advanced weapons as a deterrent.[24] Under Park, the ROK government became hyperfocused on developing the technological and technical know-how necessary to produce its own weapons, and as a result, abstract, academically oriented science was deprioritized.[25] It was at this juncture that the ADD was created.

Founding the Agency for Defense Development

Negotiations with the United States over troop reductions following the announcement of the Nixon Doctrine had just begun when, on February 2, 1970, Park ordered the Ministry of National Defense (MND) to establish a new division exclusively dedicated to defense industry development. In late April, Park called for a strategy to establish the foundation for the defense industry by fostering private industry growth.[26] He then ordered Minister of National Defense Chŏng Raehyŏk to explore plans for creating a civilian-staffed defense research center that was comparable in terms of standards to KIST, the nation's leading scientific institute.[27]

Two events would accelerate the founding of the ADD: North Korea's capture of a South Korean fishing boat in the Yellow Sea on June 5, 1970, and a botched attempt by North Korean commandos to rig a bomb at the gate of Seoul National Cemetery around two weeks later (June 22) in an effort to assassinate Park during the annual June 25 memorial ceremony for the Korean War.[28] These incidents, coming amid the United States' continuing disengagement from South Korea, led Park and his military advisers to immediately approve the establishment of the ADD at a Blue House meeting on June 27.[29] On August 6, the ADD was set up in a facility in the Hongnŭng neighborhood in Seoul, where KIST was located, so the two research institutes could easily collaborate. Park appointed Sin Ŭnggyun, the deputy director of KIST and former army general who had previously been a superior of Park's in the ROK Army, as the inaugural director of the ADD. Sin held this position from 1970 to 1972 (fig. 4.1).

FIG. 4.1. Park (right) shakes hands with Sin Ŭnggyun (left) at his appointment as director of the ADD in 1970. *Source:* National Archives of Korea; file no. CET0018510.

The agency began with a staff of sixty employees, most of whom were recruited from the ROK military, and scientists from KIST were also brought in to assist with the ADD's projects at the start.[30]

On December 31, the National Assembly passed the Agency for Defense Development Act. Article 1 of the act stated that the agency was to "take charge of technical investigation, research, development, and testing of weapons, equipment, and materials necessary for the national defense, including the related research and testing of science and technology, with the aim of strengthening national defense capabilities and achieving self-reliant national defense."[31] Originally founded as a public research institute, the ADD was christened under the act as a "special corporation" (*t'ŭksu pŏbinch'e*) specifically assigned to research and develop new weaponry on behalf of the MND.[32]

In spite of its legal designation as a nongovernment corporate entity, the ADD was treated as a semigovernmental institute by virtue of its affiliation with and funding by the MND and its unusually close collaboration with the Second Economic Secretariat (SES) in the Blue House.[33] Operating under Blue House directives, the ADD was to perform three main tasks: lead South Korea's weapons R & D and assist contracted businesses in advancing that effort, verify the quality of the weapons and parts produced by domestic contractors, and manage the assembly and final production of domestic weapons.[34] Essentially, the ADD was authorized to manage all stages of weapons development, from research on prototypes to approval of finished products. As the only institute devoted to weapons R & D, the ADD was to oversee arms development for all branches of the military—the ROK Army, Navy (the ROK Marine Corps is a branch of the Navy), and Air Force—unlike military research institutes abroad, which typically specialize in a single branch of the military.

During the ADD's earliest years, however, its researchers had to rely on KIST and its civilian scientists for technical support, since the young agency lacked both the skilled staff and proper facilities to venture into arms development on its own. According to Yi Kyŏngsŏ, KIST's scientists handled about "90 percent of the weapon projects" during this time because ADD researchers, who were recruited from the military, did not possess the technical knowledge to research modern weapons.[35] As they worked together, tensions began to brew between KIST's civilian scientists and the ADD's military engineers.[36] Yi explained:

> At the time, there were many inter-personnel conflicts. The military engineers at the ADD had this idea that military research should be carried out by the military. But that is not how it should be done. Even in the US, the R & D is all carried out by civilians and the military's duty is to only monitor and decide the specifications. . . . However, the military personnel [engineers] in the ADD, especially those recruited from the ROK Army, had this tremendous sense of pride, believing that "if we [the Army] need it, we must be the ones to make it." As a result, they bumped heads with the KIST researchers in every matter. We [KIST researchers] would be insisting, "We are working on the projects that were assigned to us by the government," but the ADD personnel would say, "We do not have adequate workforces yet, but we will be taking over these projects eventually, so you guys stay out." They would also complain that "KIST employees are sitting in a luxurious house like noblemen, filling out forms and measuring [things], while we are working dangerously in a warehouse-like environment," and thus we had a lot of conflicts.[37]

In February 1972, on O Wŏnch'ŏl's recommendation, Sim Munt'aek, the civilian director of KIST, took over as director of the ADD.[38] A graduate of O's alma mater, Seoul National University, with a degree in chemistry and a PhD in physics from Indiana University in the United States, Sim accelerated a shift in the agency from military to civilian control. Despite the fact that Sim had civilian status (unlike his predecessor, the former general), the new ADD director was accorded ministerial treatment, equivalent to that received by the minister of national defense, as he had the full backing of President Park.[39] Sim's promotion also led to his recruitment of former colleagues at KIST who had been researching guided weapons there (some of whom had already been assisting the ADD projects), including Yi Kyŏngsŏ, An Tongman, and Kim Pyŏnggyo. Many other civilian engineers and scientists joined the ADD during Sim's eight-year tenure, taking roles as head researchers in weapons programs that had previously been run by military engineers.[40] Sim quickly built a reputation as an effective leader who brought together the old and new guard at the ADD.[41] In the words of one former military scientist at the ADD, Sim's "barrel was big, and his style was bold," whereas his predecessor was known for being careful and reserved.[42] Like O, Sim's bold style aligned with Park's preference for leaders who were willing to take risks.

Sim aggressively recruited top Korean scientists and engineers to the ADD, including those educated and living abroad.[43] The government offered them attractive financial packages and other special incentives, including housing, exemptions from military service, and even exemptions from certain taxes. Some privileges, like tax-exempt automobile purchases, were on par with the perks enjoyed by military generals.[44] ADD researchers also received opportunities to study overseas and were dispatched to US military research institutes and foreign defense firms for hands-on training.[45] Such rich career benefits led many scientific and technical experts in prominent industry positions to join the agency. In addition, ADD researchers received salaries that were 20 to 30 percent higher than their counterparts at KIST.[46] Over time, the new civilian recruits included a diverse group of elite researchers from both foreign and domestic institutions. Some of these recruits came from other research institutes or the business sector, while others joined the ADD by passing the agency's public examination.[47]

Park Chung Hee esteemed the ADD for its central role in his vision for national security and referred to the agency as "the cornerstone of self-reliant national defense" (*kukpang ŭi ch'osŏk*).[48] His deep regard for the ADD was such that it is still mentioned by former ADD researchers. As aerospace scientist Hong Chaehak, who was involved in the ADD's missile project during that time, remarked in an interview published by *Shindonga* magazine in 2006, "President Park gave wholehearted support to the scientists in weapons development. . . . It was special treatment."[49] Park is known to have visited the ADD at least once or twice a year to encourage its researchers in person.[50] Based on the recollections of Hong, Yi Kyŏngsŏ, and Ku Sanghoe, Park often ate with the researchers in their cafeteria when he visited the agency. During his visits to the construction site for the ADD's new facility in Taejŏn and to weapons-testing sites, he would stop by the makeshift restaurants where the researchers ate and order the same meal for himself. During these meals, he would tell them, "We can be a powerful nation only through making our own weapons."[51]

The Special Nature of the Agency for Defense Development

The hybrid state-corporate status of the ADD, as well as its specialized role in the defense industry, meant the agency enjoyed privileges not granted to other research institutes. Even the ADD's name in English, *Agency* for Defense Development, distinguished it from KIST as well as from the newly established government-funded research institutes (GFRIs; *chŏngbu ch'uryŏn yŏn'gu kigwan*), all of which used the term "institute" in their English names (e.g., Korea Institute of Science and Technology, Korea Advanced Institute of Science). Although the literal translation of the ADD's official Korean name, Kukpang Kwahak Yŏn'guso, is "Defense Science Research Institute," the ADD was designated an agency in English to signal its unique relationship with the government as a civilian research organization dedicated to the Blue House's mission of self-reliant national defense.[52] Its special identity equipped the ADD with the dexterity and power to carry out its mission. Thanks to its affiliation with the MND, the ADD could engage in official exchanges of technical information and form partnerships with the defense ministries and military research institutes of the United States and other allies. ADD civilian researchers, treated as state employees, were issued official government passports and received the special Blue House orders for developing confidential weapons projects.[53] At the same time, the ADD's civilian (or corporate) status meant that it had operational freedom, generous financial resources for recruitment and salaries, and flexibility in its financing of weapons purchases, because it was unencumbered by the budget restrictions and inefficiencies of government agencies.[54]

Because the ADD was funded directly by the MND and operated under an independent accounting system, it could negotiate for and purchase advanced weapons technologies that were banned in Korea by the United States and not included in US military aid. Internally, as an agency receiving its orders directly from the Blue House, its budget proposals for weapons development could bypass the MND's normal review process for defense spending.[55] For instance, the ADD could directly request and receive funds from the MND or the EPB for its weapons-development budget without justifying or even revealing how the funds would be used. Designed as a quasi-private government agency acting under Blue House guidance, it operated free of outside political intervention and was given unmatched autonomy for the development of high-grade weapons and equipment.

The public-private structure of the ADD was modeled on KIST, a civilian research institute that contracted with private firms to carry out government projects. Its model was also influenced by Canada's National Research Council, which conducted state-funded strategic research but maintained operational independence from the government.[56] Further inspiration for the ADD's design came from Japan's Technical Research and Development Institute, a federal agency that guided corporate R & D for both industrial and military purposes.[57] This hybrid makeup of the ADD distinguished it from South Korea's first R & D institute for domestic arms development, the MND's Research Institute of Science, which had operated as a state-run agency before being dismantled by Park's military junta in July 1961.[58]

The ADD also distinguished itself from KIST in important ways. First, as Park's R & D instrument for the defense industry and the highest-level lab serving his military agenda, the ADD wielded far more power than KIST did.[59] Officially under the MND, the ADD was in fact personally supervised by Park's intermediary, O Wŏnch'ŏl. With a short chain of command coming straight from the Blue House, the ADD had an exclusive license to procure state-of-the-art technologies through both domestic R & D and foreign transfers (from both US and non-US suppliers), beyond what KIST could ever access, shackled as it was to US aid and oversight. Having been established with seed funding from the US Agency for International Development, KIST was hamstrung from the start by that agency's restrictions; furthermore, US aid regulations, study teams, and technical supports limited the independence of KIST researchers. From 1966 to 1971, as previously mentioned, KIST also relied heavily on the Battelle Memorial Institute, its "sister" research institute.[60] In contrast, the ADD remained relatively independent of US oversight and foreign aid. As the ADD matured into its central role in R & D for advanced military technologies, KIST scaled back its involvement in arms-related projects and shifted its focus more exclusively toward the development of commercial-industrial technologies.[61]

According to Ku Sanghoe, the United States was never supportive of the ADD and had always been concerned about its purpose, and the Americans' suspicions only intensified when the ADD set out to develop independent weapon capacities beyond what the United States was willing to offer KIST.[62] All ADD researchers had to sign strict secrecy agreements, promising not to expose any matters related to ROK weapons programs—not even to American researchers who came to assist the ADD. The Korean researchers also had to circumvent arms restrictions imposed by the United States. After Clyde Hardin and his Advanced Research Projects Agency team visited the ADD in 1972 (see chapter 2), the Joint US Military Affairs Group–Korea (JUSMAG–K) established an office within the ADD and filled it with personnel from the Eighth Infantry Division of the United States Forces Korea.[63] This office functioned as the liaison between the ADD and the US Department of Defense to facilitate US technical assistance. In reality, however, all ADD researchers recognized that the office had a surveillance role and understood that JUSMAG–K officials were informants, charged with monitoring Korean researchers and reporting them in case they violated any US weapons regulations. As Kim Ch'angsik, former ADD researcher who specialized in explosives, attested, "The JUSMAG had its office in the ADD, but there was an underlying (or secretive) divide between the ADD and JUSMAG."[64] Indeed, when it came to ROK weapons programs, the distrust was deep and wide between the two allies. Nonetheless, US military aid, though unstable, remained the largest source of external assistance for the ROK's military modernization throughout the 1970s. When the Nixon administration agreed in 1971 to support Park's new Five-Year Military Modernization Plan, the arrangement covered transfers of technical data packages (TDPs) that included weapons R & D data and technical documents—such as design templates, operation manuals, and manufacturing instructions—along with coproduction licenses for US weapons.[65] Even though the United States held back from delivering a substantial number of TDPs to South Korea until 1974, when these data packages finally arrived they quickly aided the ADD's effort to expedite its weapons programs.[66]

The National Scientization Movement

Although the ADD improved the ROK's research capacity, when it came to the civilian industrial sectors that would produce Korea's new weapons, South Korea lacked both a skilled workforce and the business infrastructure necessary for weapons manufacturing. The NSM that Park announced in 1973 operated in lockstep with his overall strategy for independent military modernization, contributing in many ways to the ADD's development of private industry–based weapons manufacturing. To build a defense industry under the HCI Policy and support the expansion of ADD's weapons development, South Korea needed a stronger technological foundation. To that end, the NSM promoted an attitude of "scientific nationalism," a sense of national identity and strength based on scientific and technological achievement, to galvanize support for scientization. The movement also introduced education reforms to develop a skilled workforce and created new policies and research institutes that formed the domestic R & D infrastructure needed to advance private-sector research. Ultimately, the NSM merged with the ADD's efforts in the 1970s, powering a mutually reinforcing support system for defense industrialization.

When Park announced his HCI Policy on January 23, 1973, he declared that the "scientization of all people" (*chŏn kungmin ŭi kwahakhwa*) was not only vital to South Korea's heavy and chemical industrialization (HCI) but also the only way to strengthen the nation. In his words, "We will all commence the 'Scientization of All People' movement from this time forth. All Koreans must learn, adopt, and develop science and technology. It is the only way to rapidly strengthen our nation. We can never become an advanced country without the development of science and technology. . . . From primary school children to college students and all adults, all people, regardless of age or gender, need to learn skills. Only then can we gain national strength."[67] As demonstrated below, the NSM was designed to serve Park's priority of producing domestic weapons and weapons parts by developing a technical workforce and the scientific infrastructure necessary to manufacture such products. At the same time, the movement was the culmination of Park's campaign for the "modernization of the fatherland" that had been launched in the mid-1960s; by declaring national scientization as part of HCI, he officially integrated technological development with his vision for national self-reliance.[68]

Prior to the initiation of the HCI Policy, Park's government, including Park himself, had addressed South Korea's pressing need to groom a population of knowledge-based and highly skilled workers, a group

Park called "scientific workforce," to support national industrialization.[69] In February 1970, for example, the Economy and Science Council of the MST presented a ten-year plan (1972–81) to cultivate "science and technology manpower": scientists, technicians, and craftspeople. The council noted that more than 80 percent of new employees in South Korea in 1969 were unskilled workers who did not meet middle-school educational benchmarks. It cited several reasons for the scarcity of skilled workers: the lack of an education policy for training them; businesses' failure to provide field training; poor vocational training in general; the shortage of students entering technical fields; a lack of correspondence between formal education and the requirements for highly skilled technical work; low wages for manufacturing jobs; and "remnants of outdated, social bias" against those who perform physical labor, such as craftspeople and technicians.[70]

In 1971, when O was promoted to head the SES and tasked with building the defense industry, he immediately prioritized the development of the nation's technical workforce. Understanding from the start that modern weapons production hinges on technical specialists with precision manufacturing skills, without whom any planned weapons facilities would be useless, O incorporated policies for training these highly skilled workers into his HCI proposal.[71] The SES's plans to train civilian workers on a massive scale was moved to the top of the agenda at the 1972 meetings of the Defense Industry Promotion Council, where it was decided that the state would subsidize technological education in high school.[72] The council agreed that "the total empowerment of the trinity of military, business, and science" would be needed for defense industrialization (see chapter 2).[73]

When Park declared the goal of national scientization in his announcement of the HCI Policy, he stressed the need to develop a highly educated national workforce. According to O in his memoir, the phrase "national scientization" was his brainchild: he wrote that during a late-1972 meeting with Park about developing a skilled workforce for HCI, he had recommended merging the ongoing New Village Movement with a "National Scientization Movement."[74] Just as the main objective of HCI was defense industry buildup, the NSM's core mission would be to build a workforce for that industry, through technical education and training for jobs in weapons production.[75]

A memo outlining O's briefing to Park and his advisers on plans for HCI and the defense industry, written a week after the announcement of the HCI Policy, underscores O's insistence that "the most important matter in the heavy and chemical industrialization policy is to train engineers and craftsmen, and to take measures to reinforce this."[76] The NSM followed the policy recommendations in O and Kim Kwangmo's HCI plan, *Kaep'yŏnnon*, especially regarding the domestic workforce and S & T development.[77] The SES technocrats prioritized such advances in the technical landscape because they were critical to localized weapons production.[78] Among various measures to promote S & T, R & D, and upgraded manufacturing, *Kaep'yŏnnon* proposed putting education reforms and requirements in place for training the first generation of technical workers for the heavy and chemical industries (which would of course bolster defense industrialization). Overall, the government set a goal of educating approximately 2 million technical workers by 1981: 110,000 scientists and engineers, 150,000 technicians, and 1.7 million craftspeople.[79] The qualifications for the three categories of employees were set as shown in table 4.1.

According to Kim Kwangmo, the national scientization plan, at least when it was initially conceived and planned by the SES, was at first exclusively part of the HCI Policy; in other words, national scientization was a task under O's authority in the SES. However, Ch'oe Hyŏngsŏp, the minister of science and technology, brought the NSM under his control in the MST and incorporated it into his plans to expand the movement's reach beyond what O had planned.[80] O could not object to Ch'oe's takeover, as Ch'oe, who had served under Park since 1962, was the technocrat with the longest tenure in the administration.[81] As a result, scientization was promoted separately by Ch'oe's MST, in parallel to the HCI Policy: the programs merged for the most part, but they were not fully coordinated. O's work on HCI was focused on developing the skilled labor needed for the defense industry; Ch'oe, while he supported HCI, wished to spread scientization more broadly, so that science and technology would be integrated into all aspects of peoples' lives.[82] The MST published books on various scientific and technological disciplines, offered resources and public lectures, and worked closely with local New Village Movement committees, scientific institutes, business organizations, and rural communities

Table 4.1.
Qualifications for S & T Workers

Employee category	Qualifications	Roles
Scientists and engineers (*kwahak kisulcha*)	Master's degree or PhD in a science or engineering field University undergraduate degree in a science or engineering field	R & D Production planning and management
Technicians (or field technicians) (*kisulgong* or *hyŏnjang kisulcha*)	High school diploma 3-year junior vocational college degree *or* High school diploma 2-year junior college degree *or* Middle school graduate 5-year vocational high school diploma	Production design Technical and procedure guidance
Craftspeople (*kinŭngsa*)	Technical high school diploma *or* Vocational training	Production and operation

SOURCES: Kim Hyung-A and Ryu, "1970-yŏndae kinŭnggong yangsŏng," 109–10; H. Kim, *Korean Skilled Workers*, 26; Kwahak Kisulch'ŏ, *Kwahak kisulgye illyŏk chawŏn chosa*, 18–19. See also PS, "Kinŭnggong yangsŏng ŭl wihan chonghap chŏngch'aek," Feb. 26, 1970, EA0023181, PA (Seongnam).

to involve citizens from all demographic groups and social classes in the NSM.

The NSM quickly spread its form of scientific nationalism as part of Park's campaign for self-reliance, resonating with a Korean populace that had been yearning for national independence and modernization since at least the colonial period.[83] While Park's authoritarian mobilization strategies often incited political resistance, the NSM, which interwove S & T policy with the goals of self-reliant national defense and a self-reliant economy, met with broad support.[84] The fear of escalating threats to national security further led most Koreans to accept, if not enthusiastically support, Park's goal of national development through scientific progress. The government's slogans—"nation building with science" (*kwahak ipkuk*), "technological self-reliance" (*kisul charip*), "nation building through industrialization" (*kongŏp ipkuk*), and "the scientization of all people"—were pervasive, deeply influencing the collective mindset.[85] They projected strength and a vision of a social order centered on advances in S & T, representing ideas that Sheila Jasanoff and Sang-Hyun Kim have called "sociotechnical imaginaries."[86] These ideas had become embedded in South Korean society by the late 1970s.

The cultural and ideological dimensions of Park's campaign for scientization once again brought to light the influence of colonial Japan. The Park regime's promotion of scientific nationalism and its slogans echoed what Park and his generation of Koreans had witnessed under Japan, when "technocratic patriotism" (*gijutsu hōkoku*) was promoted amid Japan's mobilization of science and technology for total war in the 1930s and 1940s.[87] As a result of Park's similar drive throughout the 1970s, South Korea's scientists, engineers, and technical workers gained social status and enjoyed elevated prestige in the ROK's science-friendly environment.

Creating Industrial Warriors

As its most significant achievement for defense industrialization, the NSM played a critical role in grooming a massive new workforce of young, mostly male technical workers, known as *kinŭngsa* (craftspeople), to work in the heavy and chemical industries (see table 4.1).[88] State propaganda and the president himself lauded these craftspeople as "industrial warriors" and praised their contributions, both technical and moral, to the development of new industries and the export economy.[89] Together with the ADD's scientists, these skilled workers were also called "special soldiers" (*t'ŭngnyebyŏng*). The government invested heavily in education and training programs to transform the ideology and improve the technical skills of this group of specialized workers, who were regarded by Park as indispensable for militarized industrialization.

One such investment took shape with the passing of the National Technical Qualification Act at the end of 1973. This legislation streamlined and standardized a national system of qualifications for licensed industrial workers. The qualification requirements were designed to ensure that the heavy and chemical industries were staffed with highly skilled craftspeople capable of executing precision manufacturing tasks. Under this act, individuals who graduated from a technical high school (*konggo*) or completed vocational training were required to pass the National Technical Qualification Test in order to work in HCI plants.[90] This licensing process enhanced not only the quality of manufacturing and final products but also the status and prestige of the qualified workers.

The HCI Policy also subsidized the establishment of technical high schools and the expansion of vocational training programs (the latter, which were divided into public training programs and company-run on-site training programs, were in place before the HCI Policy).[91] The state adopted the Improvement Plan for Korea's Technological Education System in 1973 and the Plan for the Priority Promotion of Technical High Schools in 1975, two measures that greatly increased the number of technical high schools—and students in them—as well as the trainers, training facilities, and equipment available to support this technical education.[92] The government offered generous financial and technological support, and these top-priority schools were held to strict standards in training skilled workers. The government recruited many male students from low-income families and rural regions by offering scholarships and tuition waivers, in addition to the opportunity for military service exemption.[93]

The Military Service Special Cases Law, enacted in 1973, codified military service exemptions for skilled workers in the heavy and chemical industries.[94] Under this law, male workers could apply for an exemption from Korea's three years of compulsory military service (required for all able-bodied Korean men) if they met two qualifications: a diploma from a three-year technical high school, and a class 2 license in a corresponding HCI field upon graduation.[95] If their exemption application was approved, in lieu of military service they were obliged to work for five years for one of the companies involved in HCI (in other words, in the defense industry).[96] Students who earned an advanced degree in a scientific or engineering field, as well as university graduates in science or engineering who passed the public exam for work in top research institutions such as the ADD and KIST, were also eligible for service exemptions.[97] ADD researchers who were recruited by the government to work at the agency were also offered the exemption.

It would be a mistake to think that the exemption from military service, attractive though it was, meant less regimentation for trainees compared with their peers in the armed forces. Indeed, what was in fact an "exemption through alternative service" involved trading one form of militarism for another, as skilled workers toiled in highly militarized industrial environments under the HCI Policy and the Yusin system. Through their formal education, technical training, and licensing, and subsequently their work in the factories, the nation's new industrial warriors completely internalized Park's militarized system of thought and the priorities of security, anticommunism, and economic nationalism.

The personal interviews I conducted with individuals who had been skilled workers in the 1970s confirmed many details about the militarized education of young men during this time.[98] Technical schools were run like training camps, and students were taught to have the attitude and discipline of soldiers serving and sacrificing for a cause higher than themselves. Often, military personnel held positions as school administrators, and students were subjected to intense thought training and disciplined daily regimens, as if they were being prepared for war.[99] Following three years of a technical high school program that mimicked the rigidity and discipline of armed forces training, graduates would spend five years working in a militarized factory setting, which meant that their lives would be governed by military-style discipline for at least eight years. Vocational training centers took the same approach. Kim Hujin, who in 1977 attended the Hanbaek Vocational Training Center, which trained skilled workers for the machinery industry, said that active-duty military officers staffed the center and its dormitory. According to Kim, "Each day after we woke up at 6:00 a.m., we had to do *kubo* [a Korean version of a military running drill, similar to "double time"], led by a student department representative [who was selected based on his prior military service]. After breakfast, we would be training from 8:00 a.m. to 10:00 p.m., so no one could escape. . . . Even on the weekends, we had to receive written permission to go out. . . . After students graduated and acquired a technical license, they ended up going to work for big defense companies like Hyundai, Kia, and Korea Tacoma."[100]

From their days as student-trainees to their employment in the defense factories (as described in chapter 3), workers were required to always abide by government- and company-imposed rules and regulations: they wore uniforms, participated in group drills and exercises, and followed rules of order and hierarchy. In other words, they basically worked like members of an industrial army under a centralized command structure. Mr. Kang (full name withheld for privacy), who had a class 2 license in chemical explosives and received a military exemption in return for his tenure at the An'gang factory of Poongsan Metal Corporation, reflected on his work in the 1970s: "At that time, regardless of whether we were being recognized or feeling proud [of working in a defense firm], because of the military-style system we suffered a lot. In many situations we were subjected to personal indignities. The supervision of work was basically authoritarian and imposed from above. . . . I do believe such efforts became the foundation of our nation's development. . . . But there was definitely a sacrifice."[101]

Building the National Infrastructure for Research and Development

The broad structural changes under the NSM and the HCI Policy not only created a highly skilled workforce but also modernized the nation's technological infrastructure. The emergence of new, localized research capabilities and the indigenized production of modern weapons by the private sector in the 1970s marked a significant shift from the 1960s, when US and Japanese foreign aid had been the only sources of technological growth among large Korean corporations such as Hanjin, Daelim, and Hyundai. The reduction of US military support in the late 1960s and subsequent US arms restrictions pushed the ROK to upgrade its S & T infrastructure to establish its own defense technology base. Furthermore, because the nation faced rising costs for technology licenses and patent fees from foreign suppliers, heavy reliance on technology imports became financially untenable.[102] These challenges prompted the architects of the HCI Policy to build up the nation's R & D infrastructure and thereby improve the capabilities of the private sector. For both economic and military purposes, the government had to count on domestic companies to innovate independently. Under Park's command and through the centralized promotion of S & T, the government enacted new laws to spur businesses to invest in R & D, founded new research institutes to support corporate R & D, and created geographically concentrated research clusters to optimize technology exchanges and development. With this state support, private enterprise indigenized industrial technologies for weapons production.

In the early 1970s the government introduced several laws that offered businesses incentives to engage in R & D in the technology-intensive heavy and chemical industries. For example, the 1973 Military Procurement Law (MPL), a major legislative initiative encouraging businesses to participate in the defense industry (see chapter 3), provided publicly financed supplementary funds, low-interest loans, and tax cuts to cover the costs of weapons R & D.[103] Articles 8 and 9 of the MPL sanctioned state subsidies for businesses' procurement of technology transfers, technical training, resources, and facilities to advance R & D for independent weapons technologies.[104] Article 10 authorized the state to appoint businesses and research institutes to develop specific weapons projects of its choosing. Under this article, top companies were selected to work with the ADD on developing new weapon prototypes. In this way, the contracting system for localized arms production under the MPL made sure that the chaebol were actively involved in R & D for advanced weapons.

In addition to the MPL, in 1972 and 1973 several laws written under Park's third Five-Year Science and Technology Promotion Plan expanded private-sector technical abilities and encouraged businesses to invest in R & D. These included the Technology Development Promotion Act, the Technical Services Support Act, and the Support of Specific Research Institutes Act.[105] The resulting legal architecture created conditions favorable for the broad diffusion of R & D capabilities in the private sector. To encourage private firms to initiate R & D in support of HCI and national defense, the government offered further financial incentives, including tax exemptions to offset corporate research costs, government reserve funds for R & D, and favorable depreciation rates on purchases of equipment.[106] From 1972 to 1980 South Korea increased R & D expenditures from 12 billion won to 211.7 billion won, a nearly eighteenfold increase in less than a decade.[107]

The laws and regulations promoting R & D infrastructure had their intended effect: a rapidly increasing number of private-sector businesses, in conjunction with government-funded research institutes (GFRIs), began engaging in R & D. Before the institution of the HCI Policy, most Korean companies had been reluctant to invest in R & D. They focused on manufacturing and complacently relied on meager research funds from the state for the development of new industrial technology.[108] Eventually, in the face of the national scientization campaign and government pressure to look beyond the assembly line to R & D, the chaebol began investing in their own corporate research. Of course, their sudden increase in R & D participation must be understood in the context of the Yusin rule and its political impact on the chaebol, including both its effectiveness and its tyranny when chaebol performance was assessed as poor. The number of corporate-affiliated research institutes was soon growing rapidly and almost doubled in two years, going from 167 in 1973 to 303 in 1975. Although this rate of increase plateaued from 1975 to 1979, the number of researchers in the business sector continued to rise, increasing from 2,655 in 1975 to 4,405 in 1979.[109]

The infrastructure for R & D was further advanced by the Support of Specific Research Institutes Act of 1973, under which the state established GFRIs to specialize in research for the heavy and chemical industries. The GFRIs' raison d'être was to help corporations meet the technological demands of HCI.[110] Research organizations such as KIST, the ADD, and the Korea Advanced Institute of Science (KAIS), also categorized as GFRIs, were already in place prior to 1973. However, over the remainder of the decade the state funded thirteen new GFRIs, nearly all of which worked on research related to improving infrastructure or providing resources (such as energy) to support one or more of the six heavy and chemical industries: machinery, steels, electronics, special metals, shipbuilding, and chemicals (including petrochemicals).[111] By the end of 1978 the ROK had sixteen GFRIs: nine in Taedŏk, four in Seoul, one in Kumi, and two in Ch'angwŏn.[112] Like KIST and the ADD, the new GFRIs received financial and material support through government contracts and had to comply with government research requests, although they otherwise operated as autonomous civilian research labs.[113]

These GFRIs furnished Korean companies with R & D support and specific technologies to help them become high-tech manufacturers and exporters of HCI-sector products, with the integrated aim of creating a self-sustaining defense industry.[114] In the new business environment of the 1970s, the institutes actively collaborated with each other and with private corporations in a concentrated effort to achieve Park's HCI goals.[115] Their research network transformed domestic R & D and opened new pathways for advancing technological and industrial capabilities.

To enhance collaboration, the new GFRIs and corporate R & D laboratories established in the late 1970s were built within South Korea's newly established HCI industrial complexes in Ch'angwŏn and Kumi, or in a new research-focused complex in Taedŏk (the older government-funded research entities, including KIST and KAIS, were located in the Hongnŭng research complex in Seoul). Three of the new GFRIs were assigned to particular industrial complexes according to their fields of specialization. For example, the Korea Institute of Electronic Technology was established in the electronics industrial complex in Kumi, where electronics firms such as Goldstar also built their corporate research laboratories in order to collaborate with the institute.[116] Similarly, the Korea Institute of Machinery and Metals and the Korea Electrotechnology Research Institute were located in Ch'angwŏn, making it convenient for them to offer R & D assistance to the machinery (and some electronics) firms there. Altogether, the research complexes in Seoul and Taedŏk and the industrial complexes in Ch'angwŏn and Kumi provided infrastructure to support corporate-GFRI partnerships in each HCI sector and to help private firms maximize their R & D potential and expand their mass production capabilities.[117] The government largely used public funding sources, such as the National Investment Fund, and drew from foreign investors involved in joint projects for additional capital to build the new GFRI facilities and training centers. Additionally, companies themselves were relied upon to invest in the R & D infrastructure.[118]

Taedŏk Science Town: The Locus of Research and Development

Private-sector resources were in fact vital to the growth of South Korea's burgeoning R & D infrastructure. The new research-centered complex built under the HCI Policy, Taedŏk Science Town, is an example in microcosm of how the Blue House mobilized private companies to work with GFRIs. Prior to HCI, Seoul's Hongnŭng neighborhood, where KIST, the KAIS, and the ADD were located, had been the site of the only research complex in South Korea. However, Hongnŭng was too congested to accommodate additional research institutes, and Seoul's proximity to the Demilitarized Zone also made it vulnerable to infiltration by North Korea. With both space and security in mind, in 1974 the MST planned a second research complex to be situated in Taejŏn, in the district of Taedŏk, approximately ninety-three miles (150 km) south of Seoul. In spite of Park's enthusiasm for the project, plans for Taedŏk did not take off because the MST's budget for the new science cluster called for an enormous amount of government funding. In March 1976, when Park was briefed on the MST's lack of progress on the complex, he transferred oversight of the project to his SES technocrats in the Blue House with orders to expedite construction.[119] Significantly, according to Kim Kwangmo of the HCI Planning Corps, the shift in leadership for the construction of the Taedŏk complex also shifted authority for the National Scientization Movement from the MST to the HCI Planning Corps within the SES, because Park saw Taedŏk as critical to the success of his national scientization effort.[120]

Within a month of receiving Park's order, O Wŏnch'ŏl and Kim Kwangmo had devised a new plan. Instead of relying on government financing, the HCI Planning Corps instituted obligatory corporate funding for the development of Taedŏk's new research complex.[121] Specifically, the government would fund the construction of the GFRI facilities, but companies would be responsible for building their own R & D facilities in Taedŏk to collaborate with the GFRIs. In other words, the Blue House required that companies commit significant resources to joint research with the newly established GFRIs by financing and constructing corporate satellite laboratories, which would partner with the GFRIs to develop HCI-related technologies.[122] However, when the corporations involved showed little willingness to voluntarily relocate their research facilities to the remote new science complex, the HCI Planning Corps, backed by the Blue House, mandated the relocation of private research institutes. They even required corporations' joint investment in the construction of one of the GFRIs, the Korea Institute of Chemical Research. Putting that kind of direct pressure on businesses had been unthinkable for the MST, but it was possible for O and his crew in the HCI Planning Corps because the SES acted on direct orders from the president.[123] The government also granted tax credits and other financial incentives to companies that set up research facilities in Taedŏk. In 1976 such companies as Samsung, Hyundai, and Rakhŭi hwahak (which became LG Chemical), and their subcontractors, began to establish new R & D labs in Taedŏk Science Town. The complex had a total of nine GFRIs by the end of the decade.

The Taedŏk design for government-corporate partnerships in R & D reflected the ROK's new model for technological innovation. Under this model, the corporations' satellite laboratories began contributing to advances in domestic technology by conducting independent research and by transferring their knowledge of foreign technologies, which they had acquired from overseas corporations, to the GFRIs.[124] The research infrastructure established at Taedŏk—with corporate laboratories working around a central government-funded institute—illustrates how R & D in South Korea was fed by two streams: one from the government and the other from private-company labs that imported foreign technology. Taedŏk's organization fostered collaborations among GFRIs as well, because their proximity in the same complex allowed them to easily share knowledge and resources. And because the GFRIs developed technologies beneficial to the defense industry, the ADD was involved in both their construction and their research.[125]

Localizing Military Technology

While GFRIs and the new research cluster in Taedŏk Science Town formed the technological base for South Korea's defense-related heavy and chemical industries, the ADD retained its unique role as the only research body specializing in weapons R & D. Because it operated under Park's direct oversight and engaged in advanced weapons development, the ADD received more state assistance than the other GFRIs and was able to acquire technologies that were unavailable to the others. Government spending on the ADD's weapons R & D increased more than fourfold in the late 1970s, from 349.4 billion won in 1975 to 1.5 trillion won in 1979.[126] The number of employees at the agency also increased throughout the decade, from 60 in 1970 to 2,810 in 1979.[127] With these advantages and full support from the Blue House, the ADD became the leading force in advancing the nation's R & D efforts.

Individual Efforts of Korean Researchers

Although macroeconomic factors, such as US military aid and the ROK's technocratic policies, were important in furthering South Korea's military modernization, microeconomic factors also played a valuable role. These included the efforts of the Korean scientists and engineers (whom I collectively refer to as "researchers" in the ADD context) who worked tirelessly, often at the risk of personal health and safety, to manufacture weapons and develop new defense technologies. Internal documents, in-person and published interviews, and the memoirs of former ADD researchers make it clear that the ROK's military advances in weaponry depended on the commitment, sacrifice, ingenuity, and even stealth of individual ADD researchers who devoted themselves to the cause of self-reliant national defense (fig. 4.2).[128]

FIG. 4.2. A team of ADD scientists (along with several external visitors) at the agency's testing site in Anhŭng, South Korea, in 1979. The group includes in the back row (all from the left) Kim Ch'angsik (third), Sim Munt'aek (seventh), Yi Kyŏngsŏ (eighth), and Ku Sanghoe (tenth). *Source:* Photo courtesy of Kim Ch'angsik.

In the beginning, the ADD's researchers had to work from scratch. Because they lacked both the knowledge and the facilities to manufacture most of the weapons they were assigned to produce, they were forced to reverse engineer them from US models. Working against the odds and under a very tight deadline, the researchers adopted a militarized mindset, seeing themselves as scientific soldiers (or "special soldiers," as the government called them) serving under Blue House orders to produce South Korea's first independently manufactured weapons. In the context of escalating threats from the DPRK and the withdrawal of US ground troops, the researchers joined forces with Park for the cause of national security, their relentless efforts for weapons development embodying Park's campaign for "technological self-reliance" (*kisul charip*) and "localized production" (*kuksanhwa*) to achieve independent national defense.[129] Ku Sanghoe, who led the ADD's Lightning Operation (discussed in chapter 2), said he and his colleagues were dedicated to acquiring "the ability to make the weapons we wanted, with our own hands" with the goal of establishing South Korea's sovereignty over weapon technologies.[130]

Some of the ADD researchers' early achievements are still celebrated because they prevailed over such incredible challenges. The following anecdotes illustrate how those involved in the defense industry's earliest projects overcame significant obstacles to develop the weapons ordered by the Blue House.[131] According to the researchers, technology in South Korea at that time was critically underdeveloped, and companies lacked the precision machine skills required to produce modern firearms for the military.[132] Said An Tongman, an ADD researcher in the 1970s who was the agency's director from 2005 to 2008, "At a time when there were no specialized [raw] materials or machine processing facilities [for weapons production], and there was no proper system for test and evaluation [T & E] or quality assurance, everything had to be developed over and over again, with constant trials and errors."[133] Yet O Wŏnch'ŏl's orders to the ADD in 1971 for the Lightning Operation were to produce prototypes based on US weapons.

Han P'ilsun recalled that when he was first assigned the task of making grenades for the Lightning Operation, he had to create something out of virtually nothing—and he had no access to a facility nor to any equipment for testing grenade prototypes. At the time, according to

Han, he and his colleagues were unsure whether 380-gram grenades should be designed with an apple shape (spherical) or a sweet potato shape (ovoid). The question was which shape would give grenades the longer range. With limited resources, Han used unconventional methods, such as throwing stones of both shapes, to determine the optimal design for the grenades. Based on these experiments, he chose a spherical grenade. Han, who became the first Korean scientist to develop domestically produced grenades, proved to be a major innovator with his independent development of other essential military products as well.[134]

A former officer in the ROK Air Force and one of the original scientists recruited from the military by the ADD in 1970, Han wrote in his memoir that he was motivated in his work by a mix of personal pride and competitive spirit, particularly toward the civilian scientists Sim Munt'aek brought on after becoming the ADD's director in 1972.[135] Han also clashed with O, whose sudden promotion to Park's senior presidential secretary had given him complete oversight of the ADD, despite his civilian background.[136] When Han proposed the development of laser weapons and night vision equipment, O rejected the idea, preferring to delegate laser development to the civilian scientists at KIST or the Korea Atomic Energy Research Institute (KAERI), whom O believed to be more technically qualified.[137] Despite O's rejection, Han persisted in pursuing the laser development project. He collaborated with university and military scientists, invited foreign technical experts to seminars, and experimented relentlessly through many nights in the lab. In 1973, Han succeeded in developing a carbon dioxide laser, South Korea's first domestically produced laser.[138] Han also developed a Korean-made bulletproof helmet—after borrowing 200,000 won from his wife to fund that project.[139] His ability to innovate and improvise played a critical role in the success of the ADD's weapons-development program.

Like Han, who was willing to do whatever it took to achieve his goals, other ADD researchers dug into new weapons projects with their bare hands. Sŏ Chŏnguk, for example, developed Korea's first military radio-communication device, the KPRC-6, a lightweight, transistor-type military radio that replaced the heavier model the ROK military had been using.[140] The military had often conducted its training exercises without radios because its devices were outdated. Recognizing the need for a newer model of military radio, Sŏ and his ADD team collaborated with an outside company and worked independently, without government aid or funding, due to budget limitations. Sŏ even paid for the research expenses out of his own pocket.[141] After Sŏ made a test transmission on their prototype radio with President Park on July 7, 1972, Park was impressed and offered Sŏ his full support to indigenize military radio technology. Sŏ's work led to the first generation of Korean telecommunications equipment.[142] Through the independent agency of researchers who, like Han and Sŏ, went beyond the work orders that came down from O and the Blue House, the ADD pursued and developed many new technologies.

To produce new weapons within the government's minimal time frame, ADD researchers expedited the manufacturing of weapons parts and applicable technologies through rigorous but often unsafe experimentation. Kim Ch'angsik, who was assigned to develop antipersonnel mines and grenades in 1972, said in an interview, "I had only samples [from which] to make the new weapons." He added, "I had to develop the weapons in the face of danger because time was against us. . . . I worked day and night, risking my life, working with dangerous gunpowder. . . . [W]ithout the TDP [technical data package from the United States], . . . I learned the technology by disassembling the sample and reassembling it."[143] Kim worked on the initiators for high explosives, a task that could trigger accidental explosions with slight changes in temperature or friction. He stated that the researchers who, like him, worked directly in the labs (he called them "practitioners in the field" [*silmuja*]) could not have worked under such dangerous conditions, putting their lives at stake, without some deep sense of patriotic duty. The ADD promoted these efforts and encouraged the researchers' competitive spirit by offering material performance incentives—including Olympic-style medals, orders of merit, and presidential awards—for those who succeeded in developing new weapons. Researchers' dangerous working conditions worsened with Park's secret Yulgok Operation, starting in 1974, when the state ordered the covert development of advanced weapons that had been withheld from Korea by the United States, including guided missiles and nuclear arms.

As another strategy to localize weapon technologies, in its procurement deals with foreign firms the ADD increasingly demanded that it receive the licensed transfer of original technologies from foreign suppliers, rather than purchase final products.[144] As the ADD secured foreign technologies, it transferred them to defense contractors, who in turn adapted the new technologies to improve their own R & D and domesticate production.

Bringing Technology to the Private Sector

When ADD researchers pioneered new research and weapons products, they introduced the resulting new technologies and equipment to Korean industries, thus helping them upgrade their method of arms development and manufacturing. However, the process of transferring and disseminating advanced foreign technologies and redesigning them for use in Korea required many adaptations on the part of the ADD to make up for differences in technical knowledge, language, procedures, and measurement systems between foreign and domestic manufacturers.

Even when the United States offered TDPs, the technical data could not be directly applied by Korean manufacturers. For example, US blueprints were in English, with measurements in inches and feet, whereas South Korea used the metric system. Furthermore, US blueprints often did not include all the information needed for manufacturing the products, such as the raw materials used. Therefore Korean engineers could not produce US-model weapons simply by looking at the original blueprints. It was up to the ADD researchers to "Koreanize" (*han'gukhwa*) the Americans' blueprints, revising and adapting them to fit the Korean manufacturing system before transferring them to company engineers to apply in the field.[145] According to Kim Kyegwan, a former mechanical engineer with Daewoo Heavy Industries, "The ADD provided a standard technical manual for manufacturing weapons, customized for Korean design engineers, and we made each product based on that. The ADD also converted all numbers in the US blueprints from inches to meters."[146]

Initially, because Korean corporate engineers lacked the high-level machining skills required to make weapons, the ADD researchers themselves received training in precision manufacturing at the Fine Instrument Center, a government institute for the education of workers in heavy industries.[147] They underwent this training so that they could then teach the engineers themselves. After their training the ADD researchers performed hands-on demonstrations for corporate engineers on the use of new precision equipment, to ensure the production of high-quality weapon parts.[148] This practical guidance, along with the ADD's data transfers, broadened the dissemination of critical knowledge and aided localized production.[149]

As the corporations improved their weapons production, R & D tasks were gradually divided between the ADD and businesses: the ADD focused on system design, and manufacturers focused on licensed production, including process engineering and the detailed design of product parts.[150] Kim Yŏngsu, who formerly served as deputy director of the ADD and led the development of Korea's first submarine and torpedo at the ADD's Chinhae Machinery Depot, described the process as follows:

> During my time at Chinhae [in the 1970s], the ADD mainly concentrated on the conceptual design [in weapon development]. We first designed the concept, then analyzed [any possible] threats to the concept. The next step was to set up a target performance of the product, and then we would do a simulation [responding to a threat]. And then we calculated the price and the period for development—this was all included in the conceptual engineering stage. . . . Afterward, we approached companies to participate in the project. In some cases only one company could do it, but when that company was not set, or when the field itself was too new, we selected multiple companies for the detailed design of the product and then the manufacturing of the weapon. . . . [In one case,] corporate engineers from Goldstar came to the ADD to work together with the agency on the detailed design and manufacture of a part [for the Korean-model torpedo]. . . . After the part was produced, the ADD ran the test and evaluation [T & E] of the part with the company.[151]

Kim emphasized that the ADD's role in managing its relationships with private firms was critical for the success of weapons projects:

> The ADD had to be very good at evaluating as well as respecting the companies' capabilities and knowing their limits, and guiding them to make the most of their capabilities as a part of our system. Since all the

> weapon parts had to be assembled, the ADD and all companies involved shared a common destiny (*kongdong unmyŏng*), which meant that even if all went well except for one part, then everything would be a failure. There are so many parts and factors that went into a weapon. . . . In my view, the ADD was excellent at managing these aspects of relationships with the companies, including selecting the right corporations, for example, for precision missile development as well as for the military projects at Chinhae.[152]

According to Kim, "At times the corporations refused the contracts because they felt the projects were not profitable or they could not meet the quantity demanded. The ADD sometimes had to plead with the corporations to take on projects. On the flip side, there were [other] companies that were begging to take on projects."[153] The contracting process also varied with different weapon projects, Kim said. For example, regular defense contracts were arranged by the MND with select corporations, but for certain projects, like the submarine, the ADD selected the primary contractors and contracted with them directly.

On the other side of the relationship, the businesses that entered into contracts had to strictly abide by ADD regulations on product quality, which was subject to verification by the ADD itself. Im Haesu, a former skilled worker who, in the late 1970s, was involved with developing the barrels of the US-model 105 mm and 155 mm howitzers as well as the missile launch pad at Kia's factory, described his work with the ADD as follows: "When we produced the [weapon] parts, the personnel would come from the ADD to examine all the parts. They checked the measurement of each weapon part and tested its performance, and only after passing this test could the weapon parts be approved and sent over [for assembly]."[154]

Despite the dogged efforts and achievements of ADD researchers and corporate engineers, technical issues festered below the surface, causing cracks in the foundation hastily laid by Park's government in its expedited push to develop a defense industry. As a result, the ADD was sometimes unable to maintain and repair domestically produced weapons or troubleshoot malfunctions. As a case in point, the MND discovered in 1977 that some Korean-made Vulcan antiaircraft guns that had been installed on active-duty navy speedboats were exhibiting breechblock failures when fired. This problem arose even though the ADD and its contractors had worked from original data supplied in US-provided TDPs for Vulcan parts and ammunition.[155] The ADD struggled to resolve the issue. In July, SES undersecretary Yi Sŏkp'yo, who oversaw reporting on Vulcan development to the Blue House, was fatally injured during a failed test launch of Vulcan at the ADD test site. Subsequent investigations revealed that defective detonator materials, produced by Olin Corporation of the United States, had caused the malfunctions in the Vulcan ammunition.[156] Thus even when the agency worked from technical data made available by the United States, weapons manufacturing was not always successful. Yi's high-profile death was one of the few publicized mishaps in weapons experiments. Many other deaths of scientists, engineers, and skilled workers occurred behind the scenes in South Korea's labs, testing sites, and defense factories, as technical problems and malfunctions persisted throughout the 1970s.[157]

Building Polar Bear

A prime example of the agency of ADD researchers is their role in the undercover development of South Korea's first ballistic missile, Polar Bear (Paekkom).[158] Polar Bear, a variant of a guided surface-to-surface missile, would later be recognized as the most iconic achievement of Park's self-reliant national defense policy, especially as it was carried out in the face of US arms control efforts.[159] The missile program, backed by 200 billion won in government funds (about $440 million), ran from 1972 to 1979.[160] Yet even with the government's extensive investment and involvement, Polar Bear succeeded largely through the efforts of individual researchers who strove mightily to overcome technical barriers and lead South Korea to become only the seventh nation to build its own ballistic missile.[161] Through these endeavors, researchers at the ADD far exceeded the expectations set by state policies, government incentives, and foreign technical aid. The project leader, Yi Kyŏngsŏ, called their achievement a "miracle."[162]

In April 1972, two months after Sim became director of the ADD, Park issued an order for the agency to develop a precision-guided ballistic missile.[163] The best and brightest researchers from the ADD and outside research institutions were recruited for the assignment, including

Yi, who was then a KIST researcher and a mechanical engineer with a degree from the Massachusetts Institute of Technology. Despite being just thirty-four years old, and already spearheading KIST's missile research, Yi was named project manager of what he and Sim codenamed "Aviation Industry Development."[164]

Following the launch of the Yulgok Operation, Aviation Industry Development was officially implemented on May 14, 1974, and it quickly expanded to become the ADD's top project. Because the United States, which constantly surveilled the ADD, was opposed to South Korea's development of long-range missiles, the Polar Bear project was conducted in great secrecy. Researchers recruited for the project were told that they would not be allowed to return home for more than four months. They were not told where they would be going or how long the journey would take. Director Sim invited the researchers' wives to a dinner at which he explained: "Your husbands are going on a four-month business trip abroad to carry out the most important and most secretive mission in the country. They cannot engage in any outside correspondence during this time. Do not try to find out where they're going and why they're going. Don't ask when they're coming back. I will guarantee their safety."[165]

The project's recruits could not use research facilities at ADD headquarters, since JUSMAG–K had its office there. Under the cover of night, the group of elite researchers was ushered to a "safe house," a remote apartment complex where the following rules were issued by security personnel: "The window[s] must be closed twenty-four hours a day; never open the curtains; don't go outside during the day; and restrict phone use to work-related purposes by designated persons."[166] The ADD researchers, including Ku Sanghoe, Yi Kyŏngsŏ, Hong Chaehak, and An Tongman, lived and worked together at the safe house. As Ku recalled, they had to endure the sizzling heat of summer inside the house, as they could not go out or open a window because "we had to avoid the eyes of the United States."[167]

According to a memoir written by An, Kim Pyŏnggyo, and Cho T'aehwan, all of whom were involved in the Polar Bear program at the time, the ADD researchers struggled to devise an initial development plan, since only six countries in the world had the surface-to-surface missile technology that they were tasked with creating from scratch.[168]

Pak Chunbok, another ADD researcher involved in the program, wrote in his memoir, "To produce a guided missile propulsion system, we needed a propellant, along with technology from various fields, and we needed a combustion tube and nozzle to charge the propellant, and the propellant-charging equipment and facilities, all of which were like 'blank sheets' [for us] at the time."[169] The lack of raw materials was another challenge. As An Tongman noted in an interview, missile construction required seamless pipes made of stainless steel, but South Korea lacked the appropriate raw materials as well as the welding and rolling skills and heat-mitigation technology for casting the pipes. As previously mentioned, Korean manufacturers at the time also lacked the precision machining skills required to cut steel for weapon parts.[170]

According to An, Kim, and Cho, while the ADD debated what the project's first step should be, O Wŏnch'ŏl clashed with Yi.[171] O argued that they should first develop small, short-range missiles and then transition to long-range missiles, but Yi insisted that they should work on long-range missiles first—because their development (which required technology superior to that used in short-range missiles) would naturally encompass the technology they would need for short-range missiles. When the issue was brought to Park, he sided with Yi, giving him full authority over missile development.[172] Under Yi, the ADD naturally decided to pursue the long-range missile first, but to do so it had to acquire technologies and skills from abroad.

When the ADD first approached US missile manufacturer McDonnell Douglas to purchase ballistic missile technology in 1974, the US Department of State intervened and rejected the ADD's request. However, a rare opportunity presented itself a year later. Yi, who headed the ADD's negotiations with McDonnell Douglas, said the ADD got very "lucky" when some US defense companies, including McDonnell Douglas, started to see sales dwindle with the thaw of Cold War relations and the new East-West détente.[173] This situation prompted the US companies to be more willing to sell their technologies to the Koreans.[174] Furthermore, South Korea's aggressive efforts to procure missile technologies from alternative foreign suppliers in 1974 and 1975 put pressure on the Ford administration to approve Park's longstanding request for missile propulsion technology, despite ongoing objections from the Department of State.[175] In the end, McDonnell Douglas managed to persuade the Department of State to approve its contract with the ADD, under the condition that the agreement would only involve the ADD's participation in the company's missile research, without any actual technology transfer.[176] Subsequently, under the terms of a joint research agreement, ADD researchers were given the opportunity to participate in McDonnell Douglas's development of an upgraded surface-to-surface version of the company's Nike Hercules (NH) missile.[177] With what its researchers learned through their work with McDonnell Douglas, the ADD hoped to design a Korean version of the NH for the Polar Bear program. At first the US company refused to allow the Korean scientists to participate in the research for the preliminary design stage—the first of three stages—of the converted NH, saying that they could only be involved in the later design stages. However, when Yi insisted that his researchers had to participate in R & D from the beginning, McDonnell Douglas conceded, provided that the ADD would complete and pay for the remaining stages as part of their contract, which covered all three stages.[178]

Once the agreement was reached, the ADD sent fifteen of its researchers to the McDonnell Douglas facility in California. They worked there for six months, from July 1975 to January 1976, with a team of twenty Americans on the preliminary design for the modified NH missile.[179] The Koreans acquired far more data from the US company than the "preliminary design" phase of the contract formally allowed. According to Yi, McDonnell Douglas employees did not hold back from sharing technical secrets in their conversations with and around their visitors from the ADD, and they did not always restrict the Koreans from viewing company data and documents.[180] ADD team members took copious notes, writing down entire discussions with the American engineers, and took advantage of their sharing of information at every opportunity.

Often working through the night after returning to their housing, the ADD researchers cataloged findings and data that were unavailable to them in Korea, especially on surface-to-surface missile guidance and control system requirements.[181] They even secretly secured a trove of internal data by "borrowing" documents from the company's files, hiding them in their clothes as they left the facility, and photocopying them overnight before returning the papers the next day.[182] In the end, their six months with McDonell Douglas allowed ADD's researchers to acquire most of the technical data they needed to proceed with missile design and development. As Yi has acknowledged, if the ADD had had to conduct the same R & D on its own, it would have cost considerably more money and time.[183] After completing the preliminary design stage of its joint research with McDonnell Douglas, the ADD concluded that it could now independently design missiles with the technology it had already acquired. The agency reneged on the remaining two stages of its contract—valued at $20 million for the design phase—citing a shortage of funds as the reason.[184]

On a related assignment, the ADD dispatched a ten-member team to the Picatinny Arsenal in Dover, New Jersey, where the Koreans stayed from September 1975 to February 1976 as part of the US-ROK Scientists and Engineers Exchange Program sponsored by the US Department of Defense; this program allowed ADD researchers to receive technical training at US military research institutes and arsenals.[185] Kim Ch'angsik, the aforementioned explosives researcher in the ADD, was one of the participants (figs. 4.3 and 4.4). A member of an R & D division working on the composite propellant used in missile propulsion, he was

FIG. 4.3. Kim Ch'angsik receiving the certification of his completion of the Scientists and Engineers Exchange Program at Picatinny Arsenal in New Jersey in February 1976. *Source:* Photo courtesy of Kim Ch'angsik.

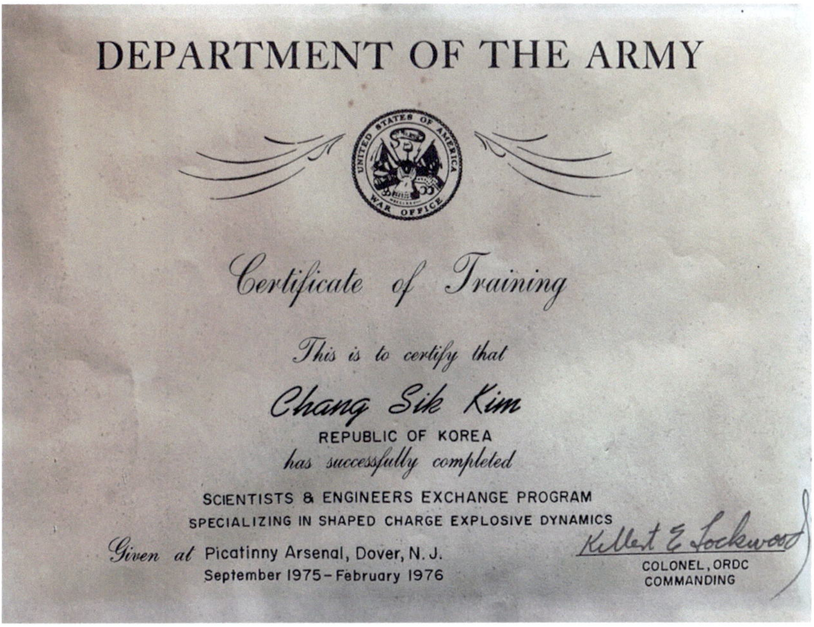

FIG. 4.4. Kim Ch'angsik's certificate from the Scientists and Engineers Exchange Program sponsored by the US Department of the Army. *Source:* Photo courtesy of Kim Ch'angsik.

also tasked with learning how to develop the shaped charge for antitank explosives. Kim reflected in an interview on the challenges and hardships ADD researchers faced, as the group started with little technical knowledge of military explosives and had to overcome language barriers: "Most of us on these missions abroad," he said, "had to resort to 'stealing' the technologies [copying documents, pilfering samples], since there was no way we could acquire them on our own. . . . These were not the types of technologies that we could acquire by merely purchasing [them] or asking questions."[186]

Because the ROK government feared that its engineers might refuse to return to Korea, or might sell classified information to the Americans, participants in such exchange programs had to leave their family members behind when they went abroad. Nonetheless, for the Korean researchers such trips were worth the trouble in order to fulfill their defense assignments. On Kim's training expedition, he gained access to technical manuals and acquired valuable knowledge about explosives and propellants; he was also able to bring back to Korea critical samples, which contributed to the development of other types of high-grade military explosives.

In 1976 the ADD sent another research team abroad, this time to the Société nationale des poudres et explosifs (SNPE) in France, as part of the ADD's contract with SNPE to receive training in the manufacturing of missile propellant.[187] On returning to South Korea, ADD scientists who had received training in France, along with those who had trained in the United States, were tasked with combining and applying their new skills to advance domestic missile technology. In addition to contracting for missile-related training and technology, the ADD purchased a propellant plant from the Lockheed Propulsion Company in the United States and then managed to secure technical assistance and on-site training in propulsion technology from both Lockheed and SNPE.[188]

The propellant facilities from Lockheed were installed in 1977 in the ADD's secret plant in Taejŏn, which was disguised as a machinery factory called "Taejŏn Machinery Depot" (Taejŏn Kikyech'ang).[189] Construction of this factory, spanning from 1974 to 1977, had been conducted under the cover name "Sacred Farm," with stringent security measures in place throughout the period.[190] Every individual associated with the construction, including representatives of the construction company and their workers, underwent rigorous background checks. Only government-approved individuals were allowed inside the construction site—even the governor of South Ch'ungchŏng Province was denied access at one point due to his failure to apply for permission in advance. Within the factory itself, a strict access control system was maintained, and only a limited number of authorized personnel could gain entry to certain areas. According to Kim Kwangmo, who reported on the planning and construction of the factory under the auspices of the SES, the Taejŏn Machinery Depot was basically "a missile factory"—the development site for Korea's ballistic missiles.[191]

On September 26, 1978, the ADD successfully launched South Korea's first indigenously developed ballistic missile, the Polar Bear. Officially known as the NHK-1, Polar Bear was a modified version of the NH and functioned as a guided surface-to-surface missile (see figs. 4.5 and 4.6).[192] Behind the scenes, according to Ku and An, ADD researchers

FIG. 4.5. South Korea's first ballistic missile, Polar Bear, in 1978. *Source:* National Archives of Korea; file no. CET0034427.

had dealt with many technical failures and issues, even up until the night before the launch.[193] The biggest problem was that the tracking radar could not lock on with the guidance system of the missile on the launch pad. The researchers eventually discovered they needed to put an attenuator cap on the antenna of the missile to regulate the electronic signal it received from the tracking radar. An attenuator cap was not immediately available, however, so they tore off the foil inside a cigarette pack and wrapped that around the tip of the antenna. With this temporary fix, the tracking radar finally locked with the guided missile.[194] The following day, with Park in attendance at the launch, researchers watched nervously, their palms sweating, until the missile

FIG. 4.6. An Tongman (right) shaking hands with President Park after the launch of Polar Bear on September 26, 1978. *Source*: Photo courtesy of An Tongman.

had been launched and sailed through the air. Their hard work had paid off. A year later, in October 1979, the ADD purchased new missile navigation technology, the Inertial Navigation System, from England to replace the radar-based system of the NHK-1, thus upgrading the missile to the NHK-2 (or Polar Bear 2, which evolved into the Hyunmoo-1 missile in the 1980s).[195] As a result, the ADD ultimately created a hybrid ballistic missile system based on American, French, British, and Korean engineering.

As the stories told by the ADD researchers and the corporate engineers who worked with them reveal, South Korea's method of developing US-model weapons often involved illegal copying and outright stealing from the Americans.[196] Nonetheless, suggesting that they created only copycat technology would undermine the complexity of their work and imply that modeling weapons on US technologies was a simple task; it would also dilute some of the most fascinating aspects of the history of S & T development in this part of the world. For a country with no defense industry and no ability to manufacture its own arms, mimicking, acquiring, and even bootlegging US technologies offered a practical route to sovereignty. The stories recounted by these researchers demonstrate that copying technologies was neither a passive act nor an easy process; it required ingenuity and strategic, proactive efforts on the part of ADD scientists and engineers, who eventually innovated and created indigenized hybrids—missiles built from multiple countries' technologies but designed to accomplish specifically Korean purposes. Their memoirs and my interviews reveal the challenges these researchers faced and overcame to develop the weapons ordered by the state—even in defiance of its superpower patron, the United States, and despite numerous risks, internal rivalries, and conflicts at the ADD. The process was rife with human error, failure, and sacrifice. Nonetheless, they prevailed through a creative and intentional process of imitation and hybridization. Through their tenacity and commitment to the cause, along with attentive learning from and participation with scientists and engineers abroad, the ADD's researchers had managed to acquire the vital missile technologies they needed.[197]

Science and Technology Spin-Offs

The pursuit of weapons for national security promoted South Korea's scientific and technological expansion in multiple ways.[198] First, the ADD's research forged a new system for domestic and international scientific collaboration. With the agency operating as the central manager of weapons-development projects, other national research organizations, particularly the GFRIs such as KIST and KAERI, along with civilian companies and military arsenals, worked together to support ADD-led weapons programs.[199] Having public and private entities combine forces for research in this way, under ADD guidance, gave rise to a development approach to R & D that is both government-led and business-driven—a hallmark that continues to characterize South Korean R & D policy.[200] Scientific research that was once carried out in small, insulated military labs was being conducted on a national scale, with the benefit of expanded civilian facilities and government directives, funding, and other supports. According to the historian Geun Bae Kim, the weapons R & D projects run by the ADD "served as the template for contemporary national R&D research in Korea."[201] Beyond its domestic impact, the

ADD-led indigenization of weapons technology deepened and broadened South Korea's international collaboration. Through programs with the United States, such as Foreign Military Sales, which provided TDPs, the Data Exchange Agreement, and the US Army's Scientist and Engineer Exchange Program, as well as research expeditions to other nations, the ADD improved research and technical training for Korean scientists and strengthened the ROK's cooperative efforts with foreign researchers and institutions.[202] ADD scientists expanded their research collaborations with US military research teams and defense corporations, and for weapons technology not supplied by the United States, the agency diversified South Korea's suppliers to include sources in France, Japan, Taiwan, Israel, England, Germany, Italy, and other nations.[203] As South Korea gathered technology from all over the world, the results went into creating the hybrid technologies that distinguish many high-tech Korean products in the automobile, shipbuilding, heavy machinery, and information and communications technology sectors today.

The ADD served as South Korea's gateway to cutting-edge military technology, whether in the form of TDPs from the United States or weapons technologies from other countries. For most of the Park government's military projects—ammunitions, heavy artillery, rotary cannons, patrol boats, armored vehicles, tanks, helicopters, and fighter jets—the ADD facilitated the transfer of a significant amount of technologies and technical skills from foreign suppliers to domestic contractors through its coproduction efforts and licensing agreements.[204] From 1975 to 1980 the ADD supplied Korean defense manufacturers with approximately 160,000 pieces of technical data and 36,000 types of item specifications, along with technical manuals, supply catalogs, research reports, and handbooks.[205] These transfers helped ensure the broad dissemination of critical knowledge and facilitated the localization of production.[206] Previously, Korean manufacturers had relied exclusively on offshore procurement agreements with US defense firms to obtain their military technologies, a monopolized process that was tightly controlled by US license providers and the US government.[207] After the establishment of the ADD in 1970, Korean defense manufacturers could procure many of the needed technologies domestically through the technical transfers and aid of the ADD, which also closely supported their advances in R & D and diversified overseas technology suppliers.

Beyond fostering collaboration and disseminating new technologies, one of the ADD's most significant contributions was the strictly enforced quality-control system it introduced for defense manufacturing. The adoption of quality standards among weapons manufacturers contributed to standardization in South Korean industries generally, which was critical to South Korea's becoming an export-led economy in the 1970s.[208] Even though large Korean manufacturers were familiar with the "total quality control" system that had been practiced by Japanese conglomerates since the 1960s, and certain quality standards had been codified in 1963 in the Korean Industrial Standards (KS) marking system, quality-control practices in South Korea were weak and not rigorously enforced prior to HCI.[209] Under the MPL of 1973, state-mandated standards (and penalties for failures to meet them) were introduced in the defense industry. In the same year, the ADD formed a quality-assurance team to conduct inspections of all domestically produced defense products and materials.[210] Only those products and parts that passed muster were sent to the military arsenals for assembly. All ADD contractors, under the MPL's demands, had to outfit their factories with the latest technology and equipment and adopt science-based research practices and evaluation methods for developing and testing high-quality weapons. These practices spread throughout the exporting heavy and chemical industries, which essentially constituted South Korea's military-industrial complex.

Quality standards were tightened further in the mid-1970s, as South Korea pursued coproduction contracts with US weapons companies and sought to establish Korean corporations as parts suppliers for US defense corporations.[211] The ADD officially adopted the US Military Standard-120 (MIL-STD-120), which was part of military specifications (MIL-SPEC), the US Department of Defense's official standard for inspecting and guaranteeing the quality of manufactured weapons.[212] Meeting those standards required the highest-level precision machine work, specialized tools and equipment, and stringent procedures to check product reliability and ensure parts were interchangeable with those in US weapons.[213] The effort catalyzed major improvements in the quality of Korean defense products, as evidenced by reports to

Park on tests that demonstrated Korean-made heavy artillery was outperforming older US models and on the exportation of arms parts to the US manufacturers.[214]

Engineers and technicians at defense corporations such as Hanwha, Kia, Hyundai, Daewoo, Tongil (now SNT Heavy Industries), and Samsung recall the impact of the ADD's quality standards for military products.[215] According to Kim Kyegwan of Daewoo Heavy Industries, prior to his company's work on defense projects with the ADD, Daewoo's factory did not have a separate quality-control department staffed with professional specialists; instead, workers within the production unit checked the quality of items produced.[216] But in accord with the ADD's criteria, Daewoo established a quality-control unit specifically responsible for testing the performance and durability of each product. By Kim's reckoning, the quality-control practices that began in Daewoo's weapons division spread through the entire company as it adopted scientific practices for quality assurance overall. Similarly, Yu Hansik, who worked in Kia Machine Tools' factory in Ch'angwŏn from 1976 to 2003, noted in an interview that the superior scientific techniques and quality-control systems used in defense production were adopted by Kia to improve its overall product quality management.[217] This, in turn, increased the marketability of the company's export products. In Yu's words, "We have to remember that *perfection* is the key to the defense industry [dysfunctional weapons would be disastrous in battle]. The standards and skills that required *perfection* were transferred to industrial technology."[218] Clearly, the ADD's enforcement of scientific quality-control standards for weapons production in the HCI corporations in turn raised quality thresholds for commercial products, including exports, thereby contributing to South Korea's export-oriented industrialization.[219]

Ultimately, the ADD had its most lasting impact in advancing the technological capabilities of South Korea's private companies. As in more technologically developed countries like the United States, Germany, and Japan, where the private sector is the major investor in R & D, South Korea's technocrats intentionally transferred contracts to private companies, the chaebol, which coordinated weapons projects with their own business interests. From firearms and ammunition to heavy artillery, military vehicles, tanks, helicopters, military telecommunications equipment, missiles, battleships, submarines, and fighter jets, the ADD worked with the chaebol to improve weapons R & D. As a secondary outcome, the latest weapons technologies, procured and distributed by the ADD to private manufacturers, sparked concentrated growth in related technology-intensive businesses. In this way, the interlocking civilian and military projects created by the ADD facilitated the spillover of advanced technologies and skills into commercial manufacturing.

The ADD's integration of military modernization with commercial technological advancement generated long-lasting spin-off ventures in the private-sector economy. Throughout the 1970s the ADD trained South Korea's best scientists and engineers, arranging opportunities for them to learn new skills and providing private-sector companies with foreign technical assistance, such as the TDPs granted by the United States.[220] Owing to the ADD's training and its dissemination of new technologies, the ROK's industries succeeded in drastically flattening their high-tech learning curve. It was not long before companies were spinning off their advances in military technology into new commercial ventures in automobile manufacturing, heavy machinery, shipbuilding, electronics, telecommunications, and the aerospace industry.[221]

The machinery sector, which had been the weakest sector in South Korea prior to HCI, was the greatest beneficiary of technology spin-offs from defense industrialization. The ADD's transfer of technical skills for manufacturing the parts and special plates for howitzers, for example, expedited the development of the domestic machinery industry, which in turn contributed to commercial production.[222] Former skilled workers for Kia, Tongil, Daewoo, and Samsung, all of which collaborated with the ADD on heavy artillery projects, have testified that acquiring the technical skills involved in producing military machinery—precision manufacturing, steel welding, developing machine tools and automated assembly systems for manufacturing weapons parts, as well as R & D and T & E methods—opened doors for their companies to develop a wide range of commercial heavy equipment, engines, and vehicles.[223] Technologies involved in the manufacture of tanks, military vehicles, and jet fighters were likewise applied to the production of railcars, buses, trucks, and engines for commercial airlines.[224]

In another important spin-off, the ADD's production of military telecommunication devices was transferred directly into what would become South Korea's globally competitive commercial telecommunications industry.[225] For instance, to manufacture military radios, which required extreme durability, shock and heat resistance, and paint-free surfaces, Sŏ Chŏnguk and his team at the ADD developed methods for casting, precision cutting, plating, and sealing the radio bodies, while also devising basic wireless technologies used in military communications.[226] By combining Sŏ's technology and US technical data for a US-model military radio (the AN/PRC-77), the Oriental Precision Corporation produced a new Korean-made military radio, the KAN/PRC-77.[227] The manufacturing of military telecommunications equipment contributed to the development of South Korea's electronic exchange system (Time Division Exchange), which was foundational for later advances in information technology and telecommunications products, such as cellular phones.[228] Similarly, military fire-control systems and navigation systems used in ranged weapons and missiles that employ precision targeting technology were spun off into commercial navigational devices and domestic global positioning system (GPS) products.[229] These technologies would eventually catapult South Korea forward in the information and communications technology sector in the 1990s, accelerating its exportation of products that today have large shares of the global market.[230]

The electronic communication technologies and components in sophisticated weapons like the Polar Bear missile are still being spun off today for use in Korea's space industry. One such spin-off was South Korea's recent successful satellite launch using the Korean-made Nuri space-launch vehicle (Korean Space Launch Vehicle-II, or KSLV-II) in June 2022.[231] Nuri, which uses only Korean rocket technologies, is the country's first domestically built space-launch vehicle. It was a direct beneficiary of the rocket technology developed during the Park government's Polar Bear project. Precision-guided systems created for Polar Bear, such as missile-tracking devices, fire-control systems, and radar-based equipment, were also instrumental in the development of technology for Nuri.[232]

Eventually, companies' rapid progress in commercial technologies also fed back into Korea's military technology through "spin-on" effects, enabling the ROK military to expand applications of the new civilian technologies.[233] Drawing on private-sector advances in information and communication technology, the MND upgraded new military equipment with civilian-made parts for global positioning systems, air-traffic control systems, and satellite and telecommunications technology, and in more recent years it has integrated commercial technologies for artificial intelligence, virtual reality, and big-data analytics into military systems.[234] Most of the latest developments in South Korea's military technology come from the chaebol that now possess these advanced, state-of-the-art technologies.[235] As a sign of even greater integration between military technologies and private-sector R & D, the MND has been increasing its investment in "spin-up" technologies intentionally developed for dual military and commercial applications.[236] In sum, the system for military weapons production that Park established in the 1970s and merged with private industry led to spin-off, spin-on, and spin-up effects that engendered a highly productive development loop in South Korea's S & T industries.

Conclusion

Science and technology would not have developed as rapidly or forcefully in South Korea without the impetus of national security and defense building. Defense industrialization spurred the Park government's NSM, within which the state expanded public contributions to defense production by training technical specialists needed for weapons development and by fostering collaborations between government-funded research and civilian industries to execute defense contracts. The process forged national research collaborations that also advanced private-sector R & D capabilities and increased private investment. Just as important as state policymaking, the nation's breakthroughs in R & D were led by scientists and engineers committed to the goal of self-reliant national defense.

Defense industrialization catalyzed active transfers of technology between the military and civilian spheres by merging military R & D with private enterprise, thereby promoting collaboration and integration. As the lines of exchange multiplied, they established a core technology base that would uphold both the emerging defense industry and commercial manufacturing. The ADD played the central role in facilitating private-sector R & D and promoting cooperation between domestic and foreign firms to achieve advances in defense technology. Although structural and institutional arrangements were crafted from the top down by the Blue House, the bottom-up efforts and innovations of ADD researchers and corporate engineers significantly influenced technological outcomes and also facilitated the spin-off of technologies that strengthened industry generally.

The results of South Korea's R & D efforts may not have been immediately apparent in the 1970s, but the rise of S & T during this decade set a successful trajectory for the ROK's technological boom in the 1980s and 1990s. The 1970s can be seen as the developmental stage, when the ROK built its "R&D hardware" in response to military-industrial demands, and the government, through GFRIs, promoted new R & D infrastructure for Korean industries.[237] Government-funded research entities, led by the ADD, provided Korean businesses with R & D, and the HCI Policy enforced the creation of corporate satellite laboratories to collaborate in state-sponsored research. In the 1980s, when the chaebol took on a more prominent role in leading domestic R & D, they drew from the basic institutional supports established in the 1970s—GFRIs, a highly educated workforce, and state subsidies, tax credits, and public procurements for corporate R & D—to generate new and more advanced technologies for their products.[238] At the same time, the Park government's push for private-sector engagement with defense research paved the way for the chaebol to establish their own in-house R & D capabilities by the mid-1980s. Soon the chaebol were innovating through their own research and developing the competitive products and technologies that would carry them into the international market on the tide of globalization in the 1980s and 1990s.[239]

CHAPTER FIVE

Mobilizing to Weaponize the Nation

Train an army of 100,000 in advance to prepare for any exigency. Otherwise a calamity of our realm's total collapse will befall [us] before ten years pass.
—Yulgok Yiyi, 1583

Growing impatient with the Nixon administration's reluctance to send the agreed-upon aid for modernizing the ROK Armed Forces, President Park instituted a covert military modernization program in March 1974. This program, code-named the Yulgok Operation (Yulgok Saŏp), was named after a revered Confucian scholar from the Chosŏn period, Yi I (1536–84), also known by the pen name Yulgok. Yi had urged the Chosŏn king to train 100,000 reserve troops in peacetime as a preventive measure against future invasions. However, the king rejected Yi's idea, and a decade later, Japan launched the Hideyoshi invasions (1592–98), leading to the complete defeat of the unprepared Chosŏn army. In his speeches, President Park often cited such historical examples of Korea's military failures as a way to solicit public support for his pursuit of self-reliant national defense.[1] Hence, the name Yulgok reflected the inspiration, philosophy, and aims of his government's top military program.

The primary goal of the Yulgok Operation was to localize the production of advanced weapons and corresponding technologies to ensure South Korea's combat readiness and independent military modernization. Yulgok revamped military-civilian dynamics within South Korea and drastically changed its relations with the United States, as the ROK not only demonstrated its capability to arm itself but also pursued the development of a nuclear missile program forbidden by its ally. As the most controversial, bold, and costly undertaking of the Park government, Yulgok accelerated South Korea's military modernization from 1974 until Park's death in 1979, despite growing US surveillance and interference. Outlasting Park, the operation remained South Korea's central military modernization program until 1995.

The Yulgok Operation was the most clandestine mission of the Park government, known only to Park and a tight circle of his government and military advisers. All data pertaining to the operation were classified by Park's insiders to prevent leaks to US intelligence.[2] As O Wŏnch'ŏl explained, Park and his officials left "no [written] documents about the Yulgok Operation because it was a secret matter."[3] Despite its secrecy, the operation was almost entirely financed by donations and taxes collected from citizens who were both pressed to contribute and convinced of the need to enhance national defense. The Park government launched the National Defense Donation (NDD; *pangwi sŏnggum*) drive in the early 1970s (although the unofficial collection of donations had begun in the late 1960s in response to North Korea's infiltrations) and then instituted the National Defense Tax (NDT; *pangwise*) in 1975, thus mobilizing civilian contributions to support self-reliant national defense. While the NDD and NDT functioned as part of Park's broader campaign to secure political and social support for his defense initiatives, they most directly contributed to national security by funding Yulgok. As their revenue was secretly funneled into Yulgok projects, the operation came to be fiscally sustained by South Korea's thirty-five million citizens, a fundraising effort that essentially required a collective shift in the entire populace's culture and ideology. Through the NDD and NDT, the state enlisted ordinary individual civilians as agents and owners of South Korea's national security.

Laying the Groundwork: The US–South Korea Rift and Yulgok

In exchange for Park's agreement to deploy ROK troops to Vietnam, with the Brown Memorandum of 1966 the US government had offered a five-year military aid package (1966–71) to support a long-overdue modernization of the ROK Armed Forces.[4] Park had sought the aid to advance domestic weapons production, both to reduce the ROK's dependence on US military arms and supplies and to catch up with North Korea's weapon production capacity. However, large reductions in US military aid undercut the five-year plan and left South Korea with only partial subsidies for military modernization.[5] The plan was further hindered by the unwillingness of the United States to cooperate fully with Park's efforts to develop military technologies required for weapons production. Because Korean manufacturers lacked the infrastructure as well as the technical specialists who could produce, repair, and upgrade advanced parts of existing US-model weapons and equipment, the ROK Armed Forces faced a chronic and critical shortage of spare parts for maintaining military equipment.[6] Even US military leaders and policymakers acknowledged that such disrepair and deficiencies prevented South Korea from being combat ready. In October 1969, US Major General L. N. Taylor, the chief of the Joint US Military Affairs Group–Korea, sent a letter to South Korea's deputy prime minister, Kim Hangnyŏl, noting that "some 25% of the vehicles in the ROK Army are inoperable due to lack of spare parts. This high deadline rate seriously impairs the combat readiness of the [ROK] Army. . . . At the current Military Assistance level [by the United States], there is no prospect of improving the spare part stockage level."[7] In February 1970 a review of the ROK military by the US Senate Subcommittee on US Security Agreements and Commitments Abroad confirmed that the United States had made inadequate progress toward modernizing the ROK's military equipment for defense against a North Korean invasion.[8] In the same month, in opposition to Nixon's plan to rush the withdrawal of United States Forces Korea (USFK) troops, a memo from the US Joint Chiefs of Staff to National Security Advisor Henry Kissinger noted the ROK's insufficient military and technical capabilities, arguing that "substantial improvements" needed to be made to the existing ROK military, especially the air and naval forces, in advance of any withdrawal of US troops.[9]

In 1971, when the Nixon administration agreed to support Park's Five-Year Military Modernization Plan (1971–76) as part of its agreement to advance the ROK's "self-defense capabilities," the deal this time included giving South Korea technical data packages (TDPs) and rights to the domestic production of basic US weapons.[10] These upgraded benefits granted South Korea access to US weapons technologies that the previous five-year plan under the Brown Memorandum had failed to provide. However, most of the TDPs granted to Korea were for low-level technologies used in producing basic conventional weapons (and often outdated models), which frustrated Park's plans (see the discussions of US arms restrictions in chapters 1 and 4).[11] Furthermore, the new five-year plan faced problems almost immediately when the financially strapped US government, which had already spent heavily on the war in Vietnam, again began cutting promised military aid.[12] A 1978 report by the US Central Intelligence Agency (CIA) states that by 1973 "the 1971 US-Korean arms modernization plan was in disarray, and domestic defense production was limited essentially to crew-served infantry weapons and small arms ammunition."[13] Park faced still more new challenges with the US-China détente, the withdrawal of US troops from Indochina, and the DPRK's aggressive arms procurements. These international developments unsettled US-ROK security arrangements and compounded the shortcomings of US military aid, intensifying Park's sense of urgency for independent military modernization.

As the United States proceeded with planned troop withdrawals from Korea in 1971, Park seized the reins of military modernization and appointed O Wŏnch'ŏl as head of a program for domestic arms production (see chapter 2). After the Lightning Operation's first successful exhibition in December 1971, Park ordered O to proceed with plans for a national defense industry and also tasked him with developing guided missiles, whose production in South Korea was not supported by the United States.[14] Earlier in that year Park had also begun pushing the Korea Atomic Energy Research Institute (KAERI) to procure foreign nuclear-fuel fabrication and reprocessing technologies, looking toward the development of domestic nuclear power for both economic (energy) and military (nuclear missiles) purposes.[15] Under Park, who saw nuclear projects as necessary for both industrialization and security needs, the government had already begun building the "Kori 1" nuclear power plant in March 1971 in the village of Kori, near Pusan.[16]

As South Korea began developing its defense industry, the Park government came to realize that its biggest bargaining chip for obtaining US military assistance was South Korea's ability to develop advanced weapons on its own. US arms policy on South Korea was inconsistent from the late 1960s through the 1970s, owing not only to the budget crisis related to the war in Vietnam but also to disagreements between the Department of Defense and the Department of State over the best approach to the ROK's militarization.[17] Partisan politics added further disruptions, as Democrats and Republicans in Congress were divided over whether to support Park's repressive regime, which received international criticism over its human rights violations.[18] Perhaps most consequential, though, was the fact that US foreign policy in Asia, which prioritized Japan, lacked a clear, long-term approach to South Korea—which meant that US policies on the ROK fluctuated with changes at home in domestic politics, budget constraints, and administrations.[19]

Over time, however, the United States fell into three patterns of response to South Korea's independent military development.[20] First, whenever the ROK's progress in weapons development alarmed Washington, US officials would dispatch "technical assistance" teams to South Korea. These teams actually functioned as informants for the US government and were assigned to monitor the ROK's development of prohibited technologies.[21] Second, when the ROK procured a technology withheld by the United States from another foreign supplier, or when the Agency for Defense Development (ADD) came close to producing such a technology on its own, the United States often opted to sell its technology to Korea. These sales were usually accompanied by discounts and other favorable terms by the relevant US manufacturing company.[22] As the ROK's principal military supplier, the United States had a large stake in sales to South Korea, especially given that US defense firms wanted to maintain their business in one of their most profitable markets.[23] Third, as Korean corporations revealed their ability to produce weapons parts, particularly after the Yulgok Operation was underway, US companies became more receptive to subcontracting with Korean manufacturers to serve as parts suppliers, or to contracting with them as coproducers, because manufacturing in South Korea was more cost-effective than in the United States.[24] Permitting the ROK to supply parts for older-generation US weapons in use by other US allies also reduced the cost of US military aid to those countries. Moreover, since the United States was no longer producing many of those outdated weapons, the Department of Defense saw the mutual benefits in allowing South Korea to produce and export US weapons to other allied governments.[25] Overall, despite its reluctance to support the South Korean defense industry, Washington was motivated to stay involved with the ROK military because of its economic interest in keeping the ROK dependent on the US military-industrial complex, and because of its strategic interests in controlling the ROK's arms capabilities and improving military interoperability within the existing US-ROK security structure.

For his part, Park was able to exploit Washington's inconsistency in its approach to South Korea by forcing the US government to react to the ROK's show of strength. Prior to Yulgok, South Korea's immediate goal under its Heavy and Chemical Industrialization Policy (HCI Policy) had been to mass-produce basic US weaponry to meet the nation's urgent security needs, rather than to pursue a complete modernization of the military. However, the aforementioned patterns of US responses to the ROK's militarization convinced Park and his technocrats to adopt increasingly aggressive procurement strategies, culminating in their launch of the Yulgok Operation as Park's signature initiative for independent military modernization. But the scale of modernization Park strove to achieve required the engagement and sacrifice of the entire citizenry, and thus the story of the Yulgok Operation sheds light on how South Korea mobilized its people to support this national quest.

The Two Branches of Yulgok

Today the Yulgok Operation is best known in South Korea for its dark controversies, including its association with the nuclear arms program under Park that drove the US-ROK alliance to the brink of collapse, and for its connection to high-profile financial scandals that shocked the general public in the early 1990s. Existing scholarship on Park's independent military modernization efforts has largely focused on the nuclear missile aspect of the operation.[26] Yet Yulgok was far more varied and comprehensive than has been appreciated, and its broader influence is yet to be explored. Besides being at the center of US-ROK nuclear weapons conflicts, Yulgok supplied Park with the political weapons he needed to stand up to the United States. It set a new direction for South Korea that initiated a nationalistic quest for security independence and injected powerful South Korean agency into the US-ROK relationship. Ultimately, South Korea's assertive enhancement of its military capabilities reshaped the nature of the alliance between the two nations, helping to transform what had been a rigid patron-client alliance into a more equal and reciprocal partnership.

Declassified presidential documents and military material on the defense industry reveal that the Yulgok Operation was strictly bifurcated and then rigidly compartmentalized. In the first of its two main branches, the Ministry of National Defense (MND) led classified military projects under the Force Improvement Plan (FIP; Chŏllyŏk Chŭnggang Kyehoek), an operation focused on immediately modernizing the ROK military with domestically produced weapons and equipment upgrades. With the aim of bolstering independent defense against the DPRK, the FIP projects developed conventional weapons, including firearms, heavy artillery, ammunition, explosives, military vehicles, tanks, naval vessels, armored helicopters, and fighter jets, most of which were tied to technical support from the United States via the US-sponsored Five-Year Military Modernization Plan.[27] While this branch of Yulgok was officially under MND oversight, the Second Economic Secretariat (SES) monitored the FIP projects and reported to Park on their progress. Most of the weapons developed through FIP were manufactured by civilian contractors in their plants, with technical assistance from the ADD and resource support from the Ministry of Commerce and Industry.[28] Since the ADD welcomed the technical data the United States offered as official military aid, the United States was aware of these officially sanctioned and classified projects.

The other main branch of the Yulgok Operation involved Park's top secret plans for nuclear arms and surface-to-surface missiles (SSMs;

see chapter 4), separate projects that were bundled together into one ambitious program to develop nuclear missiles. Heavily concealed even from the United States, the projects in this branch of Yulgok were micromanaged by Park's SES technocrats in the Blue House, in close coordination with a small cadre of elite scientists (mostly non-military civilians) affiliated with the ADD and KAERI.[29] As unofficial projects, they remained autonomous, separate from the MND and other military authorities.[30] Park and O Wŏnch'ŏl excluded the MND from decision-making processes related to these top secret projects for two primary reasons. First, they believed that military officials lacked the necessary technical expertise, and they wanted top civilian specialists in charge of all program development. Second, given the complete integration of the ROK Armed Forces with USFK, they determined that involving the defense ministry would render it impossible to evade US surveillance.[31] Besides a select few corporations that assisted in constructing facilities or producing specialized parts for these confidential projects, only the most exclusive teams of handpicked scientists were involved in developing the program's key components, including nuclear warheads and the missile system.[32]

Although the FIP and the nuclear missile program functioned as two separate parts of the Yulgok Operation, with administrative responsibility divided between the MND and SES, both parts operated under the ultimate oversight of the Blue House through the direction of O Wŏnch'ŏl. In his work on the defense industry, O was assisted by his right-hand man, Kim Kwangmo, who was also deeply involved in the HCI Policy, and O's undersecretary Yi Sŏkp'yo until his sudden death in 1977. Kim and Yi each monitored the progress of the projects they were individually assigned to oversee, compiling reports for Park that O presented during his meetings with the president. Declassified SES reports on Yulgok reveal that Park had complete control over weapons-procurement initiatives, with almost all research and development (R & D) projects for the ADD operating through inputs by the SES.[33] Working through his SES technocrats, Park was directly involved at every stage of weapons acquisition, from the selection of weapons for development and import to budget planning for each project, and from negotiations on procurement contracts to final purchases—all of which required his personal approval.[34]

The Force Improvement Plan

Whereas the origins of the top secret branch of the Yulgok Operation can be traced to 1971, when Park ordered O to develop a guided missile, the FIP was conceived in 1973, closely following promulgation of the HCI Policy. The FIP was intended to upgrade ROK weapon systems and equipment in order to address urgent security needs. Notably, the FIP was strategically designed to align the development of its weapons programs with South Korea's heavy and chemical industrialization (HCI). On April 19, 1973, three months after Park announced the HCI Policy, he delivered the following instructions to the ROK Joint Chiefs of Staff (JCS):

1. Formulate the military plans for participation in self-reliant national defense and the military buildup.
2. Formulate a long-term military strategy for the transfer of operational control [or OPCON, from the United States to South Korea].
3. Localize the production of necessary weapons and military equipment to align with the promotion of HCI, except for advanced fighter jets and missiles.[35]
4. Develop independent military strategies and a force improvement plan, with the expectation that no US troops [would] remain in South Korea by the 1980s.[36]

The plan referred to in Park's fourth directive became the formalized FIP, the centerpiece of the MND's military modernization initiative. The third directive ensured that, under the HCI Policy, FIP projects would be carried out in collaboration with contracted firms.

In February 1974, when the North Korean Navy abducted two fishing boats near Paengnyŏng Island in the Yellow Sea, Park issued emergency orders for the immediate modernization of guns and equipment used by ROK maritime forces to protect the island's security. These orders pushed the MND to expedite comprehensive military modernization with its FIP.[37] The JCS devised the Eight-Year National Defense Plan (1974–81) for military modernization, which was adopted by the MND as its plan for the first stage of the FIP (called the "first FIP").[38] On March 15 the MND launched the first FIP, which at this point served as the ministry's code name for the classified Yulgok Operation.[39] The MND subsequently established the Yulgok Enforcement Agency (Yulgok Chiphaengdan) within each military branch—army, navy, and air force—to coordinate and execute the FIP's new weapons projects.[40] For the first FIP, the MND contracted with private firms to produce weapons required by the military, and the ADD assisted contractors with the TDPs granted by the United States to support the Five-Year Military Modernization Plan.[41] The FIP program oversaw the construction of an M16 factory and a ball-powder factory, as well as the production of howitzers, mortars, rotary cannons, rocket launchers, grenades, land mines, patrol boats, armored helicopters, upgraded tanks, and military communication devices.[42] Eventually, it even extended to the production of fighter jets.

The first FIP quickly advanced the modernization of Korean infantry weapons and ammunition—supplies that needed immediate attention. Whereas North Korean troops were equipped with modern Soviet AK-47s and submachine guns, ROK troops were still carrying outdated American M1 rifles.[43] Even though the MND's purchase of an M16 factory from US-based Colt Industries (see chapter 1) had enabled South Korea to begin producing US-model M16s, Park pursued a South Korean line of guns produced independently of Colt's licensing and renewal requirements. In fact, two years before the first FIP had even begun, under Park's orders the ADD was already developing what its researchers code-named the "Korean Model A," a Korean-made 7.62 mm submachine gun.[44] In October 1974, the Korea Institute of Science and Technology (KIST) completed an experimental prototype of the XB-1 rifle, the first of the Korean Model B gun series, which was based on the American M16. Subsequently, the first FIP promoted collaboration between KIST's Korean Model B project and the ADD's development of the Korean Model A guns. Due to the specialized nature of the work, development of new gun prototypes was kept strictly under the purview of the ADD and KIST. The joint R & D carried out by those elite institutions was foundational to the emergence of the Korean K2 rifles that began to replace the M16s as the standard-issue rifle for the ROK military in the 1980s.[45]

Since artillery bombing would be critical in any warfare with North Korea, given Seoul's proximity to the Demilitarized Zone, Yulgok funds were immediately invested in producing heavy artillery to replace the ROK's outdated US artillery from World War II. The ADD collaborated with Kia Machine Tools, Daewoo Heavy Industries, Korea Heavy Industries, and Tongil Heavy Industries to manufacture Korean-model howitzers, mortars, rotary cannons, and recoilless cannons.[46] South Korea's expeditious development and mass production of these types of heavy artillery was one of the FIP's major achievements. Poongsan Metal Corporation and Hanwha supplied ammunition for the newly developed weapons.

Because the United States had initially refused the ROK's request for production contracts for military vehicles, the FIP also invested in their domestic production, which proved successful. Under Park's orders, the ADD and Kia Motors joined forces to produce armored personnel carriers, jeeps, and military trucks—all of which had previously been imported with US military aid.[47] Other domestic automakers, such as Shinjin Motors, Asia Motors, and Hyundai Motors, also engaged in the manufacturing of military vehicles.

For the domestic production of tanks, which Park prioritized under Yulgok, the ADD received US technical assistance to aid Hyundai Heavy Industries and its subcontractors in constructing production facilities and developing the necessary technology for manufacturing individual tank parts.[48] The technical assistance offered under the Foreign Military Sales (FMS) program allowed the ADD and Hyundai to upgrade South Korea's existing US M48 tanks by June 1974, and to upgrade another US model, the M48A1 tank, in May 1976.[49] By 1983, under Yulgok's second FIP (1982–86), Hyundai Rotem, a division of Hyundai, had developed the first prototype for a Korean-model tank, the K1, modeled on the United States' M1 Abrams.[50]

To counter the DPRK's superior naval power, the first FIP upgraded the ROK Navy by constructing high-speed coastal patrol boats (the PGM, PKM, and PK) and developing antisubmarine torpedoes, magnetic mines, and the 20 mm Vulcan cannon for arming navy vessels.[51] Hyundai Heavy Industries, Korea Tacoma Marine Industries, and the Korean Shipbuilding and Engineering Corporation built patrol boats, frigates, and corvettes. With the expansion of shipbuilding, new companies, such as Daewoo Shipbuilding and Marine Engineering (founded in 1973) and STX Engine (founded in 1976), emerged to supply key components and hardware for navy vessels. The first FIP also initiated several long-term naval projects. In 1975, for example, at Park's direction to produce battleships, the MND selected Hyundai Heavy Industries to develop a Korean-made battleship.[52] The project was completed in five years. The ADD began working with Korea Tacoma Marine Industries in 1977 to build South Korea's first submarine, which was completed in 1984.[53]

Growing confident in the progress of the FIP, the Park government next set its sights on modernizing the ROK Air Force. Again, the government relied on purchasing coproduction contracts from US corporations to procure the necessary advanced technologies. The ROK's strategy prioritized bringing in American know-how for key aviation technologies as part of all purchases and deals. In its contractual negotiations with US aerospace manufacturers, the ROK government insisted on receiving licensed transfers of original US technologies so that Korean manufacturers could acquire the skills required for localized production.[54] Korean Air's coproduction agreement with US-based Hughes Aircraft Company in 1976, for example, enabled the domestic production of US-model MD 500 helicopters at Korean Air's assembly plant in Kimhae.[55] Park's ambition to gain advanced aerospace technology was especially evident in his effort to domesticate the production of fighter jets in the late 1970s. South Korea produced key parts for American fighter jets, such as the McDonnell Douglas F-4 Phantom Fighter and the Northrop F-5, by acquiring US approval for coproduction with the Korean manufacturers.[56] Samsung Precision, established as a business subsidiary of Samsung, secured technological assistance from General Electric for the production of the F-4 and F-5 engines, which localized the production of fighter jet engines in 1978.[57] From 1977 to 1978 the government also aggressively pursued an agreement with the United States for licensed transfers of technology, facilities, and training for Korea's coproduction of then state-of-the-art F-16s, with General Dynamics.[58] However, this plan was abandoned after Park's death in 1979, when the new regime of Chun Doo-hwan opted to pursue F-5 production instead.[59]

Although South Korea realized significant gains in the modernization of its military under Yulgok, the FIP's focus on reproducing

US-model weapons for its projects underscores the indispensable role of US TDPs in this development.[60] Yulgok was therefore never unfettered from US influence: even its efforts to achieve self-reliant national defense were heavily reliant on US technical assistance, necessitated by the ROK military's adoption of US weapons systems since the Korean War. When the ADD sought alternative suppliers of weapons technology in the mid- to late 1970s, it did so only after facing rejections from the United States. Furthermore, as previously discussed, the United States often relented and sold South Korea the technologies it needed only when it got close to acquiring them from another source. As a result, while Yulgok was able to capitalize on US weapons expertise, it also saturated the domestic defense industry with US technology. This had another consequence as well, because the more US military technology South Korea acquired, whether through licenses and coproduction or subcontracting, the more control the United States gained over the Korean defense industry and ROK exports of military products. Therefore, even though South Korea successfully mass-produced weapons for export as early as the mid-1970s, the US Department of State, which exercised legal control over any exports of US-licensed weaponry or weapons technologies, curtailed Korean attempts to sell certain US weapons, such as M16s, to other countries.[61]

At the same time, South Korea skillfully appropriated US-granted technologies to its advantage. For example, Korean manufacturers modified and redesigned numerous components for US weapons systems, integrating them into their own hybridized systems to meet specific Korean needs.[62] During this process of customizing US manufacturing methods, former technicians at Daewoo Heavy Industries noted that US weapons-production machinery in use in Korea was further enhanced in terms of precision and quality. This was possible because Korean engineers, who had to start from scratch, followed principles in the original US manuals more strictly than American engineers did.[63] In a sense, what the FIP achieved was a blended Korean-American defense industry, as the Korean defense infrastructure was set up to produce hybrid US-model weapons. Overall, with the first FIP, the ROK made significant strides in the development of modernized weapons in the late 1970s. This progress was achieved by building on the industrial infrastructure initiated under the HCI Policy and rapidly indigenizing weapons technologies.

The Secret Nuclear Missile Program

The branch of the Yulgok Operation dedicated to the nuclear missile program was Park's most guarded project. (This branch included the development of Polar Bear, the missile project discussed in chapter 4.) Although US tactical nuclear weapons were stationed at US military bases in South Korea, in his anticipation of the eventual US withdrawal, Park determined that the ROK should possess its own nuclear missiles as a deterrent against a North Korean invasion.[64] Because Park was concerned about how his development of nuclear arms would affect the already deteriorating US-ROK relationship, the mission was completely classified. In November 1971, O Wŏnch'ŏl had met with Ch'oe Hyŏngsŏp, the minister of science and technology, and Yun Yong-gu, the director of KAERI, to plan a covert exploration of foreign resources to develop South Korea's ability to produce nuclear arms.[65] Under the aegis of the Blue House, KAERI, the ADD, and Park's Weapons Exploitation Committee began pursuing advanced nuclear technology.[66] In May 1972 Ch'oe was sent on a secret mission to France to negotiate a deal for acquiring French nuclear reprocessing technology and facilities.[67] Although KAERI already had a commercial nuclear energy program centered on the Kori 1 power plant, South Korea could not reprocess the spent fuel rods from that plant to acquire weapons-grade fissile material because of US participation in Kori 1's construction.[68] To make nuclear weapons, KAERI required clandestine, self-governing facilities to produce weapons-grade plutonium or enriched uranium.

In September 1972, under O's direction, KAERI's Yun Yong-gu and his team prepared an official plan for developing domestic nuclear fuel.[69] This plan, which the SES presented to Park in a classified report, proposed constructing new heavy-water reactors—capable of producing extremely pure plutonium—starting in 1974.[70] The report also explained the advantages of choosing plutonium over uranium as the fissile material for nuclear fuel, emphasizing the ease and cost-effectiveness of obtaining pure plutonium compared with enriched uranium.[71] The ultimate goal was to domestically produce weapons-grade plutonium by the early 1980s. The report also outlined plans for training Korean nuclear scientists.[72] According to Kim Kwangmo, even though Park never gave an official order to develop nuclear arms—to ensure the project's secrecy—he was regularly briefed by O on its progress.[73] In addition to nuclear fuel, the development of nuclear missiles required designs for nuclear warheads and carrier missiles; together, these three developments constituted the essential components of Yulgok's nuclear missile project.

When Yulgok formally commenced in 1974, the Blue House instituted a two-pronged approach to nuclear missile development. Research on SSMs, including the design of nuclear warheads, was led by ADD researchers, and the development of nuclear fuel (plutonium) for the warhead was carried out by KAERI's nuclear engineers. The ADD launched its SSM project in May 1974, and from late 1974 to 1975 it negotiated with the United States and France, as well as suppliers in other countries, to procure rocket propulsion, guidance, and other missile-related technologies.[74] These efforts rankled Henry Kissinger, then secretary of state and chief architect of the US policy of détente, who saw nuclear missiles in the hands of South Korea as a greater danger to regional stability than any threat posed by North Korea.[75] In February 1975 the US Department of State intervened in South Korea's negotiations to purchase a rocket propulsion plant from the US-based Lockheed Propulsion Company.[76] South Korea then turned to Société nationale des poudres et explosifs (SNPE) of France and signed a deal with it to receive technical aid for missile propulsion technology.[77]

As South Korea negotiated the acquisition of nuclear technologies from abroad, declassified documents from the CIA show that an ADD project specifically dedicated to designing components of nuclear missiles, code-named Project 890, emerged between 1974 and 1975.[78] According to a CIA report, this project was carried out in the ADD's Taejŏn Machinery Depot, and its work was divided among three teams of elite Korean scientists: one team worked on the design of nuclear warheads, another on chemical warheads, and the third on missiles.[79] The report provides additional details on the organization of Project 890 as follows:

> The [nuclear warhead] design team took clear shape in mid-1975, when it was divided into three substantive subgroups working on warhead structure, high explosives fabrication, and computer codes. It is believed that the total warhead design effort employed no more than a few dozen

> scientists holding doctoral degrees[,] backed by a somewhat larger number of technicians. Little information is available on the warhead design(s) investigated, but it is known that the group suffered from internal squabbling and technical incompetence and apparently made little progress. The chemical warhead team, apparently established at ADD in February 1975, employed about 10 principal researchers. By mid-1976, in contrast, the missile team reportedly employed more than 250 researchers and technicians. In addition to several administrative units, the team encompassed five substantive divisions: propellants, mechanics, electronics, testing and evaluation, and computer support.[80]

The CIA's description of the ADD missile team, with "more than 250 researchers and technicians," some of whom were Korean-born scientists recruited from abroad, indicates that South Korea was fully pursuing the development of advanced missiles at the time, and that the program had expanded considerably by mid-1976.[81] In fact, the project was even larger in scale and growing more quickly than the CIA reported.[82] As the program expanded, the report notes, "strict compartmentation was apparently enforced" between the three main teams (for nuclear warhead, chemical warhead, and missile design, respectively) for the duration of Project 890.[83]

Based on the testimony of ADD missile researchers at the time, secrecy and security around the project was so strict from the start that the team of ADD researchers working on missile design would not have known anything about the work of the teams developing warheads.[84] The security regulations also applied to private contractors and their technicians involved in producing parts for the project.[85] Each working group's knowledge of and responsibilities for a set of specific components were separate and restricted from other groups assigned to different components. According to Hong Yongsik, who joined the ADD in 1974 to develop a missile propulsion system, "The government never officially announced or acknowledged nuclear missiles, and the ADD's official organizational chart had no indication of a nuclear weapons project nor of the division in charge of it."[86] The only time Hong heard directly about the prospect of nuclear arms development was in private, during an informal gathering between Prime Minister Kim Chongp'il and a few ADD executives in 1974: "I remember him [Kim] laughing and saying, 'If successful in developing nuclear arms, we'll give 100 million won per person [to everyone in the ADD].'"[87] To this day, neither the ADD nor the ROK government has formally acknowledged South Korea's attempt to develop nuclear arms under Park, despite the well-documented historical accounts of South Korea's conflict with the United States over this issue.

In an interview televised in June 2018, the ADD's Yi Kyŏngsŏ (see chapters 2 and 4) publicly revealed that, under Park, the ADD had been secretly working on a nuclear detonator in a restricted zone of its Taejŏn Machinery Depot.[88] Remarkably, Yi, who headed the Polar Bear (SSM) project, claimed he had not been directly aware of the nuclear detonator project until after Park's death because access to the area in which the project was being worked on was tightly restricted.[89] In a separate interview I conducted with Yi, he disclosed that during his tenure as manager of the division specializing in missile technology at the Taejŏn Machinery Depot, a mysterious division existed within the same depot.[90] It was kept so isolated that he did not even know the faces of his colleagues who worked there. This division was likely the nuclear warhead design team for Project 890, which was mentioned in the CIA report.[91] Yi also said he figured that nuclear arms were being developed but chose to focus on his own task at hand—the missile—with an understanding that whatever was carried by it would be up to the president.[92] Yi's account points to an unspoken understanding among the ADD researchers that Park intended to develop a nuclear missile, even though this was never formally communicated. As Yi recounts, during one of Park's visits to the Taejŏn Machinery Depot, he told the ADD researchers, "What I want from the ADD is something that can get us a win without even having to resort to a war." Added Yi, "So what the president said then was very clear. The ADD's mission was to develop nuclear weapons and develop guided missiles that could carry them. . . . There was no one there who understood differently."[93]

While the ADD focused on missiles and warheads, KAERI sought to develop the nuclear fissile material (plutonium) for the warhead. Both efforts proceeded without much interference from the United States, until India successfully tested a nuclear weapon in May 1974. Newly wary of other nations that might be secretly developing nuclear technology, the United States began to increase the surveillance of its allies to enforce the Treaty on the Non-Proliferation of Nuclear Weapons (the Non-Proliferation Treaty, or NPT), which it had signed in 1968. In conjunction with stepped-up surveillance, the US Department of State tried to prevent South Korea from procuring advanced nuclear technology from abroad. However, by the mid-1970s KAERI's nuclear program had gained considerable momentum. In 1975 the institute secured a deal with the French company Saint-Gobain Techniques Nouvelles for the construction of a pilot reprocessing plant in South Korea.[94] KAERI also engaged in talks with Canada and Belgium in 1974 and 1975 to purchase nuclear reprocessing facilities and technology.[95]

After reporting its suspicions in December 1974 about the ROK's intention to develop nuclear weapons, the US Department of State confirmed the existence of Park's secret nuclear program in March 1975.[96] Henry Kissinger correctly perceived that South Korea's newly acquired reprocessing equipment might be used to produce weapons-grade plutonium, giving the ROK the potential to produce nuclear warheads for the ADD's missile program.[97] In response, the United States applied maximum diplomatic pressure on the governments of France and South Korea to halt the construction of the reprocessing plant, and also intervened to end KAERI's negotiations with Canada and Belgium.[98] With its allies, the United States pressured Park into signing the NPT as well, in April 1975.[99] Nevertheless, the ROK government persisted in its efforts to procure nuclear technology from France, claiming it was for producing energy for commercial use.[100] According to Kim Chongp'il, the US embassy in South Korea and the CIA joined forces to monitor the research sites of KAERI and the ADD, and US officials and CIA agents were dispatched to "cling" to top officials in the Blue House, the prime minister's office, the Ministry of Finance, MND, and KIST, to surveil and to directly press them to convince the ROK government to give up its pursuit of nuclear weapons.[101] It became increasingly difficult for South Korea to keep nuclear secrets from the United States—partly due to some Korean insiders who, according to Kim, "snitched" to the Americans about domestic nuclear activities.

Under strong US pressure, South Korea eventually dismantled its nuclear program, but not all was lost from the failed deal with France. In return for Park's adherence to the NPT, the Ford administration pledged the United States' commitment to ROK security as well as continued assistance for South Korea's development of commercial nuclear technology (that is, technology for peaceful use only).[102] Seeing the US monopoly on Korea's defense market threatened by a foreign competitor like France, the Ford administration even allowed the previously denied purchase of missile propulsion facilities from Lockheed, which were sold to Korea in December 1975.[103] The United States believed that even with Lockheed's facilities, the ROK would not be able to develop an advanced missile on its own. The Department of State also ensured that manufacturing technology was not included in the deal with Lockheed, although the company's engineers who helped set up Lockheed's facilities in Taejŏn did end up providing more assistance on missile technologies than was allowed, such as showing Korean engineers how to produce and test large-scale solid-fuel motors.[104] Furthermore, unbeknownst to the Americans, ADD and Hanwha engineers had by this time made great strides in propulsion technology through an earlier deal with France that had supplied viable substitutes for the propulsion technologies withheld by the United States. Still, South Korea acquiesced to US demands: in exchange for US technical assistance, such as the ADD's joint research with McDonnell Douglas discussed in chapter 4, the ROK government agreed to limit the range of domestically produced missiles to 180 kilometers (112 miles) and limit warheads to 1,000 pounds, or about 454 kilograms (an agreement later formalized in a 1979 memorandum of understanding signed by the United States and the ROK).[105] Therefore, the purchase of US missile technology came at the cost of further military restrictions.

Park did not abandon his nuclear activities for long. In November 1976 Jimmy Carter was elected president of the United States, which gravely concerned Park and his policymakers. Carter had long argued for US military disengagement from Korea, including the removal of all US ground troops and even US nuclear weapons.[106] When he took office Carter sought to complete the withdrawal plan that Nixon had introduced but that had been delayed under the Ford administration. In anticipation of this shift in US policy, in the month following Carter's election Park established the Korea Nuclear Fuel Development Corporation, which in effect replaced KAERI as the locus of South Korea's nuclear research activities and expanded the domestic nuclear program. In official communications, the government represented to the public and US officials that the new corporation had been created to develop commercial nuclear energy, not nuclear weapons.[107] Located in Taedŏk, near the Taejŏn Machinery Depot (ADD's missile factory), the corporation in effect maintained South Korea's potential ability to shift to nuclear arms production (including the production of nuclear missiles) in the event of any large-scale US exit from South Korea.[108]

The Carter administration announced in 1977 that it planned to withdraw 33,000 American ground troops from Korea by 1982, leaving only 7,000 US Air Force personnel and 4,000 to 6,000 troops involved in communications, logistics, and intelligence.[109] As Carter also began tightening restrictions on the US weapons technologies that South Korea could acquire, Park hastened the missile development under Yulgok, using missile propulsion technologies secured from the United States and France prior to Carter's inauguration. When, in spite of US restrictions and surveillance, the ADD successfully test-launched the Polar Bear ballistic missile in September 1978, US officials were caught off guard by how quickly the ROK's missile technology had progressed. In fact, this reflected an ironic pattern: the United States, which had been closely involved in the ADD's technical efforts since the Advanced Research Projects Agency team's arrival in 1972, was often caught by surprise by the ADD's activities. This demonstrated both the well-guarded secrecy of Park's weapons programs (despite snitching Korean insiders, as Kim Chongp'il previously noted) and the lack of consistent, long-term vigilance across US administrations over the development of these programs in South Korea.

The launch of Polar Bear escalated US concerns about the ROK's military capabilities and marked a turning point in the Carter administration's arms restrictions and withdrawal plans.[110] US officials saw the ADD's missile development as the most convincing sign to date that Park would acquire dangerous weapons technology on his own if he was not given US support. A CIA report in April 1977 had cautioned that the withdrawal of US ground troops could "stimulate President Park to attempt to reactivate South Korea's nuclear and long-range missile programs."[111] After the Polar Bear launch, Carter shifted his stance and began to offer more coproduction opportunities for Park's weapons programs, eventually approving sales of US missile technology to South Korea—which he had previously denied.[112] Like his predecessors in previous US administrations, Carter agreed to such deals only when South Korea had independently secured military technologies that the United States had earlier refused to transfer and when the concessions provided additional means to surveil the Koreans.

Polar Bear not only impressed on US leaders South Korea's arms potential in the event of US abandonment, but it also reinforced the arguments of the US military leaders and legislators who opposed Carter's withdrawal policy.[113] They believed that the presence of US troops was a necessary deterrent to Park's full development of nuclear arms, as well as to a North Korean invasion.[114] At this juncture, South Korea's ability to acquire banned weapons technology through domestic R & D and alternative suppliers also pressured Carter to protect the United States' dominant market share in the Korean defense industry and maintain US leverage over the ROK military. All in all, South Korea's growing potential to develop nuclear missiles compounded the pressure on Carter to make additional concessions in the alliance. Recognizing South Korea's increasing ability to defend itself, in November 1978 the Carter administration created the US-ROK Combined Forces Command. Under this new joint command structure, South Korea was for the first time granted authority over operational decisions for the ROK military.[115] By July 1979, faced with rising opposition at home, Carter had reversed both his troop withdrawal policy and the removal of US nuclear weapons.[116] Plans for the removal of troops from South Korea came to a complete halt. Thereafter, the new Republican administration of Ronald Reagan discarded the entire withdrawal plan in the first month of his presidency, in January 1981. Ultimately, then, Yulgok not only forced US policy to shift in favor of Park's demands for greater military aid, but it also wrung from the United States a stronger commitment to South Korea's defense.[117] In this regard, Park's defense industrialization dissuaded the United States from withdrawing from the ROK as it had Vietnam. Unlike Vietnam, which was an agricultural nation, South Korea had made swift advances in high-tech weapons capabilities and industrialization. The country's new status as an industrialized arms producer meant that the United States could not risk losing this ally, with all its weapons and weapon technologies, to a communist power.[118]

Mobilizing Civilian Revenue

With its mission to modernize the military, the Yulgok Operation required tremendous amounts of capital to pay for its projects. The magnitude and the scale of Yulgok's funding requirements necessitated a level of social and institutional support far in excess of the state's prior mobilization efforts. And because the operation was classified and involved weapons banned by the United States, its funding could not rely on foreign military aid. Although investments in the heavy and chemical industries by the chaebol aided the government in financing basic infrastructure related to weapons manufacturing, Yulgok's advanced projects required additional internal sources of capital.

To fund the Yulgok Operation, the Park state drew massive amounts of financial and other resources from individual citizens. It was able to do this through a mixture of state directives and civilian participation. In the process, a distinct form of national cohesion emerged that was at once forcefully channeled by the state and fueled in part by the people's shared experiences—ranging from their colonial legacy and wartime experiences to a collective fear of communist threats. This well-coordinated program of state-society engagement distinguished the military modernization process in South Korea from such processes in other areas of the world. Amid the state's efforts to garner support from all sectors of society, Yulgok succeeded in indigenizing the production of advanced weapons, thereby transforming South Korea from a dependent client nation into a country capable of asserting its own sovereignty.

The Colonial Precedent for Donations

Long before Yulgok, the Korean people were familiar with mass mobilization (*tongwŏn*) and the practice of making individual wartime sacrifices and donations because of their experiences under Japanese colonialism.[119] During the Asia-Pacific War, the Japanese state conducted highly organized mass fundraising campaigns to pay for industrialization and military expenditures. As the war escalated, all residents in the Japanese Empire were pressed to donate funds as well as household items made from raw materials that could be recycled, such as rubber and special metals, to support resource-deficient Japan.[120] Over time, donating to the government in times of national emergency became customary in Japan and its colonies.[121] In spite of the fact that such donation drives were tools of colonial extraction, these experiences nurtured a culture of civic responsibility, and they influenced how the Korean people more readily adapted to Park's mass fundraising campaign later.

In 1931, Japan's invasion of Manchuria sparked the *imon* ("consolation"; 慰問) movement in Imperial Japan, in which local citizens sent war-relief packages, including letters and gifts, to support recruits from their respective hometowns fighting in Manchuria.[122] Of all the groups collecting and donating money, the ones organized at the city and prefecture levels were the most effective. In these regions, entities such as local governments, press outlets, business and professional organizations, and student groups organized fundraisers to help pay for military supplies and equipment, even airplanes, for the Japanese Kwantung Army in Manchuria.[123] Citizen-financed "patriotic planes" were inscribed with the names of the regions or groups that had contributed to their funding.[124] The *imon* movement, which ballooned with the support of local initiatives, soon joined with the government's national fundraising drive to collect defense donations (*kokubō kenkin*) for the Japanese army and navy throughout the war period, from the 1930s until 1945.[125] With the enactment of the National Mobilization Law (Kokka Sōdōin Hō) in 1938, the donation movement expanded even further, as the Japanese government established a system to mobilize all citizens and their resources.[126]

Japan's total war effort spread to all citizens of the Japanese Empire.[127] Koreans in their colonized homeland, along with Korean businesses and workers located in Japan, other colonies such as Taiwan and Sakhalin, and Manchuria, were all mobilized to contribute to the donation drives. The largest collections often came from businesses and business associations, which donated to support Japan's purchases of warplanes, vehicles, and military equipment.[128] Businesses also contributed war-related supplies, such as tires and machinery. In addition, a wide range of city-, district-, and neighborhood-based organizations in Korea—including educators' groups, student associations, social clubs, women's groups, local community groups, health-care workers, laborers, and religious groups—collected defense donations to support Japan's total war effort, passing the funds they raised to officials at colonial police stations and military headquarters.[129] "Patriotic" individuals and organizations in Korea were celebrated in media headlines for donating to the Japanese army and navy.[130] Regardless of the growing Korean nationalist movement against Japan, many Koreans still willingly donated to support the local Korean troops and reserves who had been drafted into the Japanese military.[131]

After Korea's liberation from Japanese rule in 1945, the US Army Military Government in Korea, which held governing authority in South Korea from 1945 to 1948, left colonial administrative structures largely intact for the newly founded ROK government that took over in 1948.[132] The violently anticommunist regime of Rhee Syngman was widely unpopular, however. Beset by frequent domestic uprisings, Rhee's administration never found a way to effectively tap the inherited institutional structures or their capacity for drawing civilian support to advance state projects. Yet, in the face of North Korean threats and civil war, people offered patriotic donations called "national citizens' donations" (*kungmin sŏnggŭm*) that funded the government's purchase of airplanes and other defense-related supplies.[133] While the tradition of donating continued sporadically, the Rhee administration, plagued by failed economic policies and wide-ranging corruption, could not develop a broad base of social support and lacked the strength to organize or sustain donation campaigns. It was not until the advent of Park's militarized administration that the donation culture of the colonial era was resurrected and the state was able to amass donations on a national scale through the unified effort of the populace.

The National Defense Donation

Under Park and the Yusin state, people felt compelled to contribute money to support national defense for many reasons, given the diverse ways the state's mobilization campaign was carried out and impinged on their personal lives. From its beginning, the Park regime had been much more effective than the previous administrations of Rhee and Chang Myŏn in using the practices and structures of Korea's colonial experience to mobilize civilians for the state's goals. Starting in the mid-1960s, to assist the families of Korean troops fighting in Vietnam, the government instituted the large-scale collection of consolation (*wimun*; the Korean equivalent of the Japanese word *imon* above) donations from civilians and public employees.[134] Then, in 1968, following North Korea's Blue House Raid, the terror that gripped South Korean citizens helped the state to begin raising local donations for defense strengthening, in the form of the National Defense Donation. For the Park government, still hampered by an underdeveloped economy and a very limited defense budget, the NDD provided critical financial aid for independent military modernization. The initial withdrawal of US troops in 1971, combined with the government's propaganda promoting self-reliant national defense, added more fuel to the wildfire of public fear, bringing in further support for Park's independent military modernization.

By encouraging informal defense collection drives through the New Village Movement (NVM), schools, businesses, and the media, the Park government harked back to the strategic mobilizations employed by wartime Japan and revived the tradition of locally organized, nationally coordinated donation drives, making donations an indispensable part of national citizenship. First, through its extensive bureaucratic outreach, the Park administration established what eventually became community-driven efforts to extract citizens' financial support. To promote local defense collections, the government used the NVM, which had already proved its effectiveness in channeling local efforts toward rural development. The NVM, together with the highly organized Homeland Reserve Forces, institutionalized social networks that rapidly expanded locally driven defense donations into a national movement.[135] Accordingly, the NVM emerged as a powerful tool for mobilizing civilian material and ideological support for defense industrialization. Collection efforts were coordinated by provincial, metropolitan, and neighborhood NVM branches, and by the movement's regional promotion committees.[136] Additional support was provided by a program of monthly government-led neighborhood meetings, known as *pansanghoe*, that were held throughout the country, in which groups of ten to twenty households came together for NVM education.[137] Eventually, swept up in the state's self-reliant national defense campaign, civilians began to organize donation efforts on their own. These grassroots initiatives were bolstered by local neighborhood business associations, churches and other religious groups, labor unions, youth groups, social clubs, senior community centers, public employees, and even clan gatherings (*chongch'inhoe*).[138] Provincial governments, city councils, and district heads (*tongjang*) also contributed by collecting defense donations. The collected donations were delivered to local government offices or nearby military headquarters, or sent directly to the MND or the Blue House. Together, these highly organized, closely interwoven local fundraising efforts reinforced the practice of making patriotic donations among South Korea's population.

Second, the government mobilized the public schools, emulating the former colonial state's strategy of involving young students in wartime donations as a character-building exercise and a means of fostering loyalty to the state.[139] In 1968, reforms introduced by the National Charter on Education had incorporated an anticommunist, nationalistic curriculum in the schools (see chapter 1).[140] From that point on, the Ministry of Education increasingly rallied students and educators around national security issues.[141] The school boards and principals in each province organized school-wide and local fundraising activities to collect the NDD.[142] To raise money for school donation campaigns, students in all grades across the nation collected and sold secondhand items, set up barley and rice gleaning programs, harvested edible plants, cleaned public places, recycled materials, worked part-time jobs, and held special "save your pocket money" days, among other activities.[143] Teachers also asked students to bring in donations from home. One interview subject, Mrs. Kim, who attended high school in South Korea in the mid-1970s, said: "I remember that we regularly got an envelope for the defense donation from the school. Parents would put money in there for us to turn in."[144]

Student donations were highlighted in the national media, with the collected funds being ceremoniously received by the state at the Blue House or by the minister of education. These public celebrations of students' collections doubled as public relations platforms to invigorate Koreans' allegiance to Park's self-reliant national defense agenda. For example, the government invited 350 students from across the nation to attend a ceremony in November 1971 that marked the completion of two seventy-ton PK speedboats funded with donations from elementary school students.[145] To thank the students publicly for their donations and acknowledge their sacrifice and effort, Park called the new vessels "PK Student Ships." Schools were a steady source of funding for Park's military projects every year, with students and teachers from elementary through high schools continually organizing collections within their districts.[146]

Third, in addition to regional donation campaigns and public-school fundraising, the business sector was another active participant in the state's defense donation drives. The chaebol often made headlines with their hefty donations of expensive equipment or funds to the NDD.[147] These generous offerings ensured government reciprocation in the form of favors, as well as positive media coverage. When the MND faced severe shortages of funds for its military projects, chaebol executives—including Chung Ju-yung (of Hyundai), Ku Chagyŏng (Lucky Group), Kim Chonghŭi (Hanwha), Yi Pyŏngch'ŏl (Samsung), Kim Sangha (Samyang Corporation), Pak Pyŏnggyu (Haitai), Yi Chaejun (Daelim), Cho Chunghun (Hanjin), and Pak Hŭngsik (Hwasin)—not only donated personally but also collected donations from their employees that were then delivered to the ministry.[148] When the media publicized the contributions made by one well-known chaebol, rival companies would be challenged to match or exceed those donations, creating a cycle that not only heightened awareness of the state's expectations but also energized the donation culture.[149] Corporations even collected cash donations from local citizens to help purchase new lathes and other training equipment needed for students enrolled in technical high schools that trained HCI workers.[150] As in the colonial era, in the 1970s defense donations represented one way in which businesses became supporters of the state—to ensure their own prosperity and even survival.

Finally, like the colonial state, the Park government used mass media and media corporations to organize local fundraising efforts.[151] With South Korea's highly literate populace, newspapers effectively disseminated Park's nationalistic messages, promoted financial contributions to support self-reliant national defense, and publicized the donations others were making.[152] In January 1972, for example, the *Kyŏnghyang* newspaper featured the story of Yi Suam, a rural tenant farmer with physical disabilities, who had made a defense donation.[153] The head of a seven-member household, Yi donated all his personal gains from working in other men's fields to express his gratitude for the military's protection. He explained that this was his way of making up for the physical disabilities that had prevented him from serving in the military. Nationalistic sentiments and sacrifices like Yi's were regarded as supremely moral acts that served the greater good of the nation. Many such individual patriots were treated as heroes in the media and were rewarded by the government for their sacrifices.[154]

In his public addresses, Park lauded Koreans from all walks of life for donating to the best of their abilities for the sake of national defense.[155] Indeed, internal government records on the NDD document a wide collection of donations from men and women of all ages, social groups, professions, and regions, revealing the breadth and depth of civilian participation.[156] The nationalistic donation campaign was so far-reaching and pervasive that even politically and economically marginalized groups, such as laborers and women, actively participated (figs. 5.1a and 5.1b).[157] And even the impoverished residents of *p'anjach'on*, the Korean equivalent of shantytowns, who had been displaced by various state projects and survived as manual laborers, collected spare change and sent their hard-earned money to the MND. In July 1975, a mothers' association from a *p'anjach'on* made headlines by organizing a donation effort in their local district (*tong*); they collected money from residents and encouraged those without money to gather and sell recyclable refuse to raise money for donations.[158] Expatriate Korean communities abroad also contributed, sending money to their local embassies for forwarding to the ROK government.[159] Whether willingly or out of obligation, the Korean people responded to the NDD drives and made significant contributions to support national security. The projects that began with NDD funding in the early 1970s, including the manufacture of basic infantry weapons and patrol boats, became the first programs undertaken by the FIP in the Yulgok Operation, in 1974.[160]

Over time, NDD collections became a part of people's everyday lives. Both the top-down and grassroots collection efforts further instilled Park's ideology of self-reliant national defense throughout South Korean society. While Park followed the coercive methods of

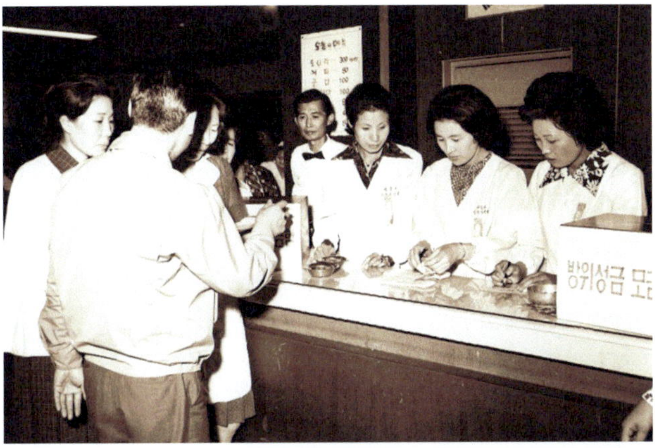

FIGURES 5.1A AND 5.1B. A group of Korean women sells refreshments and snacks as part of their fundraising efforts to gather defense donations in June 1975. *Source:* Courtesy of Seoul Metropolitan Archives; file no. IT3502.

colonial mobilization, his government was more effective than Japan's in driving the citizenry to achieve the state's goals by merging their nationalism with the government's vision of self-reliant national defense. Although the state certainly did not receive unanimous support, in light of people's unfulfilled demands for democracy, it adeptly used diverse social and ideological mechanisms to promote coactions and ties between citizens and the state in a mutual quest for security independence.

The Launch of Yulgok

The growing number of intrusions into South Korean waters by North Korean ships in late 1973 and the reduction of US military aid for Park's Five-Year Military Modernization Plan prompted Park to increase domestic funding for weapons manufacturing and to formalize what had begun as an unofficial, locally driven campaign to raise donations five years earlier.[161] By the end of 1973, defense donations had become an official government program. With the commencement of the Yulgok Operation in March 1974, unbeknown to the public, government insiders began to refer to the revenue from the NDD (and later from the NDT as well) as "Yulgok funds" (*Yulgok chagŭm*).[162] Park's public campaign for the NDD, which he began in December 1973, raised approximately 6.45 billion won (approximately $13 million) in the first ten months, and by November 1975 a total of 16.13 billion won (approximately $33 million) had been raised for defense strengthening (which was secretly allocated to Yulgok projects).[163] The MND immediately directed the funds to domestic arms production and the purchase of new weaponry.[164] The funds were also used to boost maritime security by expanding and equipping the maritime forces, addressing South Korea's vulnerability from the sea exposed in the Paengnyŏng Island incident. Table 5.1 shows how the NDD funds collected between 1974 and 1975 were distributed.

While the NDD was amassing funds to modernize weapons and equipment, the government increased its investment in weapons R & D. The funding for R & D undertaken by the ADD saw a sixfold increase from 1974 to 1975, jumping from 4.6 billion won (which constituted 1.3 percent of the government's defense budget in 1974) to 28.1 billion won (accounting for 8 percent of the 1975 defense budget).[165] Reports from the MND to President Park also disclose other uses of the NDD in 1974, including the construction of troop facilities such as barracks, underground bunkers, apartments, and dormitories for army officers, all as part of Yulgok.[166] The NDD was the primary source of revenue for all early Yulgok projects until Park established the compulsory NDT, which officially replaced the NDD as Yulgok's funding stream. However, even after the institution of the NDT in 1975, defense donations from Korean civilians continued to pour in.

Table 5.1.
Distribution of National Defense Donation Funds Collected in 1974 and 1975

Defense project	Amount allocated
Defense of islands in the Yellow Sea	728 million won ($1.50 million)
Construction of ROK Navy speedboats	673 million won ($1.39 million)
Maritime Police communication equipment	300 million won ($0.62 million)
Security in Seoul	4,270 million won ($8.82 million)
Homeland Reserve Forces equipment	1,950 million won ($4.03 million)
Ground forces equipment (purchases)	1,215 million won ($2.51 million)
ROK Air Force planes	6,900 million won ($14.26 million)

SOURCES: O W., "25-cho wŏn Yulgok," 422; Sŏ U., Sin, and Chang, *Pangwi sanŏp*, 62; *HGKK*, 5:238.
NOTES: The allocated amounts are based on the 1975 KRW-USD exchange rate of 484 won to the dollar. In 1974 and 1975, 16,130 million won (16.13 billion won, or $33 million) were distributed. The exchange rate was obtained from "Official Exchange Rate (LCU per US$, Period Average)—Korea, Rep.," World Bank, accessed April 11, 2023, https://data.worldbank.org/indicator/PA.NUS.FCRF?locations=KR&view=chart.

The National Defense Tax

Despite fundraising efforts through the NDD, Yulgok projects were becoming expensive. In February 1974 the JCS had estimated that Yulgok's first FIP would cost approximately $1.526 billion over the plan's eight-year period.[167] But after the launch of the FIP in March, the JCS raised the projected cost to $1.668 billion in June and then to $2.14 billion in August.[168] By this time, continual cuts in US military aid for Park's Five-Year Military Modernization Program had also substantially reduced grants from the US under the Military Assistance Program (MAP).[169] Whereas US grant aid through the MAP made up 14.5 percent of South Korea's total defense budget in 1974, it accounted for only 8.6 percent in 1975.[170] Attempting to make up for the shortage, the United States offered loans through the FMS program, which obligated South Korea to purchase US weapons and military equipment through a loan-credit system.[171] The US decision to cut aid was ostensibly a result of budget constraints and concerns over Park's human rights violations, but the United States also took into consideration South Korea's own rising military and economic strength.[172]

Due to insufficient funding by the United States, Park's Five-Year Military Modernization Plan "achieved a 69 percent level of the original target by 1976, causing a two-year delay in the completion of the program."[173]

Meanwhile, the ROK was deeply engaged in an arms race with the DPRK, which Park believed to have superior military capabilities thanks to Kim Il Sung's head start via Soviet-backed defense industrialization that began in the early 1960s.[174] Although data on North Korea's military spending are elusive and imprecise, it was widely believed at the time that Pyongyang was spending between 10 and 25 percent of its annual gross national product (GNP) on its military by the mid-1970s; by comparison, South Korea spent 4.4 percent of its GNP on national defense in 1974 and 5.1 percent in 1975.[175] Even prominent US experts, the CIA, and international think tanks like the International Institute for Strategic Studies (IISS) estimated that North Korea had significant advantages in terms of troop strength, ground firepower (including tanks, armored personnel carriers, and artillery), military aircraft, ships, and reserve supplies.[176] The perceived gap between the two Koreas only hardened Park's resolve to develop a self-reliant and modernized military. Moreover, the fall of South Vietnam to communist North Vietnam in April 1975 further eroded his trust in the United States and its commitment to the ROK. Limited by an inadequate defense budget and reduced US military aid, Park urgently needed additional revenue to fund Yulgok's modernization of the military, and once again he turned to the Korean people themselves.

Shortly after the fall of South Vietnam, the Park government drafted a new national tax. In June 1975, his administration submitted the National Defense Tax Law to the National Assembly as a bill. The bill stated that it was being introduced "in response to recent developments in the international situation and the increased threat of a North Korean invasion, which create an unprecedented need to strengthen defensive capabilities for homeland security." The objective of the law was "to secure the finances required to establish an independent defense posture."[177] With Park pushing hard, the National Assembly passed the new law in just one month.

On July 16, 1975, the government promulgated the National Defense Tax Law, which was introduced as a public tax to help meet the rising cost of South Korea's defense needs. However, the compulsory NDT, or *pangwise*, as it was known to the people, was actually intended to finance the classified Yulgok Operation. From 1975 on, the NDT created a much larger internal pool of funds for the defense budget. The NDT was a surtax, or value-added tax, that raised tax rates in a range of categories, including the income tax, import tax, corporate tax, inheritance or gift tax, registration tax, liquor tax, commodity tax, admissions tax, resident tax, property tax, car tax, entertainment tax (e.g., purchases at bars, restaurants, and motels), and land tax (on ownership of farmland, rice paddies, and mountain land).[178] Considering the wide reach of this surtax, virtually all Koreans who spent money were contributing to the Yulgok Operation. For security purposes, since the tax revenue was to be spent on classified operations, the money collected was delivered directly to the MND, bypassing all public and legislative oversight and budgeting.[179]

For Park, the new tax signified more than revenue collecting. The NDT materialized his total security system by institutionalizing national allegiance to self-reliant national defense through personal sacrifice, in the form of the tax. Three days after the promulgation of the NDT, in a speech at Korea National Defense University's graduation ceremony, Park thanked the people for their defense donations and reiterated that such sacrifices were vital. Warning against relying on a faltering US security commitment, Park asserted, "We must bear in mind that the fundamental responsibilities for our national defense lie with us, ourselves." With the implementation of the NDT, Park said, an "indistinguishable oneness of the military and civilians" would establish the nation's "total security posture [*ch'ongnyŏk anbo t'aese*]," in which civilians at home, through their financial donations, taxes, and other support, would strengthen the military's efforts on the battlefront.[180] The NDT put into practice Park's conviction that every South Korean had to act to protect national security, to the extent that there was no distinction between the military and the citizenry.

When the NDT went into effect in 1976, revenue from the surtax amounted to 233.8 billion won (approximately $483 million), or approximately 2 percent of GNP, all of which was spent on Yulgok.[181] Combining the government's preexisting defense budget (4 percent of GNP) with the NDT revenue, South Korea spent a total of 6.1 percent of its GNP on national defense in 1976 (or 32.7 percent of the state budget that year), a huge percentage for any economy.[182] In comparison, the United States spent 5.4 percent of its GNP on defense in 1976, India spent 3.3 percent, France 3.8 percent, Japan 0.9 percent, and the United Kingdom 5.0 percent.[183]

The NDT had an immediate impact on the arms race between the two Koreas by rapidly and drastically expanding the ROK's defense spending. As noted, available data indicate a significant gap in military spending between the DPRK and the ROK in the early 1970s, but in 1976, fueled by NDT revenue, the ROK began surpassing its northern rival in annual military expenditure.[184] According to the Stockholm International Peace Research Institute (SIPRI), for example, the ROK's annual defense spending jumped from $1.69 billion in 1975 to $2.43 billion in 1976, compared with the DPRK's, which went from $2.14 billion in 1975 to $2.36 billion in 1976—although, again, statistics on the DPRK's defense expenditures are almost impossible to verify.[185] It should also be noted that the task of comparing the military spending of two such disparate economies, based on absolute dollar figures or even percentages of GNP, is fraught with problems.[186] Nonetheless, the NDT clearly boosted the ROK's defense expenditures by a large margin. Since then, as the economic performance gap between the two Koreas has continued to widen, the ROK has likely not lost its lead in this aspect of the arms race.

In the late 1970s, the ROK government continued to depend on the people's defense donations and taxes to keep pace with Yulgok's swiftly rising budget requirements and to compensate for the declining US military grants.[187] In 1976 the JCS again increased the total estimated cost for Yulgok's first FIP, raising it to $4.6 billion; by 1977 the estimate had gone up to $5 billion, and by 1978 it was $5.5 billion.[188] The state increasingly relied on the NDT to meet the cost of Yulgok's projects (table 5.2). From 1976 to 1979, the NDT covered an average of 37.5 percent of the Park government's annual defense expenditures. From 1977 onward, with the NDT and its own defense budget the ROK government could meet its annual defense-spending benchmarks solely with domestic revenue, a remarkable feat considering that until 1969 South Korea had relied on US military aid for up to 50 percent of its annual defense costs.[189] The NDT funds collected were used entirely for Yulgok projects until 1978. From 1979 onward,

Table 5.2.
South Korea's National Defense Tax, 1975–88

Year	Percentage of total taxes	Percentage of government defense expenditures
1975	3.8	14
1976	11.3	38
1977	11.4	36
1978	11.7	36
1979	11.5	40
1980	12.9	37
1981	13.4	40
1982	12.3	37
1983	12.1	40
1984	12.5	42
1985	12.8	44
1986	12.5	43
1987	13.0	48
1988	14.0	43

SOURCE: Hyŏn, *Han'guk ŭi pangwibi*, 91.

as the combined total of NDT revenue and the government defense budget began to exceed Yulgok's projected costs, the government diverted excess funds to defense expenditures beyond Yulgok.[190]

With the defense tax, the government collected a cumulative total of $5.148 billion (2.6 trillion won) between 1976 and 1980.[191] During that period, the NDT represented, on average, nearly 12 percent of the annual national tax revenue (table 5.2). The state invested a total of approximately $5.4 billion (3.14 trillion won) in the Yulgok Operation's first FIP from 1974 to 1981, allocated as follows: 43.3 percent went to projects for the ROK Army, 15.8 percent was dedicated to Navy modernization, 22 percent to Air Force projects, and the remaining 18.9 percent was spent on other costs.[192] Although Yulgok ended up costing more than three times the $1.5 billion that both the Nixon administration and the JCS had originally estimated for South Korea's military modernization, the expanded cost was covered by public funding. This outcome reflects the tightly forged coalition of polity and society that supported South Korea's military development, as well as the massive civic extractions the government carried out to fund Yulgok. Remarkably, although an immense amount was spent on Yulgok, South Korea's

GNP, as well as its volume of exports, increased at the same time so that the country's economy experienced no substitution effect.[193]

Surveillance over Yulgok Spending

The Blue House's financial oversight rendered Yulgok spending surprisingly efficient and limited corruption.[194] O Wŏnch'ŏl and Kim Kwangmo have both attested that Park emphasized the importance of financial cleanliness in all transactions related to Yulgok, to protect the use of citizens' money.[195] To that end, Park himself monitored Yulgok closely. He directly supervised the MND's allocations of Yulgok funds, requiring the ministry to report all activities to him via the SES.[196] And SES technocrats regularly sought his approval on all military projects and procurement deals.

Park was known to have established a multilayered surveillance system to monitor Yulgok's spending and ensure strict oversight of the use of NDT and NDD funds. He ordered the MND to install the Five-Member Committee (Oin Wiwŏnhoe) as an exclusive, covert task force to run the Yulgok Operation and regulate its spending.[197] This special auditing committee was under the jurisdiction of the MND, led by the deputy minister of national defense. Its four other members were the chair of the JCS, the deputy minister for weapons supplies in the MND, the director of the ADD, and O, whom Park included as both a watchdog and his liaison for decision making.[198] In July 1975, the MND's Five-Member Committee expanded into the Six-Member Committee when Park added the deputy minister of the Economic Planning Board to the committee. As a result, three of the six committee members were civilian officials (O, the ADD director, and the deputy minister of the Economic Planning Board), reflecting Park's intent to increase civilian supervision of military spending—that is, the MND's use of public tax revenue. In January 1978, the MND's committee expanded further with the addition of four more members, including another civilian official (from the Office of the Prime Minister), forming the Ten-Member Committee. By November 1978, it was expanded still further and renamed the Force Improvement Plan Promotion Committee.[199]

As an additional layer of surveillance over the MND's committee, Park set up his own separate committee in the Blue House, known as the Blue House Five-Member Committee (Ch'ŏngwadae Oin Wiwŏnhoe). Park's creation of an additional committee was likely motivated by his lack of trust in the MND and its military leadership over Yulgok's spending.[200] The Blue House Five-Member Committee oversaw and audited every proposal and financial decision related to Yulgok. It was led by O and included four of Park's closest advisers in the Blue House: Park's special adviser for national security, his special adviser for economic policy, the special secretary for administration, and the first senior presidential secretary for the economy.[201] As the presidentially appointed overseer of and intermediary on both committees, O was involved in every deliberation and meeting on decisions about Yulgok. Based on O's reports on Yulgok's financial plans and activities, Park delivered his own instructions to improve and support its projects.[202]

In sum, all Yulgok-related policies, transactions, and purchases, as well as all spending of NDD and NDT revenue, came under the inspection of two committees, one led by the MND and the other led by members of the Blue House; together the two committees worked as a dual surveillance system over Yulgok.[203] The system was suited to Yulgok's secrecy, whose clandestine projects already bypassed the government's normal budget-authorization process, which included review by the Economic Planning Board and deliberation by the National Assembly prior to presidential approval. Yulgok budget decisions were instead finalized under rigorous verification and regulation procedures in an alternative process: a review by the MND's committee, a reverification audit by the Blue House Five-Member Committee, and a final review and approval by the president via the SES reports.[204] This exclusive and highly centralized system gave the Blue House technocrats total control over Yulgok's planning and development, independent of outside pressure and out of the sight of politicians, legislators, and the United States.

In spite of the layers of surveillance, the Yulgok funding process was not free from scandal or misappropriation, and the lack of transparency surrounding such enormous military expenditures and huge amounts of tax revenue did not sit well with some public officials. Already concerned about the 1973 Military Procurement Law, these legislators increased their objections to the Park administration's revisions of the law in 1977 and 1979, which further concentrated the power over weapons procurement in the office of the president.[205] The Military Procurement Law had initially granted the president latitude to intervene in all MND weapons deals as part of Park's effort to promote financial transparency in military transactions. During their review of the government's proposed revisions of the law in 1977, however, members of the National Assembly's National Defense Committee expressed growing concern that the new revisions would basically give the president "a political blank check" in all aspects of the defense industry.[206] In October of the same year, during the National Assembly's review of state spending, legislators demanded surveillance powers over government defense expenditures, especially in dealings with corporate defense contractors.[207]

Newspaper articles and reports to President Park on the NDD mention cases in which local authorities did not deliver defense collections directly to the government or to the MND.[208] The autonomy of local governments and the lack of centralized regulation sometimes helped local governments disguise their misappropriations of donations collected for national defense. For example, a report from July 26, 1977, prepared by the director of the Board of Audit and Inspection (Kamsawŏn) and submitted to Park, states that from 1973 to 1977 the city of Pusan did not deliver to the MND all of the defense donations collected from its residents.[209] In its defense, the Pusan city council claimed to have used the undelivered funds to invest in the city's own security, by building new facilities, supporting local surveillance against spies, and training reserve troops. In relation to Pusan's undelivered donations, the report points to the varying effectiveness of regional offices overseeing the NDD and a central surveillance system too weak to guarantee complete deliveries of collected donations. The report concludes by recommending corrections in the delivery process as well as greater intervention by the MND and the Ministry of Home Affairs to ensure that all local donations reached the MND.

Regardless of such evident loopholes, Park's surveillance system proved relatively effective in preventing large-scale misuse of public defense funds. In fact, after Park's surveillance system shut down following his death in 1979, both the NDT and the NDD became rife with corruption, demonstrating the crucial role that Park's rigorous oversight must have played in deterring it. Following his successful military coup in December 1979, Chun Doo-hwan abolished the SES, which had overseen Yulgok's weapons development, and put the MND back in charge of the defense industry. This decision effectively reopened the doors to the financial mismanagement and scandal that had festered under the military's watch before Park had seized control. Under the MND's management of secret Yulgok projects in the 1980s, and without oversight from either the Blue House or the National Assembly, rampant financial abuse plagued the military sector. The NDD was finally discontinued in 1988 amid growing public distrust over where the money was being spent.

Corruption and the misuse of funds were publicly exposed during the anticorruption campaign of the subsequent government of Kim Young-sam, in its investigation of the preceding military regimes. The public learned of the Yulgok Operation in 1993 when it was implicated in financial scandals involving Hanahoe, the group of military elites under former president Chun.[210] What came to be known as "*Yulgok piri*" (Yulgok corruption) eventually led to the official dismantling of the Yulgok Operation in 1995, although its projects continued under different names.[211] While Chun and his successor, Roh Tae-woo, were both imprisoned for their misuse of Yulgok funds and for accepting bribes from chaebol, among other crimes, Kim's anticorruption investigation did not discover any evidence of financial misconduct on the part of Park, or at least none that could be traced to him at the time of his death—which implies Park's relative "cleanliness" in terms of his financing of self-reliant national defense.[212]

The Transformative Impact of Donations and Taxes

When Park introduced the bill for the National Defense Tax Law in the National Assembly in June 1975, the members of the New Democratic Party opposed it, citing the financial hardship it would impose on the Korean populace, especially low-income households.[213] Aside from this initial resistance by the major opposition party, however, there is hardly any record of organized opposition or publicly demonstrated resistance by the Korean people against either the NDD or the NDT in the 1970s.[214]

Political and social acceptance of the defense tax was influenced by the design of the NDT as a progressive tax, which required the rich to pay a larger portion (through surtaxes imposed on existing income tax and property tax, for example).[215] In general, South Koreans did not pay a large percentage of their income in taxes at this point, which also may have made the NDT more acceptable.[216] Nonetheless, the NDT still disproportionately affected poorer families because it included value-added taxes on purchases of everyday commodities like rice and ramen, as well as on phone bills, cars, liquor, and soft drinks; it thus functioned partly as a sales tax. For example, if a household's phone bill tax prior to the NDT was 15 percent of the bill, it increased to 25 percent with the defense tax (the NDT added 10 percent to the existing phone bill tax). For a phone bill of 2,000 won per month, the tax rose from 300 won to 500 won.[217] The NDT also added a surtax to items and services classified as "luxury consumption": when people went out for drinks, played golf, bought jewelry or electric appliances, or went to a restaurant, they had to pay an additional 10 to 20 percent tax on top of the existing liquor, commodity, admissions, or entertainment taxes on those goods and services. Adding the surtaxes was essentially the same as increasing the prices of those goods for all consumers. A former US Peace Corps worker in Seoul in the late 1970s said, "I remember this [NDT] well and was quite annoyed that I had to pay this tax on nearly everything I bought or did. I'm sure many Koreans felt that way too."[218] Still, the lack of resistance to such a major financial extraction by the state contrasts starkly with the ample record of political and social resistance to other policies under the Yusin rule in the same period. People could more readily accept this ad hoc tax because most Koreans believed Park's message that the security threats the country faced could only be staved off through a strong and independent national defense, which the NDT would finance. Notwithstanding passionate and unyielding protests by activists against Park's undemocratic modus operandi, in general South Koreans were on board with the government's prioritization of national security.

Social Response

The foreboding sense that South Korea's national security was under threat was not limited to the president; it was a sentiment shared nationwide (see chapter 1). With the memory of North Korea's invasion—and the devastating civil war it had brought just twenty years prior—still fresh in people's minds, the major changes in the United States' force posture were enough to instill fear in most of the South Korean population. In a national survey conducted by the *Maeil Kyŏngje* newspaper in March 1974, people were asked for their opinions on a range of political, sociocultural, economic, psychological, and regional issues. One area of exceptional consensus regardless of one's place of birth, generation, or gender was concern for "national security." In the survey, 52 percent of respondents agreed with the idea that "freedom can be deferred in order to ensure a total effort for national security."[219] In another national survey conducted by the same newspaper in June 1976, 14.7 percent of the respondents prioritized "freedom"—as in political freedom, democracy—over national security, whereas 29 percent believed that freedom and national security could be developed in parallel, and the remaining 56.3 percent indicated that national security took priority over all else, including freedom.[220] While the validity of surveys conducted by state-controlled media under the Yusin regime should certainly be questioned, their results may also be interpreted as affirming the effectiveness of the state's campaign for self-reliant national defense—especially amid the prospect of the ROK's abandonment by USFK troops, which deeply alarmed most Korean leaders and citizens alike, regardless of their political differences. Even Park's detractors yielded to the defense tax as a necessary measure and joined with the government in desperate attempts to persuade US policymakers to change their position on troop withdrawals.[221]

By the mid-1970s, the shocking discovery of secret tunnels running from North Korea into South Korea, combined with communist expansion in Indochina and the US withdrawal from Vietnam, heightened security concerns among South Korean citizens. However, not everyone accepted without question the Park government's views on national security and its portrayal of external threats. Those most fiercely opposed to Park's policies on national welfare and political freedom, including many dissident intellectuals, religious leaders, and university students, certainly did not accept Park's warnings about North Korean threats to the same degree. Some even accused Park of fabricating these threats. In response, Park publicly criticized his detractors for compromising national security by downplaying the threats.[222] And the evolving security situation favored Park's position.

Even longtime opposition leaders such as Kim Young-sam, despite their ongoing criticism of Park's authoritarian rule, agreed with the government on the importance of keeping the US military presence in South Korea for the protection it provided.[223]

Overall, the prevalent sense of peril broke down some otherwise rigid divisions between the government and society, and even brought together rivals within each sector. For example, in response to communist invasions in South Vietnam and Cambodia in April 1975, the often-divided denominations of the Korean Christian church publicly declared their united stance with the government against the growing communist threat.[224] By this time, an increasing number of activist churches had participated in democratic struggles against the repressive policies of Park's Yusin regime. However, in a significant display of unity in support of Park's anticommunist policies, representatives of the eighteen Christian denominations came together and issued a joint statement: "The recent attacks by the communists in Indochina present a threat to South Korea as well as all free allied nations of Asia. . . . [T]he Korean church, facing the large task of resisting communist invasion, pledges to transcend trivial differences over doctrinal or interpretative matters to stand as one."[225] Acknowledging recent tensions between the church and the government, the statement also included a pledge to prioritize concerns for national defense in collaboration with the state.

Such public declarations, as well as petitions and mass rallies calling for greater national security, were widespread. In line with messages from the state's propaganda machine, schools, religious organizations, and social organizations from all levels of society declared their commitment to the government's total security system and vowed to defend the nation against communists.[226] The Park government, in collaboration with the police and the Korean Central Intelligence Agency, took advantage of the public's fear and framed domestic protesters who opposed Park as communists and North Korean sympathizers or spies, to bolster the regime and rally the people behind the government's anticommunist campaign.[227] The people's shared sense of national crisis, along with Park's campaign for self-reliant national defense, created relatively widespread support for public financial collections, even amid social unrest and continued resistance to the Yusin state. Urgent and impassioned donation drives, inspired by patriotism mixed with fear, prompted many citizens to donate large amounts and even pay extra defense taxes to support national security.[228] Not all Koreans agreed with Park's politics, nor did all willingly take part in his programs to strengthen defense, but all were impelled, as national citizens (*kungmin*), to participate in one way or another.[229]

It is difficult, if not impossible, to provide evidence of the extent to which Koreans enthusiastically complied with or merely acquiesced to the mobilization and coercion carried out by the Yusin state. Nonetheless, in my surveys of 313 Korean civilians who lived in South Korea during the Park regime, 265 respondents (84.7 percent) answered yes when asked if they had supported the NDT and NDD as necessary measures for national defense, while 27 said no and 21 did not respond to that question.[230] The respondents came from various regions and socioeconomic backgrounds, and all were at least in their teens when the NDD and NDT were collected in the 1970s. When asked if they "agreed with" President Park's self-reliant national defense policy at the time, 275 respondents answered yes (87.9 percent), 16 said no, and 22 did not respond or wrote "I don't know." Owing to the limited sample size, these results are suggestive, not determinative, and it must also be considered that the surveys were conducted several decades after the Park era. Still, the vast majority of those I surveyed said that they had agreed with Park's national-security objectives and supported his defense-financing efforts in the 1970s. The survey results also reflect that the defense tax and donations were experienced as ubiquitous, everyday facts of life. In response to open-ended questions about their personal experiences with the NDD or NDT, respondents said they recalled contributing through donation drives or taxes collected at work (through payroll deductions), at school (where they contributed as students), at Homeland Reserve Forces training sessions, and in the context of civic and social affairs (including at community and neighborhood events, through social groups, and even at large family gatherings). Respondents also made donations through the NVM. According to my survey, whether because of the state's mobilization efforts or the prevailing national security situation, in the 1970s the majority of the respondents had accepted NDT and defense donations as normal civic responsibilities.

Notwithstanding the apparent support of many Korean citizens, the coercive aspect of the NDD and NDT as state extraction tools can neither be denied nor underestimated. Public cooperation was influenced by the power of the Yusin state and its total co-optation of the populace: Park's defense agenda demanded the performed material and cultural commitment of all people and businesses to his state programs. The prevailing security climate made it extremely difficult for both the general public and the legislators to resist the security-related agenda under Yusin. For large corporations, the NDD functioned almost as a double defense tax forced on businesses. Many people and companies felt pressure from all directions to cough up money and to make their quotas for the defense budget, for fear of being branded unpatriotic.

In my interviews with ordinary civilians of the Park era, some respondents described feelings of resistance and resentment toward the defense donation campaigns and the compulsory defense tax.[231] Ms. Kim, who worked in Taejŏn in the 1970s, explained: "I made defense donations but not voluntarily. . . . I participated more out of obligation."[232] Ms. Paek, who attended public schools in South Korea in the 1970s, stated: "We were forced to donate [at school], and it was definitely not voluntary. Teachers would criticize me if I didn't bring money to school for the [defense] donation."[233] Mr. Pak, another interviewee, recalled his experience in elementary school during the same period: "We couldn't get good marks from teachers without making defense donations, so some of the poor students had to go sell newspapers in order to donate."[234] As another interviewee claimed, "Considering the nation's overall 'mood' [*punwigi*] at the time, no one could possibly oppose the National Defense Donation or National Defense Tax, especially amid the ongoing [state of civil] war [with North Korea] and living under the National Security Law. . . . The Korean Central Intelligence Agency would take away anybody who publicly opposed it."[235]

Beyond Coercion and Consent

Whether participation was compulsory, voluntary, or a mixture of both, the defense tax and defense donations shaped a new sociopolitical discourse on civilian participation in the ROK's self-reliant national defense. Despite the ongoing, contentious debate surrounding state-society relations under Park, it is hard to deny that the Park regime operated with broad societal support, especially in matters related to security and economic growth.

Challenging static portrayals of the Park era as a binary opposition between (state) coercion and (people's) resistance, a group of scholars, most notably Jie-Hyun Lim, have used the concept of "mass dictatorship" to incorporate the notion of the people's "consent" to the Park state, in spite of its coercion of society.[236] According to Lim and Paul Corner, mass dictatorship refers to "the attempted mobilisation of the masses for state projects which frequently secured voluntary mass participation and support."[237] They add:

> In the context of twentieth century dictatorships, coercion and consent, domination and hegemony, forced mobilization and self-mobilization cannot be seen as polar opposites to each other; rather they should be understood as integral parts of dictatorship in which one concept does not necessarily exclude the other. In fact, seen from the view-point of history from below, consent and coercion are not exclusive opposites; they can and do co-exist. Coercion itself is a multi-layered experience spanning many definitions—internalised coercion, forced consent, passive conformity, and silent resignation are just some of them. The realities of coercion and consent are subject to negotiations and interactions between individual historical actors and the mass dictatorship regime.[238]

Pointing to the example of post-1956 communist Eastern Europe, Lim argues that a dictatorship that functions with the people's consent, whether active or passive (nonvoluntary but compliant), constitutes a "consensus dictatorship" or a "dictatorship of consent," a form of modern mass dictatorship.[239] In fact, the defense donation movement during the Park era represents a powerful instance in which the people of South Korea were forcibly mobilized to participate in a state-sponsored program, while at the same time, the program drew strength from many participants who were motivated to support the state's mission and the values undergirding defense industrialization. The top-down policymaking and bottom-up efforts enabled a greater convergence of forces to achieve total security. This presents a more complex picture of the state–civil society relationship in the ROK under

Park, far different from the clear-cut dichotomy depicted in politicized views of the period. If we view state power in the Gramscian sense, as a combination of coercion and consent, we can see that by combining his authority and policies with historical precedent and the people's collective experience and demands, Park built up a level of political consent that supported and funded national defense.[240]

While fear of the regime drove mass compliance, in the long run the NDD and NDT were instrumental in intertwining the public's sense of patriotism with the state's military aspirations, resulting in broad support for self-reliant national defense. Beyond functioning merely as propaganda or military doctrine, Park's movement for self-reliant national defense, as a comprehensive national program, created a new "value system" that socialized people to uphold his security goals.[241] The continued outpouring of voluntary defense donations long after Park's death in 1979, and even after the termination of the NDT in 1990, suggests that the Korean populace had come to regard such contributions as an a priori aspect of citizenship.[242] In fact, the salience of the self-reliant national defense policy, the impetus behind the defense tax and donations, remains visible today in the strong public support for South Korea's ongoing pursuit of security independence.

After Park, Chun Doo-hwan's military regime (1980–88) continued to collect formal defense donations until the end of his rule. Following the June Democracy Movement in 1987, which forced Chun to institute a presidential election and other democratic reforms, the newly elected president Roh Tae-woo finally abolished the NDD in August 1988. Roh also discontinued all other official donation programs that had been initiated under Park, such as the Saemaŭl (New Village) donations. However, the practice of making donations to support national security remained vibrant for some time.[243] Defense donations were actively made even during the government of Kim Young-sam (1993–98), the first civilian president in three decades and a former pro-democracy activist. Even after Kim banned defense donations as a part of his anticorruption campaign, South Koreans, partly driven by the rising nuclear threat from North Korea, continued their contributions into the 1990s.[244]

Indeed, the tradition of making defense donations has been carried on mainly by the generation of Koreans who lived through the

Park era, especially in times of national crisis and conflict with North Korea.[245] This was demonstrated in the aftermath of an incident in March 2010, when a North Korean submarine torpedoed and sank the ROKS *Cheonan*, a Pohang-class corvette of the ROK Navy, in the Yellow Sea off the west coast of South Korea, resulting in the loss of forty-six seamen's lives. In response to this tragedy, citizens and corporations immediately organized defense donation campaigns to provide financial support to the bereaved families and to strengthen national security.[246] A foundation was also established to support these efforts.[247] In particular, many individual donations came from elderly Koreans, such as eighty-nine-year-old Kim Yongch'ŏl, who made headlines when he donated his entire life's savings in response to the *Cheonan* incident, asking that the money be spent on national security.[248] The grassroots donation drive to raise funds in response to the *Cheonan* incident has continued even without government sponsorship.[249]

Older Koreans who had been the main contributors to the NDD under Park, particularly those who were at least teenagers or young adults in the 1970s (born before 1960), have done the most to keep the defense donation culture going.[250] Today, they also constitute the core of South Korean conservatism, as many from this generation remain steadfast in their commitment to a strong defense against North Korea. Their stance reflects the enduring culture of voluntary donations and profound concern for national security that were prevalent when these people came of age—not to mention the entrenched spirit of anticommunism that was at its height then. These sentiments were exemplified in 2013 when Chŏng Hŭisu (b. 1953), a conservative politician and member of the then-ruling Saenuri Party and the National Assembly's National Defense Committee, proposed formally reinstituting the NDD in response to North Korea's nuclear arms development.[251] Today, many of these citizens continue to passionately advocate for a stringent policy against North Korea, a position contrasting starkly with the more liberal views of the younger generation.

In sum, Park's efforts to heighten public awareness of the nation's defense needs and to engage them in national security affairs built up an allegiance to self-reliant national defense among the people and helped to create a culture of voluntary defense donations. One way he did this was by exhibiting and publicly celebrating newly developed weapons funded by defense donations and taxes. On October 1, 1979, during a nationally televised military parade for Armed Forces Day, Park's government proudly displayed the Polar Bear missile, the crowning achievement of the Yulgok Operation. Thereafter, the missile became a regular feature of the annual parade.[252] Following the ceremony that day, Park wrote in his diary:

> We celebrated the 30th anniversary of the establishment of the ROK Armed Forces on Armed Forces Day. . . . [O]ur military has now developed into a formidable force. Since the 1970s, through our dedication and efforts to establish a self-reliant national defense, the military has become fortified each year. I was proud to learn that 70–80 percent of the military equipment displayed as part of today's event was domestically developed. In particular, the multiple launch rockets as well as medium- and long-range ballistic missiles that successfully test-fired on September 26 last year were introduced to the public for the first time, drawing enthusiastic applause and welcome from citizens. Our military has grown and become so much stronger both internally and externally that its transformation can be felt in the skin. Our men in uniform are full of spirit. Perhaps this is the first time in our history that we are equipped with such a powerful military. Soldiers, I implore you to continue to strive harder to bring glory to our nation. God bless our soldiers.[253]

According to O Wŏnch'ŏl, "This diary entry in some ways became the last will of President Park, a man who devoted his life to Korea's establishment of a self-defense capacity."[254] Park was assassinated less than a month after he made that diary entry, but not before he had established Yulgok as the cornerstone of South Korea's independent national defense.

Conclusion

The Yulgok Operation epitomized the thrust of Park's defense policy: advancing security independence, rallying civilians to finance military modernization, and shaping Korean attitudes toward a lasting commitment to self-reliant national defense. By channeling revenue from the NDD and the NDT to Yulgok projects, Park's government established an independent and continuous stream of civilian funding for his signature military modernization program, relegating to the citizenry the lion's share of responsibility for financing national defense. Yulgok and its weapons programs fundamentally shifted South Korea's defense posture by cutting a new path away from total reliance on US military aid and equipping the military with domestically produced arms.

The story of the NDD collections that went to Yulgok tells how the state engineered and capitalized on a distinctively Korean interplay between polity and society, using local citizens to mobilize their own donation efforts in support of the nation. This unique dynamic was rooted in patterns reaching back to Korea's colonial wartime experience, and perhaps even further back to its long history of strong and autonomous local communities.[255] Nonetheless, historical precedent alone does not explain the magnitude of the contributions that went to Yulgok. Park's Yusin system both forcefully and strategically incorporated elements of the older donation practices into new structures, fashioning a national movement to achieve his military goals.

Far from solely functioning as an instrument of mobilization and extraction of civilian resources, the Yusin state impelled important cultural and ideological shifts that transformed civilians into active stakeholders in national security. The system of public funding not only financed South Korea's arms production but also reinforced the people's collective commitment to their nation and its safety. With the NDD, the NDT, and the NVM as mobilizing forces, the Park state adroitly used ideology to build consensus among a vast majority of South Korea's citizens. This comports with Jie-hyun Lim's notion of a "dictatorship of consent" and Antonio Gramsci's emphasis on the social consensus that a state builds through cultural leadership—that is, how the state promotes acceptance and normalization of its ideas among the masses to uphold political and economic order.[256] The consensus-building aspect of Park's mobilization strategy has not been widely appreciated in scholarship on the Park era. State-led campaigns spread Park's ideas through the populace and mobilized social and community groups. As part of this cultural movement, the NDD and NDT were powerful mechanisms by which the Park regime conscripted civilians to support national defense. In this sense, the most profound impacts of the NDD and the NDT were cultural, rather than strictly material or even military, owing to the influence these institutions had on many Koreans' everyday lives and beliefs.

The people's newly adopted commitments to security and the spirit of self-reliant national defense that powered the Yulgok Operation led to further, more tangible results. By strategically mobilizing citizens ideologically and connecting their nationalism and safety concerns with Park's self-reliant national defense policy, the Yusin state was able to wield far greater power for resource extraction than it would have had through coercion alone. In addition, the success of the NDD and NDT, along with the HCI Policy, signified the state's newfound ability to fund large-scale development projects internally, instead of depending on foreign financial aid and investment as it had done previously. The collection campaigns also expanded on the tax reforms Park instituted in the late 1960s and the 1970s by fusing financial contributions and national defense, thereby justifying the increased donations and taxes, and broadening public compliance.[257] In general, the nationwide collection efforts converged with Park's defense policy to legitimize and strengthen the state's extraction powers, while also seeding a tax and donation culture that would endure for generations. Clearly the power to mobilize citizens and extract domestic resources was key not only to the buildup of South Korea's defense industry but also to its overall economic development.

CONCLUSION

Self-Reliant National Defense

The Cornerstone of Modern Korea

> The defense industry is the project that most simply and directly displayed President Park Chung Hee's ideology and philosophy for national development.
> —Kim Kwangmo, interview, July 29, 2021

In his quest to establish the ROK's self-reliant national defense, Park Chung Hee pursued the total merging of state and society in the cause of domestic arms production. By rallying all forces for military modernization, his regime fundamentally transformed the economy, the polity, and the very soul of the nation. The urgent need for weapons and a modernized military drove Park's policies for heavy and chemical industrialization (HCI) and economic expansion; in turn, progress made in these areas fueled both military and industrial advancements. The rapid growth of a powerful new military-industrial complex reflects the Park state's orchestrated strategy of dual development of industry and defense.

External historical forces and internal actions together paved the way for the convergence of public and private interests in the service of national security. The national security emergency presented by threats and attacks coming from communist North Korea, combined with the softening of US military protection, spurred the president's radical call for self-reliant national defense through indigenized arms production and a total security state. An external influence from Korea's past was also important, as Park and his technocrats looked to Japan—Korea's former colonizer—and how it had achieved its own export-led HCI in the 1960s, also in tandem with arms manufacturing and based on the state's partnership with a few large conglomerates. Furthermore, Park's deployment of locally organized civilian forces in his mobilization of South Korean society expanded on colonial structures he had known under Japanese rule.

The key internal measures that contributed to the Park government's total security system were Park's presidential directives system and the Yusin Constitution he imposed. These measures provided him the executive power necessary to launch South Korea's Heavy and Chemical Industrialization Policy (HCI Policy), which operated as the government's grand strategy to maximize civilian entrepreneurship, infrastructure, capital, and labor to benefit domestic arms production. Notwithstanding his full authority under Yusin, Park understood that the success of his defense industrialization plan also depended on substantial citizen cooperation and support from the ground up. To that end, he constantly stoked the fire of ideological and cultural support for his total security system through distinct but interlocking programs, such as the New Village Movement (NVM), the National Scientization Movement (NSM), the National Defense Donation (NDD), and the National Defense Tax (NDT). The Park state carried out its self-reliant national defense campaign in concert with efforts to reform the people's mindset to prioritize national defense goals and, in so doing, built a new cultural superstructure that powerfully infused the state's goals throughout civil society.[1] With the resulting shift in the collective national consciousness that accommodated and even reinforced the nation's historic changes, the political and socioeconomic order remained relatively stable, in spite of growing antiauthoritarian opposition.

The Interplay of the State and the People

The story of the South Korean defense industry sheds light on the indigenous forces that worked to achieve military modernization and economic growth under Park. This book reveals how various state and nonstate actors—including military and civilian forces, as well as entities from both the public and private sectors—collectively shaped the South Korean model of militarized industrialization. Notwithstanding the United States' broad influence on South Korea during the Cold War, these distinct Korean actors and institutions played pivotal roles.[2] Although the Park administration has been criticized for its insular and top-down approach to policymaking, newly available evidence from archival materials and my interviews with contemporaneous participant-observers show the extent to which Park's policies fostered collaboration between a diverse range of agencies, both within and outside the state apparatus.

The Second Economic Secretariat (SES) in the Blue House spearheaded the efforts toward Park's goal of establishing a civilian-based arms production system. However, the success of this system relied on the coordinated efforts of an extensive network of national and local organizations. Entities such as the Factory NVM committees, local manufacturers, educational institutions, and grassroots fundraisers for the NDD, as well as coordinating ministries—including the Ministry of National Defense, Ministry of Commerce and Industry, Ministry of Education, and Ministry of Science and Technology—all provided multilevel support. Likewise, in line with Blue House orders, newly established government-funded research institutes advanced the nation's research and development (R & D) and distributed technology to civilian industries to expedite domestic technological growth and weapons development.

The Agency for Defense Development (ADD), one of the government-funded research institutes and the weapons-research arm of the Blue House, played a vital role in transferring cutting-edge science and technology (S & T) to domestic private industries. The agency was also critical to advancing R & D and standardizing quality control for both weapons and commercial products. Individual testimonies from ADD researchers (as presented in chapter 4) show that they were proactive, innovative, and resourceful in acquiring new technologies. This entailed undertaking high-risk research, engaging in relentless experimentation, and actively sourcing technology from overseas. The commitment, sacrifice, stealth, and ingenuity of these researchers were indispensable to the ROK's military modernization efforts.

In close collaboration with the ADD and other government-funded research institutes, the chaebol also strove to indigenize technologies and skills for weapons production. Their level of engagement far exceeded simply following state directives. As new defense contractors, they overcame previous boundaries and expanded their operations by investing in R & D, developing new prototypes, competing with other firms, and negotiating for foreign technical aid—all activities that involved risks. The chaebol eventually exerted their own push to advance weapons manufacturing beyond state provisions through the independent efforts of corporate executives, engineers, technicians, and craftspeople. In this aspect, the chaebol and their workers represented the drive of civilians in the workplace to achieve national security.

Outside the defense labs and factories, civilian participation in the self-reliant national defense movement involved citizens of all stripes, including individual taxpayers, donors, local groups, and residents from every region. This widespread involvement can largely be attributed to the success of the state's mobilization mechanisms—namely, the NVM, NDD, and NDT. The financial contributions garnered through these mechanisms proved essential to Park's weapons development, particularly his efforts in the secret Yulgok Operation. Civilians also carried an additional burden for national security as reserve troops in Park's Homeland Reserve Forces.

Examining the efforts of these diverse actors shows us that the government's operations were more complex than the exclusively state-centric narratives of the era have appreciated.[3] While South Korea's defense industry development was certainly steered by a top-down, technocratic state, we cannot underestimate the contributions of an engaged citizenry. A wide range of civilians driven by patriotism, profit motives, fear, or a sense of responsibility joined Park and his Blue House technocrats—along with entire ministries, research institutes, corporations, and industrial labor—to actively and critically support it.

The dynamics at work between the strong state and its mobilized and militarized citizens blurred conventional lines between coercion and consent. In addition to exerting disciplinary power, the Park government skillfully persuaded many South Koreans to willingly conform to its agenda. This nuanced, dialogic aspect of the state-society relationship operated alongside and despite the prevailing military influences. The narrative of defense industry development presented in these chapters reveals how extensively the state coupled its policies with larger societal concerns and sentiments, even as it was also successful in amplifying those concerns. Undoubtedly, popular protest against the Park government was a defining feature of the era and has been the focal point of much scholarly research. However, only limited attention has been given to the ways in which the regime effectively engaged with and integrated citizens' ideological and material interests into its own goals.

If we view Park's rule in a Gramscian sense, it is clear that his state recognized the need to exercise "cultural leadership" to both co-opt and change people's beliefs and attitudes to obtain their support for national security and the defense industry.[4] Through the regime's bureaucratic expansion into social and cultural structures—schools, workplaces, public events, community organizations—and through Park's repeated articulation of national concerns, the state constantly engaged citizens with its message. To further his agenda, Park consistently promoted principles of civilian ownership and responsibility for national defense, eventually asking all civilians to make active contributions to meet national security needs. The levers of coercion and consent were also applied in other areas of the state's mobilization for rapid development. As Byeong-ju Hwang writes, "The developmental mobilization from the top was intimately conjoined with the *desire* of a great number of Koreans. The state unified and collectivized with its own code the dispersed desires of its citizens. As such, Park's regime was not only the politics of repression but *of desire*."[5]

The total convergence of state and society for militarized industrialization shaped South Korea's sociopolitical and cultural processes in a powerful way and re-formed the national identity. Park connected with South Koreans strongly where national security was concerned, and through that connection, he was able to forge broad coalitions among industrialists, scientists, workers, and ordinary tax-paying citizens for his program of militarized industrialization. National security became the basis for national unity.

Legacies of Militarization

For more than four decades, the principles that guided the ROK under Park have continued to reverberate through subsequent governments. This legacy is particularly evident in several key areas. First, Park's techno-nationalist fervor, which shaped his regime's philosophy, continues to influence contemporary policymaking. Second, successive ROK governments have upheld the dual-purpose defense industry that his regime built through the HCI Policy. Third, the symbiotic cooperation between the public and private sectors, cultivated during the Park era, remains a vibrant aspect of South Korea's commercial and military landscape. Finally, the cultural and ideological systems that underpinned the concept of self-reliant national defense are still prominent in South Korea today.

Techno-nationalism

Although the country has gone through significant political transformations through democratization since the 1990s, Park's technology-driven modernization and the NSM remain deeply embedded in South Korea's governance, which continues to prioritize S & T and self-reliant national defense.[6] This dual commitment to technology and security is not confined to the realm of state policy but is also widespread among the populace. All administrations since Park's have adhered to his vision of "technological self-reliance" (*kisul charip*) and furthered the nation's embrace of S & T for the good of both the economy and national defense.[7] The defense industry in South Korea remains closely involved with domestic technological development, and the country's ongoing efforts to achieve indigenized weapons production epitomize the quest for technological self-reliance that began with Park. At the ground level, the NSM's promotion of technical education and training has had a lasting benefit for South Korean industries by nurturing a highly sophisticated workforce essential for economic growth.

Immediately after Park's rule, the heavy and chemical industries experienced a steep decline, partly owing to the Park regime's overinvestment in those few industries. However, many principles established under the HCI Policy were upheld by the administration of Park's successor, Chun Doo-hwan. While Chun reduced state subsidies for HCI in response to inflation and the economic crisis of the early 1980s, and he also downsized the domestic defense industry in favor of increased imports of US weapons, his government invested heavily in S & T and technical skills, thus continuing the Park state's pursuit of technological independence.[8] Under the fifth Five-Year Economic Development Plan (1982–86), for example, Chun's government made big investments in high-tech electronics, semiconductors, telecommunications, information systems, and commercial R & D.[9] The Ministry of Science and Technology's "technology drive policy" under Chun expanded the government's R & D contracting with various civilian sectors and adopted the ADD's R & D method as a model for reforming the national R & D management system.[10] The knowledge gained by scientists and engineers who worked on ADD projects under Park also helped improve civilian S & T.[11] Chun's industrial policies not only retained the Park-era system for technical training of skilled workers but also assigned the chaebol a leading role by supporting their development of in-house R & D. In this regard, Chun followed the course set by Park's principles of "nation building through industrialization" and "technological self-reliance," phrases that still express deeply held priorities and values for government and industry in South Korea.[12]

Roh Tae-woo (1988–93), another general and Chun's handpicked successor, instituted a policy of "Koreanization of Korean defense" (*Han'guk pangwi ŭi han'gukhwa*).[13] Roh aimed to reduce South Korea's military dependence on the United States by reinvigorating the defense industry and reasserting its self-reliant posture through the procurement of new weapons and the modernization of the ROK Air Force and Navy. Like his predecessors, Roh promoted the advancement of indigenous technology to boost localized manufacturing in technology-intensive industries. However, that goal was overshadowed by his preoccupation with the rising demand for democratization and the ROK's evolving policy toward China, Russia, and North Korea during the waning years of the Cold War.[14]

Following Chun and the semi-military regime of Roh Tae-woo, three consecutive civilian governments—headed by Kim Young-sam (1993–98), Kim Dae-jung (1998–2003), and Roh Moo-hyun (2003–8)—continued to prioritize S & T as the basis for growth. Although those democratic administrations introduced a series of political and economic liberalization measures, they also adopted the pro–S & T approach that Park had fostered with the NSM. This commitment was particularly evident in their advancements in biotechnology and nuclear power, even in the face of social protests over ethical concerns surrounding the state's S & T policies promoting these sectors.[15] Under Kim Young-sam, who was focused on eliminating the military's influence on domestic politics, the defense industry was relegated to a lower priority. The onset of the Asian financial crisis further limited Kim's attention to the industry. However, the subsequent administrations of Kim Dae-jung and Roh Moo-hyun, who both emphasized military self-reliance, advanced the technological capabilities of local defense manufacturers.[16] Ironically, it was Kim Dae-jung, a liberal critic and former political rival of Park, who resuscitated Park's strategy of investing in dual-purpose technology (for both civil and military use) and incorporating civilian industries in domestic weapons production.[17] The following administration of Roh Moo-hyun, another liberal opponent of Park's authoritarianism, expanded on Kim's efforts by making major investments in the technical capabilities of private defense manufacturers and founding the Defense Acquisition Program Administration (DAPA) to foster growth in the defense industry.[18] Despite their liberal Sunshine Policy for reconciliation and engagement with North Korea, Kim and Roh pushed for militarization for at least two political reasons: first, to counter the perception that liberal governments were soft on national security and lenient toward the DPRK, and second, to promote the ROK's independence from its patron, the United States.[19] As a result, the defense industry made major strides under their administrations.

Efforts to expand localized arms manufacturing continued under the subsequent conservative administrations of Lee Myung-bak (2008–13) and Park Geun-hye (2013–17), as well as under the liberal administration of Moon Jae-in (2017–22), all of whom displayed unwavering commitment to the development of homegrown weapons and related technologies.[20] Even though he reinstituted the Sunshine Policy to improve relations with North Korea and vowed to bring a formal end to the Korean War through dialogue, Moon was particularly supportive of domestic arms manufacturing: following his inauguration, he immediately declared his commitment to self-reliant national defense and earmarked billions of dollars for defense R & D.[21] Moon increased the ROK's defense budget by a yearly average of 7 percent from 2017 through 2021, outpacing the annual increase of 4 to 6 percent under Park and Lee, who were much more hawkish toward North Korea.[22]

Despite Moon's progressive stance on environmental and economic issues, including his pledge to curtail the power of the chaebol, his administration pursued pro-technology policies that were wedded to a traditional growth-oriented approach and benefited large corporations. Moon employed the phrase "Fourth Industrial Revolution"—which refers to the latest wave in the technological and digital advancements in areas such as artificial intelligence, big-data technology, robots, drones, 3D printing, and the "Internet of Things"—almost as a military and economic slogan.[23] With his Defense Reform 2.0 plan, Moon expanded government support for the development and application of these new technologies for the ROK's military.[24]

Moon's assertive efforts to indigenize new dual-purpose technologies mirrored the techno-nationalist defense policy that had developed through Park's implementation of self-reliant national defense. In its pursuit of defense-technological autonomy and accelerated independent military modernization, Moon's administration echoed the objectives set by Park. Yet, their motivations differed: Park sought independent military technology, particularly for nuclear missiles, to prevent the United States from withdrawing from Korea, whereas Moon pursued independent military capabilities as a means to reduce US involvement on the peninsula. Moon's heavy investment in the domestic weapons industry was driven by the goal of persuading the United States to approve the transfer of wartime operational control (OPCON) from Washington to Seoul—an effort that had begun with his liberal predecessor Roh Moo-hyun in 2005.[25] Moon's substantial defense investment also reflected his objective of decreasing the ROK's reliance on the United States for advanced military technology related to naval and aerial defense.[26]

Like Roh's previous efforts, Moon's push for the OPCON transfer and investments in independent military technology can be viewed as a liberal-nationalist form of self-reliant national defense. This discourse, driven by a desire for greater autonomy from the United States, reflects the sentiments of many South Koreans who hold critical views of past US interventions in Korea. Unlike liberals, who see OPCON transfer as an inevitable step in the ROK's achievement of full sovereignty, conservatives see the US maintenance of wartime OPCON as an affirmation of a strong US-ROK security alliance.[27] Accordingly, Yoon Suk-yeol, the conservative president-elect in 2022, pledged to strengthen Seoul's combined defense posture with Washington as a primary goal of his new administration.[28] This commitment was formalized a year later in the "Washington Declaration," jointly issued by US president Joe Biden and Yoon in April 2023.[29]

Indeed, liberals and conservatives have come to diverge on the main goals of self-reliant national defense. Liberals, who advocate for reconciliation with the DPRK and view US intervention as an obstacle to Korean reunification, have directed their efforts for self-reliant national defense toward the ROK's attainment of full autonomy from the United States.[30] Conservatives, on the other hand, seek to achieve an independent defense posture by fortifying the existing US-ROK military alliance against the traditional enemies, the DPRK and, by association, China. At the same time, both forms of self-reliant national defense seek to give South Korea greater ownership of defense technology and more political leverage in the asymmetrical US-ROK relationship, and thus both approaches can be traced to Park's assertion of self-reliance vis-à-vis the United States.

Furthermore, both liberals and conservatives share a common commitment to science and technology as the pillar of South Korean sovereignty. Administrations from both political camps have consistently prioritized advancements in domestic R & D, recognizing the strong correlation between technological growth and national security independence. President Yoon highlighted this connection explicitly in his statement in June 2023 when he declared, "National security and high-tech industries are directly connected."[31] In line with this vision, Yoon has pledged to transform the ROK military into "a strong force of science and technology" under his

Defense Innovation 4.0 plan.[32] This plan essentially continues the previous Moon administration's efforts to build up the ROK military as a high-tech force by leveraging technologies like artificial intelligence, big data, and robotics.[33] In this sense, Park's fervent techno-nationalist drive for self-reliance supplied the template for South Korea's strategy of building up its S & T sectors in parallel with independent arms development. The ongoing military quest for technological independence as a shared doctrine among both the liberal and conservative political elites, and their collective commitment to achieving self-reliant national defense despite their radically different agendas, are distinct features of the nation's discourse.

The Dual Pursuit of Growth and Security

Administrations since Park's have mostly stayed on the parallel tracks of economic growth and security as the founding principles of self-reliant national defense, developing robust indigenous industries both to supply the ROK military and to expand South Korea's commercial export industries.[34] This parallel military-economic development structure in Korea originally derives from Park's conviction that a strong economy is foundational to national strength and vice versa, the principle encapsulated in the catchphrase "rich nation, strong army." The nation's rivalry with the DPRK has naturally extended the dual pursuit of growth and security. However, it was the Park government that first worked the idea into a practical plan and drew up a national blueprint for future administrations to follow. Most ROK administrations, whether conservative or liberal, have remained committed to continuing Park's dual-purpose defense development even throughout major changes in the years since Park, including the end of the Cold War, evolving US-ROK relations, the rise of democracy, and decreases in the overall proportion of defense spending in South Korea.[35] In fact, apart from the aforementioned efforts to advance domestic military technology, the drive to promote defense industry exports has been one of the few continuities between the current conservative administration of Yoon and the preceding administration of Moon.[36] Yoon and Moon, as well as Moon's predecessors Lee and Park Geun-hye, have publicly supported and invested in defense industry exports as an "engine of economic growth."[37] In the past decade alone, South Korea rose quickly in the international defense market. According to the Stockholm International Peace Research Institute, the country was the fourteenth largest arms exporter in the world for the five-year period of 2012–16, and then moved up to eighth place for 2017–21.[38] Between 2012 and 2016 South Korea's share of global arms exports was about 1 percent. That number nearly tripled, to 2.8 percent, during the subsequent five-year period, when Korea's export sales were 177 percent higher than in the previous five-year period—by far the greatest growth among the top twenty exporters.[39] South Korea's weapons exports in recent years have included sales of patrol corvettes to Malaysia; light combat aircraft to the Philippines and Poland; advanced training aircraft to Indonesia and Thailand; howitzers to India, Turkey, Finland, Norway, Poland, Egypt, and Australia; military vehicles to the Philippines, Poland, and Australia; midrange surface-to-air missiles to the United Arab Emirates; and various weapon supplies to Saudi Arabia.[40]

Under President Yoon, the ROK's arms exports have continued to soar and expand. Since the beginning of his presidency, Yoon has consistently affirmed his commitment to turn the defense industry into South Korea's engine of economic growth, establishing himself as a leading advocate of this vision.[41] In June 2022, Minister of National Defense Yi Chongsŏp declared that "the defense industry will become an industry that feeds the ROK in the future."[42] Two months later, Yoon unveiled his ambitious goal to elevate South Korea into one of the world's top four defense exporters, after the United States, Russia, and France, by 2027.[43] The steadfast bipartisan support for defense exports, coupled with the rising global demands for Korean weapons in the aftermath of Russia's invasion of Ukraine in 2022, ensures that Yoon is well positioned to pursue his goal.[44] During the biennial International Maritime Defense Industry Exhibition in Pusan in June 2023, Yoon reiterated his commitment to defense exports by pledging to assume the role of the "No. 1 salesperson" for the exports of local defense companies.[45]

Today Park Chung Hee's dual-purpose defense industrialization might be aptly described as a form of "defenomics," a portmanteau that combines "defense" and "economics" to refer to the idea that the defense industry can act as a high-tech engine for both national security and economic development. This term is popular among South Korean government and military leaders who promote the potential of the Korean defense industry to spur economic development—especially as the competitiveness of South Korea's HCI sector, which once led the global market in industries like shipbuilding and heavy machinery, has waned in the face of increasing competition from China and Japan.[46]

For five decades, beginning with Park, the ROK has worked toward Park's benchmark of self-reliant defense by closely linking defense industrialization to national economic goals and to expanding technology sectors, as well as to the goal of self-sufficiency in arms production.[47] This integrated approach has empowered the South Korean defense industry to rapidly and cost-effectively produce advanced weapons utilizing cutting-edge technology, thereby enhancing national security and elevating the ROK's position as a global player in both commercial and defense technology and innovation.

Continuing Public- and Private-Sector Cooperation

Always seeking to improve competitiveness and exports, successive ROK governments have promoted active business participation in weapons development and R & D—another legacy of Park-era militarization. The government-led, business-driven model of South Korea's defense industry reflects Park's vision of a defense industry built on private-sector cooperation. In the Park regime's design for the defense industry, the role of the government (that is, the Blue House) was to provide strong guidance and a comprehensive framework to effectively manage and promote the efforts of the private companies engaged in defense development. Fundamentally, defense production was expected to thrive on close cooperation and coordination between government and business.

Government-business ties in the defense sector weakened after Park, especially after the decision-making power for the defense industry shifted from the Blue House to the Ministry of National Defense in the 1980s. According to Pak Ch'anggyu, director of the ADD from 2008 to 2011, despite the ADD's efforts to revitalize government-business cooperation in the defense industry, the agency found it difficult to cultivate private-sector initiative in R & D and improve companies' profitability in the defense market.[48] Pak cited as the defense industry's main challenges the lack of assertive efforts by private companies and the limited government budget allocated to support the industry's growth. Observing these trends, one can discern the critical role that state support and strategic planning played at the inception of the defense industry. Indeed, the Park government's active support for the defense industry, as well as its long-term strategies for weapons development, had clearly been important for the industry's growth.

With renewed attention to the economic potential of the defense industry, recent administrations have again taken up Park Chung Hee's approach to public- and private-sector cooperation. Specifically, they have followed the SES's original strategy of directly engaging with the private sector by investing in business suppliers of military hardware, supporting corporate participation in domestic weapons R & D and production, and aiding the marketization and export of defense products.[49] With their military reforms, Presidents Yoon, Moon, Park Geunhye, and Lee have sought to recharge Korea's indigenous weapons production through closer civil-military technical cooperation and increased public investment in businesses specializing in information technology and weapons-related R & D.

The military-civilian weapons collaborations forged under Park Chung Hee had a lasting impact on the industries of South Korea. Chaebol that served as defense contractors during the Park government, including Hyundai, LG, Hanwha, Kia, Hanjin, Daewoo Shipbuilding and Marine Engineering (now Hanwha Ocean, as of 2023), and formerly Samsung (until its recent exit from the defense industry), as well as Korea Aerospace Industries (a government-supported corporation with roots in the chaebol), continue to operate as principal players in both the economy and military technology.[50] These industry leaders continually contribute to the advancement of military technology through research collaboration with the ADD. The cross-sectoral channels created in the 1970s that led to spin-off and spin-on effects in manufacturing also reinforced technological links between military and commercial production. Today, top firms in South Korea still engage in both commercial and military production, an arrangement that maintains the cycle between defense and commercial manufacturing established by Park's HCI Policy. South Korea's rise as a global arms exporter is largely attributed to its dynamic public-private sector partnership, centered on the military (and the state) and chaebol. This partnership involves a close collaboration between the robust private-sector manufacturing base, particularly in Ch'angwŏn, and the national arms production system. As a result, South Korea has been able to achieve swift manufacturing and delivery of weapons to international customers, outpacing countries like the United States and Germany. "They assemble things in weeks or months that would take us years," a European defense industry executive said in May 2023.[51]

Various negative outcomes of the state-chaebol collusion under Park's militarized industrialization also persist. The Park state's defense building entrenched chaebol-led development in South Korea, which resulted in an oligarchic economic system dominated by a few powerful conglomerates that gradually extended their "octopus-like" reach into many sectors. This system limited business diversification and led to overinvestment in a small number of suppliers, an outcome many critics have cited as a major reason for South Korea's economic collapse in 1997 during the Asian financial crisis.[52] Close government-business ties also resulted in cronyism, coercion of labor, policy priorities of business growth and scientific development at the expense of social equity and welfare, and, ultimately, an ever-widening socioeconomic gap. The *minjung* ("mass" or "people") democratization movement that rose up in protest brought with it a reassessment of Park's economic achievements.

The Korean defense industry has challenges to overcome, as well, many of which began under Park. The Park government's concentrated procurement of US weapons technologies in building up its own defense-technology base forced Korean manufacturers into a systematic dependence on the American military-industrial complex, subjecting them to foreign suppliers' controls and regulations, which limited South Korea's exports of weapons and related products.[53] Notwithstanding South Korea's recent success with exports of domestic arms products, such as howitzers, military vehicles, and combat aircraft, the defense industry at large has not kept up with the ROK's ascent in commercial exports, including smartphones, computers, integrated circuits, ships, and automobiles. Except for a few major defense exporters, like Hanwha Aerospace and LIG Nex1, without the level of government support it enjoyed under Park, the ROK defense industry has become a high-cost, low-profit business sector with a corporate profit margin of only 3 to 5 percent.[54] This has pushed some companies away from defense manufacturing, including Samsung (as mentioned earlier)—which averages profits of more than 12 percent on its commercial electronic products.[55] Today the ROK's defense industry supply chain still lacks diversity and is dominated by a few conglomerates, most of which are companies that have been in business since the Park era.

Another major impediment to growth has been the negative public perception of the industry and, consequently, its overregulation. The revelations of financial corruption in the Yulgok Operation in 1993, compounded by continuing military financial scandals from the mid-1990s to the 2010s, solidified a sense of "defense industry corruption" (*pangsan piri*) in the public's mind that overshadowed the industry's contributions to the Korean economy and national security.[56] Partly to curb corruption, the Roh Moo-hyun government in 2006 created DAPA, which began a trend of heavy regulation and monitoring of the defense sector by civilian officials.[57] Such monitoring intensified under the administrations of Lee, Park Geun-hye, and Moon, whose highly publicized pledges and campaigns to combat corruption in the industry perpetuated the defense industry's poor public image, even as arms exports expanded.[58] According to one longtime defense industry worker, "The defense businesses have been viewed and treated as thieves (*todungnom*) under both liberal and conservative governments."[59] An Tongman, former ADD director, remarked: "The defense industry is a business that protects national security. We should instill pride in those who say they will protect national security. . . . [But] just as in the 1970s, the military still doesn't believe in domestically produced weapons. . . . The Korean people's view of the military industry is also a mess; in general, the public distrust of domestic weapons is too strong. In my view, only when the Korean people start trusting the Korean weapons will the national identity and industrialization also be strengthened."[60]

An and Ch'ae Usŏk, president of the Korean Association of Defense Industry Studies, an academic forum, both cite strong presidential management as key to the defense industry's development. Ch'ae argues that the solution to growing the industry lies in the role of the most powerful government institution, the Blue House. He states: "The

Blue House should take the role of a control tower and lead the efforts to remove excessive regulations and shorten defense acquisition procedures, and then guarantee the independence of defense companies [to develop products more freely on their own]."[61] As part of this initiative, Ch'ae proposes that the Blue House should assume responsibility for overseeing agencies involved in the defense industry, such as the Ministry of National Defense and DAPA. An also shared the view that the defense industry is a special sector that requires active leadership and support from the Blue House.[62] It is worth noting that the only administration to have directed defense industry development through extensive and active Blue House guidance was that of Park Chung Hee. President Park's complete and dedicated support was indispensable in nurturing Korea's weapons-production system.

Amid the ongoing and deep left-right political divide, the country's rapidly declining birth rate and shrinking pool of military conscripts, and the existential threats posed by the DPRK's nuclear missiles, the ROK may require a new, comprehensive, and unifying "total security system"—one that combines the strengths of the state, the military, industry, and society, but through democratic channels. South Korea's formation of a new total security posture (*sin ch'ŏngnyŏk anbo t'aese*) that can meet and withstand the challenges of the twenty-first century may be the most paramount task for the ROK leadership going forward.

Chaju Kukpang: The Tie That Binds the Nation

Today, as a movement deeply interwoven with the rise of modern nationalism, Park's self-reliant national defense agenda remains salient not only in military and state policymaking but also in popular culture, education, and the social, economic, and technological landscape. Even in the hotly charged and highly polarized realm of Korean politics, the pursuit of self-reliant national defense remains a strong tie that binds the state and the people, with the term *chaju kukpang* itself representing the entrenched nationalist ideology that unites South Koreans in valuing a strong, independent system for national security.[63] Korea's campaign under Park for self-reliant defense may represent an extreme expression of nationalism that developed out of the security needs of the 1960s and 1970s, but the spirit of *chaju kukpang* has remained and continues to inspire the political drive for complete self-reliance through a strong military and economy.

As corroborated by recently declassified documents and the personal accounts of individuals who worked under the Park state, modern South Korea grew out of the joint civilian-military venture that was launched with the goal of self-reliant national defense. Despite politicized interpretations of the Park era that portray the military and civilian sectors as opposing forces, the significant cross-fertilization between the two cannot be overlooked in any holistic examination of Korea's development under Park. As the evidence suggests, Park's policies were effective in merging military and civilian forces and dismantling many of the barriers between them.[64] South Korea's development benefited from the combined strength of military discipline and civilian prowess.

The modernization of South Korea presents an intriguing case for evolving theoretical discussions on the relationship between militarism and capitalism as it has played out around the globe. In the post–World War II period, military production, once monopolized by state industries, was integrated into capitalist market economies worldwide. The process was accelerated in newly liberated or decolonized developing nations, such as South Korea, the Philippines, India, and Indonesia, which were eager to pursue their own defense industries. The connection between security-driven states and technological innovation was pronounced in South Korea's neighbors, as well—North Korea, China, and Japan—all of which invested heavily in dual-purpose industrialization as the basis for self-reliance. Military and civilian industries became more thoroughly intertwined with the rise of the Cold War military-industrial complex, which reconfigured the technological landscape in industrial economies. Since the end of the Cold War, the proliferation of transnational arms production and exports by multinational defense contractors, along with the "revolution in military affairs" led by the United States, has expedited privatization in the national security arena by synchronizing weapons procurement with the private sector's development of advanced technology.[65]

The emergence of a militarized South Korea as a global economic force vividly illustrates the intricate connections between militarism and national capitalist development, signifying that more should be said about how military developments during the Cold War shaped the diverse paths of modernization around the globe. South Korea's market economy grew as a function of its total militarization, which drove industrial acceleration and vice versa. The extent to which militarization and industrialization simultaneously propelled each other forward distinguishes the South Korean model of development from the approaches adopted by other industrialized economies in the postwar world. No other country in the post–World War II era, perhaps aside from Israel, merged its military and civilian sectors as rapidly or completely, nor with such dramatic results, and then emerged from total poverty to become a global economic power.[66] While South Korea's journey was not without flaws, its militarized industrialization exemplifies the transformative power of strategic focus, collective will, human agency, resilience, and visionary leadership. As a modern nation forged in the crucible of militarism amid a national security crisis, South Korea's simultaneous commitment to a strong economy and strong defense as the path to independence will continue to be integral to her national identity. This commitment will also serve as the cornerstone of the ROK's power as the country rises to the challenges presented by an increasingly nuclear-armed North Korea, a rapidly ascending China, the growing Sino-Russian entente, and its own evolving alliances with Japan and the United States.

Notes

Introduction

1 This term has its roots in C. Wright Mills's *The Power Elites*, but it was popularized by President Dwight Eisenhower in his 1961 presidential farewell address, in which he warned the US public against the "unwarranted influence" of the military-industrial complex and the threat it posed to American democracy. "Eisenhower's Farewell Address to the Nation," National Archives, Jan. 17, 1961, https://www.archives.gov/milestone-documents/president-dwight-d-eisenhowers-farewell-address.

2 Like Park, Kim viewed self-reliance (*chaju*), which signifies political independence, as being founded on two key pillars: self-sustainability (*charip*), representing an independent economy, and self-defense (*chawi*), denoting an independent military. See French, *North Korea*, 30. See also Taet'ongnyŏng Pisŏsil, *Pak Chŏnghŭi Taet'ongnyŏng yŏnsŏl munjip* [President Park Chung Hee's speeches collection (*PPCHS*)], 7:5.

3 The literal translation of *juche* (主體) is "main body," but it has also been translated as "independent stand" and "self-reliance." *Juche* expresses a Korean form of ultranationalism in which the ethnic Korean nation (*minjok* 民族) must be completely independent of foreign powers. See Suh, *Korean Communism*, xi; G. Lee, "Political Philosophy of *Juche*," 105. See also Suh, Lee, and Lee, *North Korean Modern History*, 2:573.

4 Even a cursory glance at Korea's history explains why the notion of self-reliance would resonate with the Korean people. The peninsula had long experienced invasions, by Han Chinese, Mongols, Manchurians, and even pirates from the Japanese archipelago. After five centuries as a vassal state under the Chinese imperial system, at the close of the nineteenth century Chosŏn Korea's internal affairs were encroached on by Qing China, Meiji Japan, czarist Russia, and the United States. Japan subsequently colonized and ruled Korea for thirty-five years. When the Japanese occupation of Korea ended after World War II, the Soviet Union and the United States occupied northern and southern Korea, respectively, from 1945 to 1948. The subsequent Korean War (1950–53) involved major interventions by the United States and China. In short, Koreans' collective experiences of invasion and occupation by foreign powers, along with the

nationalist movement and writings (by nationalist intellectuals) highlighting that long history, had created fertile ground for the ideal of self-reliance. See G. Shin, *Ethnic Nationalism in Korea*, 100.

5 For example, in a speech on April 12, 2019, to the First Session of the Fourteenth Supreme People's Assembly, Kim Jong Un declared, "Self-reliance is the political philosophy of our Republic, and it constitutes the core of the 'Kim Il Sung–ist/ Kim Jong Il–ist' ideology of nation building" (*Maeil Kyŏngje*, April 12, 2019, www.mk.co.kr/news/politics/view/2019/04/228114/). See also "Supreme Leader Kim Jong Un's Policy Speech," *KCNA Watch*, April 17, 2019, https://kcnawatch.org/newstream/1555477236-190851832/supreme-leader-kim-jong-uns-policy-speech/.

6 Kim Jong Un implemented the *pyŏngjin* policy in 2013 as an attempt to simultaneously develop economic and military strength (including nuclear arms). Despite having the same name as the policy instituted by Kim Il Sung, Kim Jong Un's *pyŏngjin* policy sought to prioritize both economic and military development, whereas the earlier regime aimed to improve the economy primarily to support national defense. In April 2018, Kim announced a shift from *pyŏngjin* to the "new strategic line" policy of concentrating all efforts on economic development. Nonetheless, irrespective of official policies, Pyongyang has clearly maintained a strong prioritization of national defense. With its aggressive expansion of nuclear and missile capabilities, Kim Jong Un's policy has not diverged much from the past regime's maintenance of the military as the basis of the regime's political power. See R. Lee, "Kim Jong Un's Tortuous Path."

7 GlobalFirePower.com, "Active Military Manpower."

8 *Pusan Ilbo*, July 19, 2019, http://www.busan.com/view/busan/view.php?code=20190719152355593l4.

9 GlobalFirePower.com, "2023 Military Strength Ranking"; GlobalFirePower.com, "Active Military Manpower."

10 Bitzinger and Kim, "Why Do Small States Produce Arms?," 183 and 205.

11 Given US military aid, the heavy financial burden of research and development (R & D), and the ROK's comparative disadvantage in manufacturing advanced and diverse military products for the international market, its pursuit of independent arms production has been widely viewed as strategically and economically impractical. This perception has only started to shift in recent years, thanks to South Korea's growing success with its defense exports. See Cha, "Strategic Culture and Military Modernization," 100–101; Bitzinger, *Towards a Brave New Arms Industry?*, 49. See also Cheon and Park, "Is South Korea's Booming Defence Industry Here to Stay?"

12 See Cha, "Strategic Culture and Military Modernization"; Jiyul Kim, "Strategic Culture of the Republic of Korea"; Kang and Bang, "Pursuit of Autonomy."

13 While many scholars underscore the 1966 Brown Memorandum—an agreement between the US and ROK that established a US-backed five-year plan for military

aid (1966–71)—as the initial catalyst for the ROK's military modernization, this book prioritizes developments in the 1970s. It emphasizes milestones such as Park's establishment of the Agency for Defense Development (ADD), the enactment of the Heavy and Chemical Industrialization Policy (HCI Policy), and the initiation of the Yulgok Operation.

14 By "modernization" I do not mean to imply a linear, progressive model of development. Although many traits of South Korea's modernization under Park, such as technological advancement, industrialization, urbanization, and marketization, derive from economically advanced Western nations, South Korea did not necessarily adopt the same models and institutions. In this book, "modernization" refers to a process of economic change closely linked to military development, which is how Park envisioned South Korea's modernization. For Park, the pursuit of economic modernization was intricately tied to the nation's achievement of independent national security. See Y. Kim, "Park Chung Hee's Governing Ideas," 98–99.

15 Eckert, *Park Chung Hee and Modern Korea*, 21 and 27.

16 Seungsook Moon, *Militarized Modernity.*

17 Eckert, *Park Chung Hee and Modern Korea*, 2; Kwŏn Insuk, *Taehan Min'guk ŭn kundaeda*; Yi Pyŏngch'ŏn, *Kaebal tokchae*; Choi and Chung, "Divergent Paths toward Militarized Citizenship"; Tikhonov, "Militarism and Anti-Militarism in South Korea"; Henry, "Ch'anggyŏng Garden as Neocolonial Space"; Kwon, "Building Bombs"; H. Kim, *Korean Skilled Workers.* Among Korean scholars, terms like militarist ideology (*kunsajuŭi*), militarization (*kunsahwa*), and militarism (*kun'gukchuŭi*) have been used to describe Park Chung Hee's model of development. See Rhyu, "Stirring Up Debate," 128.

18 See, for example, Chŏng Y. et al., *Kusul ro pon Han'guk hyŏndaesa wa kun.*

19 It is not an exaggeration to say that the current political view of the average Korean citizen is closely tied to that individual's view of Park and his legacy. Indeed, divisiveness around Park's legacy arguably intensified with the 2012 presidential election of his daughter, Park Geun-hye, and the massive demonstrations of 2016–17 that led to her impeachment in 2017.

20 Pak H., *Pangwi sanŏp piri (pangsan piri) pŏmjoe ŭi ch'ŏbŏl*, 16–18; 20–23.

21 Eckert, *Park Chung Hee and Modern Korea*, 4.

22 Eckert, *Park Chung Hee and Modern Korea*, 2.

23 Article 2 of the 1973 Law on Special Measures for Military Procurement defined the "arms industry" (*kunsuŏp*)—soon termed "defense industry"—as "an industry that produces military products (through manufacturing, processing, assembling, fixing, reproducing, mass-producing, or remodeling), or one that engages in the R & D of such products." Presidential Secretariat, "Kunsu Chodal e kwanhan T'ŭkpyŏl Choch'ibŏp," Feb. 16, 1973, 1A00614175010714, Presidential Archives (PA) (Sejong).

24 Only a few studies have investigated the relationship between the defense industry and the chaebol. See, for example, Kwon, "Building Bombs." For more discussion about chaebol's participation in the defense industry, see chapter 3.

25 The seven-volume memoir by O Wŏnch'ŏl has for a long time served as the main source on Park's HCI Policy and the development of the defense industry (*Han'gukhyŏng kyŏngje kŏnsŏl*, 7 vols.).

26 H. Kim, *Korea's Development*; Kim Chin'gi, "Han'guk pangwi sanŏp"; Ryu, "Pak Chŏnghŭi ŭi chunghwahak"; Nishino, "Ilbon model esŏ Han'gukchŏk."

27 Kim Kwangmo, *Chunghwahak kongŏp e Pak Chŏnghŭi* and *Odyssey of Korean Heavy and Chemical Industrialization*; Chung-yum Kim, *From Despair to Hope*.

28 The most comprehensive and up-to-date work on HCI is by Pak Yŏnggu, whose empirical studies based on policy documents and interviews contain historical background as well as analyses of the HCI Policy and its broad effects on the national industries (*Han'guk ŭi chunghwahak kongŏphwa kongŏppyŏl yŏn'gu: Chosŏn kongŏp*, *Han'guk ŭi chunghwahak kongŏphwa kongŏppyŏl yŏn'gu: Kigye kongŏp*, and *Han'guk ŭi chunghwahak kongŏphwa: Kwajŏng kwa naeyong*).

29 It was not until around 1995, when O Wŏnch'ŏl's testimonies and memoirs were published, that the link between HCI and defense industry development came into public view. Although scholars have acknowledged HCI's ties to the defense industry since then, only a handful have made use of the latest declassified materials to scrutinize these connections from an empirical, historical perspective.

30 On this point Ch'ae Usŏk, president of the Korean Association of Defense Industry Studies, observes: "There is a popular negative assessment that views heavy and chemical industrialization in the 1970s as causing the problems, such as overinvestment [in limited suppliers], that led, in turn, to economic crisis, the fall of the Park Chung Hee regime, and political and economic instability in the early 1980s; such an assessment seems like an attempt to sully HCI and its historical significance owing to its association with the Yusin system" (*Hwanggŭmal ŭl nannŭn*, 138–39).

31 See, for example, Kukpangbu, *Kukpangsa*; Han'guk Pangwi Sanŏp Chinhŭnghoe, *Pangjinhoesa*; Sŏ U., Sin, and Chang, *Pangwi sanŏp*.

32 For example, no defense white papers were written or published by the ROK Ministry of National Defense for the years 1969–87.

33 The public had no knowledge of the Yulgok Operation until it was implicated in widespread financial scandals in 1993.

34 The only major work on the history of the Korean defense industry is a 2015 publication by the Korean Association of Defense Industry Studies in South Korea. Authored by Sŏ Udŏk, Sin Inho, and Chang Samyŏl, and titled *Pangwi sanŏp 40-yŏn: Kkŭt ŏmnŭn tojŏn ŭi yŏksa*, this work covers a broad forty-year history of the Korean Defense Industry from the 1970s to the 2010s. However, it does not specifically focus on the construction of the defense industry during the Park era and its impact on South Korea's development.

35 For example, since the opening of the Presidential Archives in South Korea in 2008, newly available declassified presidential documents have allowed Korean scholars to undertake retrospective examinations of Park's policies for military modernization. As new documents continue to be released, updated analyses have illuminated the internal process, including the Park government's independent policies for arms production and South Korea's adaptations and applications of US military supports, all of which were critical to the rise of domestic defense industry. See, for example, Pak P., "1970-yŏndae Han'guk chaju kukpang"; Ŏm, "Pak Chŏnghŭi chŏngbu ŭi chaju kukpang."

36 For example, official company sources and interviewees from Hanwha (Korea Explosives, or Han'guk Hwayak, as it was called in the 1970s) provide detailed accounts of a collaborative state-chaebol relationship that focused on advancing national defense policy.

37 I accessed South Korean newspaper archives online, including the Naver News Library database and the Newspaper Archives of the Republic of Korea (National Library of Korea), as well as other news archives available online from *Tonga Ilbo*, *Chosŏn Ilbo*, and *Chungang Ilbo*. Additionally, I utilized the online archives of the *Japan Times & Mail* (the name for the *Japan Times* in 1918–40) and the *New York Times*.

38 Following Chalmers Johnson's classic 1982 study of Japan's Ministry of International Trade and Industry and its role in leading Japan's postwar industrialization, *MITI and the Japanese Miracle*, scholars of South Korea have emphasized the dirigiste role of the Korean developmental state, based on the heavy-handed policies that guided economic growth. As a result, South Korea under Park has been likened to other Asian countries such as Japan, Taiwan, Hong Kong, and Singapore—all of which experienced state-led industrialization. For other works on the developmental state, see Amsden, *Asia's Next Giant*; Wade, *Governing the Market*; Woo-Cumings, *Developmental State*; Vogel, *Four Little Dragons*.

39 For example, see Deyo, *Beneath the Miracle*; Koo, *Korean Workers*; Johnson, "Political Institutions and Economic Performance." See also Migdal, *Strong Societies and Weak States*.

40 See J. Lim, "Conference Report: Coercion and Consent," 252; Im C. and Kim, *Taejung tokchae*; Corner and Lim, *Palgrave Handbook of Mass Dictatorship*.

41 Im C., "Taejung tokchae ŭi chihyŏngdo kŭrigi."

42 Gramsci, *Prison Notebooks*, 1:153. See also J. Lim, "Conference Report: Coercion and Consent" and "Historiographical Perspectives on 'Mass Dictatorship,'" 327.

43 In alignment with the expansion of the literature on East Asian economies, scholarly inquiry on the developmental state has evolved since Johnson's work to include new interpretations of state-society relations. See Evans, *Embedded Autonomy*; Hundt and Uttam, *Varieties of Capitalism in Asia*; Taekyoon Kim, "History of the Developmental State," 89–92. Seok-Choon Lew and Hye Suk

Wang directly challenge the traditional "strong state and weak society" depiction of the Park era with their own "strong state and strong society" theory ("Generalized Reciprocity between Strong State and Strong Society," 119 and 120). Other Korean scholars have highlighted the role of nonstate actors, such as businesses and workers, in driving or competing against Park's developmental policies. See E. Kim, *Big Business, Strong State*; Nam, *Building Ships*.

44 *PPCHS*, 9:24. The concept of a total war system refers to wartime mass mobilization of not only a country's military but also its civilian arenas, including its politics, economy, education, and culture. See Hedinger, "Introduction," 287–88.

45 Bandow, "Free Rider," 1. See also, for example, Cumings, "Power and Plenty." For more recent literature on the US-centric view of South Korea's development, see Pak K., *Pak Chŏnghŭi kyŏngje sinhwa haebu*.

46 See, for example, Hwang T., "Miguk ŭi tae-Han anbo"; C. Moon, "U.S. Third Country Arms Sales Regulation"; Yi T., "Yi Sŭngman chŏnggwŏn'gi Miguk"; Pak K., *Pak Chŏnghŭi kyŏngje sinhwa haebu*.

47 See Glassman and Choi, "*Chaebol* and the US Military-Industrial Complex"; T. Park, "Roles of the United States and Japan"; P. Chung, "From Korea to Vietnam"; Chang Y., "Pet'ŭnam Chŏnjaeng i Han'guk kun"; Woo, *Race to the Swift*.

48 The US-centric view has largely resulted from the scarcity of Korean primary sources in comparison with more readily available American foreign policy materials on the US-ROK security alliance. See S. Hong, "Search for Deterrence"; Cho C., "Pak Chŏnghŭi ŭi chaju kukpang kwa haek kaebal"; Ŏm, "Miguk mugi ijŏn chŏngch'aek."

49 See chapter 5 for a discussion of Yulgok and its impact on the US-ROK relations.

50 This more nuanced understanding aligns with the work of historians Tae Gyun Park and Gregg Brazinsky, who, through their examination of both US and Korean archival documents, have emphasized the more reciprocal dynamics at play in the US-ROK alliance in the post–World War II era. See Tae Gyun Park, *An Ally and Empire*; and Brazinsky, *Nation Building in South Korea*. For an example of literature focusing on the patron-client relationship of the US and the ROK, see W. Shin, *Dynamics of Patron-Client State Relations*.

51 See, for example, Mizuno, Moore, and DiMoia, *Engineering Asia*.

52 The literature on Japan's militarization, technological transformation, advancement of skilled workers, and heavy industrialization through the war and postwar periods identifies important parallels between Japanese industrialization and the Park regime's developmental strategies. See, for example, Barnhart, *Japan Prepares for Total War*; Gordon, *Evolution of Labor Relations in Japan*; Morris-Suzuki, *Technological Transformation of Japan*; Samuels, *Rich Nation, Strong Army*; Mizuno, *Science for the Empire*.

53 Through case studies of Hanwha (chapter 3) and other defense contractors that worked with the ADD (chapter 4), the book reveals the militarization of heavy

and chemical industry factories and their workers, the critical role played by the defense industry in Korea's development, and the link between defense technology growth and national scientization.

54 Classic liberalist and mercantilist literature views capitalism and militarism as dichotomous forces. For example, the classic writers on nineteenth-century liberalism, such as Herbert Spencer, believed that the growth of modern industrialism would quickly relegate militarism to a minor role in modern affairs. See Mills, *Power Elites*, 215. After the Cold War, as the arms race wound down, pressure increased to reduce military spending; many scholars and peace activists argued that reduced defense spending would lead to increased investment in economic growth (the so-called peace dividend). See Heo and DeRouen, "Military Expenditures," 830. See also Seungsook Moon, "Legacies of Militarism," 9–10.

55 Benoit, *Defense and Economic Growth*; Gansler, *Defense Industry*; Neuman, "Arms Transfers"; Sanders, *Arms Industries*; Weiss, *America Inc.?*; O'Mara, *The Code*; Neuman and Kurç, "Defence Industries."

56 See Seungsook Moon, "Cultural Politics of Remembering Park."

57 Although I use Hanwha as a representative case, chapter 3 includes examples from other corporations (e.g., Kia, Daewoo, Tongil, Samsung) in discussing the impact of defense industrialization on all chaebol.

1. Park Chung Hee's Total Security System

1 In the 1960s and 1970s, many scholars of Soviet foreign policy assumed that Moscow was responsible for Pyongyang's political and military actions, including Kim Il Sung's decision to invade the South at the start of the Korean War. In the 1970s and 1980s, established scholars of North Korea, such as Dae-Sook Suh (*Kim Il Sung*) and Robert Scalapino and Chong-Sik Lee (*Communism in Korea*), continued to emphasize the so-called sovietization of North Korean communism. See also Rees, *Korea*, 19; Dallin, *Soviet Foreign Policy after Stalin*, 60; Slusser, "Soviet Far Eastern Policy"; and C. Lee, *Korean Workers' Party*. However, US Central Intelligence Agency (CIA) reports during this period interpreted the North Korean aggressions in the late 1960s as resulting from an independent policy of Kim Il Sung. See CIA, "North Korean Intentions," 7, and "Kim Il Sung's New Military Adventurism."

2 See Bolger, *Scenes from an Unfinished War*; Lerner, *Pueblo Incident*; Radchenko, "Soviet Union"; Schaefer, "North Korean 'Adventurism'"; Ryu, "1960-yŏndae mal Pukhan ŭi tobal." See also Yang, Pak, and Yun, *Pak Chŏnghŭi*, vol. 2.

3 Schaefer, "North Korean 'Adventurism,'" 2.

4 A 1965 report from East Germany notes that Kim Il Sung lamented to his communist allies that no other country had suffered as much from the split between

China and the Soviet Union as North Korea ("Changes in the Leadership of the Korean Workers Party and the Government of North Korea," July 12, 1965, History and Public Policy Program, Wilson Center Digital Archive [HPPP], http://digitalarchive.wilsoncenter.org/document/111822).

5 See Szalontai and Radchenko, "North Korea's Efforts," 27. The DPRK also strongly opposed the Limited Nuclear Test Ban Treaty that was signed by the Soviet Union, United States, and United Kingdom on August 5, 1963, and did not ratify it.

6 Szalontai and Radchenko, "North Korea's Efforts," 27.

7 After the confrontation in October 1962 between the Soviet Union and the United States over Soviet missiles stationed in Cuba—the Cuban Missile Crisis—Moscow ordered Cuba to remove the missiles, a decision Kim Il Sung criticized publicly. See Szalontai, *Kim Il Sung in the Khrushchev Era*, 191.

8 See Szalontai, *Kim Il Sung in the Khrushchev Era*, 191–93. Moscow did not resume military aid to North Korea until 1966.

9 Kim Ilsŏng, *Nam Chosŏn hyŏngmyŏng*, 272–73; Bolger, *Scenes from an Unfinished War*, 3.

10 Kukpangbu Kunsa P'yŏnch'an Yŏn'guso, *Kukpang sagŏnsa*, 1:48.

11 However, Park had written about industrialization as a mechanism for economic and security independence as early as 1963. See Pak Chŏnghŭi, *Kukka wa hyŏngmyŏng kwa na*, 262–66 and 271–72.

12 *Kim Il Sung Works*, 20:383. See also *Kim Il Sung Works*, 20:368 and 383–85; Hamm, *Arming the Two Koreas*, 71.

13 In May 1965 József Kovács, the Hungarian ambassador to North Korea, received information about the status of the Korean People's Army (KPA) from Colonel L. Borsky, head of the Czechoslovak section of the Neutral Nations Supervisory Commission, who had participated in a KPA military exercise. According to Kovács, Borsky stated that the KPA was equipped with "15–20-year-old, obsolete military technology." The outmoded tanks, which the KPA had used in the Korean War, performed very poorly during the exercise, with some even breaking down. ("Report, Embassy of Hungary in North Korea to the Hungarian Foreign Ministry," May 15, 1965, Hungarian National Archives, XIX-J-1-j Korea, 1965, 73. doboz, IV-20, 003662/1965. Translated by Balázs Szalontai [the translated document was given to the author by Professor Szalontai].)

14 Schaefer, "North Korean 'Adventurism,'" 39.

15 Schaefer, "North Korean 'Adventurism,'" 4.

16 "The DPRK Attitude toward the So-Called 'Cultural Revolution' in China," March 7, 1967, HPPP, http://digitalarchive.wilsoncenter.org/document/114570.

17 Schaefer, "North Korean 'Adventurism,'" 3.

18 Bolger, *Scenes from an Unfinished War*, 127. See also Sarantakes, "Quiet War," 441–42.

19 See Bolger, *Scenes from an Unfinished War*, 4, 35, and 61–71. See also CIA, "North Korean Intentions," 7; Lerner, "'Mostly Propaganda in Nature,'" and "Second

Korean War," HPPP, https://digitalarchive.wilsoncenter.org/essays/second-korean-war.

20 It should be acknowledged that each of the DPRK's actions against South Korea in the late 1960s had its distinct factors, and that determining Kim's precise motive may be impossible due to the limitations of currently available sources. For a detailed overview of the scholarly interpretations of North Korean militancy in the late 1960s, see Lerner, "'Mostly Propaganda in Nature,'" 4–10.

21 Kim Il Sung's aggressive tactics in the late 1960s have been interpreted by some scholars as deliberate attempts to disrupt US and South Korean efforts in Vietnam. See Downs, *Over the Line*; Koh, "Pueblo Incident in Perspective"; Michishita, *North Korea's Military-Diplomatic Campaigns*. See also CIA, "North Korean Intentions," 4. In a more recent analysis, Balázs Szalontai argues that the Vietnam War played a far more marginal role in incidents such as North Korea's seizure of the *Pueblo* ("In the Shadow of Vietnam," 125).

22 See, for example, Kim's October 1966 speech on the Vietnam War (*Kim Il Sung Works*, 20:332–35).

23 "Report on a Meeting between Enver Hoxha and DPRK Ambassador An Yong," June 20, 1966, HPPP, https://digitalarchive.wilsoncenter.org/document/114407. The discussion between Enver Hoxha, first secretary of the Central Committee of the Albanian Labor Party, and An Yong, North Korea's ambassador to Albania, reveals the significance DPRK leaders placed on the Vietnam War, and their motive for giving military aid to the Vietcong for their fight against the United States and South Korea.

24 CIA reports on North Korea's aggression in the late 1960s also interpreted it as Kim's opportunistic attempt to disrupt the combined US-ROK campaign in Vietnam ("North Korean Intentions," 4–7, and "Confrontation in Korea," 5).

25 Martin, *Under the Loving Care*, 127.

26 *Kim Il Sung Works*, 20:397; see also 398–404.

27 See, for example, Yim, "Dynamics of North Korean Military Doctrine," 124–26. See also Sin C., "Han'guk chŏngch'i ŭi Pukhan yoin," 125.

28 O, *Korea Story*, 117.

29 Weathersby, "Dependence and Mistrust," 14; Martin, *Under the Loving Care*, 121–25; Soon Sung Cho, "North and South Korea," 35–37. See also Lerner, "'Mostly Propaganda in Nature,'" 6–7.

30 Lerner, "'Mostly Propaganda in Nature,'" 9–10 and 47.

31 Joo-Hong Kim, "Armed Forces," 176. According to a 1968 CIA report, Kim Il Sung sent KPA officers to Vietnam to "copy North Vietnamese guerrilla warfare tactics" ("Kim Il Sung's New Military Adventurism," 34).

32 See Ryu, "1960-yŏndae mal Pukhan ŭi tobal," 186. See also O, *Korea Story*, 119. US reports indicate that military incidents in the DMZ had increased from 42 in 1966 to more than 300 in 1967 and that there were "nearly 300 US/ROK casualties [in 1967] compared with less than 70 in 1966" ("Memorandum of Conversation,"

September 15, 1967, document 127 in US Department of State, *Foreign Relations of the United States* [*FRUS*], *1964–1968*, vol. 29, https://history.state.gov/historical documents/frus1964-68v29p1/d127). South Korea's countermeasures included military incursions into North Korea in 1967. In response to the Blue House Raid, the ROK's secret Unit 684 was trained for a mission to kill Kim Il Sung; the assassination plan was canceled by the ROK government when it entered into talks with the DPRK. See T. Park, *Ally and Empire*, 292.

33 H. Kim, *Korea's Development*, 104. See also *Kyŏnghyang Sinmun*, Jan. 26, 1968.

34 Kim S., *Na ŭi chan*, 794–95.

35 Kim S., *Na ŭi chan*, 785.

36 Kukpangbu Kunsa P'yŏnch'an Yŏn'guso, *Kukpang sagŏnsa*, 1:121–26.

37 *Tonga Ilbo*, Jan. 22, 1968; *Kyŏnghyang Sinmun*, Jan. 22, 1968.

38 *Tonga Ilbo*, Jan. 22, 1968.

39 *Tonga Ilbo*, Jan. 25, 1968.

40 *Tonga Ilbo*, Jan. 22, 1968.

41 "Pueblo and the US–South Korean Relations: Political Report No. 11," Feb. 9, 1968, HPPP, https://digitalarchive.wilsoncenter.org/document/116725.

42 "Pueblo and the US–South Korean Relations."

43 Im T., *P'isŭmeik'ŏ*, 146.

44 "Memorandum of the Foreign Ministry of the DPRK for the Ambassadors and Acting Ambassadors of All Socialist Countries Accredited to the DPRK," Jan. 24, 1968, HPPP, http://digitalarchive.wilsoncenter.org/document/113715.

45 Tae Gyun Park notes, "Only one spy infiltration mission [into North Korea by the United States and South Korea] had succeeded . . . between 1965 and 1967, and independent South Korean infiltration missions into North Korea had a low success rate" (*Ally and Empire*, 293).

46 "Mission of Cyrus R. Vance: Special Instruction," Feb. 8, 1968, *Pueblo Crisis 1968*, vol. 3: *Day-by-Day Documents*, Part 11, Box 29, National Security File, Lyndon B. Johnson Presidential Library. In Yang, Pak, and Yun, *Pak Chŏnghŭi*, 2:21.

47 Lerner argues, "In planning and executing the *Pueblo* mission, American advisers neglected to do the one thing that was needed above all else: evaluate North Korea as North Korea rather than as a generic communist nation" (*Pueblo Incident*, 232). See also Radchenko, "Soviet Union," 13.

48 Radchenko, "Soviet Union," 1–2 and 20.

49 "Telegram from Pyongyang to Bucharest, Top Secret, No. 76.017, Flash," Jan. 25, 1968, HPPP, http://digitalarchive.wilsoncenter.org/document/113944. Parentheses and brackets are in the original.

50 For a collection of diplomatic sources related to North Korea's capture of the USS *Pueblo*, see "USS Pueblo Crisis," HPPP, https://digitalarchive.wilsoncenter.org/collection/85/uss-pueblo-crisis.

51 "Excellency," Feb. 20, 1968, *Korea*, vol. 1: *President Park Correspondence*, Box 5, National Security File, Lyndon B. Johnson Presidential Library. In Yang, Pak, and Yun, *Pak Chŏnghŭi*, 2:191–93.

52 Taet'ongnyŏng Pisŏsil, *Pak Chŏnghŭi Taet'ongnyŏng yŏnsŏl munjip* [President Park Chung Hee's speeches collection (*PPCHS*)], 5:77. See also H. Kim, *Korea's Development*, 111–12.

53 Nam, "Taehan Min'guk ŭi sumŭn chŏllyŏk."

54 CIA, "North Korean Intentions," 8–9; Bolger, *Scenes from an Unfinished War*, 33. See also Kukpangbu Kukpang Kunsa Yŏn'guso, *Tae pijŏnggyujŏnsa II*, 360.

55 *PPCHS*, 5:77.

56 *PPCHS*, 5:80.

57 *PPCHS*, 5:76–77.

58 *PPCHS*, 5:142.

59 *Chungang Ilbo*, April 2, 1969; "Hyangt'o Yebigun sŏlch'ibŏp," Kukka Pŏmnyŏng Chŏngbo Sent'ŏ, https://law.go.kr/LSW/lsInfoP.do?lsiSeq=48528#0000.

60 *PPCHS*, 5:80. See also "Hyangt'o Yebigun sŏlch'ibŏp."

61 Park's HRF program was similar to Kim Il Sung's "armament of all North Korean people" policy, which Kim began implementing in the 1960s in keeping with the expansion of reserve forces required by the Four Military Doctrines (Kukpangbu Kunsa P'yŏnch'an Yŏn'guso, *Kukpang sagŏnsa*, 1:48).

62 See Federal Research Division, Library of Congress, *South Korea*, 287–88; Kungnip Yŏnghwa Chejakso, "Chikchang yebigun kyedo."

63 *PPCHS*, 5:80; H. Kim, *Korea's Development*, 112.

64 Bolger, *Scenes from an Unfinished War*, 86.

65 Kukpangbu Kukpang Kunsa Yŏn'guso, *Tae pijŏnggyujŏnsa II*, 48.

66 Chung-yum Kim, *From Despair to Hope*, 402; Kukpangbu Kukpang Kunsa Yŏn'guso, *Tae pijŏnggyujŏnsa II*, 56.

67 Pak P., "1970-yŏndae Han'guk chaju kukpang," 174 and 179. Testimonies by Im Tongwŏn, the aforementioned military strategist and policymaker under Park, and Pae Yŏngil, a former colonel and military adviser in the ROK Army's 27th Infantry Division (1976–77) and the ROK-US Combined Field Army (1977–80), confirm that South Korea's top military leaders concurred with Park's reaction to North Korea's threats in the late 1960s. See Sin U. and Cho, *Kowi kwallyodŭl*, 168. See also Pae Yŏngil, interview with the author, Feb. 2, 2012, Seoul.

68 For scholarship challenging the authenticity of the North Korean threat, see, for example, Hong S., "1960-yŏndae Han-Mi kwan'gye"; T. Park, "Beyond the Myth." See also Pak T., "1960-yŏndae chungban anbo." Other studies based on declassified documents in Korean, American, Russian, and Eastern European diplomatic archives reveal that the Kim Il Sung regime was indeed the aggressor responsible for initiating the 1968 attacks and escalating tensions on the Korean peninsula. See Lerner and Shin, "New Romanian Evidence"; Ryu, "1960-yŏndae mal Pukhan

ŭi tobal"; Schaefer, "North Korean 'Adventurism'"; Sin C., "Han'guk chŏngch'i ŭi Pukhan yoin"; Radchenko, "Soviet Union." See also Lerner, "'Mostly Propaganda in Nature,'" 5.

69 Two national surveys conducted by the newspaper *Maeil Kyŏngje* in 1974 and 1976 assessed people's opinions on national security (*Maeil Kyŏngje*, March 24, 1974, and June 5, 1976). See also chapter 5 for a discussion of my own surveys. See also Sin C., "Han'guk chŏngch'i ŭi Pukhan yoin," 321–28.

70 Sin C., "Han'guk chŏngch'i ŭi Pukhan yoin," 158, 277–78.

71 Their concerns were legitimate. Reports by the Ministries of Home Affairs and National Defense document the reserve troops' unreadiness for battle, poor equipment, and lack of discipline, and cite numerous problems, including accidental shootings, mismanagement of weapons, equipment theft, absenteeism or falsified attendance at mandatory training sessions, and financial mismanagement. See Presidential Secretariat (PS), "Naemu, kukpang yebigun kwan'gyegwan hoeŭi kyŏlgwa pogo," May 6, 1970, EA0004329; "Yebigun haptong kamsa kyŏlgwa pogo," July 1, 1970, EA0004355; "Naemu, kukpang yebigun kwan'gyegwan hoeŭi kyŏlgwa pogo," Jan. 29, 1971, EA0004425, Presidential Archives (PA) (Seongnam).

72 *Kyŏnghyang Sinmun*, April 27, 1968.

73 *Tonga Ilbo*, May 6, 1968; *Kyŏnghyang Sinmun*, May 2, 1968.

74 By the time of Park's death in 1979, the number of reserves would reach 2.8 million. See International Institute for Strategic Studies, *Military Balance 1979–1980*, 69.

75 "Telegram from the Commander in Chief, United Nations Command, and Commander of United States, Korea (Bonesteel) to the Commander in Chief, Pacific (Sharp)," Jan. 23, 1968, HPPP, http://digitalarchive.wilsoncenter.org/document/113368.

76 After a series of negotiations between North Korea and the United States, the crew members were released on December 23, 1968.

77 "Notes of the President's Meeting with Cyrus R. Vance," Feb. 15, 1968, document 180 in US Department of State, *FRUS, 1964–1968*, vol. 29, https://history.state.gov/historicaldocuments/frus1964-68v29p1/d180.

78 Sarantakes, "Quiet War," 450–52.

79 "Telegram from the Commander, Military Assistance Command, Vietnam (Westmoreland) to the Chairman of the Joint Chiefs of Staff (Wheeler)," Feb. 1, 1968, document 43 in US Department of State, *FRUS, 1964–1968*, vol. 6, https://history.state.gov/historicaldocuments/frus1964-68v06/d43.

80 "Special National Intelligence Estimate," May 16, 1968, document 200 in US Department of State, *FRUS, 1964–1968*, vol. 29, https://history.state.gov/historicaldocuments/frus1964-68v29p1/d200.

81 See "North Korean Aggression and the Pueblo Incident, Possible Future Strategies," n.d., *Pueblo Crisis 1968*, vol. 3: *Day-by-Day Documents*, Part 12, Box 29, National Security File, Lyndon B. Johnson Presidential Library. In Yang, Pak, and Yun, *Pak Chŏnghŭi*, 2:203. See also Yang, Pak, and Yun, *Pak Chŏnghŭi*, 2:22–23.

82 "Mission of Cyrus R. Vance: Special Instruction," Feb. 8, 1968, *Pueblo Crisis 1968*, vol. 3: *Day-by-Day Documents*, Part 11, Box 29, National Security File, Lyndon B. Johnson Presidential Library. In Yang, Pak, and Yun, *Pak Chŏnghŭi*, 2:198–99. See also H. Kim, *Korea's Development*, 105.

83 T. Park, *Ally and Empire*, 295–96.

84 "Notes of the President's Meeting with Cyrus R. Vance."

85 "Telegram from the Embassy in Korea to the Department of State," April 18, 1969, document 18 in US Department of State, *FRUS, 1969–1976*, vol. 19, part 1, https://history.state.gov/historicaldocuments/frus1969-76v19p1/d18. See also H. Kim, *Korea's Development*, 106.

86 Revealed during Nixon's stopover in Guam, the Nixon Doctrine signaled a move toward rapprochement with communist powers. This policy shift led to the reduction of US troops in Korea in March 1971, shortly before Henry Kissinger's visit to China in July that led to East-West détente.

87 "Editorial Note," July 25, 1969, document 29 in US Department of State, *FRUS, 1969–1976*, vol. 1, https://history.state.gov/historicaldocuments/frus1969-76v01/d29.

88 "Editorial Note"; Nixon, "Informal Remarks in Guam."

89 "Memorandum of Conversation," July 29, 1969, document 31 in US Department of State, *FRUS, 1969–1976*, vol. 1, http://history.state.gov/historicaldocuments/frus1969-76v01/d31.

90 "Memorandum of Conversation: Talks between President Nixon and President Park," Aug. 21, 1969, document 35 in US Department of State, *FRUS, 1969–1976*, vol. 19, part 1, https://history.state.gov/historicaldocuments/frus1969-76v19p1/d35.

91 "Memorandum of Conversation: Talks between President Nixon and President Park."

92 As a result of Nixon's shift, by 1970 "the development of South Korean self-sufficiency in the production of defense materiel [essentially became] the formal policy of the United States" (US Congress, House Committee on International Relations, *Investigation of Korean-American Relations*, 78). Although challenged, that policy would endure through the 1970s.

93 "Memorandum of Conversation: Talks between President Nixon and President Park." See also Ma, "Pak Chŏnghŭi wa Nambuk taehwa," 138–39.

94 "National Security Decision Memorandum 48," March 20, 1970, document 56 in US Department of State, *FRUS, 1969–1976*, vol. 19, part 1, https://history.state.gov/historicaldocuments/frus1969-76v19p1/d56.

95 Ma, "Pak Chŏnghŭi wa Nambuk taehwa," 146.

96 "Letter, UNCURK Principal Secretary Kuzbari to UN Chef de Cabinet Narasimhan," July 31, 1970, HPPP, http://digitalarchive.wilsoncenter.org/document/117445. See also "Chuhan Migun kamch'uksŏr e ttarŭn taejŏngbu kŏnŭi (che 60-hoe)," Aug. 1970, Kukka Kirogwŏn, http://theme.archives.go.kr/viewer/common/archWebViewer.do?bsid=200300839394&dsid=000000000011&gubun=search.

97 Chung-yum Kim, *From Despair to Hope*, 396.

98 Chung-yum Kim, *From Despair to Hope*, 396.

99 O, *Korea Story*, 121 and 123.

100 James M. Naughton, "Agnew Says U.S. Aims at Full Pullout in Korea," *New York Times*, Aug. 27, 1970.

101 Chung-yum Kim, *From Despair to Hope*, 398; O W., *Han'gukhyŏng kyŏngje kŏnsŏl*, 5:22; O, *Korea Story*, 121.

102 See PS, "Chuhan Mi 7-sadan e taehan kakha ŭi ch'iha ch'insŏ kŏnŭi," March 25, 1971, EA0004436, PA (Seongnam).

103 "Memorandum from Laurence E. Lynn, Jr., of the National Security Council Staff to the President's Assistant for National Security Affairs (Kissinger)," Feb. 26, 1970, document 53 in US Department of State, *FRUS, 1969–1976*, vol. 19, part 1, https://history.state.gov/historicaldocuments/frus1969-76v19p1/d53.

104 "Draft Minutes of a National Security Council Meeting," March 4, 1970, document 55 in US Department of State, *FRUS, 1969–1976*, vol. 19, part 1, https://history.state.gov/historicaldocuments/frus1969-76v19p1/d55. See also Ma, "Pak Chŏnghŭi wa Nambuk taehwa," 140.

105 US Department of State, "United States Air Force Pacific Bases," 5. See also "Draft Minutes of a National Security Council Meeting."

106 Ma, "Pak Chŏnghŭi wa Nambuk taehwa," 142.

107 Joo-Hong Kim, "Armed Forces," 174–75.

108 CIA, "North Korea: Foreign Trade," 7. See also *Kim Il Sung Works*, 20:362.

109 By 1968 North Korea had the capacity to produce its own heavy artillery, ammunition, explosives, and automatic firearms, including modern Soviet-style AK-47s. See PS, "Mi Kukpangsŏng Kukche Anjŏn Tamdangbu Ch'agwanbo wa ŭi hoedam kyŏlgwa pogo," Nov. 4, 1968, EA0002502, PA (Seongnam). See also "Report, Embassy of Hungary in North Korea to the Hungarian Foreign Ministry," March 10, 1967, HPPP, https://digitalarchive.wilsoncenter.org/document/110620; CIA, "North Korea: Foreign Trade," 7 and 9.

110 Despite being promised a five-year aid package (1966–71) by the United States for military modernization as a reward for its participation in the Vietnam War, South Korea did not receive all of this aid. This caused setbacks in Park's modernization plan, as discussed in chapter 5.

111 PS, "Mi Kukpangsŏng Kukche Anjŏn Tamdangbu." Because of the M1 rifle's size and weight, South Korean soldiers had trouble using them effectively in battle.

112 See US Congress, House Committee on International Relations, *Investigation of Korean-American Relations*, 77; Chung-Yum Kim, *From Despair to Hope*, 403. This approval followed the US agreement, made by Cyrus Vance in February 1968, to fund the construction of a South Korean M-16 factory.

113 See An, Kim, and Cho, *Taehan Min'guk ch'oech'o ŭi chidaeji*, 113–14; Kim Chin'gi, "Pak Chŏnghŭi wa Han'guk ŭi mugi," 208; Ku, "Ku Sanghoe."

114 US Congress, House Committee on International Relations, *Investigation of Korean-American Relations*, 79.

115 US Congress, House Committee on International Relations, *Investigation of Korean-American Relations*, 79–80. See also Im T., *P'isŭmeik'ŏ*, 146.

116 As stipulated in the agreement, the Seventh Infantry Division withdrew from South Korea in the following month. See Joo-Hong Kim, "Armed Forces," 177.

117 Negotiations over building the M16 plant, which began in 1968, had dragged on partly because Colt Industries wanted South Korea to keep purchasing M16s from the company instead of purchasing the right to manufacture them. Even after the 1971 agreement, Americans delayed building the factory until 1973. See US Congress, House Committee on International Relations, *Investigation of Korean-American Relations*, 76–77, 82, and 352; Chung-yum Kim, *From Despair to Hope*, 402–4.

118 US Congress, House Committee on International Relations, *Investigation of Korean-American Relations*, 78. Before this time, the ROK was not given access to the necessary technology to produce US weapons domestically.

119 See US Congress, House Committee on International Relations, *Investigation of Korean-American Relations*, 55. US restrictions on the ROK's arms development in fact extended back to the regime of Rhee Syngman, who had publicly endorsed reunification with North Korea through military means. See M. Park, "The 'American Boundary,'" 40.

120 On several occasions in the mid-1970s, then–Secretary of State Kissinger (1973–77) and the US National Security Council expressed concern about the impact that South Korea's armament and nuclear capability could have on Japan's potential nuclear proliferation. See, for example, "Draft US Department of State Cable on Approach to South Korea on French Reprocessing Plant," July 11, 1975, HPPP, https://digitalarchive.wilsoncenter.org/document/114623; "US Department of State Cable, ROK Plans to Develop Nuclear Weapons and Missiles," March 4, 1975, HPPP, https://digitalarchive.wilsoncenter.org/document/114616.

121 See US Congress, House Committee on International Relations, *Investigation of Korean-American Relations*, 79–80.

122 Nolan, *Military Industry*, 25.

123 US Congress, House Committee on International Relations, *Investigation of Korean-American Relations*, 87. See also Nolan, *Military Industry*, 24–25.

124 PS, "6.22 Reŏdŭ Changgwan ŭi Miguk sangwŏn esŏ ŭi chŭngŏn naeyong (Chumi Taesa pogo)," July 20, 1971, EA0002985, PA (Seongnam).

125 *PPCHS*, 9:24, 34.

126 *Tonga Ilbo*, Jan. 11, 1972; *Kyŏnghyang Sinmun*, Jan. 17, 1972; *PPCHS*, 9:34.

127 Hedinger, "Introduction," 287–88. During World War I, the level of destruction and the warring states' mass mobilization of people and resources spread the war's impact through all aspects of life. The phrase "total war state" is generally used to describe a state that engages in such a complete mobilization for war. Leon Daudet (1869–1942), a French royalist, introduced the theory of total war in his 1918 *La Guerre Totale* [The total war]. See Koketsu, "Total War and Japan," 62.

128 Uchiyama, "Munitions Worker as Trickster," 656.

129 Yun, *Pet'ŭnam Chŏnjaeng ŭi Han'guk sahoesa*, 42–43. Regarding the timeline of the Asia-Pacific War (1931–45), it is widely accepted in the West that the war, more commonly known as the Pacific War (1941–45), began after Imperial Japan attacked Pearl Harbor on December 7, 1941. However, many influential historians of Asia argue that the war had actually begun much earlier, on September 18, 1931, when the Imperial Japanese Army attacked and occupied Manchuria in northeastern China. See, for example, Ienaga, *The Pacific War*, 3.

130 See Sang-Hyun Kim, "Science, Technology, and the Imaginaries," 322.

131 Eckert, *Park Chung Hee and Modern Korea*, 229–30.

132 Eckert, *Park Chung Hee and Modern Korea*, 230. The Japanese textbook Park and his military cohorts studied at the time taught that "successful prosecution of the war . . . depended on the 'combined strength of matter and mind,' but ultimately it depended on 'internal spiritual power,' which rested on the eradication of enemy thought, the elimination of the threat from air attacks and other machinations, and the stabilization of the people's livelihood" (Eckert, *Park Chung Hee and Modern Korea*, 230).

133 Monica Kim, *Interrogation Rooms*, 7.

134 Yun, *Pet'ŭnam Chŏnjaeng ŭi Han'guk sahoesa*, 63.

135 Yun, *Pet'ŭnam Chŏnjaeng ŭi Han'guk sahoesa*, 184–85 and 196.

136 *PPCHS*, 5:96.

137 *Kyŏnghyang Sinmun*, March 6, 1968.

138 *PPCHS*, 5:122 and 125–26; *Maeil Kyŏngje*, March 7, 1968.

139 *PPCHS*, 5:142.

140 *PPCHS*, 7:28–29.

141 *PPCHS*, 5:125. See also *PPCHS*, 5:80, 122, 125–26, and 141.

142 *PPCHS*, 5:80 and 108.

143 Im T., *P'isŭmeik'ŏ*, 146–47; Ku, "Ku Sanghoe."

144 Im T., *P'isŭmeik'ŏ*, 146. See also PS, "Isŭrael sich'al (kunsa punya) kwiguk pogo kŏnŭi," July 18, 1970, EA0004367, PA (Seongnam).

145 Chungang Ilbo T'ŭkpyŏl Ch'wijaet'im, *Sillok Pak Chŏnghŭi*, 117–18; Kim Chŏngnyŏm, *A Pak Chŏnghŭi*, 116–17; *Kyŏnghyang Sinmun*, Jan. 15, 1971.
146 See Y. Kim, "Park Chung Hee's Governing Ideas," 96–99.
147 Park, *Our Nation's Path*, 122.
148 Park, *Our Nation's Path*, 122.
149 President Rhee Syngman's staunch anticommunism and his regime's efforts to deter it at home during the 1950s had already imbued South Korean society with anticommunist ideals.
150 C. Moon and Jun, "Modernization Strategy," 138–39.
151 *PPCHS*, 5:78.
152 Park had been discussing what he called *chŏngsinjŏk hyŏkmyŏng*, or mental (spiritual) revolution, since the beginning of his military regime in 1961 (Pak C., *Uri minjok ŭi nagal kil*). However, it was not until the late 1960s that he started actively promoting the internalized aspect of national transformation.
153 Pak T., "1960-yŏndae chungban anbo," 147–48.
154 *PPCHS*, 4:411–12. See also "Che 4-hoe such'ul ŭi nal," Nov. 3, 1967, Yŏnsŏl kirok, Taet'ongnyŏng Kirokkwan, https://www.pa.go.kr/research/contents/speech/index.jsp.
155 Han and Downey, *Engineers for Korea*, 69.
156 Pak T., "1960-yŏndae chungban anbo," 148–49.
157 *PPCHS*, 5:35 (italics added).
158 *PPCHS*, 5:37.
159 Three days later, on January 18, Park's ruling party formed a committee to implement the Second Economy Movement, with the goal of achieving an average annual per capita income of $200 by 1969. See Chŏng Chaegyŏng, *Pak Chŏnghŭi silgi*, 252. See also H. Kim, *Korea's Development*, 136.
160 Kim Yonghwan, *Kaebal nyŏndae wa IMF*, 284.
161 Robinson, *Cultural Nationalism*, 71–75.
162 Park, *Our Nation's Path*, 216. This cited work is an English version of Park's book published in 1964. The original Korean version was published in 1962. See also Park, *Our Nation's Path*, 216–47; Han and Downey, *Engineers for Korea*, 66–70.
163 See also Jiyul Kim, "War, Diplomacy, Mobilization," 12–16.
164 For example, because Park had first introduced the idea of the second economy as a spiritual transformation for the purpose of economic development, critics in the media interpreted his use of the term to mean that the human spirit should be subordinate to material development. See H. Kim, *Korea's Development*, 136. See also Pak T., "1960-yŏndae chungban anbo." Park himself addressed such criticisms in his defense. See *PPCHS*, 5:40.
165 H. Kim, *Korea's Development*, 136.
166 See Jiyul Kim, "Crisis and Ideology," 12.
167 Cho H., "Pak Chŏnghŭi sidae ŭi kangap," 177. See also Han and Downey, *Engineers for Korea*, 68–70.

168 Pak C., "1968-yŏn chejŏng toen kungmin kyoyuk hŏnjang."

169 Mun'gyobu, *Anbo kyoyuk mit Saemaŭl kyoyuk*, 11–29. See also H. Kim, *Korea's Development*, 112.

170 Han and Downey, *Engineers for Korea*, 70.

171 While Park believed that many premodern traditions and past patterns should be eliminated for Korea's modernization, he also believed that the nation could more speedily modernize by "reawakening the strength of our long traditions" (G. Shin, *Ethnic Nationalism in Korea*, 106–7).

172 *PPCHS*, 8:501.

173 *PPCHS*, 9:24.

174 *PPCHS*, 9:34 and 67.

175 See also *Kyŏnghyang Sinmun*, Dec. 21, 1972.

176 *PPCHS*, 9:129–36.

177 *Kyŏnghyang Sinmun*, March 24, 1972; *Kyŏnghyang Sinmun*, Aug. 18, 1972. See also Mun'gyobu, *Anbo kyoyuk mit Saemaŭl kyoyuk*.

178 PS, "Chaju kukpang undong saŏp ch'ujin hyŏnhwang pogo (hyanggun hoe)," 1A00614174958511, Feb. 17, 1972, PA (Sejong). In 1975 the government created the Student National Defense Corps and the Civilian Defense Corps to expand civilian participation in national defense. See *Kyŏnghyang Sinmun,* Oct. 10, 1975.

179 See *Kyŏnghyang Sinmun*, Dec. 11, 1971. As mentioned above, many scholars support this reasoning, arguing that Park meticulously planned his path to totalitarian rule under Yusin. See Hong S., "1960-yŏndae Han-Mi kwan'gye," 297 and 301; Han Hongguk, *Ojik han saram ŭl wihan sidae*.

180 *Kyŏnghyang Sinmun*, April 22, 1971; *Kyŏnghyang Sinmun*, Dec. 11, 1971. See also Ma, "Tet'angt'ŭ ŭi wihŏm," 118.

181 With the establishment of the total security system in 1972, the government and the MND officially switched the defense policy from *chawi kukpang*, or "national self-defense," a purely defensive concept, to *chaju kukpang*, or "self-reliant national defense," which underscored the importance of autonomy and ownership (O W., *Han'gukhyŏng kyŏngje kŏnsŏl*, 7:420–22). See also Kukpangbu, *Kukpangsa*, 4:177.

2. "Rich Nation, Strong Army"

1 On January 1, 1962, for example, Park said, "While we need formidable national-defense strength to protect our freedom from the Communists' threats, national economic reconstruction must be achieved to obtain such freedom" (Pak C., *Han'guk kungmin ege koham*, 33).

2 Taet'ongnyŏng Pisŏsil, *Pak Chŏnghŭi Taet'ongnyŏng yŏnsŏl munjip* [President Park Chung Hee's speeches collection (*PPCHS*)], 8:19.

3 *Tonga Ilbo*, Feb. 20, 1969; *Kyŏnghyang Sinmun*, April 13, 1971; *Maeil Kyŏngje*, March 28, 1972; *Maeil Kyŏngje*, Oct. 12, 1978. The importance of having both a strong defense and a strong economy was a prominent theme in Meiji Japan (from which Park inherited this slogan, as noted in chapter 1). A similar philosophy has been emphasized by other nations as well, including the People's Republic of China, North Korea, Argentina, Brazil, Indonesia, and Israel. See Bitzinger, *Towards a Brave New Arms Industry?*, 15.

4 *Tonga Ilbo*, July 20, 1971. See also *PPCHS*, 7:28.

5 *PPCHS*, 8:163 and 7:28.

6 "10-wŏl 17-il Taet'ongnyŏng t'ŭkpyŏl sŏnŏn," Oct. 17, 1972, Yŏnsŏl kirok, Taet'ongnyŏng Kirokkwan, https://www.pa.go.kr/research/contents/speech/index.jsp. See also Y. Kim, "Park Chung Hee's Governing Ideas," 98.

7 Compared with Park's Heavy and Chemical Industrialization Policy (HCI Policy), Rhee's three-year plan was much more limited in terms of the industries it planned to develop. Chŏng China argues that, nevertheless, the Rhee government's formation of state-led industrialization policies centered on heavy and chemical industries were important precedents for Park's economic development plans promoting heavy and chemical industrialization (HCI) ("Yi Sŭngman chŏnggwŏn'gi," 373 and 376; see also Chŏng C., "Che-1 Konghwakukki").

8 Rhyu and Lew, "Pohang Iron," 322.

9 Park tried and failed to establish an integrated steel mill in 1962, 1964, and 1967. See Rhyu and Lew, "Pohang Iron," 325 and 328–32.

10 The aid was promised in a document known as the Brown Memorandum (see chapter 5), which stipulated that the United States would subsidize military equipment modernization by the ROK Armed Forces according to a five-year plan (1966–71). Presidential Secretariat (PS), "Kunwŏn igwan ŏmmu hyŏnhwang pogo," Feb. 19, 1970, EA0004298, Presidential Archives (PA) (Seongnam).

11 See Kim Kwangmo, *Han'guk ŭi sanŏp*, 300; *Tonga Ilbo*, Feb. 10, 1968. See also *Kyŏnghyang Sinmun*, July 5, 1968.

12 The Agency for Defense Development (ADD) began working with Hanwha, for example, in 1968 to research and develop basic munitions and military explosives in its factory (see chapter 3). See Hanwha Inch'ŏn Kongjang 50-yŏn P'yŏnch'an Wiwŏn, *Hanwha Inch'ŏn Kongjang 50-yŏn*, 183. For other examples of the government's mobilization of local factories for arms production, see *Chosŏn Ilbo*, Feb. 24, 1968; *Chosŏn Ilbo*, July 27, 1968; *Maeil Kyŏngje*, July 20, 1968. See also PS, "FRP-che kyŏngbijŏng sijaksŏn chun'gong pogo," Feb. 4, 1969, EA0001873, PA (Seongnam).

13 For example, this information about "economic militarization" is presented in a 1967 course text published by the ROK Army Staff College (Yukkun Taehak, *Kukpangbi wa kunwŏn*, 11).

14 The abovementioned Army Staff College text (in the previous endnote) taught the notion of a "national defense economy," which was based on developing civilian peacetime industries that could also be used for defense production. The text described the "national defense economy as equivalent to the economy of the national citizens" and emphasized that the civilian economy serves as the backbone of the nation's military strength (Yukkun Taehak, *Kukpangbi wa kunwŏn*, 11; see also 25–26).

15 Pak Chŏnghŭi Taet'ongnyŏng Yuk Yŏngsu Yŏsa Kinyŏm Saŏphoe, *Kyŏre ŭi chidoja*, 291. See also Pak Y., *Han'guk ŭi chunghwahak kongŏphwa: Kwajŏng kwa naeyong*, 1:72.

16 Chŏng Chaegyŏng, *Pak Chŏnghŭi silgi*, 326. See also *Chosŏn Ilbo*, July 5, 1970.

17 Pak Y., *Han'guk ŭi chunghwahak kongŏphwa: Kwajŏng kwa naeyong*, 1:72.

18 See, for example, *Maeil Kyŏngje*, March 25, 1970; *Kyŏnghyang Sinmun*, April 12, 1971; PS, "Pangwi sŏnggŭm e ŭihan kosokchŏng kŏnjo kyehoek kŏnŭi (Kukpangbu)," March 2, 1971, EA0004431, PA (Seongnam).

19 PS, "Chuyo kiŏpch'e pisang kyehoekkwan paech'i hyŏnhwang," June 12, 1970, EA0004343, PA (Seongnam).

20 *Tonga Ilbo*, April 12, 1971.

21 The term "technocratic state" refers to a form of the ROK government that was heavily influenced by industrial and economic policymaking led by a new group of technocrats from the Ministry of Commerce and Industry (MCI) during the nation's HCI from 1973 to 1979. Key figures in this group included O Wŏnch'ŏl, Kim Chŏngnyŏm, and Kim Kwangmo. The few studies that examine South Korea's defense industry efforts in the 1960s and early 1970s (prior to the introduction of the HCI Policy in 1973) include Pak Y., "4 Taehaek Kongjang," and Glassman and Choi, "Geopolitical Economy." Other studies on South Korea's defense development in this period have focused on the external impact of US military aid, with little attention to Park's domestic policies.

22 This focus on O Wŏnch'ŏl's policies has limited the discussion of other factors at play in the development of the HCI plan. In volume 5 of *Han'gukhyŏng kyŏngje kŏnsŏl* (*HGKK*), O mainly attributes defense industry development to policies he created as Park's second senior presidential secretary for the economy from 1971 to 1979. Using this volume and personal interviews with O, scholars have concentrated their analyses of the defense industry on O's role, due to his status as chief policymaker for defense industrialization and the paucity of alternative domestic sources on the Korean defense industry in the 1970s until recently. See H. Kim, *Korea's Development*; Kim Chin'gi, "Han'guk pangwi sanŏp"; Nishino, "Ilbon model esŏ Han'gukchŏk"; Horikane, "Political Economy," 369–97.

23 Park's speeches from the late 1960s clearly show his intention to develop heavy and chemical industries as part of his second FYEDP. See Park's following speeches: "Chŏnju yuse yŏnsŏl," April 18, 1967, and "1969-yŏn sinnyŏnsa." Jan. 1,

1969, Yŏnsŏl kirok, Taet'ongnyŏng Kirokkwan, https://www.pa.go.kr/research/contents/speech/index.jsp.

24 PS, "Kyŏngje kukpang t'aese kanghwa e kwanhan kŏn (ŭian 3-ho)," EA0023140, Feb. 22, 1968, PA (Seongnam).

25 Rhyu and Lew, "Pohang Iron," 322 and 325. On April 1, 1970, Park stated, "To foster and develop the military industry, we must first develop the steel industry" (P'ohang Chonghap Chech'ŏl Chusik Hoesa, *P'ohang Chech'ŏl 10-yŏnsa*, 9).

26 Rhyu and Lew, "Pohang Iron," 336. See also "History of POSCO," POSCO, accessed June 22, 2023, https://www.posco.co.kr/homepage/docs/eng6/jsp/company/posco/s91a1000012c.jsp.

27 Pak T'aejun served as president of POSCO from its founding until October 1992.

28 The funds came from war reparations paid as a result of the Treaty on Basic Relations between Japan and the Republic of Korea (also known as the 1965 Japan-Korea Normalization Treaty), in which Japan agreed to compensate Korea for its previous colonization. Reparations took the form of loans and financial support for economic development.

29 Pak Y., "4 Taehaek Kongjang," 85.

30 An, Kim, and Cho, *Taehan Min'guk ch'oech'o ŭi chidaeji*, 56–57 and 59.

31 Korea Institute of Science and Technology (KIST), *Plan for Development*, 5–6 and 215.

32 KIST, *Plan for Development*, 216.

33 *HGKK*, 7:152–53.

34 An, Kim, and Cho, *Taehan Min'guk ch'oech'o ŭi chidaeji*, 57.

35 Yi Ŭ., "ADD mugi kaebal," 4.

36 Yi Kyŏngsŏ, interview with the author, July 13, 2021, Anyang, South Korea.

37 According to Yi, he and O clashed often in their work as principal weapons advisers under Park, a rivalry that continued when Yi was transferred to oversee the ADD's Polar Bear missile project (see chapter 4). Yi Kyŏngsŏ, interview with the author, July 13, 2021. See also An, Kim, and Cho, *Taehan Min'guk ch'oech'o ŭi chidaeji*, 112–13.

38 Yi, interview. One significant departure of HCI Policy from the KIST plan was the inclusion of the "chemical" component by O and his team. This addition expanded the scope of KIST's heavy industries policy to encompass both heavy and chemical industrialization.

39 Glassman and Choi, "Geopolitical Economy," 409–10.

40 C. Kim, *From Despair to Hope*, 405.

41 A militarized South Korea would have presented a direct challenge to the US foreign policy on Korea, which (as mentioned in chapter 1) opposed the ROK's development of banned weapons because of their potential to trigger a regional arms race.

42 The United States continued to maintain a large military presence in Japan after the end of the Allied occupation in 1952, and Japan was specifically banned, under its postwar constitution, from creating its own armed forces. While the United States encouraged Japan-ROK economic cooperation, it was not supportive of their arms cooperation. Japan was also wary of South Korea's nuclear ambitions, which further hampered cooperation. See Jack et al., *Regional Rivalries and Nuclear Responses*, 2:18 and 58–60.

43 Kim Chŏngnyŏm, interview with the author, April 5, 2013, Seoul.

44 "Letter from Korean Prime Minister Kim to the President's Assistant for National Security Affairs (Kissinger), Oct. 6, 1971," document 112 in US Department of State, *Foreign Relations of the United States* (*FRUS*), *1969–1976*, vol. 19, part 1, https://history.state.gov/historicaldocuments/frus1969-76v19p1/d112. See also *HGKK*, 5:25–26.

45 Kim Chŏngnyŏm, *Ch'oebin'guk*, 393–94. Following the EPB's briefing with Park, O approached Kim with a plan for developing a defense industry without foreign loans. Intrigued by O's proposal and familiar with his work in the MCI, where Kim had served as minister from 1967 to 1969, Kim immediately took O to the president to present his plan to Park directly (interview, April 5, 2013, Seoul). For more on O's background, see H. Kim, *Korea's Development*, 169–71.

46 Kim Chŏngnyŏm, *Ch'oebin'guk*, 393–94, and interview.

47 See O, *Korea Story*, 132–35.

48 O W., *Pak Chŏnghŭi nŭn ŏttŏtk'e*, 117–19.

49 PS, "Simŭi pogosŏ," Feb. 26, 1970, EA0023181, PA (Seongnam).

50 See Chŏng Chaegyŏng, *Pak Chŏnghŭi silgi*, 317. See also Pak Chŏnghŭi Taet'ongnyŏng Yuk Yŏngsu Yŏsa Kinyŏm Saŏphoe, *Kyŏre ŭi chidoja*, 328–38.

51 For example, O's January 1972 report on plans to expand domestic ammunition production indicates that he had revised an ongoing government plan to make greater use of existing plants, such as Poongsan Metal Corporation's An'gang factory, which had been operating under the guidance of the Ministry of National Defense (MND) since 1969. PS, "T'anyak kongjang hwakchang saŏp kyehoek," Jan. 25, 1972, 1A00614174958500, PA (Sejong).

52 *HGKK*, 5:25.

53 Rhyu and Lew, "Pohang Iron," 323.

54 Pak Chŏnghŭi Taet'ongnyŏng Yuk Yŏngsu Yŏsa Kinyŏm Saŏphoe, *Kyŏre ŭi chidoja*, 328–38.

55 C. Kim, *From Despair to Hope*, 157–58.

56 O W., *Pak Chŏnghŭi nŭn ŏttŏtk'e*, 118.

57 Yukkun Taehak, *Kukpangbi wa kunwŏn*, 11; PS, "Kyŏngje kukpang t'aese kanghwa e kwanhan kŏn (ŭian 3-ho)," EA0023140, Feb. 22, 1968, PA (Seongnam).

58 After its defense industry's existence was exposed to the outside world, the ROK government used "defense industry" (*pangwi sanŏp*) in place of the terms

"military-industrial complex" (*kunsu sanŏp tanji*) or "military (or arms) industry" (*kunsu sanŏp*), which most other nations used. The Park government called its MIC a defense industry to emphasize that its primary purpose was defensive, in an effort to alleviate the concerns of neighboring nations and the United States, which did not welcome South Korea's arms development. See An, Kim, and Cho, *Taehan Min'guk ch'oech'o ŭi chidaeji*, 114.

59 *HGKK*, 5:26–27; Kim Kwangmo, interview with the author, April 16, 2013, Seoul.

60 Kim Kwangmo, interview with the author, April 18, 2014, Seoul.

61 Kim Kwangmo, interview, April 18, 2014.

62 H. Kim, *Korea's Development*, 168.

63 *HGKK*, 5:29–31.

64 H. Kim, *Korea's Development*, 168.

65 H. Kim, *Korea's Development*, 78.

66 Nishino, "Ilbon model," 186.

67 O, *Korea Story*, 132–34.

68 Ku, "Ku Sanghoe."

69 An, Kim, and Cho, *Taehan Min'guk ch'oech'o ŭi chidaeji*, 33 and 74.

70 Han, *Suryut'an esŏ*, 4–5.

71 Sin was replaced three months later, in February 1972, by Sim Munt'aek, who was O's choice for the new director of the ADD. Han, *Suryut'an esŏ*, 24. See also An, Kim, and Cho, *Taehan Min'guk ch'oech'o ŭi chidaeji*, 71.

72 *HGKK*, 5:38; Ku, "Ku Sanghoe."

73 Ku Sanghoe, interview with the author, July 14, 2021, Bundang, South Korea, and "Ku Sanghoe."

74 Ku, interview.

75 Ku, interview.

76 Ku, "Ku Sanghoe."

77 *HGKK*, 7:418–19.

78 *PPCHS*, 9:13.

79 The DIPC's core members were President Park, the prime minister, the vice prime minister, the minister of national defense, and the director of the ADD.

80 *HGKK*, 5:78.

81 *HGKK*, 5:78.

82 *HGKK*, 5:120.

83 For example, the MND began holding an annual Defense Products Evaluation Conference, inviting personnel from the government, military, businesses, research institutes, and academia to evaluate the latest Korean-made military products. The feedback collected was used to enhance product quality and economic competitiveness. See PS, "Kunsup'um p'yŏnggahoe silsi kyŏlgwa pogo," Sept. 19, 1972, EA0004621, and "73-yŏndo kunsup'um p'yŏnggahoe silsi kyŏlgwa pogo (Kukpangbu)," Dec. 15, 1973, EA0004759, PA (Seongnam).

84 The second point also includes, "Utilize the existing [civilian] facilities to the fullest extent and provide major support for their development" (*HGKK*, 5:135).

85 This system was designed to safeguard against US and North Korean surveillance. With individual parts assigned to different civilian manufacturers and the military arsenals responsible for the final assembly of the weapons, even the manufacturers often did not know exactly what they were making.

86 *HGKK*, 5:134–35.

87 Kim Chin'gi, "Han'guk pangwi sanŏp," 113.

88 Kim Kwangmo, "Such'ul 100-ŏkpul," 51; *HGKK*, 5:137.

89 *P'enaendŭmaik'ŭ*, May 31, 2019, https://www.pennmike.com/news/articleView.html?idxno=19329; C. Moon and Paek, "Defense Innovation," 4.

90 *HGKK*, 5:138–39.

91 The "Weapons Production System" report is dated February 15. See PS, "Pyŏnggi saengsan ch'eje," Feb. 15, 1972, EA0004549, PA (Seongnam).

92 PS, "Pyŏnggi saengsan ch'eje."

93 The Department of Defense and the Joint US Military Affairs Group–Korea advocated for providing South Korea with aid for its military modernization, but the Department of State opposed this, viewing Park's arms ambitions as a threat to arms control efforts in Asia. See chapter 5 for more discussion on the Department of State's attempts to restrict South Korea's procurement of advanced weapons technologies; Ku, "Ku Sanghoe"; Taehan Min'guk Yŏksa Pangmulgwan, *Kukpang kwahak kisul palchŏn*, 33.

94 An Tongman, interview with the author, July 23, 2021, Taejŏn, South Korea; Ku, "Ku Sanghoe."

95 *HGKK*, 7:398–99.

96 Hardin's team was later disbanded by the United States, owing to Hardin's willingness to give classified weapons data to South Korea. See Ku, "Ku Sanghoe."

97 Yu S., "Kukka yŏn'gu kaebal saŏp," 168–69.

98 See PS, "Han'gukhyŏng sohwagi kisul chehyu," Dec. 28, 1971, EA0004526, PA (Sejong), and "Han-Chung hyŏmnyŏk," July 24, 1972, EA0004600, PA (Seongnam).

99 O, *Korea Story*, 140–41; Kukpang Kwahak Yŏn'guso, *Kukpang ŭi ch'osŏk*, 162.

100 *HGKK*, 7:40 and 405–7. See also O, *Korea Story*, 148.

101 Kim Kisŏk, "Uri nara chobyŏng kisul palchŏnsa (3)," 54. See also Kukpang Kwahak Yŏn'guso, *Kukpang Kwahak Yŏn'guso 50-yŏnsa*, 55.

102 See, for example, PS, "Pangwi sanŏpch'e chijŏng," June 3, 1972, EA0004575, PA (Seongnam); "T'ŭksu kang kongŏp yuksŏng pangan," Oct. 20, 1972, EA0004630, PA (Seongnam); and "Sije ŏpch'e chojŏng mit sŏnjŏng," Oct. (n.d.), 1972, 1A00614174958654, PA (Sejong).

103 *HGKK*, 5:76.

104 *HGKK*, 5:189–90.

105 *HGKK*, 5:204.

106 Im Tongwŏn, the chief architect of the self-reliant national defense policy within the Joint Chiefs of Staff (mentioned in chapter 1), stated that South Korea was "at the point where self-reliant national defense and heavy and chemical industrialization had to go together," as the nation's limited industrial and economic base had rendered it completely reliant on the United States for all arms products (Sin U. and Cho, *Kowi kwallyodŭl*, 167).

107 PS, "Han-Mi yŏllye anbo hyŏbŭi hoeŭi kyŏlgwa pogo (Kukpangbu)," June 28, 1972, EA0004585, PA (Seongnam).

108 *PPCHS*, 10:58.

109 *PPCHS*, 10:58–59. For more on the National Scientization Movement, see chapter 4.

110 Kim Chŏngnyŏm, interview, and *Ch'oebin'guk*, 324. See also O's testimony (*HGKK*, 5:76).

111 *HGKK*, 5:26–27.

112 PS, "Pyŏnggi saengsan nŭngnyŏk pogo," Jan. 23, 1973, EA0004651, PA (Seongnam). See also Pak Pongsu, "1970-yŏndae Han'guk chaju kukpang," 184.

113 Kyŏngje 2, *Kaep'yŏnnon*. See also Kim Kwangmo, interview, April 16, 2013. O was a man of many ideas, according to Kim Kwangmo: it was Kim's responsibility to document and organize their ideas into systematic policy, while O, a gifted presenter, was the one who persuaded Park to approve their proposed policies for HCI. Kim Kwangmo, interview, April 18, 2014.

114 Kim Kwangmo, phone interview with the author, Sept. 24, 2020.

115 According to O, "Having determined the heavy & chemical and defense industries as overlapping with one another, the two were thus integrated into one overarching project" (*Korea Story*, 246). See also PS, "Pangwi sanŏp mit chunghwahak kongŏphwa chŏngch'aek," Jan. 31, 1973, 1A00614174958687, PA (Sejong).

116 O, *Korea Story*, 249–54.

117 H. Kim, *Korea's Development*, 177.

118 The August Third Measure is discussed in more detail in chapter 3.

119 O Wonchol, "Opportunities to Participate," 1–2 and 8. Most foreign investments took the form of joint ventures with South Korean companies, in which projects were funded by the Korean manufacturers with the help of loans from the foreign investors. Kim Kwangmo, text message interview with the author, Aug. 22, 2020.

120 The NIF was launched on December 14, 1973. See Yang, *Political Economy*, 82; Heavy and Chemical Industry Promotion Council Planning Office (HCI Promotion Council), *Heavy and Chemical Industry*, 18–19.

121 Kim Kwangmo, text message interview, Aug. 22, 2020.

122 For more on the Law on Special Measures for Military Procurement, see chapter 3.

123 Kim Kwangmo, interview, April 16, 2013.

124 Kwon, "Mars and Manna," 21–24.

125 Bringing together the public and private sectors in a "system of total power" ("the total empowerment of the trinity of military, business, and science" [*HGKK*, 5:78]) was set as the government's priority at the DIPC's meetings in 1972. See also Kyŏngje 2, *Kaep'yŏnnon*, 31.

126 Kyŏngje 2, *Kaep'yŏnnon*, 31. See also O, *Korea Story*, 232.

127 Kyŏngje 2, *Kaep'yŏnnon*, 15 and 28. See also O, *Korea Story*, 221 and 230.

128 C. Kim, *From Despair to Hope*, 409.

129 Kyŏngje 2, *Kaep'yŏnnon* 18.

130 PS, "Pyŏnggi saengsan ch'eje," Feb. 15, 1972, EA0004549, PA (Seongnam).

131 Kyŏngje 2, *Kaep'yŏnnon*, 19–20; O, *Korea Story*, 135.

132 Kim Kwangmo, text message interview with the author, Feb. 24, 2020.

133 Kyŏngje 2, *Kaep'yŏnnon*, 19.

134 C. Kim, *From Despair to Hope*, 419.

135 Kyŏngje 2, *Kaep'yŏnnon*, 21–23.

136 Kyŏngje 2, *Kaep'yŏnnon*, 4 and 22.

137 Stern et al., *Industrialization and the State*, 41–42.

138 Japan, the first example in Asia of a nation that experienced rapid industrialization under a strong developmental state, has been viewed as the prototype for newly industrialized economies in the region, with South Korea, Taiwan, Hong Kong, and Singapore soon following suit with their own state-led industrialization in the 1970s and 1980s. See, for example, Gulati, "Foundations of Rapid Economic Growth"; World Bank, *East Asian Miracle*.

139 See Samuels, *Rich Nation, Strong Army*.

140 Kim Kwangmo, interview with the author, July 29, 2021, Seoul.

141 Kyŏngje 2, *Kaep'yŏnnon*, 7–8, 12–13, 19, and 29. See also O, *Korea Story*, 217–31.

142 According to Kim Kwangmo, the HCI Planning Corps studied Japan's *Shin Chōki Keizai Keikaku* (New Long-term Economic Plan), which contained policies for Japan's HCI in the 1950s and 1960s. See Kim Kwangmo, "Such'ul 100-ŏkpul," 46, and *Han'guk ŭi sanŏp*, 207–9. O Wŏnch'ŏl, in a 1972 presidential briefing, referred to Japanese prime minister Tanaka Kakuei's 1972 publication *Nippon Rettō Kaizō Ron* [A theory of Japan's reconstruction] in his effort to convince Park that South Korea needed to learn from Japan's experience with HCI and transition from labor-intensive light industries to more knowledge-based heavy industries. See *HGKK*, 7:464–68.

143 Nishino, "Ilbon model," 204–5.

144 Taiwan, Japan, and the other newly industrialized economies in Asia prioritized economic goals over national defense. Kwon, "Building Bombs," 69–70.

145 Kwon, "Building Bombs," 70.

146 *HGKK*, 5:38.

147 *HGKK*, 7:460. See H. Kim, *Korea's Development*, 168–69.
148 See, for example, PS, "Kukpang kwahak kisul simŭhoe," Feb. 7, 1974, EA0004772, PA (Seongnam). See also Chapter 5 on Park's oversight of Yulgok.
149 Kim Chin'gi, "Pak Chŏnghŭi wa Han'guk ŭi mugi," 182 and 184–85.
150 Kim Chŏngnyŏm, interview.
151 O W., "Yulgok Saŏp ch'ulpal," 469.
152 This conclusion is based on statements in my interviews with former skilled workers for Kia Machine Tools, Samsung Heavy Industries, Tongil Heavy Industries, Daewoo Heavy Industries, and Poongsan Metal Corporation. See also H. Kim, *Korean Skilled Workers*, 20–40. See chapters 3 and 4 for fuller discussions of militarized skilled workers.
153 Park often referred to Japan's modernization during the Meiji Restoration (1868–1912) (as mentioned in chapter 1) as well as postwar Japan's success with export-led HCI. He challenged his policymakers and citizens to exceed the achievements of their former colonizers. See Chungang Ilbo T'ŭkpyŏl Ch'wijaet'im, *Sillok Pak Chŏnghŭi*, 219; Pak C., *Nara ka wigŭp*, 314.
154 The Blue House's militaristic hierarchy was so rigid that even when SES technocrats like Kim Kwangmo wrote reports for Park, only O presented them to the president. Kim never reported to Park in person or communicated with him directly. Kim Kwangmo, text message interview with the author, March 26, 2021, and *Chunghwahak kongŏp*, 313.
155 *HGKK*, 5:30.
156 Though primarily run and managed by SES technocrats O and Kim Kwangmo, the HCI Planning Corps employed approximately fifty experts in different technical areas of HCI. Kim Kwangmo, text message interview with the author, March 30, 2021. See also H. Kim, *Korea's Development*, 178–79.
157 Development in Japan, given preexisting institutional ties between the Ministry of International Trade and Industry and the *zaibatsu* (large Japanese business conglomerates), required less top-down control. See Evans, *Embedded Autonomy*, 52–53. In Taiwan, public-private sector cooperation was much weaker and its export-driven industrialization was led by small and medium-size enterprises rather than conglomerates. See Nolan, *Military Industry*, 48 and 83; Nishino, "Ilbon model," 204–5. See also Kwon, "Building Bombs," 69–70.
158 Kim Kwangmo, interview, April 18, 2014.
159 Kim Kwangmo, interview, April 18, 2014; Han, *Suryut'an esŏ*, 25–29.
160 H. Kim, *Korea's Development*, 180; Yi, interview.
161 For example, in a 1972 report to Park on O's defense industry plan, critics questioned O's strategies, including his proposal to distribute the production of individual weapons parts among thirty large and medium-size corporations, citing concerns about the "poor facilities and disorderly management of existing companies" (PS, "Pangwi sanŏp pyŏnggi kaebal mit ch'ujinsang ŭi munje chŏm kŏmt'o,"

Jan. 25, 1972, A0000073100018, PA [Sejong]). Instead, the internal report suggested concentrating investment in fewer (and more qualified) large corporations that would handle the full process of arms production.

162 Kim Kwangmo, interview, April 16, 2013; Pak Y., *Han'guk ŭi chunghwahak kongŏphwa: Kwajŏng kwa naeyong*, 1:83–84; Taehan Min'guk Yŏksa Pangmulgwan, *Kukpang kwahak kisul palchŏn*, 15; O, *Korea Story*, 247.

163 For the ROK Armed Forces, using standardized weapons and hardware also employed by US forces meant that, in the event of war, they would have in common not only weapons but also ammunition, replacement parts, and training—all of which would simplify wartime logistics.

164 Ku, interview; Kim Kwangmo, interview, April 16, 2013.

165 *HGKK*, 7:420.

166 The MND had been involved in numerous financial scandals prior to the establishment of the SES in 1971, which deepened Park's distrust of military. See Pak Y., *Han'guk ŭi chunghwahak kongŏphwa: Kwajŏng kwa naeyong*, 1:83–84. See also H. Kim, *Korea's Development*, 190.

167 Hwang T., "Sŏnjin'guk ilsurok," 97–98.

168 Pak C., *Han'guk kungmin ege koham*, 32.

169 See Koo, "Labor Policy," 134–35.

170 Those who take this position include O, Hyung-A Kim, Ryu Sŏkch'un, and Cho Kapche. See also a published interview with Kim Kwangmo and Korean scholars featured in Kim Kwangmo et al., "Pak Chŏnghŭi Taet'ongnyŏng ŭi chunghwahak," 36–37. Kim Kwangmo himself, who is cited as a coauthor of this article, does not take this stance, according to my interview with him on April 18, 2014. For more about divided opinions on the origins of Yusin, see Im H., "Yusin ŭi yŏksajŏk kiwŏn," 130–32.

171 From Hyung-A Kim's interviews with O Wŏnch'ŏl (translated into English by Kim), Oct. 1996 and Jan. 2000, in H. Kim, *Korea's Development*, 175–76 (italics added).

172 Kim Chŏngnyŏm, interview. See also Kim Chŏngnyŏm, *A Pak Chŏnghŭi*, 133.

173 See H. Kim, "Heavy and Chemical Industrialization," 26; Kim Chŏngnyŏm, *A Pak Chŏnghŭi*, 271–72.

174 Kim Chŏngnyŏm noted, however, that Park's economic goals for export-oriented industrialization also factored into South Korea's shift to HCI (interview).

175 See, for example, Pak T., "1960-yŏndae chungban anbo"; Chŏng I., "Yusin ch'eje ŭi mosun"; Han H., *Ojik han saram*. See also chapter 1.

176 See, for example, Hong S., "1960-yŏndae Han-Mi kwan'gye," 297.

177 Kim Kwangmo, interview, April 18, 2014, and interview with the author, Sept. 10, 2013, Seoul. Kim, in a text message to the author, reinforced his point that Yusin was not initiated for the sake of HCI. He stated, "It makes no sense to claim that the Yusin system, enacted in October [1972], was intended to sup-

port a factory construction plan [HCI plan] that hadn't even been finalized at that time. . . . The Yusin system was already in effect when I was still drafting the official documents [for the HCI]." Kim Kwangmo, text message interview, July 8, 2023.

178 Kim Kwangmo, interview, April 18, 2014.

179 Kim Kwangmo, interview, April 18, 2014.

180 Kim Kwangmo, interview, Sept. 10, 2013. Kim's account of the origins of HCI merits serious consideration, especially since he was the person with whom O worked most closely from the establishment of the SES in 1971. Like O, Kim was a graduate of Seoul National University and had a background in chemical engineering. Before being recruited by O to the SES, he served as the MCI's director of planning for the petrochemical industry from 1969 to 1971.

181 Kim claimed in two separate interviews that he, not O, was the real author of the HCI Policy. However, because Kim had never revealed this publicly, especially when O was still alive, this claim is unverifiable. According to Kim, he had spent roughly a year studying and researching (mostly on his own) to formulate the ideas for the HCI Policy, from his recruitment to the SES in late 1971 until the plan was presented by O to Park in late 1972. Kim Kwangmo, interviews, April 18, 2014, and July 29, 2021.

182 O, *Korea Story*, 246. See also Kim Chŏngnyŏm, *Ch'oebin'guk*, 393–94.

183 Kim Kwangmo, interview, Sept. 10, 2013, and interview, April 18, 2014.

184 Kim Kwangmo, interview, April 18, 2014.

185 Kim Chongp'il, *Kim Chongp'il*, 1:403.

186 PS, "Pyŏnggi saengsan nŭngnyŏk pogo," Jan. 23, 1973, EA0004651, and "Pangwi sanŏp mit chunghwahak kongŏphwa chŏngch'aek," Jan. 31, 1973, EA0004652, PA (Seongnam).

187 Kim Kwangmo, interview, Sept. 10, 2013. Similarly, Kim Chongp'il wrote in his memoir that Park saw the need for a total mobilization system (Yusin) to execute his plans for the defense industry and HCI (*Kim Chongp'il*, 1:404–5).

188 This viewpoint is agreed upon among the technocrats responsible for HCI policymaking under Park, specifically O Wŏnch'ŏl and Kim Kwangmo. They both concur that the defense industry could not have been constructed without the HCI Policy, and that HCI would not have been feasible without the Yusin government.

189 Kim Chŏngnyŏm believed that Park's experience in Manchuria influenced his militaristic approach to industrialization in South Korea (Pae, "Taet'ongnyŏng pisŏsiljanggye"). Under the Manchukuo government (1932–45), Imperial Japan overhauled Manchuria's industry to expedite economic development. The integration of the Manchukuo state (run by the Imperial Japanese Army) and the Japanese business community (through its investments in Manchuria) showed

Park what a military-business coalition under a strong state would look like. See Young, *Japan's Total Empire*, 183–90.

190 H. Kim, *Korea's Development*, 140.

191 See Eckert, "Total War."

192 Kwon, "Mars and Manna," 27–29.

193 Kyŏngje 2, *Kaep'yŏnnon*, 27.

194 HCI Promotion Council, *Heavy and Chemical Industry*, 117.

195 HCI Promotion Council, *Heavy and Chemical Industry*, 25.

196 HCI Promotion Council, *Heavy and Chemical Industry*, 41.

197 Bruno and Tenold, "Basis for South Korea's Ascent," 208; O, *Korea Story*, 250.

198 C. Kim, *From Despair to Hope*, 409 and 414; O, *Korea Story*, 250.

199 Joo-Hong Kim, "Armed Forces," 177.

200 PS, "Pyŏnggi saengsan ch'eje," Feb. 15, 1972, EA0004549, PA (Seongnam).

201 O, *Korea Story*, 251.

202 Kwon, "Mars and Manna," 29.

203 HCI Promotion Council, *Heavy and Chemical Industry*, 67–68.

204 Hong Ŭ. and Yi, *K'orian mirak'ŭl*, 3:108–9.

205 Kyŏngsang Province's coast, where the cities Pohang, Ulsan, Pusan, Ch'angwŏn, and Chinju are located, is surrounded by the Sobaek Mountains, which provided natural protection against surveillance and infiltration. By comparison, provinces such as Chŏlla in the southwest have flat terrain and were not ideal defensively. The southeast was also favored because it was a better location for large ports. Electronics complexes could be built inland because they did not require access to ports as much as other industries did. Petrochemical complexes, which also generally did not require large seaports, were built in Yŏch'ŏn (what is now called Yŏsu) in the southwest. See Kim Kwangmo et al., "Pak Chŏnghŭi Taet'ongnyŏng ŭi chunghwahak," 56–57; Kim Kwangmo, text message interview with the author, Dec. 3, 2020.

206 Taehan Min'guk Yŏksa Pangmulgwan, *Kukpang kwahak kisul palchŏn*, 12–13.

207 Kwon, "Beyond Patron and Client," 200–201.

208 O, *Korea Story*, 150.

209 PS, "Pangwi sanŏp ŏpch'e ryangsan t'aese hwangnip," Dec. 4, 1974, EA0004816, PA (Seongnam).

210 PS, "Pangwi sanŏp," Dec. 27, 1974, EA0004825, PA (Seongnam).

211 PS, "Pangwi sanŏp," Dec. 27, 1974, EA0004825, PA (Seongnam).

212 For example, a report by a US Army review team sent to South Korea in February 1976 noted the overall success of South Korea's artillery production and praised the new Ch'angwŏn Industrial Complex, saying it "promises to upgrade both steel making and manufacturing processes to 'STATE OF THE ART' levels" (PS, "Mi Yukkun mulchach'ang kisulja chunggan pogo," Feb. 17, 1976, EA0004870, PA [Seongnam]).

213 The SES reported to President Park on a visit by the new US ambassador to the ADD's facilities in November 1974 (eight months after the start of the Yulgok Operation). In the report, Kim Kwangmo wrote that after witnessing the progress made by the defense industry, the ambassador voiced support for its further development, and even the US embassy shifted its stance toward South Korea's defense industry. As Kim noted, this was in stark contrast to the position of the previous ambassador, who had long opposed Park's defense development. See PS, "Chuhan Mi Taesa ŭi kukpang kwahak yŏn'guso pangmun," Nov. 21, 1974, EA0004813, PA (Seongnam).

214 US Congress, Office of Technology Assessment, *Arming Our Allies*, 15. See also H. Yoon, "National Security," 266–68.

215 PS, "Pangwi sanŏp," Dec. 27, 1974, EA0004825, PA (Seongnam).

216 PS, "Soch'ongt'an such'ul kŏnŭi," July 11, 1975, EA0004850; "Kuksan 81 mm pakkyŏkp'o such'ul kŏnŭi," Aug. 18, 1975, EA0004856; and "Inni e taehan kunsu chiwŏn," Feb. 5, 1976, EA0004867, PA (Seongnam). See also Central Intelligence Agency, *Arms Sales*, 7–8.

217 *HGKK*, 5:38.

218 In August 1970, Vice President Spiro Agnew declared that all American troops would exit South Korea by 1976, a plan the United States later canceled. See *HGKK*, 5:22; O, *Korea Story*, 121; James M. Naughton, "Agnew Says U.S. Aims at Full Pullout in Korea," *New York Times*, Aug. 27, 1970; "Mr. Agnew 'Shows the Flag,'" *New York Times*, Sept 1, 1970. In April 1973 Park ordered the ROK Joint Chiefs of Staff to pursue independent military modernization, with the expectation that no US soldier would remain in Korea by the 1980s. See Kukpangbu, *Yulgok Saŏp*, 22.

219 "Memorandum of Conversation," Nov. 22, 1974, Gerald R. Ford Presidential Library and Museum, https://www.fordlibrarymuseum.gov/library/document/0314/1552860.pdf. The Ford administration did not cancel the plan for eventual total withdrawal; it intended to significantly reduce the number of troops in Korea by 1978 and then completely withdraw all ground forces by 1980. See Yang, Pak, and Chang, *Pak Chŏnghŭi*, 5:39 and 46.

220 "Memorandum of Conversation," Dec. 2, 1970, document 81 in US Department of State, *FRUS, 1969–1976*, vol. 19, part 1, https://history.state.gov/historicaldocuments/frus1969-76v19p1/d81.

221 For more on this operation, see chapter 5.

222 HCI Promotion Council, *Heavy and Chemical Industry*, 99–100.

223 Pak Y., *Han'guk ŭi chunghwahak kongŏphwa: Kwajŏng kwa naeyong*, 1:104.

224 For details about Park's and the ADD's efforts to procure diverse foreign technologies for advanced weapon programs (such as ballistic missile) under the Yulgok Operation, see chapters 4 and 5.

3. The Militarization of the Chaebol

1 The chaebol are large family-owned business conglomerates composed of multiple subsidiaries. The majority of the South Korean businesses that later became chaebol were established after the Japanese colonial period ended in 1945 (including SK, Goldstar, and Hanwha). Others (such as Hyundai, Lotte, POSCO, and Daewoo) were founded after Park's rule began in 1961. However, there were no actual conglomerates until after Park initiated his HCI Policy in 1973. See E. Kim and Kim, "Chaebŏl and the Political Economy," 100.

2 Woo, *Race to the Swift*, 35.

3 E. Kim, *Big Business, Strong State*, 124–26.

4 Numerous important studies have analyzed the significant role of US economic aid and military contracts in the 1950s and 1960s in the development of the Korean companies that would later emerge as conglomerates. See P. Chung, "From Korea to Vietnam"; Glassman and Choi, "*Chaebol* and the US Military-Industrial Complex"; Pak K., *Pak Chŏnghŭi kyŏngje sinhwa haebu*; Woo, *Race to the Swift*; Ch'oe T., "Pet'ŭnam p'abyŏng i Han'guk kyŏngje"; DiMoia, "Reconfiguring Transport Infrastructure."

5 Eckert, "Total War," 8 and 13–14.

6 In return for supporting Rhee's policy of import substitution industrialization—which aimed to quickly put South Korea on a path to industrialization by replacing foreign imports with domestically manufactured products—these businesses received greater state assistance.

7 See *Tonga Ilbo*, June 25, 1960; *Chosŏn Ilbo*, July 20, 1960.

8 *Tonga Ilbo*, May 29, 1961. See also E. Kim, *Big Business, Strong State*, 113.

9 E. Kim, *Big Business, Strong State*, 114–15 and 117. See also H. Kim, *Korea's Development*, 81.

10 E. Kim and Park, "*Chaebol*," 271.

11 E. Kim, *Big Business, Strong State*, 118–19.

12 Baldwin, "America's Rented Troops," 34.

13 In 1965, in return for Park's agreement to send troops to Vietnam, Johnson promised $150 million in economic development loans, committed to maintaining US forces in South Korea, and agreed to slow the transfer of US military equipment from South Korea to Vietnam. See Text of Joint Communiqué between President Lyndon B. Johnson and His Excellency Chung Hee Park, "President of the Republic of Korea following talks in Washington, D.C. May 17 and 18, 1965," May 18, 1965, Office Files of Horace Busby, Park Visit, 5/17–5/18/1965, White House Central File, Lyndon B. Johnson Presidential Library. In Yang, Pak, and Cho, *Pak Chŏnghŭi*, 1:173-175. See also US Congress, House Committee on International Relations, *Investigation of Korean-American Relations*, 53–54.

14 For more on the Brown Memorandum, see chapter 5. Between 1965 and 1973 the ROK earned more than $9 billion from its involvement in the Vietnam War. See Kwak, "Anvil of War," 152; US Congress, House Committee on International Relations, *Investigation of Korean-American Relations*, 54.

15 P. Chung, "From Korea to Vietnam"; Hong K., "Pak Ch'ŏnghŭi Pet'ŭnamjŏn ch'amjŏn," 320–21; Woo, *Race to the Swift*, 96.

16 Glassman and Choi, "*Chaebol* and the US Military-Industrial Complex"; Yun, *Pet'ŭnam Chŏnjaeng ŭi Han'guk sahoesa*.

17 Woo, *Race to the Swift*, 95–96; Stubbs, "War and Economic Development," 348.

18 E. Kim and Park, "*Chaebol*," 284.

19 Rhyu, "Institutionalizing Property Rights," 169; E. Kim and Park, "*Chaebol*," 285.

20 Pak T., "8.3 choch'i." See also E. Kim and Kim, "Chaebŏl and the Political Economy," 106; *Tonga Ilbo*, Sept. 16, 1966; *Maeil Kyŏngje*, Oct. 11, 1967.

21 For more details about the Yusin system under Park, see chapters 1 and 2.

22 Kim Kwangmo, interview with the author, April 18, 2014, Seoul.

23 Kim Kwangmo, interview, April 18, 2014, and *Chunghwahak kongŏp e Pak Chŏnghŭi ŭi hon*, 125.

24 Kukpangbu, *Kukpangsa*, 4:175 and 185.

25 Han'guk Pangwi Sanŏp Chinhŭnghoe, *Pangjinhoesa*, 283.

26 According to article 6 of the MPL, the state was to guarantee that weapons contractors would fulfill state-set production quotas, and distribute funding and resources to support the contractors in meeting production goals. See Presidential Secretariat (PS), "Kunsu Chodal e kwanhan T'ŭkpyŏl Choch'ibŏp," Feb. 16, 1973, 1A00614175010714, Presidential Archives (PA) (Sejong). See also Han'guk Pangwi Sanŏp Chinhŭnghoe, *Pangjinhoesa*, 62, 286–87.

27 PS, "Pangwi sanŏp e taehan chiwŏn chisi," Nov. 18, 1976, EA0000236, PA (Seongnam).

28 *Tonga Ilbo*, June 24, 1977.

29 Han'guk Pangwi Sanŏp Chinhŭnghoe, *Pangjinhoesa*, 62.

30 For more on the law's support of domestic R & D, see chapter 4.

31 As articulated in article 23, fines or incarceration were the punishments for poor performance, mismanagement of state funds or resources, failure to meet state quotas or quality standards for defense products, and breaches of security at company facilities. Penalties were to be imposed not only on the individuals immediately responsible but also on the entire company. See Han'guk Pangwi Sanŏp Chinhŭnghoe, *Pangjinhoesa*, 295–96; Shaw, "South Korean Foreign Military Sales," 6–7.

32 Han'guk Pangwi Sanŏp Chinhŭnghoe, *Pangjinhoesa*, 290–92.

33 See PS, "Kunsu Chodal e kwanhan T'ŭkpyŏl Choch'ibŏp," Feb. 16, 1973, 1A00614175010714, PA (Sejong).

34 Nam, *Building Ships*, 189.

35 Shaw, "South Korean Foreign Military Sales," 7. In March 1973, Park established the Defense Industry Bureau within the MND. The creation of this bureau pressed the MND to collaborate with the MCI's own Defense Industry Bureau on decisions related to defense-related business activities. See Pak Y., *Han'guk ŭi chunghwahak kongŏphwa: Kwajŏng kwa naeyong*, 2:36–40; Kukpangbu, *Kukpangsa*, 4:794–95.

36 The MCI's expanded responsibilities over the defense sector caused the ministry and MND to clash over their respective jurisdictions. See PS, "Ilbu pangsanŏpch'e t'ŭkhye choch'i e taehan kyŏngwi pogo," June 14, 1976, EA0004881, PA (Seongnam).

37 The Korea Defense Industry Association's council meetings were chaired by Park at the Blue House and attended by military leaders, state ministers, corporate executives, and National Assembly members. The meetings expanded civilian participation in formulating policies on weapons procurement and exports. See Han'guk Pangwi Sanŏp Chinhŭnghoe, *Pangjinhoesa*, 294–95 and 299; Yi Y., "Chaju kukpang kwa Han'guk Pangwi Sanŏp Chinhŭnghoe," 6.

38 Shaw, "South Korean Foreign Military Sales," 8.

39 See Shaw, "South Korean Foreign Military Sales," 8; *Tonga Ilbo*, Oct. 20, 1977.

40 Some of the discussions and anecdotes in this chapter involving Hanwha previously appeared in my article "Building Bombs, Building a Nation: The State, *Chaebŏl*, and the Militarized Industrialization of South Korea, 1973–1979," in *Journal of Asian Studies* 79, no. 1 (Feb. 2020): 51–75. Copyright 2020, The Association for Asian Studies, Inc. All rights reserved. Republished by permission of the publisher, Duke University Press.

41 The other companies and subsidiaries that served as defense contractors in the 1970s included Hyundai, Kia, Samsung, LG (formerly Goldstar), SK, Doosan, Daewoo, and Hanjin. Some merged with or were purchased by other corporations, especially after the 1997 financial crisis in Asia, and no longer exist under their original names.

42 Hanwha Kŭrup 50-yŏnsa P'yŏnch'an Wiwŏn [Hanwha Kŭrup], *Hŭimang ŭro ŭi yŏjŏng*, text volume, 32–33.

43 Hanwha Inch'ŏn Kongjang 50-yŏn P'yŏnch'an Wiwŏn, *Hanwha Inch'ŏn Kongjang 50-yŏn* (*HIK*), 52. The phrase "*saŏp poguk*" (through business, repay the nation) was widely used by leading entrepreneurs, including Chung Ju-yung of Hyundai and Yi Pyŏngch'ŏl of Samsung, as it conveyed their commitment to businesses that would strengthen the nation. See *Maeil Kyŏngje*, Oct. 10, 1977.

44 On the business philosophy of South Korea's early entrepreneurs, see *Herŏldŭ Kyŏngje*, Aug. 31, 2012, http://news.heraldcorp.com/view.php?ud=20120831000301. See also Choong Soon Kim, *Culture of Korean Industry*, 31 and 51–52.

45 Sŏ M., "Hyŏnam Kim Chonghŭi."

46 Hanwha Kŭrup, *Hŭimang ŭro ŭi yŏjŏng*, picture volume, 21.

47 *HIK*, 57.

48 Hanwha Kŭrup, *Hŭimang ŭro ŭi yŏjŏng*, text volume, 59–61.

49 PS, "T'anyak kongjang sisŏl chŏnhwan mit hwakchang saŏp kyehoek kŏmt'o," Jan. 21, 1972, EA0004533, PA (Seongnam).

50 The twenty-nine corporations selected as defense contractors at the second meeting of the Defense Industry Promotion Council, in October 1972, were the premier manufacturers in the fields of machinery, electronics, special metals, and chemicals. The number of contractors increased to thirty-nine after the start of the Yulgok Operation in 1974 and expanded further with Park's development of the aerospace and naval industries. O Wŏnch'ŏl, *Han'gukhyŏng kyŏngje kŏnsŏl* (*HGKK*), 5:189. See also PS, "Pangwi sanŏp ŏpch'e ryangsan t'aese hwangnip," Dec. 4, 1974, EA0004816, PA (Seongnam).

51 *Kyŏnghyang Sinmun*, July 15, 1968.

52 Samsung initially delayed (and resisted) joining Park's defense industry plans as a licensed weapons producer due to the company's policy of minimizing involvement in state-subsidized enterprises. According to O Wŏnch'ŏl, Samsung was eventually compelled to join Park's plan to build an aerospace (defense) industry after O warned the company's leaders that failing to accept the defense assignment would jeopardize Samsung's relations with Park. See *HGKK*, 5:480–82. Similarly, in 1975, when O requested CEO Kim Sŏnhong of Kia Motors to build military vehicles, he initially refused. He relented only after O informed him that the request was a direct order from the president. See Kia Chunggongŏp, *Kia Chunggongŏp 20-yŏnsa*, 85–86. It should be noted, however, that Kim Kwangmo, former deputy director of HCI Planning Corps (see chapter 2), offers a contradicting account of Samsung's initial reaction to the government's invitation to join the defense projects; according to Kim, Samsung's chairman Yi Pyŏngch'ŏl was a willing participant in Park's defense projects, who "never refused to participate in the government's planned projects" (Kim Kwangmo, text message interview with the author, Feb. 10, 2023).

53 A 1972 report to Park on the defense industry notes that the state lacked the capital and resources to fully support the research, facilities, and labor required to build a defense industry. See PS, "Pangwi sanŏp pyŏnggi kaebal mit ch'ujinsang ŭi munjejŏm kŏmt'o," Jan. 25, 1972, A0000731000118, PA (Sejong). On the government's support for the technical development of Hanwha and other corporations, see *Maeil Kyŏngje*, Aug. 4, 1973.

54 Taet'ongnyŏng Pisŏsil, *Pak Chŏnghŭi Taet'ongnyŏng yŏnsŏl munjip* [President Park Chung Hee's speeches collection (*PPCHS*)], 10:222; *PPCHS*, 14:173. See also *Kyŏnghyang Sinmun*, Oct. 4, 1973; *PPCHS*, 14:166 and 174.

55 *Tonga Ilbo*, June 18, 1977; *Kyŏnghyang Sinmun*, April 15, 1977.

56 Kim Kwangmo, *Han'guk ŭi sanŏp palchŏn*, 305–6; Kim Chŏngnyŏm, interview with the author, April 5, 2013, Seoul.

57 The sentiment and pride expressed by former workers in the company memoirs and in my interviews with former workers attest to this. See, for example, *HIK*, 16; Kim Chongbong, interview with the author, June 27, 2018, Kangnŭng; Min Pyŏngman, interview with the author, Nov. 14, 2012, Inch'ŏn, South Korea.

58 For examples, see *Tonga Ilbo*, April 15, 1977; *Kyŏnghyang Sinmun*, April 27, 1977.

59 Hangnok Ryu Ch'anu Hoejang Ch'umo Wiwŏnhoe, *Hak, san ŭl kkum kkuda*, 51 and 53; Choong Soon Kim, *Culture of Korean Industry*, 31.

60 *Maeil Kyŏngje*, Oct. 10, 1977; *Kyŏnghyang Sinmun*, July 24, 1976.

61 *HIK*, 53. Inch'ŏn is on the coast to the west of Seoul and Kyŏnggi Province.

62 *HIK*, 16.

63 Min, interview, Nov. 14, 2012. Min Pyŏngman was the last plant manager of the Inch'ŏn factory, from 2004 until its closing in 2006. The factory has since been converted into the Hanwha Historical Museum ("Hanwha Kinyŏmgwan" in Korean).

64 Stringent international regulations on transporting explosives by ship limited both their import and export.

65 Hong Kwangung, email interview with the author, July 28, 2021.

66 *HIK*, 183; Min Pyŏngman, *Han'guk ŭi hwayak yŏksa*, 546.

67 Yi Ch'anggi, interview with the author, Aug. 11, 2017, Seoul.

68 *HIK*, 66.

69 Hanwha Kŭrup, *Hŭimang ŭro ŭi yŏjŏng*, text volume, 42; PS, "Pangwi sanŏp ŏpch'e ryangsan t'aese hwangnip," Dec. 4, 1974, EA0004816, PA (Seongnam).

70 PS, "Pangwi sanŏp pyŏnggi kaebal mit ch'ujinsang ŭi munjejŏm kŏmt'o," Jan. 25, 1972, A0000073l0001118, PA (Sejong); Kim Ch'angsik, phone interview with the author, August 7, 2020.

71 Yi, interview, Aug. 11, 2017. Members of Production Division 2, in charge of experimentation and R & D for military explosives, worked closely with ADD scientists to develop the new military products. See also Kim Chongbong, interview; Hanwha Kŭrup, *Hŭimang ŭro ŭi yŏjŏng*, text volume, 70; *HIK*, 158.

72 An, Kim, and Cho, *Taehan Min'guk ch'oech'o ŭi chidaeji*, 114; Yang, Pak, and Chang, *Pak Chŏnghŭi*, 5:44.

73 Yi, interview, Aug. 11, 2017. See also Kim Chongbong, interview.

74 Yi, interview, Aug. 11, 2017; Kim Ch'angsik, interview with the author, July 3, 2018, Seoul. Hanwha's failures with reverse engineering included the attempted development of US-model aerial bombs (Yi interview).

75 Yi, interview, Aug. 11, 2017. Technology transfers were usually arranged through the purchase of licensed technology and equipment from a foreign supplier (which would also include a foreign-capital loan from the same supplier). This became standard practice among HCI companies that sought to accelerate weapons production by acquiring foreign know-how. See Tenold et al., "International Transfer of Tacit Knowledge."

76 Yi Ch'anggi, interview with the author, June 28, 2018, Seoul. See also Kim Ch'angsik, interview, July 3, 2018.

77 According to Yi, for example, the Inch'ŏn factory's Special Defense Development Department, which began in 1972 as a group (*kye*) within the factory dedicated to R & D for military gunpowder, was expanded into a department (*kwa*) in 1974 and had become a full-fledged, independent research division (*pu*) by 1976 (interview, June 28, 2018).

78 Yi, interview, June 28, 2018.

79 Kim Ch'angsik, interview, July 3, 2018.

80 Hong Kwangung, interview with the author, July 9, 2021, Kwach'ŏn, and email interviews with the author, July 28 and October 1, 2021. Hong worked as a quality-control specialist at the Inch'ŏn factory from 1974 to 1975. He later oversaw Hanwha's construction of a specialized defense plant in Yŏsu from 1976 to 1980 and then served as the plant manager at Hanwha's Inch'ŏn, Yŏsu, and Poŭn factories.

81 Hong, email interview, July 28, 2021. The concept of "total quality control" was popularized by Japanese companies in the 1960s, but it is likely that Hong used the term here to convey an upgraded and comprehensive quality-control system based on the high standards set by the United States for military explosives.

82 Hong, email interview, July 28, 2021.

83 *Kyŏnghyang Sinmun*, April 15, 1977.

84 Sŏ U., Sin, and Chang, *Pangwi sanŏp*, 59.

85 Shaw, "South Korean Foreign Military Sales," 6–7; Han'guk Pangwi Sanŏp Chinhŭnghoe, *Pangjinhoesa*, 295.

86 Kim Ch'angsik, interview, July 3, 2018.

87 *HIK*, 158.

88 See, for example, Kim Kyegwan, interview with the author, Aug. 5, 2021, Ch'angwŏn; Cho Kilsu, interview with the author, July 21, 2021, Ch'angwŏn; Yu Hansik, interview with the author, Aug. 5, 2021, Ch'angwŏn.

89 Kim Ch'angsik, interview, July 3, 2018; Hong, interview, July 9, 2021, and email interview, July 28, 2021.

90 PS, "Han'guk Hwayak Chusik Hoesa," Dec. 31, 1976, EA0001048, PA (Seongnam).

91 Hanwha had indigenized the production of black powder in 1972. See Hanwha Kŭrup, *Hŭimang ŭro ŭi yŏjŏng*, text volume, 42.

92 Hanwha and other HCI companies sought contracts for foreign-capital loans that would allow them to purchase technical aid and equipment from the same foreign lenders that sold them.

93 PS, "Isŭrael kunsu ch'agwan toip munje," June 19, 1973, 1A00614174956424, PA (Sejong).

94 Hanwha became known as a corporation that largely covered its own expenses in defense production. See *Maeil Kyŏngje*, Aug. 18, 1977; Yi, interview, Aug. 11, 2017; Hanwha Kŭrup, *Hŭimang ŭro ŭi yŏjŏng*, text volume, 74.

95 Chibber, "Developmental State," 43.
96 *HGKK*, 5:171–72.
97 As the sole domestic producer of gunpowder, Hanwha claimed that it should also produce ball powder—a type of gunpowder. Poongsan, which manufactured ammunition shells, argued that its production of ball powder would establish the company as a complete vertical producer of M16 ammunition, from the powder to the shells, and thus streamline the production process.
98 Hanwha Kŭrup, *Hŭimang ŭro ŭi yŏjŏng*, text volume, 74. See also PS, "Kunsu simŭihoe ŭigyŏl sahang pogo," Nov. 11, 1975, EA0004861, PA (Seongnam).
99 PS, "Han'guk Hwayak Chusik Hoesa," Dec. 31, 1976, EA0001048, PA (Seongnam).
100 ADD scientists who visited the United States in the mid-1970s sought to acquire such proprietary knowledge through field training with US corporations. See Seltzer, "Baekgom," 290. See also chapter 4.
101 Yi, interview, Aug. 11, 2017; Ch'oe Pyŏngyun, interview with the author, June 29, 2018, Inch'ŏn.
102 Kim Chongbong, interview; Hanwha Kŭrup, *Hŭimang ŭro ŭi yŏjŏng*, text volume, 75.
103 Yi, interview, Aug. 11, 2017, and interview with the author, Jan. 6, 2022, Seoul.
104 Yi, interview, June 28, 2018.
105 Yi, interview, Jan. 6, 2022.
106 Yi, interview, June 28, 2018.
107 Yi, phone interview with the author, Jan. 22, 2020. See also chapter 4. Hanwha engineers played a key role in the design and overall performance of the propulsion engine for South Korea's first ballistic missile. See An, Kim, and Cho, *Taehan Min'guk ch'oech'o ŭi chidaeji*, 240–41. Like Hanwha, the ADD got technical aid from the United States and France to develop missile propellant technologies, as discussed in chapter 4.
108 Hong Kwangung, email interview with the author, April 12, 2022.
109 The geographical vulnerability of the Inch'ŏn factory, located near both the DMZ and the coast, prompted the government to select Yŏsu, a location in the southwestern part of the peninsula, to safeguard Hanwha's new factory should the North Korean military invade. See Han'guk Pangwi Sanŏp Chinhŭnghoe, *Pangjinhoesa*, 291.
110 The first petrochemical complex was located in Ulsan.
111 Although the factory began operating in 1978, Hanwha's full transfer of military gunpowder facilities from Inch'ŏn to Yŏsu was completed only in 1980. Hanwha Kŭrup, *Hŭimang ŭro ŭi yŏjŏng*, text volume, 75.
112 Ch'oe, interview; Cho Pyŏngch'ŏl, interview with the author, June 29, 2018, Inch'ŏn; Yi, interview, Aug. 11, 2017; Kim Chongbong, interview; *HIK*, 17.
113 Ch'oe, interview.

114 See Kungnip Yŏnghwa Chejakso, "Chikchang yebigun kyedo."

115 See Kungnip Yŏnghwa Chejakso, "Mangjŏn p'irwi."

116 *Kyŏnghyang Sinmun*, April 15, 1977.

117 Hanwha Kŭrup, *Hŭimang ŭro ŭi yŏjŏng*, text volume, 42. PS, "T'anyak kongjang sisŏl chŏnhwan mit hwakchang saŏp kyehoek kŏmt'o," Jan. 21, 1972, EA0004533, PA (Seongnam).

118 See Kukpangbu Kukpang Kunsa Yŏn'guso, *Tae pijŏnggyujŏnsa II*, 236–38. See also *Kyŏnghyang Sinmun*, June 5, 1973.

119 *Tonga Ilbo*, Nov. 19, 1973. See also Kukpangbu Kukpang Kunsa Yŏn'guso, *Tae pijŏnggyujŏnsa II*, 238.

120 Kim Chongbong, interview; Min Pyŏngman, interview with the author, March 13, 2014, Inch'ŏn, South Korea.

121 Yu Hansik, interview with the author, June 27, 2013, Ch'angwŏn. Kia Machine Tools is the former name of Kia Heavy Industries, a subsidiary of the Kia Group that was founded in 1976.

122 Cho Pyŏngch'ŏl, interview.

123 Min, interview, March 13, 2014.

124 *HIK*, 90.

125 Kim Chongbong, interview; Ch'oe, interview.

126 Hanwha Kŭrup, *Hŭimang ŭro ŭi yŏjŏng*, text volume, 119.

127 *HIK*, 86, 96–97; Kim Chongbong, interview; Cho Pyŏngch'ŏl, interview; Yi, interview, June 28, 2018. See also Hanwha Kŭrup, *Hŭimang ŭro ŭi yŏjŏng*, text volume, 43.

128 Kim Chongbong, interview. The number of deaths recalled by Kim during his tenure at the Inch'ŏn factory is much higher than what is officially reported in the Inch'ŏn factory's published data. See *HIK*, 96–97.

129 Hong, email interview, July 28, 2021.

130 Hanwha's safety measures included implementing stringent security guard training to protect the factory and requiring mandatory safety education for all workers in the production divisions every morning. See, for example, *HIK*, 87.

131 *HIK*, 86; Hanwha Kŭrup, *Hŭimang ŭro ŭi yŏjŏng*, text volume, 43; Yi, interview, June 28, 2018.

132 Such rituals included *kosa*, a shamanistic ritual in which people bowed before a disembodied pig head to avoid misfortune. Kim Chongbong, interview. See also *HIK*, 87.

133 Yi, interview, June 28, 2018.

134 Hanwha Kinyŏmgwan, *Sajin ŭro tasi*, 104 and 183; Min, interview, March 13, 2014.

135 Hanwha Kinyŏmgwan, *Sajin ŭro tasi*, 330. See also Kim Chongbong, interview.

136 The findings are based on my visits in 2012 and 2013 to the Hanwha Historical Museum, which maintains the original facilities and records from the Inch'ŏn factory, including the safety oaths and the company songs.

137 Hanwha Kinyŏmgwan, *Sajin ŭro tasi*, 331.

138 Hanwha Kinyŏmgwan, *Sajin ŭro tasi*, 330.

139 *HIK*, 87.

140 *HIK*, 86. See also Min, interview, Nov. 14, 2012; Ch'oe, interview; Yi, interview, June 28, 2018.

141 *HIK*, 84–85.

142 Kim Chongbong, interview; Cho Pyŏngch'ŏl, interview.

143 This statement is based on my interviews with former skilled workers at various companies. See, for example, Kim Hujin (Daewoo), interview with the author, Aug. 5, 2021, Ch'angwŏn; Kim Kwŏnjung (Samsung), interview with the author, Dec. 29, 2021, Seoul; Im Haesu (Kia), interview with the author, July 21, 2021, Ch'angwŏn; Cho Kilsu (Tongil), interview; Kim Kyegwan (Daewoo), interview; anonymous interviewee (a former electrical engineer at Hyundai Heavy Industries [HHI]), phone interview with the author, April 24, 2022.

144 Kim Hujin, interview.

145 Kim Hujin, interview.

146 Kim Hujin, interview.

147 Anonymous interviewee, phone interview. HHI was founded in 1972 as a division of the Hyundai Group that specialized in shipbuilding but manufactured other products as well.

148 In the phrase "*hoesik munhwa*," *hoesik* means "get together and dine" and *munhwa* means "culture." This after-work dining tradition is still widely practiced by Korean corporations today. Its origin is often attributed to the shared experience of military service required of all Korean men.

149 According to the anonymous former engineer, many accidents were not revealed to the public because of the company's sensitive management-labor relationship amid the rising democracy movement (phone interview).

150 Min, interview, Nov. 14, 2012; Cho Pyŏngch'ŏl, interview; Ch'oe, interview.

151 *Maeil Kyŏngje*, Nov. 5, 1973.

152 Nam, *Building Ships*, 191. See also *PPCHS*, 14:171.

153 Nam, *Building Ships*, 191.

154 Ch'oe Changjip, *Han'guk ŭi nodong undong*, 208–9.

155 From 1944 to 1945, around 1.5 million Korean workers, along with other colonial subjects, were put to work in Japan's munitions factories. See Uchiyama, "Munitions Worker as Trickster," 668–69. See also Michael Kim, "Industrial Warriors."

156 This observation is based on my visits in 2012 and 2013 to the Hanwha Historical Museum, which showcases original buildings from the Inch'ŏn factory. The museum's walls display framed lyrics of company songs and slogans, such as an old company song that included the phrase "*sanŏp ŭi yŏkkun*." *Sanŏp ŭi yŏkkun* was a popular phrase for industrial workers, used by both the state and

corporations. The characters that make up the word *yŏkkun* (*yŏk* meaning "to work" and *kun* meaning "military") conjure up an image of workers as soldiers. See also Hanwha Kinyŏmgwan, *Sajin ŭro tasi*, 330.

157 Cho Pyŏngch'ŏl, interview. See also *HIK*, 85.

158 Min, interview, Nov. 14, 2012; Kim Chongbong, interview.

159 *Kyŏnghyang Sinmun*, May 9, 1975; *Maeil Kyŏngje*, May 10, 1975; *Kyŏnghyang Sinmun*, Oct. 1, 1977. These messages had been echoing loudly throughout South Korea since the anticommunist regime of Rhee Syngman in the 1950s, but they became especially pronounced in the 1970s in factories like Hanwha's in Inch'ŏn, where the state required workers' complete allegiance to Park's mission of defense industrialization. See, for examples, *Tonga Ilbo*, June 29, 1978; *Tonga Ilbo*, Jan. 1, 1971.

160 See, for example, Hanwha Kinyŏmgwan, *Sajin ŭro tasi*, 19.

161 Min, interview, Nov. 14, 2012. See testimony by other former Inch'ŏn factory employees in *HIK*, 88–89. See also Hanwha Kŭrup, *Hŭimang ŭro ŭi yŏjŏng*, text volume, 119.

162 Photographs of the Inch'ŏn factory in the 1970s reveal the dissemination of nationalistic rhetoric and messages in the work environment. See Hanwha Kinyŏmgwan, *Sajin ŭro tasi*.

163 Ch'oe, interview.

164 Kim Chongbong, interview.

165 Nam, *Building Ships*, 189–92.

166 In May 1959, two hundred workers at the Inch'ŏn factory had organized the company's first labor strike. Initially denied formal recognition by Hanwha leadership, the union was officially certified in May 1960, after the April 19 Revolution. See *Tonga Ilbo*, May 1, 1959. Because lethal accidents at the factory were so common, Kim Chonghŭi and company managers made substantial efforts with union leaders early on to address workers' rights and safety. See Hanwha Kŭrup, *Hŭimang ŭro ŭi yŏjŏng*, text volume, 43; *HIK*, 83 and 85–86.

167 Yi, interview, June 28, 2018. See also Ch'oe, interview.

168 Yi, interview, June 28, 2018.

169 *Maeil Kyŏngje*, Nov. 12, 1977; Hanwha Kŭrup, *Hŭimang ŭro ŭi yŏjŏng*, text volume, 114–17.

170 *Maeil Kyŏngje*, Oct. 19, 1968, and *Maeil Kyŏngje*, Feb. 2, 1972. See also *Chosŏn Ilbo*, Nov. 15, 1977; *Tonga Ilbo*, Nov. 15, 1977.

171 *Maeil Kyŏngje*, Nov. 22, 1977.

172 *Kyŏnghyang Sinmun*, Nov. 19, 1977; *Kyŏnghyang Sinmun*, Dec. 10, 1977.

173 *Chungang Ilbo*, Aug. 5, 1978; Hanwha Kŭrup, *Hŭimang ŭro ŭi yŏjŏng*, text volume, 117.

174 See *Kyŏnghyang Sinmun*, July 13, 1978; *Maeil Kyŏngje*, April 4, 1979; *Maeil Kyŏngje*, May 30, 1980.

175 Hanwha Kŭrup, *Hŭimang ŭro ŭi yŏjŏng*, text volume, 76–77.

176 Kwon, "Building Bombs," 68.

177 J. Chung, *Born of this Land*, 130 and 136–37; Tenold et al., "International Transfer of Tacit Knowledge," 339, 344–46, 356, and 359.

178 Han'guk Pangwi Sanŏp Chinhŭnghoe, *Pangwi sanŏp kaeron*, 1:241.

179 Kia Chunggongŏp, *Kia Chunggongŏp 20-yŏnsa*, 101–3.

180 PS, "Changgapch'a saengsan ch'uljang kyŏlgwa pogo," July 20, 1976, EA0004886, PA (Seongnam).

181 *HGKK*, 5:384–99.

182 Kia Chunggongŏp, *Kia Chunggongŏp 20-yŏnsa*, 102–3.

183 *HGKK*, 5:399–400; Kukpang Kwahak Yŏn'guso, *Kukpang Kwahak Yŏn'gusosa* (*KKYS*), 3:75.

184 Cho Kilsu, interview, July 21, 2021.

185 A former Kia employee, who was part of a team from Kia Machine Tools that visited Hitachi's factory in Japan in 1978–79, said that he would secretly take Hitachi's product drawings into the factory bathroom to sketch copies of them, so he could bring the information back to Korea. He acknowledged that "we forcibly brought many technologies from Japan that it would not give" (anonymous interviewees, former workers for Kia Machine Tools, interview with the author, July 21, 2021, Ch'angwŏn).

186 Amsden, *Asia's Next Giant*, 329.

187 See the discussion about the spin-off effects on civilian corporations in chapter 4.

188 Kwon, "Mars and Manna," 33.

189 Samsung Precision evolved into Samsung Techwin, which was later acquired by Hanwha and became Hanwha Techwin. Most recently, the company has been renamed as Hanwha Vision.

190 In addition, the most capable major companies, such as Kia and Hyundai, were able to take on multiple military projects, whereas smaller corporations specialized as subcontractors in small projects. Kia Group's subsidiaries Kia Motors and Kia Heavy Industries produced jeeps, military trucks, and armored vehicles as well as heavy artillery and rocket launchers. *KKYS*, 3:75.

191 Daewoo and Hyundai, for example, were known to have had excellent relationships with the state because they did whatever President Park ordered them to do. From the start of HCI, they were placed at the forefront of the push for industrialization. See E. Kim, *Big Business, Strong State*, 156; D. Choi, "Limits of State Strength," 85.

192 E. Kim, *Big Business, Strong State*, 156.

193 In 1976 Samsung Heavy Industries (a Samsung subsidiary specializing in shipbuilding) received government financial and technical support for the construction of a new machinery plant in the Ch'angwŏn Industrial Complex. Likewise,

through government aid for HCI, Goldstar established a factory in the Kumi Industrial Complex and received R & D assistance from a government-funded research institute. PS, "Samsung chonhap kigye kongjang kŏnsŏl kyehoek," EA0006186, Aug. 14, 1976, PA (Seongnam), and "Taedŏk Chŏnmun Yŏn'gu Tanji kŏnsŏl kyehoek," 1A00614174951517, April 14, 1976, PA (Sejong). See also E. Kim and Park, "*Chaebol*," 293; L. Jones and Sakong, *Government, Business, and Entrepreneurship*, 353–54.

194 Samsung undertook defense-related shipbuilding after 1974 and entered the aerospace industry after 1977, when its new subsidiary Samsung Precision became a government-contracted aircraft engine producer. LG's telecommunication sector has its roots in the defense contractor Goldstar Precision Company (a subsidiary of Goldstar), which was established in 1976 and became a defense contractor the same year; in 1995 the company became part of LG Precision. See Han'guk Pangwi Sanŏp Chinhŭnghoe, *Pangwi sanŏp kaeron*, 1:238–39 and 247; Sŏ U., Sin, and Chang, *Pangwi sanŏp*, 328. See also Kwon, "Mars and Manna," 35.

195 When Samsung Precision secured a licensing agreement with US-based General Electric in 1978 for the production of engines for American F-4 and F-5 jet fighters, the engines had to pass the same quality-control tests as the ones produced by the US company, which led to upgrades in Samsung's technology and quality. See *HGKK*, 5:488, 490, and 492. Samsung Heavy Industries also helped its parent company reduce its long-standing reliance on Japanese technology by aggressively procuring machinery technologies from other foreign suppliers for its products in shipbuilding and heavy industry. Pak Y., *Han'guk ŭi chunghwahak kongŏphwa kongŏppyŏl yŏn'gu: Chosŏn kongŏp*, 477–80.

196 Hanwha has maintained its leading position in explosives and is one of South Korea's largest chaebol. Today, it has a market presence in multiple industries, including sectors as diverse as solar energy and hotels and resorts—it even owns a professional baseball team. Hanwha is also South Korea's top defense manufacturer and exporter of military products. See "Top 100 for 2022."

197 Kim Kwangmo, interview with the author, July 29, 2021, Seoul; Ku Sanghoe, interview with the author, July 14, 2021, Bundang, South Korea.

198 Kim Kwŏnjung, interview with the author, Dec. 29, 2021, Seoul.

199 Kwŏn Insuk, *Taehan Min'guk ŭn kundaeda*; Han and Downey, *Engineers for Korea*, 141–43.

200 Korea's regimented corporate environment has been widely documented by both academic and nonacademic writers. See, for example, Surdej, *Han'gugin ŭn mich'yŏtta* (the memoir of a French executive who worked for LG Electronics for ten years), which was published originally in French as *Ils sont fous ces Coréens!* See also Prentice, *Supercorporate*, 162–63.

201 E. Kim, *Big Business, Strong State*, 4–6, 15, and 17.

4. National Scientization and the Agency for Defense Development

1 The Agency for Defense Development (ADD) has received limited scholarly attention in the literature about South Korea's development. Most relevant sources of information about the agency remain inaccessible due to national security concerns, especially amid the ongoing conflict with North Korea. Most official records on ADD weapons programs in the 1970s, which included nuclear missile development, remain classified. Given the agency's implication in controversial military financial scandals since the 1990s, academicians have been reluctant to examine its contributions to Korea's development. For two of few works that have analyzed the ADD and its connection to the national technological growth, see Kwon, "Defender of the Nation, Champion of Science"; Yu S., "Kukka yŏn'gu kaebal saŏp."

2 See T. Park, "Roles of the United States and Japan"; Pak K., *Pak Chŏnghŭi kyŏngje sinhwa*; Glassman and Choi, "*Chaebol* and the US Military-Industrial Complex"; P. Chung, "From Korea to Vietnam"; DiMoia, "Han-Mi Hyŏpcho."

3 See, for example, Mun and Kang, "Pak Chŏnghŭi sidae kwahak kisul"; Ch'oe and Im, "Ch'oe Hyŏngsŏp."

4 For examples of recent literature on South Korea's S & T development, see S. Kim and Ku, *Future Yet to Come*; Kim T., *"Kwahak taet'ongnyŏng Pak Chŏnghŭi" sinhwa rŭl nŏmŏ*; and Mun, *Han'guk kwahak kisul yŏn'gu ch'eje ŭi chinhwa.*

5 M. Moon, "Postcolonial Desire," 166–67 and 170; Bitzinger, "Defense Industries in Asia."

6 T. Park, "Roles of the United States and Japan," 215 and 218–19. The Atomic Energy Research Institute was later reestablished as the Korea Atomic Energy Research Institute (KAERI), one of the government-funded research institutes (GFRIs) founded under the HCI Policy in 1973.

7 The 1962 plan was called the First Five-Year Technology Promotion Plan; "Science" was added to the name of the second and third plans. These five-year plans operated in tandem with the economic development plans of the Economic Planning Board (EPB) for fifteen years, from 1962 to 1976.

8 Taet'ongnyŏng Pisŏsil, *Pak Chŏnghŭi Taet'ongnyŏng yŏnsŏl munjip* [President Park Chung Hee's speeches collection (*PPCHS*)], 3:189–92.

9 Sang-Hyun Kim, "Science, Technology, and the Imaginaries," 330. The 1965 treaty reestablished diplomatic relations between Japan and South Korea.

10 Amsden, *Asia's Next Giant*, 231–32.

11 T. Park, "Roles of the United States and Japan," 219.

12 Paupe, "Korea Institute of Science and Technology," 7.

13 Mun, "KIST esŏ Taedŏk Yŏn'gu," 82–83.

14 KIST's contractual arrangements with private companies served as an organizational prototype for the more than one dozen additional GFRIs that would help Korean firms develop technologies for HCI in the 1970s. See Ch'oe and Im, "Ch'oe Hyŏngsŏp."

15 Both Kim Chŏngnyŏm (Park's former chief of staff) and Kim Kwangmo (former deputy director of the HCI Corps) state in their memoirs that KIST was underequipped to provide technical support when the HCI Policy was launched in 1973. And according to former ADD scientists, South Korea's research facilities were too outmoded to manufacture modern weapons when the defense industry began to operate in the early 1970s. See Chung-yum Kim, *From Despair to Hope*, 447; K. Kim, *Odyssey*, 272; An, Kim, and Cho, *Taehan Min'guk ch'oech'o ŭi chidaeji*, 66–69; Han, *Suryut'an esŏ wŏnjaro*, 1–2; Ku, *Han'guk ŭi pangwi sanŏp*, 30.

16 G. Kim, "Political Power–Mediated Expansion," 124.

17 DiMoia, "Han-Mi Hyŏpcho," 434. KIST in the late 1960s largely functioned as an intermediary between foreign exporters of technology (especially those in the United States, Western Europe, and Japan) and domestic firms, not as a bona fide R & D institute (DiMoia, "Han-Mi Hyŏpcho," 433–34). See also D. Kim, "Transfer of 'Engineer's Mind,'" 88.

18 Glassman and Choi, "Geopolitical Economy," 409.

19 Ku, *Han'guk ŭi pangwi sanŏp*, 52; An, Kim, and Cho, *Taehan Min'guk ch'oech'o ŭi chidaeji*, 146.

20 C. Moon and Paek, "Defense Innovation," 2. See also chapter 1.

21 Yi Kyŏngsŏ, interview with the author, July 13, 2021, Anyang, South Korea. Missile development was only in the planning stage at this time. The first domestic project to develop a guided missile would be officially launched by the ADD in May 1974 (as discussed below in the chapter).

22 However, it should be noted that Yi's reported start date for this missile research by KIST varies in his memoir published in 2023. In this memoir, which was released two years after my interview with him in July 2021, Yi's writing suggests that it was 2 to 3 months prior to April 1972 when he began exploring the development of guided missiles under the president's instruction. Yi Kyŏngsŏ, *Pak Chŏnghŭi ŭi chaju kukpang*, 131–32.

23 Ku, "Ku Sanghoe"; O W., *Han'gukhyŏng kyŏngje kŏnsŏl (HGKK)*, 7:418.

24 Ku Sanghoe, interview with the author, July 14, 2021, Bundang, South Korea. See also Seltzer, "Baekgom," 299.

25 According to the historian Geun Bae Kim, the increasing emphasis of the Park regime on applied science over basic science in the late 1960s and 1970s can be attributed to two significant factors: the S & T policies implemented by Minister of Science and Technology Ch'oe Hyŏngsŏp and the utilization of reverse engineering methods by the ADD. These factors not only promoted a more practical application of science and technology but also influenced the prioritization

of applied research within the regime. See G. Kim, "Political Power–Mediated Expansion," 124–25.

26 An, Kim, and Cho, *Taehan Min'guk ch'oech'o ŭi chidaeji*, 38.

27 An, Kim, and Cho, *Taehan Min'guk ch'oech'o ŭi chidaeji*, 38. See also Seltzer, "Baekgom," 295.

28 Sŏ U., Sin, and Chang, *Pangwi sanŏp*, 39.

29 Kukpang Kwahak Yŏn'guso, *Kukpang ŭi ch'osŏk*, 208–9.

30 Kukpang Kwahak Yŏn'guso, *Kukpang ŭi ch'osŏk*, 209. See also Seltzer, "Baekgom," 295.

31 Presidential Secretariat (PS), "Kukpang Kwahak Yŏn'gusobŏp," Dec. 31, 1970, EA0011800, Presidential Archives (PA) (Seongnam).

32 Kukpang Kwahak Yŏn'guso, *Kukpang Kwahak Yŏn'guso 50-yŏnsa*, 44. See also Kukpang Kwahak Yŏn'guso, *Kukpang Kwahak Yŏn'guso 50-yŏnsa*, 45–46.

33 Seltzer, "Baekgom," 295–96.

34 *HGKK*, 5:120–22; Yu S., "Kukka yŏn'gu kaebal saŏp," 169. See also Kukpang Kwahak Yŏn'guso, *Kukpang Kwahak Yŏn'gusosa* (*KKYS*), 3:57, 63.

35 Yi, interview.

36 *HGKK*, 5:61–63.

37 Yi, interview.

38 *HGKK*, 7:398.

39 Song M., "Kukpang Kwahak Yŏn'guso," 407.

40 Han, *Suryut'an esŏ wŏnjaro*, 22–23; *KKYS*, 3:97. Eventually most of the founding members of the ADD were replaced, except for top military engineers with PhDs, such as Ku Sanghoe, Sŏ Chŏnguk, and Han P'ilsun.

41 Former ADD scientist Ku Sanghoe, despite his own background as a military scientist, lauded Sim's leadership and his ability to overcome the numerous challenges the ADD faced in its early days. Ku, interview.

42 Han, *Suryut'an esŏ wŏnjaro*, 24.

43 In the context of the chapter's discussion about the ADD, I generally use the term "researchers" as a collective designation for ADD personnel, including both those trained as scientists and those trained as engineers. This term is meant to highlight their mutual role in conducting research related to weaponry, regardless of their field of expertise. Whether they were applying the methods of scientific inquiry or applying the problem-solving and design skills of engineering, these individuals collectively contributed to the research objectives of the ADD, and thus I refer to them under the umbrella term "researchers."

44 PS, "Kukpang Kwahak Yŏn'guso chiwŏn taech'aek pogo," Feb. 5, 1975, EA0006423, PA (Seongnam); Yi Ŭ., "ADD mugi kaebal," 5.

45 Educational opportunities for ADD researchers included scholarships for earning advanced university degrees abroad. Seltzer, "Baekgom," 307–8.

46 Song M., "Kukpang Kwahak Yŏn'guso," 407.

47 In 1971, the ADD initiated a public exam to hire more civilian technical experts.
48 Hong C., "Kukpang Kwahak Yŏn'guso," 499. A reproduction of the phrase in Park's calligraphy carved in a monumental stone is in front of the ADD's current headquarters in Taejŏn.
49 Yi Ŭ., "ADD mugi kaebal," 5.
50 Hong C., "Kukpang Kwahak Yŏn'guso," 487.
51 Yi Ŭ., "ADD mugi kaebal," 6.
52 An, Kim, and Cho, *Taehan Min'guk ch'oech'o ŭi chidaeji*, 48. See also Seltzer, "Baekgom," 295–96.
53 Hong C., "Kukpang Kwahak Yŏn'guso," 487. See also Seltzer, "Baekgom," 295.
54 *KKYS*, 3:56–57 and 98.
55 Hong C., "Kukpang Kwahak Yŏn'guso," 487.
56 Ch'oe H., *Ch'oe Hyŏngsŏp hoegorok*, 63; Kukpang Kwahak Yŏn'guso, *Kukpang Kwahak Yŏn'guso 50-yŏnsa*, 39–40.
57 An Tongman, interview with the author, Dec. 16, 2021, Taejŏn; An, Kim, and Cho, *Taehan Min'guk ch'oech'o ŭi chidaeji*, 70.
58 The Research Institute of Science and Technology was established on June 15, 1950. In 1954 the Rhee government renamed it the Research Institute of Science. According to an insider at the institute, when Park came to power in 1961 and shut down the institute, some speculated that Park's military junta aimed to redirect the lab's budget to address pressing financial requirements elsewhere. There were others who postulated that Park feared potential retaliation from the United States for the institute's autonomous arms development, which might lead Washington to replace military grants with loan-based military sales. See Kukpang Kwahak Yŏn'guso, *Ŏttŏk'e haegyŏl haetchi?*, 408–9; M. Moon, "Postcolonial Desire," 171–72.
59 An Tongman, interview, Dec. 16, 2021.
60 Han'guk Kwahak Kisul Yŏn'guwŏn, *KIST 30-yŏnsa*, 108–9.
61 M. Moon, "Postcolonial Desire," 182.
62 Ku, interview. See also An, Kim, and Cho, *Taehan Min'guk ch'oech'o ŭi chidaeji*, 114–15.
63 Kim Ch'angsik, interview with the author, July 3, 2018, Seoul. See also Hong Yongsik, "Han'guk ŭi misail kaebal," *Korea Times*, Sept. 25, 2018, http://sf.koreatimes.com/article/20180925/1204892. Until the 1980s the "A" in JUSMAG-K stood for "Assistance."
64 Kim Ch'angsik, interview.
65 C. Moon, "U.S. Third Country Arms Sales," 82.
66 Ku, *Han'guk ŭi pangwi sanŏp*, 53; An Tongman, interview with the author, July 23, 2021, Taejŏn.
67 *PPCHS*, 10:58–59.
68 Beginning with his New Year's address on January 10, 1964, Park often used the phrase "modernization of the fatherland" when he spoke of achieving "national

restoration" ("1964-yŏn taet'ongnyŏng yŏndu kyosŏ," Jan. 10, 1964, Yŏnsŏl kirok, Taet'ongnyŏng Kirokkwan). For Park, this essentially meant attaining self-reliance by modernizing both the economy and defense. See also Park's speeches in "Chinhae che-4 piryo kongjang kigongsik ch'isa," May 2, 1965; "Che 1-hoe chŏn'guk kwahak kisulcha taehoe ch'isa," May 19, 1966; and "Che-2 kyŏngje undong silch'ŏn kungmin kwŏlgi taehoe ch'isa," Sept. 28, 1968, in Yŏnsŏl kirok, Taet'ongnyŏng Kirokkwan, https://www.pa.go.kr/research/contents/speech/index.jsp.

69 Chŏng Chaegyŏng, *Pak Chŏnghŭi silgi*, 317; see also Chŏng Chaegyŏng, *Pak Chŏnghŭi silgi*, 318–19 and 321. See also Pak Chŏnghŭi Taet'ongnyŏng Yuk Yŏngsu Yŏsa Kinyŏm Saŏphoe, *Kyŏre ŭi chidoja*, 328–38.

70 PS, "Kinŭnggong yangsŏng ŭl wihan chonghap taech'aek," Feb. 26, 1970, EA0023181, PA (Seongnam). See also H. Kim, *Korean Skilled Workers*, 26.

71 *HGKK*, 5:195 and 203–4.

72 *HGKK*, 5:76 and 78.

73 *HGKK*, 5:78.

74 *HGKK*, 7:538–39.

75 H. Kim, *Korean Skilled Workers*, 21.

76 PS, "Pangwi sanŏp mit chunghwahak kongŏphwa chŏngch'aek," Jan. 31, 1973, 1A00614174958687, PA (Sejong).

77 Kyŏngje 2, *Chunghwahak kongŏphwa chŏngch'aek sŏnŏn e ttarŭn kongŏp kujo kaep'yŏnnon* [*Kaep'yŏnnon*], 21–23. See also K. Kim, *Odyssey*, 164–79. For more on *Kaep'yŏnnon*, see chapter 2.

78 O, *Korea Story*, 224–26.

79 K. Kim, *Odyssey*, 252–53.

80 Kim Kwangmo, text message interview, Sept. 17, 2020.

81 As director of the KAERI (1962–66) and KIST (1966–71) and the minister of science and technology (1972–78), Ch'oe was a towering figure in the Park government. Testimonies from Kim Kwangmo and Han P'ilsun, who was one of the chief ADD researchers at the time, indicate that O's sudden rise to top policymaker in charge of HCI incited some rivalry between him and Ch'oe. Despite O's elevated status and unmatched power, Ch'oe was the more senior official and was eight years older than O. See Kim Kwangmo, text message interview, Sept. 17, 2020; Han, *Suryut'an esŏ wŏnjaro*, 56.

82 Mun, "'Chŏn kungmin ŭi kwahakhwa,'" 187–88. According to Han P'ilsun, Ch'oe and O cooperated with each other but also "kept each other in check" (*Suryut'an esŏ wŏnjaro*, 47). Their goals and spheres of interest were different, however: O focused on building the defense industry under the HCI Policy, and Ch'oe served more broadly as the government's "science emissary," connecting the administration's scientization efforts with the people. See Mun and Kang, "Pak Chŏnghŭi sidae kwahak kisul," 230.

83 For example, Korean scientists had sought to develop an indigenous and modernized research infrastructure since the 1930s, and the "new farmer" movement of the mid-1960s had encouraged science-based agricultural advancements for Korean farmers. See M. Moon, "Postcolonial Desire," 166–68 and 174–76; Mun, "'Chŏn kungmin ŭi kwahakhwa,'" 182–83.

84 Sang-Hyun Kim, "Science and Technology," 87. See also O, *Korea Story*, 406.

85 See, for example, *Tonga Ilbo*, Feb. 10, 1976; *Chosŏn Ilbo*, Feb. 9, 1977.

86 Jasanoff, "Future Imperfect," 4; Sang-Hyun Kim, "Science, Technology, and the Imaginaries," 334.

87 Mizuno, *Science for the Empire*, 43. The powerful merger of nationalism and technology was a defining aspect of Imperial Japan's militarized discourse, as reflected in its government slogans like "rich nation, strong army" (*fukokyu kyōhei*), "serving the nation through science" (*kagaku hōkoku*), and "nation building through technology" (*gijutsu rikkoku*), all of which Park adopted. Park and his technocrats also used the term "science-technology" (*kwahak kisul* in Korean), which was derived from the Japanese compound *kagaku gijutsu*, as part of their campaign for technoscientific development. This compound word gained widespread usage among Koreans in all business and scientific domains, as well as among the labor force. See Mizuno, *Science for the Empire*, 43–44; Sang-Hyun Kim, "Science and Technology," 84, and "Science, Technology, and the Imaginaries," 324–25; Han and Downey, *Engineers for Korea*, 90.

88 H. Kim, "Industrial Warriors," 580; H. Kim, *Korean Skilled Workers*, 21.

89 See, for example, *PPCHS*, 12:233–34 and 255–56.

90 EPB, *Economic Survey of the 1973 Korean Economy*, 174–75. Administration of the National Technical Qualification Test began in 1974.

91 In 1967 the state had passed the Vocational Training Act, which was designed to address South Korea's shortage of skilled labor by establishing new vocational training institutes and funding the expansion of existing vocational training programs run by government and nonprofit organizations and by companies in their own facilities. See H. Kim, "Industrial Warriors," 583 and 585. In 1974 the Vocational Training Special Measure Act was also passed. This required large companies to guarantee that at least 15 percent of their total workforce would be newly trained by the company. See H. Kim, *Korean Skilled Workers*, 36–37.

92 H. Kim, *Korean Skilled Workers*, 28.

93 For example, to pass the qualification test and earn the required class 2 license for work in the machinery sector, students had to demonstrate machining skills with a level of precision to within 1/100 mm. That standard was raised to 7/1,000 mm in 1979. H. Kim, *Korean Skilled Workers*, 29–30. See also Pak Chŏnghŭi Taet'ongnyŏng Yuk Yŏngsu Yŏsa Kinyŏm Saŏphoe, *Kyŏre ŭi chidoja*, 328–38.

94 Han'guk Pangwi Sanŏp Chinhŭnghoe, *Pangjinhoesa*, 62; "Pyŏngyŏk ŭimu ŭi t'ŭngnye kyuje e kwanhan pŏmnyul," Kukka Pŏmnyŏng Chŏngbo Sent'ŏ, https://www.law.go.kr/lsInfoP.do?lsiSeq=5564&viewCls=lsRvsDocInfoR#.
95 Seungsook Moon, *Militarized Modernity*, 60.
96 PS, "Pangwi sanŏp ŏpch'e ŭi tangmyŏn munje e taehan taech'aek kanggu," July 5, 1974, EA0004797, PA (Seongnam).
97 Sŏ U., Sin, and Chang, *Pangwi sanŏp*, 108.
98 Kim Hujin, interview with the author, Aug. 5, 2021, Ch'angwŏn; Kang, Kwŏn, and Yu (former Poongsan skilled workers; full names withheld), interview with the author, Nov. 27, 2012, An'gang, South Korea; Ch'oe Pyŏngyun, interview with the author, June 29, 2018, Inch'ŏn; Yu Hansik, interview with the author, June 28, 2018, Ch'angwŏn; Kim Kwŏnjung, interview with the author, Dec. 29, 2021, Seoul; Im Haesu, interview with the author, July 21, 2021, Ch'angwŏn.
99 H. Kim, *Korean Skilled Workers*, 33.
100 Kim Hujin, interview.
101 Kang, interview with the author, Nov. 27, 2012, An'gang.
102 K. Kim, *Odyssey*, 267–68.
103 The MPL's tax benefits also included corporate income tax breaks and special protective excise taxes and tariffs. See PS, "Kunsu Chodal e kwanhan T'ŭkpyŏl Choch'ibŏp," Feb. 16, 1973, 1A00614175010714, PA (Sejong); Han'guk Pangwi Sanŏp Chinhŭnghoe, *Pangjinhoesa*, 283–93.
104 Han'guk Pangwi Sanŏp Chinhŭnghoe, *Pangjinhoesa*, 288–89.
105 Han and Downey, *Engineers for Korea*, 85.
106 Jung and Mah, "R&D Policies of Korea," 170.
107 Pak Y., *Han'guk ŭi chunghwahak kongŏphwa: Kwajŏng kwa naeyong*, 2:322.
108 Pak Y., *Han'guk ŭi chunghwahak kongŏphwa: Kwajŏng kwa naeyong*, 2:344.
109 Pak Y., *Han'guk ŭi chunghwahak kongŏphwa: Kwajŏng kwa naeyong*, 2:345.
110 Mun, "KIST esŏ Taedŏk Yŏn'gu," 99.
111 Y. Lim, *Technology and Productivity*, 136.
112 K. Kim, *Odyssey*, 268–69 and 274.
113 Mun, "KIST esŏ Taedŏk Yŏn'gu," 90; Han and Downey, *Engineers for Korea*, 85.
114 K. Kim, *Odyssey*, 267–73; Kim Kwangmo, interview with the author, July 29, 2021, Seoul.
115 Mun, "KIST esŏ Taedŏk Yŏn'gu," 90–91.
116 PS, "Kumi Kongŏp Tanji e taehan chisi sahang choch'i kyŏlgwa," May 9, 1973, A000007310000965, PA (Sejong).
117 EPB, *Economic Survey of the 1973 Korean Economy*, 177.
118 Kim Kwangmo, *Chunghwahak kongŏp e Pak Chŏnghŭi*, 109–15; Kim Chŏngnyŏm, interview with the author, April 5, 2013, Seoul.
119 Kim Kwangmo, text message interviews, Sept. 17, 2020, and April 28, 2021.

120 According to Kim, the Taedŏk research cluster was originally part of O's HCI plan, but Ch'oe, as head of the Ministry of Science and Technology (MST), had assumed the lead on the project in 1973 (text message interview, Sept. 17, 2020, and *Ch'ŏngwadae pisŏgwan ŭi Pak Chŏnghŭi*, 143–44).

121 Kim Kwangmo, text message interview, Sept. 17, 2020.

122 PS, "Taedŏk Chŏnmun Yŏn'gu Tanji kŏnsŏl kyehoek," 1A00614174951517, April 14, 1976, PA (Sejong), 27; K. Kim, *Odyssey*, 270.

123 Kim Kwangmo, text message interview, Sept. 17, 2020.

124 Amsden, *Asia's Next Giant*, 328–29.

125 For example, the ADD was involved in the development of the Maritime Research Institute, a GFRI in Taedŏk devoted to shipbuilding. PS, "Taedŏk Chŏnmun Yŏn'gu Tanji kŏnsŏl kyehoek."

126 *KKYS*, 3:64.

127 *KKYS*, 3:65.

128 Some of the discussions and anecdotes in this chapter involving the ADD previously appeared in in my article "Defender of the Nation, Champion of Science: The Agency for Defense Development as a Nexus for the Technological Transformation of South Korea" in *Journal of Korean Studies* 28, no. 1 (March 2023): 59–90. Copyright 2023, Duke University Press. All rights reserved. Republished by permission of the publisher, Duke University Press.

129 An Tongman, interview with the author, July 30, 2021, Taejŏn.

130 Ku, interview.

131 In 2021 and 2022 I interviewed former ADD scientists who had worked on the earliest defense projects in the 1970s, including Yi Kyŏngsŏ, Ku Sanghoe, An Tongman, Kim Pyŏnggyo, Kim Ch'angsik, Kim Yŏngsu, and an individual who wished to remain anonymous. I also interviewed two former ADD directors: Pak Ch'angsik in 2012 and Chŏng Hongyong in 2013. I also consulted memoirs and articles published by former ADD scientists.

132 An, Kim, and Cho, *Taehan Min'guk ch'oech'o ŭi chidaeji*, 74; anonymous interviewee (a former ADD scientist), interview with the author, July 13, 2021; *Hankyŏng nyusŭ*, Sept. 9, 1996, https://www.hankyung.com/news/article/1996091602611.

133 An, interview, July 30, 2021.

134 Sŏ U., Sin, and Chang, *Pangwi sanŏp*, 45; Han, *Suryut'an esŏ wŏnjaro*, 4–5. See also *Chungchung Today*, July 2, 2020, https://www.cctoday.co.kr/news/articleView.html?idxno=2079621.

135 Han, *Suryut'an esŏ wŏnjaro*, 26. Most of the ADD's first sixty employees had been military academy instructors who had PhDs, officials in the MND, or military reserve officers. *KKYS*, 3:65.

136 Han, *Suryut'an esŏ wŏnjaro*, 26.

137 Han, *Suryut'an esŏ wŏnjaro*, 25–35.

138 Han, *Suryut'an esŏ wŏnjaro*, 30–31.

139 Han, *Suryut'an esŏ wŏnjaro*, 6–9.

140 An, Kim, and Cho, *Taehan Min'guk ch'oech'o ŭi chidaeji*, 77; *Science Times*, Oct. 22, 2006, http://www.sciencetimes.co.kr/news/군용-무전기-개발에서-tdx-개발로/.

141 *Science Times*, Oct. 22, 2006.

142 Sŏ U., Sin, and Chang, *Pangwi sanŏp*, 327–29.

143 Kim Ch'angsik, phone interview with the author, Aug. 7, 2020.

144 Kwon, "Anatomy of *Chaju Kukpang*," 233.

145 Kim Ch'angsik, phone interview; An, interview, July 23, 2021; Kim Hujin, interview. See also Kukpang Kwahak Yŏn'guso, *Kukpang Kwahak Yŏn'guso 50-yŏnsa*, 62.

146 Kim Kyegwan, interview with the author, Aug. 5, 2021, Ch'angwŏn.

147 An, Kim, and Cho, *Taehan Min'guk ch'oech'o ŭi chidaeji*, 234.

148 An, interview, Dec. 16, 2021.

149 Sŏ U., Sin, and Chang, *Pangwi sanŏp*, 96–97; Ku, "Ku Sanghoe."

150 H. Yoon, "National Security," 242. As businesses gradually took on greater responsibility for weapons production, the ADD shifted its focus to the development of core defense technologies, allowing for a more efficient division of labor.

151 Kim Yŏngsu, interview with the author, Dec. 16, 2021, Taejŏn.

152 Kim Yŏngsu, interview.

153 Kim Yŏngsu, interview.

154 Im Haesu, interview.

155 PS, "Kunsu simŭihoe ŭigyŏl sahang pogo," Nov. 12, 1975, EA0004861, and "Palk'anp'o ryangsan kyehoek," May 3, 1976, EA0004874, PA (Seongnam).

156 Han, *Suryut'an esŏ wŏnjaro*, 62–63, 68–70, and 72–73.

157 For examples of the sacrifices made by participants in the defense industry, see Kukpang Kwahak Yŏn'guso, *Ŏttŏk'e haegyŏl haetchi?*; O W., "Pak Chŏnghŭi chŏnggwŏn Yulgok," 387–88; Kim Chongbong, interview with the author, June 27, 2018, Kangnŭng; Kim Kwŏnjung, interview.

158 Polar Bear was a part of Park's top secret program to develop a nuclear missile under the Yulgok Operation (for more on the operation, see chapter 5).

159 Polar Bear was a surface-to-surface ballistic missile that also featured a guidance system (it used radar technology in 1978 and then the Inertial Navigation Technology in 1979), making it a type of guided missile as well. It is important to note the distinction among the terms "guided missile," "surface-to-surface missile," and "ballistic missile" due to their different functionalities, but in the case of Polar Bear, these terms can be used interchangeably to describe the missile's capabilities. See Seltzer, "Baekgom," 298 and 304.

160 G. Kim, "Political Power–Mediated Expansion," 125.

161 O, *Korea Story*, 418.

162 Yi Ŭ., "ADD mugi kaebal," 4.

163 Kukpang Kwahak Yŏn'guso, *Kukpang ŭi ch'osŏk*, 210. According to O Wŏnch'ŏl's memoir, Park first ordered O to plan the development of a guided missile in December 1971 (*HGKK*, 7:418–19). But as noted above, Yi Kyŏngsŏ stated in an interview with me that KIST had already embarked on the preliminary exploration of a guided missile project in 1969 (or early 1972, according to his new memoir, Yi Kyŏngsŏ, *Pak Chŏnghŭi ŭi chaju kukpang*, 132); however, this project by KIST only reached the setup stage (Yi Kyŏngsŏ, interview). It was the Polar Bear project that became the first official endeavor to develop an actual missile.

164 An, Kim, and Cho, *Taehan Min'guk ch'oech'o ŭi chidaeji*, 108–9. While the ADD's missile in development was initially modeled on the US Pershing surface-to-surface missile (MGM-31), the agency later replaced it with a different model, the Nike Hercules (NH) missile. See *KKYS*, 3:76.

165 An, Kim, and Cho, *Taehan Min'guk ch'oech'o ŭi chidaeji*, 109–10.

166 Yi Ŭ., "ADD mugi kaebal," 4.

167 Yi Ŭ., "ADD mugi kaebal," 4.

168 An, Kim, and Cho, *Taehan Min'guk ch'oech'o ŭi chidaeji*, 111.

169 Pak Chunbok, *Han'guk misail*, 35.

170 To gather the needed materials, An said his team scoured local hardware stores along the Ch'ŏnggye Stream, a tributary of the Han River that runs through Seoul, looking for seamless pipes and other items that had been smuggled out of US military bases by Korean workers and then pawned (interview with the author, July 23, 2021).

171 An, Kim, and Cho, *Taehan Min'guk ch'oech'o ŭi chidaeji*, 112–13. See also Yi Kyŏngsŏ, *Pak Chŏnghŭi ŭi chaju kukpang*, 145.

172 An, Kim, and Cho, *Taehan Min'guk ch'oech'o ŭi chidaeji*, 113. See also Yi Kyŏngsŏ, *Pak Chŏnghŭi ŭi chaju kukpang*, 154–55.

173 Yi Ŭ., "ADD mugi kaebal," 4; An, Kim, and Cho, *Taehan Min'guk ch'oech'o ŭi chidaeji*, 150. See also Yi Kyŏngsŏ, *Pak Chŏnghŭi ŭi chaju kukpang*, 169–70; and Hong, "Search for Deterrence," 495.

174 An, Kim, and Cho, *Taehan Min'guk ch'oech'o ŭi chidaeji*, 150–51.

175 For more information about Park's quest to procure foreign missile technologies and its opposition by the US Department of State, see chapter 5. See also Hong, "Search for Deterrence," 495–96; Ŏm, "Pak Chŏnghŭi chŏngbu ŭi chaju kukpang," 17–18.

176 An, Kim, and Cho, *Taehan Min'guk ch'oech'o ŭi chidaeji*, 153. See also Yi Kyŏngsŏ, *Pak Chŏnghŭi ŭi chaju kukpang*, 171.

177 The original NH was a surface-to-air missile controlled remotely to its target in the air, rather than by a preset ballistic trajectory—and McDonnell Douglas engineers sought to convert the missile's guidance and control system to that of a surface-to-surface ballistic missile. See Seltzer, "Baekgom," 304.

178 Seltzer, "Baekgom," 311.
179 Sŏ U., Sin, and Chang, *Pangwi sanŏp*, 131.
180 Sŏ U., Sin, and Chang, *Pangwi sanŏp*, 131. See also An, Kim, and Cho, *Taehan Min'guk ch'oech'o ŭi chidaeji*, 154.
181 Seltzer, "Baekgom," 312.
182 Yi Ŭ., "ADD mugi kaebal," 4.
183 An, Kim, and Cho, *Taehan Min'guk ch'oech'o ŭi chidaeji*, 154.
184 Sŏ U., Sin, and Chang, *Pangwi sanŏp*, 131.
185 The program was later called the Engineer and Scientist Exchange Program.
186 Kim Ch'angsik, interview.
187 An, Kim, and Cho, *Taehan Min'guk ch'oech'o ŭi chidaeji*, 171 and 242.
188 Seltzer, "Baekgom," 311 and 318–20. See also Robert Lindsey, "Lockheed Rocket Facility Is Sold Indirectly to Seoul," *New York Times*, Dec. 17, 1975.
189 *KKYS*, 3:76 and 94.
190 *KKYS*, 3:96; Yi Kyŏngsŏ, interview.
191 Kim Kwangmo, interview with the author, April 15, 2021.
192 Yi Ŭ., "ADD mugi kaebal," 1.
193 Ku, interview; An, interview, July 30, 2021.
194 Ku, interview.
195 An, Kim, and Cho, *Taehan Min'guk ch'oech'o ŭi chidaeji*, 391; Yi, interview; Kim Pyŏnggyo, interview with the author, July 13, 2021, Anyang, South Korea.
196 The experience was similar to what Yi Ch'anggi, a Hanwha engineer, reported happening during his team's visit to an NH factory in New Jersey in 1976 (see chapter 3).
197 An, Kim, and Cho, *Taehan Min'guk ch'oech'o ŭi chidaeji*, 75–77.
198 See Kwon, "Defender of the Nation, Champion of Science," 78–81.
199 D. Hwang, "Role of Defense Industry," 164; Sŏ U., Sin, and Chang, *Pangwi sanŏp*, 122 and 128; Kukpang Kwahak Yŏn'guso, *Kukpang ŭi ch'osŏk*, 209; Kukpang Kwahak Yŏn'guso, *Kukpang Kwahak Yŏn'guso 50-yŏnsa*, 55.
200 G. Kim, "Political Power–Mediated Expansion," 138; Kim Kwangmo, *Odyssey*, 270.
201 G. Kim, "Political Power–Mediated Expansion," 125; see also 134.
202 *KKYS*, 3:70–71.
203 See, for example, PS, "Han'gukhyŏng sohwagi kisul chehyu," Dec. 28, 1971, EA0004526; "Han-Chung hyŏmnyŏk," July 24, 1972, EA0004600; "Eksose yudot'an toip munje e kwanhan myŏndam naeyong," Nov. 23, 1974, EA0003465; Isŭrael kwa ŭi hyŏpcho pangan," Dec. 18, 1974, EA0004811; "Kwaesokchŏng misail kuip munje tŭng e kwanhan mich'ŭk ipchang," Jan. 13, 1975, EA0003473; "Ilbon kwa ŭi t'ŭksu hyŏmnyŏk," June 13, 1975, EA0004846; and "Yŏngguk Taesa wa pangsan hyŏbŭi," Aug. 13, 1975, EA0004854, PA (Seongnam). See also Hayes and Moon, "Park Chung Hee"; *KKYS*, 3:71; An, Kim, and Cho, *Taehan Min'guk ch'oech'o ŭi chidaeji*, 70.

204 See, for example, PS, "Chŏnch'a kaebal kyehoek," July 13, 1974, EA0004802, and "Pangwi sanŏp," Dec. 27, 1974, EA0004825, PA (Seongnam).

205 Kukpang Kwahak Yŏn'guso, *Kukpang Kwahak Yŏn'guso 50-yŏnsa*, 64.

206 Sŏ U., Sin, and Chang, *Pangwi sanŏp*, 96–97. See also Ku, "Ku Sanghoe."

207 Glassman and Choi, "*Chaebol* and the US Military-Industrial Complex."

208 An, Kim, and Cho, *Taehan Min'guk ch'oech'o ŭi chidaeji*, 78 and 81.

209 South Korean corporations that had served as contractors for the US military in Vietnam in the 1960s, such as Hyundai Construction Company, had upgraded their quality standards to meet US federal regulations. However, such quality assurance standards were seldom used in domestic production and did not become widely adopted until the HCI initiative in the 1970s. See Amsden, *Asia's Next Giant*, 232, 280–81, and 310.

210 The team consisted of ADD scientists and inspection officers from the military. See An, Kim, and Cho, *Taehan Min'guk ch'oech'o ŭi chidaeji*, 81; Kukpang Kwahak Yŏn'guso, *Kukpang Kwahak Yŏn'guso 50-yŏnsa*, 65–66.

211 PS, "Kuksan 81 mm pakkyŏkp'o such'ul kŏnŭi," Aug. 18, 1975, EA0004856, and "Pangwi sanŏp," Dec. 27, 1974, EA0004825, PA (Seongnam).

212 Kukpang Kwahak Yŏn'guso, *Kukpang Kwahak Yŏn'guso 50-yŏnsa*, 65–66.

213 Kukpang Kwahak Yŏn'guso, *Kukpang Kwahak Yŏn'guso 50-yŏnsa*, 79. For example, the production of US jet engines required Samsung to adopt technology capable of precision work to within 1/1,000 mm. See *HGKK*, 5:490–91.

214 For example, see PS, "Kuksanp'o wa kunwŏnp'o ŭi pigyo pogo," Nov. 22, 1977, EA0004915, PA (Seongnam).

215 Kim Kwŏnjung, interview; Cho Kilsu, interview with the author, July 21, 2021, Ch'angwŏn. See also chapter 3.

216 Kim Kyegwan, interview.

217 Yu, text message interview with the author, April 24, 2021. See also Yu, interview with the author, Aug. 5, 2021, Ch'angwŏn.

218 Yu, interview with the author, Aug. 19, 2017, Ch'angwŏn (italics added).

219 Kukpang Kwahak Yŏn'guso, *Kukpang Kwahak Yŏn'guso 50-yŏnsa*, 79; PS, "Minkun kyŏmyong kisul kaebal ch'ujin pangan"; An, Kim, and Cho, *Taehan Min'guk ch'oech'o ŭi chidaeji*, 78 and 81.

220 Kukpang Kwahak Yŏn'guso, *Kukpang Kwahak Yŏn'guso 50-yŏnsa*, 57, 63, 79; Ku, interview.

221 Kwon, "Mars and Manna," 32.

222 Sŏ U., Sin, and Chang, *Pangwi sanŏp*, 96–97.

223 Kim Kyegwan, interview; Kim Kwŏnjung, interview; Cho, interview; Im, interview.

224 Kia Chunggongŏp, *Kia Chunggongŏp 20-yŏnsa*, 355; D. Hwang, "Role of Defense Industry," 165; Min S., *Kisul chugwŏn hoebok ŭi chuyŏk*, 96, 135–36.

225 Sŏ U., Sin, and Chang, *Pangwi sanŏp*, 328–29; An, Kim, and Cho, *Taehan Min'guk ch'oech'o ŭi chidaeji*, 77; Min S., *Kisul chugwŏn hoebok ŭi chuyŏk*, 96–97.

226 *Science Times*, Oct. 22, 2006, http://www.sciencetimes.co.kr/news/군용-무전기-개발에서-tdx-개발로/.

227 Sŏ U., Sin, and Chang, *Pangwi sanŏp*, 327–29. The Oriental Precision Company later merged with Goldstar Precision Company to become LG, South Korea's flagship manufacturer of electronic products.

228 *Science Times*, Oct. 22, 2006. Military telecommunications technology was spun off into the development of cameras, video recorders, copy machines, printers, and marine electronics as well. See D. Hwang, "Role of Defense Industry," 165; PS, "Min-kun kyŏmyong kisul kaebal hwalsŏng hwa pangan," Dec. 1, 1996, 1A20620161519964, PA (Sejong).

229 An, Kim, and Cho, *Taehan Min'guk ch'oech'o ŭi chidaeji*, 320; Yu, interview, Aug. 19, 2017.

230 PS, "Min-kun kyŏmyong kisul kaebal ch'ujin pangan," April 23, 1997, 1A2062 0161644257, PA (Sejong), 2.

231 Associated Press, "South Korea Launches First Satellite," *U.S. News & World Report*, June 21, 2022.

232 *Tonga Saiŏnsŭ*, Sept. 8, 2021, https://www.dongascience.com/news.php?idx=49115.

233 C. Moon and Lee, "Revolution in Military Affairs," 134.

234 MND, *2018 Defense White Paper* (English version), 146–47, and *2020 Defense White Paper* (English version), 57–58.

235 Hanwha, Hyundai, LG, Daewoo Shipbuilding and Marine Engineering (now Hanwha Ocean), Samsung Precision (now Hanwha Vision), Doosan (now Doosan Mottrol), and Korean Air have used the specialized expertise they gained from commercial production to spearhead new military weapons and weapons systems. See Kwon, "Mars and Manna," 35. See also Han'guk Pangwi Sanŏp Chinhŭnghoe, *Pangwi sanŏp kaeron*, 1:238–39, 241–47, 249–50, 253–55.

236 MND, *2018 Defense White Paper*, 153, and *2020 Defense White Paper*, 145.

237 Yi M., "Chŏngbu ch'uryŏn yŏn'guso," 19.

238 E. Shin and Welch, "Korean Science and Technology," 470 and 473.

239 Jung and Mah, "R&D Policies," 183.

5. Mobilizing to Weaponize the Nation

1 See, for example, Taet'ongnyŏng Pisŏsil, *Pak Chŏnghŭi Taet'ongnyŏng yŏnsŏl munjip* [President Park Chung Hee's speeches collection (*PPCHS*)], 5:108–9.

2 In fact, the existence of Yulgok was not made public until 1993, when the operation was implicated in major financial scandals. Yulgok has received limited coverage in academic scholarship due to the scarcity of available primary source data on the subject.

3 O W., *Han'gukhyŏng kyŏngje kŏnsŏl* (*HGKK*), 5:238.

4 Under the plan, the US Military Assistance Program (MAP) granted South Korea small arms, M16 rifles, and aircraft; improvements to military facilities, air bases, and communication facilities; tactical devices to counter infiltrations; and some technical training for Korean workers. See Presidential Secretariat (PS), "Kunwŏn igwan ŏmmu hyŏnhwang pogo," Feb. 19, 1970, EA0004298, Presidential Archives (PA) (Seongnam).

5 Ministry of Foreign Affairs (MOFA), *Symington Ch'ŏngmunhoe kibŏn munsŏch'ŏl, 1970*, vol. 1, 729.13US, file no. 3629, 24–36. In Oegyo Saryogwan [Diplomatic Archives].

6 See O W., "Yulgok Saŏp ch'ulpal," 482.

7 PS, "Kunwŏn igwan ŏmmu hyŏnhwang pogo," Feb. 19, 1970, EA0004298, PA (Seongnam).

8 Chaired by Senator Stuart Symington of Missouri, the subcommittee—later known as the Symington Subcommittee—was responsible for reviewing US defense policies toward allied nations. The subcommittee held a special hearing on South Korea from February 24 to 26, 1970. PS, "Saimingt'ŏn Sowiwŏn pogosŏ chung Han'guk kwan'gye pubun," Dec. 24, 1970, EA0002942, PA (Seongnam); MOFA, *Symington Ch'ŏngmunhoe kibŏn munsŏch'ŏl*, 203–4, 229. See also US Congress, Senate Committee on Foreign Relations, *United States Security Agreements*, 2:1621.

9 "Memorandum from the Joint Chiefs of Staff Representative to the National Security Council Review Group (Unger) to the Chairman of the Review Group (Kissinger), Washington, DC," Feb. 17, 1970, document 52 in US Department of State, *Foreign Relations of the United States* (*FRUS*), *1969–1976*, vol. 19, part 1, https://history.state.gov/historicaldocuments/frus1969-76v19p1/d52.

10 C. Moon, "U.S. Third Country Arms Sales," 82.

11 From 1971 to 1984, South Korea received 853 TDPs from the United States. However, 92 percent of them covered low-level technologies, which were used for producing basic weapons such as guns, ammunition, artillery, and basic communication devices. See H. Yoon, "National Security," 234–35; C. Moon, "Political Economy," 457. See also Ku, *Han'guk ŭi pangwi sanŏp*, 53.

12 From 1965 to 1975 the United States spent approximately $111 billion on the war in Vietnam. Daggett, "Costs of Major U.S. Wars," 2; Kukpangbu, *Kukpangsa*, 4:775. Regarding the shortcoming of the United States in fulfilling its promised aid to Park's Five-Year Military Modernization Plan, see Yi Chaehak, "Pak Chŏnghŭi chŏngbu ŭi kukpang oegyo," 224, 228–229.

13 Central Intelligence Agency (CIA), "South Korea," 3.

14 *HGKK*, 7:418–19.

15 Hong, "Search for Deterrence," 488–89.

16 However, because building Kori 1 required US technical assistance, its plant was designed for commercial energy use only. Construction was completed in 1977,

and South Korea's first domestic nuclear power plant began operating in 1978. See "Report, Embassy of Hungary in North Korea to the Hungarian Foreign Ministry," Feb. 23, 1979, History and Public Policy Program Digital Archive [HPPP], https://digitalarchive.wilsoncenter.org/document/110134.

17 The Department of State under Secretary of State Kissinger (1973–77) disagreed with the Department of Defense at various points on offering US weapons technologies to the ROK because of the potentially destabilizing effect that Korean militarization could have on East-West détente. See Hong, "Search for Deterrence," 495–96.

18 H. Kim, *Korea's Development*, 217.

19 For example, in 1977, the newly inaugurated administration of Jimmy Carter, along with the Democratic majority in Congress, imposed much stricter arms controls on South Korea compared with those under the previous Republican administrations of Gerald Ford and Richard Nixon.

20 Kwon, "Beyond Patron and Client," 195–96.

21 After the first exhibition of Korean-made weapons from the Lightning Operation, in December 1971, the United States sent an Advanced Research Projects Agency team led by Clyde D. Hardin to assist the Agency for Defense Development (ADD), as discussed in chapter 2. And when the ADD missile program showed progress in the mid-1970s, the United States dispatched a team of technical advisers to both assist and monitor missile development. See Seltzer, "Baekgom," 306.

22 Han, *Suryut'an esŏ wŏnjaro*, 86. See also Hong, "Search for Deterrence," 493.

23 The US economic stake was even higher after 1974, when it began to transfer arms to South Korea under its Foreign Military Sales (FMS) program, which required the ROK to purchase US-transferred military equipment, services, and training through loan credits. A smaller portion of the weapons sales to South Korea were conducted under the Direct Commercial Sales program. The FMS is a government-to-government sales process overseen by the Department of Defense and approved by the president. Purchases can be paid for with US grant aid, loan credit, or the purchasing country's own funds. Sales must also be approved by the Department of State. See US Department of Defense, Defense Security Cooperation Agency, "Foreign Military Sales FAQ."

24 It was shortly after witnessing the South Korean defense industry's remarkable progress in 1974, under Yulgok, that the United States decided to grant South Korean manufacturers coproduction licenses for more advanced weapons. See PS, "Pangwi sanŏp," Dec. 27, 1974, EA0004825, PA (Seongnam); Ku, "Ku Sanghoe."

25 An, Kim, and Cho, *Taehan Min'guk ch'oech'o ŭi chidaeji*, 114; Kukpang Kwahak Yŏn'guso, *Ŏttŏk'e haegyŏl haetchi?*, 167; Ku, "Ku Sanghoe." Even though in the late 1960s the Department of State had initially agreed with the Department of Defense that the ROK's exporting of US-licensed weapons would serve "a re-

gional arms supply role" for the United States, in the 1970s the Department of State became more prohibitive about the ROK's exports of US weapons (US Congress, House Committee on International Relations, *Investigation of Korean-American Relations*, 82).

26 See, for example, H. Kim, *Korea's Development*, chapter 9; Cho C., "Pak Chŏnghŭi ŭi chaju kukpang"; Hong, "Search for Deterrence"; L. Choi, "First Nuclear Crisis"; Hayes and Moon, "Park Chung Hee."

27 H. Yoon, "National Security," 204.

28 As the right arm of the SES, the Ministry of Commerce and Industry (MCI) became increasingly influential in the defense sector, particularly in areas related to weapons contracting. By the late 1970s, it had largely supplanted the role of the Ministry of National Defense (MND) in these domains (see chapter 3).

29 Kim Kwangmo, interview with the author, June 26, 2018, Seoul.

30 Although the MND, as the official governing body for the ADD, issued orders related to missile development, the close connection between the Blue House and the ADD effectively marginalized the MND's role in decision-making regarding these top secret programs. For these confidential programs like nuclear arms and ballistic missile development, SES technocrats worked directly with the ADD. PS, "Taejŏnch'ang p'ungdong sisŏl chiyŏn silt'ae ch'ŏppo e taehan kŏmt'o pogo," Nov. 22, 1977, EA0004914, PA (Seongnam); O T., "1972-yŏn O Wŏnch'ŏl."

31 Hong, "Search for Deterrence," 490.

32 For example, developing rocket propulsion technology for Yulgok's ballistic missile program involved engineers from Hanwha and other firms, as well as university researchers. See An, Kim, and Cho, *Taehan Min'guk ch'oech'o ŭi chidaeji*, 241–43. See also chapter 3, for more on Hanwha.

33 See, for example, PS, "Changgapch'a saengsan ch'uljang kyŏlgwa pogo," July 20, 1976, EA0004886; "Kuksanp'o wa kunwŏnp'o ŭi pigyo pogo," Nov. 22, 1977, EA0004915; "Chŏnch'a saengsan e taehan chisi," July 7, 1975, EA0000230; "T'ŭksu t'anyak mit sije pyŏnggi sisa kyŏlgwa pogo," Nov. 1, 1975, EA0004860; "Panggong yudot'an kaejo saŏp kyehoek," Feb. 15, 1973, EA0004655; "F-16 chŏnt'ugi hwakpo," Dec. 12, 1977, EA0004916; "Kunsu simŭihoe ŭigyŏl sahang pogo," Nov. 12, 1975, EA0004861; and "Hwap'o ilgwan saengsan kongjang kŏnsŏl," May 6, 1975, EA0000226, PA (Seongnam). See also Baradaran, "Transformation," 199.

34 O W., "25-cho wŏn Yulgok," 412 and 423; Kim Kwangmo, interviews with the author, April 16 and 22, 2013, Seoul.

35 Park excluded fighter jets and missiles in his directions to the JCS, but he had already secretly ordered O and the ADD to pursue missile development independently. As for the fighter jets, South Korea lacked aerospace technology in 1973, making immediate construction of such jets impossible at the time. However, given the early success of defense industrialization, Park eventually decided to develop the aerospace industry as part of Yulgok in the late 1970s.

36 Kukpangbu, *Yulgok Saŏp*, 22.

37 O W., "25-cho wŏn Yulgok," 414–15.

38 After Park, subsequent ROK governments would extend the original first FIP (1974–81) into the second FIP (1982–86) and the third FIP (1987–92; later extended to 1995), creating three stages in South Korea's military modernization. See Kukpangbu, *Yulgok Saŏp*, 31–33 and 34–48. See also Ch'oe S., Ko, and Yi, "Han'guk pangwi sanŏp ŭi 40-yŏn," 81.

39 *HGKK*, 5:235. According to the MND's records, Park gave his final approval for the commencement of Yulgok on February 25, 1974. See Kukpangbu, *Kukpangsa*, 4:36.

40 Basically, every weapons program under the FIP had to be coordinated with the Yulgok Enforcement Agency in each division. The agency prepared project plans and submitted them to the MND, which then forwarded them to two separate Yulgok committees—one within the MND and the other in the Blue House—for approval. These "Five-Member Committees" are discussed later in the chapter. See *HGKK*, 5:235 and 240. See also H. Kim, *Korea's Development*, 190.

41 H. Yoon, "National Security," 187.

42 Kukpangbu, *Yulgok Saŏp*, 35–36. All of these programs under FIP were aided to varying degrees by TDPs from the United States and contracts with American manufacturers. See US Congress, House Committee on International Relations, *Investigation of Korean-American Relations*, 78.

43 US Congress, Senate Committee on Foreign Relations, *United States Security Agreements*, 2:1621. See also *HGKK*, 5:296.

44 PS, "Han'gukhyŏng-A sŏlgye," Sept. 21, 1972, EA0004622, PA (Seongnam).

45 Kukpang Kwahak Yŏn'guso, *Kukpang Kwahak Yŏn'gusosa* (*KKYS*), 1:138; PS, "Han'gukhyŏng soch'ong," Dec. 1974, EA0004815, PA (Seongnam).

46 *KKYS*, 1:138–39 and 3:73; PS, "Kunsu simŭihoe ŭigyŏl sahang pogo," Nov. 12, 1975, EA0004861, PA (Seongnam), "Kuksan 81mm pakkyŏkp'o such'ul kŏnŭi," Aug. 18, 1975, EA0004856, and "Kuksanp'o wa kunwŏnp'o ŭi pigyo pogo," Nov. 22, 1977, EA0004915, PA (Seongnam); Pak P., "1970-yŏndae Han'guk chaju kukpang," 184.

47 *KKYS*, 3:75; *HGKK*, 5:317.

48 *KKYS*, 3:209. See also PS, "Yulgok Saŏp ch'ujin pogo," Dec. 18, 1974, EA0004821, and "Chŏnch'a kaebal kyehoek," July 13, 1974, EA0004802, PA (Seongnam).

49 *KKYS*, 1:142–43.

50 Kukpang Kwahak Yŏn'guso, *Kukpang ŭi ch'osŏk*, 259.

51 *KKYS*, 3:79–81. The PGM stands for "patrol gunboat, motor," PKM stands for "patrol killer medium," and PK stands for "patrol killer."

52 PS, "Hamjŏng saengsan," July 7, 1975, 1A00614174951507, PA (Sejong).

53 *KKYS*, 3:79.

54 Ŏm, "Pak Chŏnghŭi chŏngbu ŭi chaju kukpang," 22–23.

55 *HGKK*, 5:327–28.

56 Kukpangbu, *Yulgok Saŏp*, 36–37.

57 *HGKK*, 5:488, 490, and 492; Han'guk Pangwi Sanŏp Chinhŭnghoe, *Pangwi sanŏp kaeron*, 1:238–39.

58 *HGKK*, 5:504 and 530; PS, "F-16 chŏnt'ugi hwakpo," Dec. 12, 1977, EA0004916, PA (Seongnam).

59 *HGKK*, 5:537–38. South Korea did not begin producing F-16s until 1995.

60 From 1971 to 1979 the United States delivered 534 TDPs to South Korea (H. Yoon, "National Security," 236, table 7-5).

61 US Congress, House Committee on International Relations, *Investigation of Korean-American Relations*, 81–83; C. Moon, "Political Economy," 456–57; CIA, "Sale of Korean Manufactured M-16 Rifles to a Third Country."

62 H. Yoon, "National Security," 223.

63 Kim Hujin, interview with the author, Aug. 5, 2021, Ch'angwŏn; Kim Kyegwan, interview with the author, Aug. 5, 2021, Ch'angwŏn.

64 The United States had nearly 950 nuclear warheads deployed on the Korean peninsula in the mid-1960s. However, it began to withdraw them in the late 1970s and by the early 1990s, all of them had been removed. See Woolf and Chanlett-Avery, "Redeploying U.S. Nuclear Weapons," 3.

65 Hong, "Search for Deterrence," 488.

66 US Congress, House Committee on International Relations, *Investigation of Korean-American Relations*, 79–80.

67 Kim Chongp'il, *Kim Chongp'il chŭngŏnnok*, 1:427. See also Kim's testimony in "Pak Chŏnghŭi haek p'ŭrojekt'ŭ," *Chungang Ilbo*, July 9, 2015, https://www.joongang.co.kr/article/18210193#home.

68 Hong, "Search for Deterrence," 491.

69 Kim Kwangmo, text message interview with the author, July 29, 2021. In addition to this text message exchange, I also conducted an in-person interview with Kim Kwangmo on the same day. See also O T., "1972-yŏn O Wŏnch'ŏl."

70 O T., "1972-yŏn O Wŏnch'ŏl."

71 Pure plutonium could be extracted from the spent fuel of reprocessing facilities, whereas the production of enriched uranium required more expensive facilities. See Kim Kwangmo, text message interview.

72 O T., "1972-yŏn O Wŏnch'ŏl."

73 Kim Kwangmo, text message interview.

74 See, for example, PS, "Eksose yudot'an toip munje e kwanhan myŏndam naeyong," Nov. 23, 1974, EA0003465; "Kwaesokchŏng misail kuip munje tŭng e kwanhan mich'ŭk ipchang," Jan. 13, 1975, EA0003473; "Isŭrael kwa ŭi hyŏpcho pangan," Dec. 18, 1974, EA0004811; and "Yŏngguk Taesa wa pangsan hyŏbŭi," Aug. 13, 1975, EA0004854, PA (Seongnam). The SSM project is the same project as the "Aviation Industry Development" project discussed in chapter 4.

75 Burr, "Stopping Korea."

76 "US Department of State Memorandum, Sale of Rocket Propulsion Technology to South Korea," Feb. 4, 1975, History and Public Policy Program, Wilson Center Digital Archive (HPPP), http://digitalarchive.wilsoncenter.org/document/114634.

77 See the discussion in chapter 4 about the ADD's deal with SNPE.

78 CIA, "South Korea." See also An, Kim, and Cho, *Taehan Min'guk ch'oech'o ŭi chidaeji*, 345.

79 CIA, "South Korea," 6–7.

80 CIA, "South Korea," 7.

81 Hayes and Moon, "Park Chung Hee," 51.

82 According to Hong Chaehak, a former ADD missile engineer, five hundred researchers were employed at the ADD's missile factory in Taejŏn by late 1976, and there were six divisions in the missile team: system control, propellants, missile body design, missile guidance control, ground mechanics, and test and evaluation ("Kukpang Kwahak Yŏn'guso," 486).

83 CIA, "South Korea," 6.

84 Yi Kyŏngsŏ, interview with the author, July 13, 2021, Anyang, South Korea; Ku Sanghoe, interview with the author, July 14, 2021, Bundang, South Korea. See also the published testimony by former ADD researcher Hong Yongsik in "Han'guk ŭi misail kaebal," *Korea Times*, Sept. 25, 2018, http://sf.koreatimes.com/article/20180925/1204892.

85 See chapter 3 for my discussion of security protocols in defense factories based on interviews with engineers at Hanwha and other defense companies.

86 Hong Y., "Han'guk ŭi misail kaebal."

87 Hong Y., "Han'guk ŭi misail kaebal."

88 *Yi Kyuyŏn ŭi sŭp'ot'ŭrait'ŭ*, episode 152, "Yi Kyŏngsŏ Paksa ŭi chŭngŏn." The detonator is used for nuclear fission during a nuclear test.

89 *Yi Kyuyŏn ŭi sŭp'ot'ŭrait'ŭ*, episode 152, "Yi Kyŏngsŏ Paksa ŭi chŭngŏn." In my own interview with Yi Kyŏngsŏ, he stated that he learned directly about the nuclear detonator project only after Park's death, when he was ordered to investigate and report on all of the ADD's programs for the new administration of Chun Doo-hwan (interview).

90 Yi, interview.

91 CIA, "South Korea," 7.

92 Yi, interview.

93 *Yi Kyuyŏn ŭi sŭp'ot'ŭrait'ŭ*, episode 152, "Yi Kyŏngsŏ Paksa ŭi chŭngŏn."

94 Kim Chongp'il, "Pak Chŏnghŭi haek p'ŭrojekt'ŭ."

95 Hayes and Moon, "Park Chung Hee," 51; "U.S. Embassy in Republic of Korea telegram 7328 to Department of State, 'Canadian Nuclear Reactor Program in Korea,'" Nov. 4, 1974, National Security Archive, https://nsarchive.gwu.edu/document/22668-document-03-u-s-embassy-republic-korea.

96 "US Department of State Cable, ROK Plans to Develop Nuclear Weapons and Missiles," March 4, 1975, HPPP, https://digitalarchive.wilsoncenter.org/document/114616; "US Department of State Cable, ROK Plans to Develop Nuclear Weapons and Missiles," Dec. 11, 1974, HPPP, https://digitalarchive.wilsoncenter.org/document/114617.

97 Burr, "Stopping Korea."

98 "US Department of State Cable, ROK Nuclear Reprocessing," Sept. 8, 1975, HPPP, https://digitalarchive.wilsoncenter.org/document/114609.

99 Hong, "Search for Deterrence," 499.

100 PS, "Haek yŏllyo chaech'ŏri sisŏl toip e kwanhan Miguk chŏngbu ŭi ipchang (konggae)," 1A00614174956990, Dec. 13, 1975, PA (Sejong).

101 Kim Chongp'il, "Pak Chŏnghŭi haek p'ŭrojekt'ŭ."

102 Hong, "Search for Deterrence," 508.

103 Ŏm, "Pak Chŏnghŭi chŏngbu ŭi chaju kukpang," 26–27.

104 Seltzer, "Baekgom," 318–19; Hong, "Search for Deterrence," 495.

105 Seltzer, "Baekgom," 305; Hong, "Search for Deterrence," 495 and 510.

106 Don Oberdorfer, "Carter's Decision on Korea Traced Back to January 1975," *Washington Post*, June 12, 1977. See also "Forecast on Presidential Candidate Carter's Policy on ROK and Analysis on It," Nov. 1976 (n.d.), HPPP, http://digitalarchive.wilsoncenter.org/document/118400.

107 PS, "Chuhan Miguk ch'ŏlsu wa haek kaebal munje (konggae)," Aug. 13, 1977, 1A00614174957131, PA (Sejong).

108 After Park's death in 1979, Chun Doo-hwan shut down the nuclear arms program to win US political support for his new regime. See O T., "1972-yŏn O Wŏnch'ŏl," 197. However, the ROK revealed in 2004 that Chun's government had secretly conducted a plutonium-based nuclear experiment in 1982. *Korea JoongAng Daily*, Sept. 9, 2004, https://koreajoongangdaily.joins.com/2004/09/09/socialAffairs/Official-admits-plutonium-was-produced-in-82/2467315.html.

109 Bernard Weinraub, "U.S. Will Keep Bulk of Combat Forces in Korea until 1982," *New York Times*, July 27, 1977; CIA, "2 Carter Backers."

110 Kwon, "Beyond Patron and Client," 206–7.

111 CIA, "Task for the CIA," 3.

112 "Korea," Memorandum for the Secretary of Defense from Zbigniew Brzezinski, Nov. 2, 1978, Korea, Republic of 10/77–12/78, Box 43, Records of the Office of the National Security Adviser—Zbigniew Brzezinski's Country Files (NSA 6), Jimmy Carter Presidential Library; Ŏm, "Pak Chŏnghŭi chŏngbu ŭi chaju kukpang," 28, and "K'at'ŏ haengjŏngbu," 157.

113 See, for example, Donald S. Zagoria, "Why We Can't Leave Korea," *New York Times*, Oct. 2, 1977.

114 "General Vessey's Testimony on Korean Troop Withdrawals," Memorandum for Zbigniew Brzezinski from Mike Armacost, Feb. 2, 1977, Korea, Republic of 1-4/77, Box 43, Records of the Office of the National Security Advisor Zbigniew Brzezinski's Country Files (NSA 6), Jimmy Carter Presidential Library; Yang, Pak, and Chang, *Pak Chŏnghŭi*, 5:21 and 287; Rich, "U.S. Ground Force Withdrawal," 21–22.

115 Up until this establishment of the Combined Forces Command in 1978, the United States held exclusive operational control (OPCON) over the ROK military. The US transferred peacetime OPCON of the ROK military to Seoul in 1994. However, to this day the United States holds wartime OPCON of the ROK military. See Work, "Long History."
116 During the Carter presidency, the net reduction in USFK forces was a mere 3,400 out of 42,000 troops. See Rich, "U.S. Ground Force Withdrawal," ii.
117 Kwon, "Beyond Patron and Client," 208.
118 Ch'ae, *Hwanggŭmal ŭl nannŭn*, 70–71.
119 There were precolonial nationalist donation drives in Korea, like the Movement to Repay the National Debt (Kukch'ae Posang Undong) in 1907, but none was as systemically effective or long lasting as the donation campaigns carried out under the colonial regime.
120 M. Kim, "Brassware Industry."
121 Eckert, "Economic Development," 402; Young, *Japan's Total Empire*, 65–69.
122 Young, *Japan's Total Empire*, 156–58.
123 *Japan Times & Mail*, April 2, 1938, and June 24, 1936.
124 *Japan Times & Mail*, March 4, 1934.
125 *Japan Times & Mail*, March 6, 1939; Feb. 28, 1938; and Dec. 2, 1933.
126 Narita, "Women's Total War," 338.
127 Narita, "Women's Total War," 338–39.
128 *Tonga Ilbo*, Aug. 24, 1937.
129 *Tonga Ilbo*, Aug. 4, 1937, and Sept. 16, 1937.
130 *Japan Times & Mail*, Dec. 8, 1934; Dec. 18, 1934; and Aug. 21, 1937.
131 Although the exact number of Koreans who served in the Imperial Japanese Army is not known, it is estimated that the military contribution by Koreans to Japan's war effort "totaled between 286,000 and 367,000 soldiers, sailors, and military civilians" (Palmer, *Fighting for the Enemy*, 123).
132 Eckert, "Economic Development," 403.
133 *Kukpang hŏngŭm* and *kukpang sŏnggŭm* were other names for defense donations. See *Kyŏnghyang Sinmun*, Oct. 26, 1949; *Tonga Ilbo*, Sept. 5, 1951; *Chosŏn Ilbo*, July 19, 1952; *Tonga Ilbo*, Oct. 6, 1953.
134 Yun, *Pet'ŭnam Chŏnjaeng ŭi Han'guk sahoesa*, 185–86.
135 PS, "Saemaŭl sŏnggŭm chŏpsu pogo (Chusin Torik'o U Sanggi oe 2 tanch'e)," April 30, 1973, 1A00614174957465, and "Saemaŭl sŏnggŭm chŏpsu mit kamsa sŏhan palsong (Mun Sŏnmyŏng oe 10)," Nov. 28, 1973, 1A00614174957577, PA (Sejong).
136 *Kyŏnghyang Sinmun*, March 24, 1972.
137 H. Kim, *Korea's Development*, 141.
138 PS, "Pangwi sŏnggŭm ch'wigŭpsang ŭi munjejŏm e kwanhan pogo," July 26, 1977, EA0008039, PA (Seongnam). See also *Maeil Kyŏngje*, Dec. 29, 1973; *Kyŏnghyang Sinmun*, May 10, 1975; *Kyŏnghyang Sinmun*, July 17, 1973.

139 Tsurumi, "Colonial Education."
140 Han and Downey, *Engineers for Korea*, 68–70.
141 *Tonga Ilbo*, Nov. 25, 1969; *Tonga Ilbo*, March 23, 1973; *Kyŏnghyang Sinmun*, April 30, 1975.
142 *Kyŏnghyang Sinmun*, Feb. 21, 1974.
143 *Tonga Ilbo*, Nov. 8, 1972.
144 Kim (full name withheld), interview with the author, April 13, 2016, Cambridge, MA.
145 PS, "Pangwi sŏnggŭm e ŭihan pangwijŏng chinsu mit myŏngmyŏngsik kyehoek pogo," Nov. 16 1972, EA0004636, and "Pangwi sŏnggŭm e ŭihan kosokchŏng kŏnjo kyehoek kŏnŭi (Kukpangbu)," March 2, 1971, EA0004431, PA (Seongnam).
146 See, for example, *Tonga Ilbo*, Nov. 8, 1972; *Kyŏnghyang Sinmun*, Jan. 6, 1973.
147 *Tonga Ilbo*, Dec. 19, 1973; *Maeil Kyŏngje*, Sept. 5, 1974.
148 *Tonga Ilbo*, April 22, 1974; *Tonga Ilbo*, May 7, 1975; *Kyŏnghyang Sinmun*, Sept. 25, 1975.
149 *Maeil Kyŏngje*, Jan. 6, 1976; *Tonga Ilbo*, Dec. 13, 1976.
150 *Kyŏnghyang Sinmun*, July 18, 1974; *Kyŏnghyang Sinmun*, Jan. 16, 1976.
151 For more details on Imperial Japan's use of mass media to support its war efforts in the 1930s, see Young, *Japan's Total Empire*, 67–69.
152 *Kyŏnghyang Sinmun*, Oct. 8, 1974; *Tonga Ilbo*, Nov. 12, 1975.
153 *Kyŏnghyang Sinmun*, Jan. 29, 1972.
154 See, for example, *Kyŏnghyang Sinmun*, May 27, 1972, and Jan. 20, 1972.
155 *Kyŏnghyang Sinmun*, Nov. 12, 1975.
156 For example, see PS, "Kukpang hŏn'gŭm sayong kyehoek kŏnŭi (Kukpangbu)," May 8, 1973, EA0004683; "Pangwi sŏnggŭm ch'wigŭpsang ŭi munjejŏm e kwanhan pogo," July 26, 1977, EA0008039; and "Han'guk Haeyang Taehak silsŭpsŏn insu e ttarŭn pangwise kyŏngbi," Nov. 27, 1975, EA0001418, PA (Seongnam).
157 *Kyŏnghyang Sinmun*, Sept. 13, 1975.
158 *Kyŏnghyang Sinmun*, July 2, 1975.
159 *Kyŏnghyang Sinmun*, June 20, 1974; *Kyŏnghyang Sinmun*, July 26, 1975.
160 For example, some of the patrol speedboats that the MND began constructing with defense donations in 1971 were taken over and upgraded under Yulgok when it was instituted in 1974. PS, "Sohyŏng kosokchŏng kŏnjo rŭl wihan pangwi sŏnggŭm sayong," Sept. 10, 1974, EA0004808, PA (Seongnam).
161 "Pangwise," Kukka Kirogwŏn, Feb. 20, 2014, https://www.archives.go.kr/next/search/listSubjectDescription.do?id=006405&pageFlag=&sitePage=1-2-1.
162 Kim Kwangmo, interview with the author, June 13, 2017, Seoul. See also *HGKK*, 5:272.
163 *HGKK*, 5:228 and 238. See also O W., "25-cho wŏn Yulgok," 422.

164 For example, the MND used NDD funds to replace the M1 rifles used by ROK soldiers with M16s and to produce new heavy artillery, such as 106 mm recoilless cannons. PS, "106 mm mubandongch'ong saengsan," April 22, 1974, EA0004782, PA (Seongnam).

165 Kukpang Kwahak Yŏn'guso, *Kukpang Kwahak Yŏn'guso 50-yŏnsa*, 51.

166 PS, "Pangwi sŏnggŭm e ŭihan yŏnggwan ap'at'ŭ mit toksin changgyo sukso kongsa wallyo kyŏlgwa pogo," Oct. 23, 1974, EA0004810, PA (Seongnam).

167 Kukpangbu, *Yulgok Saŏp*, 23.

168 Kukpangbu, *Yulgok Saŏp*, 25.

169 The MAP provided grants that South Korea could use to procure military supplies and services from the United States. US military aid to South Korea was reduced partly due to the failure of Congress to allocate the full funding promised by the Nixon Doctrine. This shortfall resulted from budget constraints brought on by the costly war in Vietnam. A Congress dominated by Democrats further undercut the military aid promised by the Republican Nixon and Ford administrations. See US Congress, House Committee on International Relations, *Investigation of Korean-American Relations*, 204; "Memorandum of Conversation, Seoul," Nov. 22, 1974, document 258 in US Department of State, *FRUS, 1969–1976*, vol. E-12, https://history.state.gov/historicaldocuments/frus1969-76ve12/d258.

170 Kukpangbu, *Kukpangsa*, 4: 392 and 394.

171 "Memorandum from the President's Assistant for National Security Affairs (Kissinger) to President Ford, Washington," Jan. 3, 1975, document 260 in US Department of State, *FRUS, 1969–1976*, vol. E-12, https://history.state.gov/historicaldocuments/frus1969-76ve12/d260.

172 "Memorandum from the President's Assistant for National Security Affairs (Kissinger) to President Ford"; Schlesinger, *Annual Defense Department Report, FY 1975*, 92.

173 C. Moon, "U.S. Third Country Arms Sales," 82n5.

174 Ku, "Ku Sanghoe."

175 The International Institute for Strategic Studies (IISS) estimated that the DPRK spent 11.2 percent of its GNP on defense in 1976 and 10.5 percent in 1977 (*Military Balance 1979–1980*, 95). South Korea's MND estimated that DPRK's defense spending was 23.2 percent of GNP, or $1.39 billion, by 1973 (Kukpangbu, *Yulgok Saŏp*, 25). See also US Arms Control and Disarmament Agency, *World Military Expenditures and Arms Transfers*, 49. It should be noted that statistics on the DPRK's military spending are murky because of political and transparency issues and that ROK data on DPRK may be inflated. The statistics cited on the ROK's military spending as a percent of GNP are from Kukpangbu, *Kukpangsa*, 4:392 and 394. Another way of interpreting the gap in military spending would be that the DPRK had to spend a much larger share of its GNP on its military to keep up with the ROK's rapidly growing economy.

176 See CIA, "Military Balance," 1–2. See also PS, "Chuhan Migun ch'ŏlsu wa haek kaebal munje," Aug. 13, 1977, 1A00614174957131, PA (Sejong). This report to Park includes the IISS statistics on the militaries of the two Koreas as well as summaries of lectures by US academics who publicly opposed Carter's preset timetable for the US troop withdrawal from South Korea.

177 PS, "Pangwisebŏp," July 16, 1975, EA0012310, PA (Seongnam).

178 PS, "Pangwisebŏp." See also *HGKK*, 5:228.

179 O, *Korea Story*, 30.

180 *Kyŏnghyang Sinmun*, July 19, 1975.

181 Kukpangbu, *Yulgok Saŏp*, 26.

182 Kukpangbu, *Kukpangsa*, 4:396.

183 IISS, *Military Balance 1979–1980*, 94–95; US Arms Control and Disarmament Agency, *World Military Expenditures and Arms Transfers*, 42, 46, 65.

184 See, for example, Stockholm International Peace Research Institute (SIPRI), *World Armaments and Disarmament*, 163–64. See also Wolf et al., "Changing Balance," 46–47; Hyŏn, *Han'guk ŭi pangwibi*, 81.

185 SIPRI, *World Armaments and Disarmament*, 163–64. The figures are based on 1980 prices and exchange rates.

186 Furthermore, most international statistics on DPRK defense expenditures, including the figures from SIPRI, are based on data reported by the DPRK government itself. See SIPRI, *SIPRI Yearbook 2011*, 221. For a fuller discussion of the problems associated with comparing the arms expenditures of two Koreas, see C. Moon and Lee, "Military Spending and the Arms Race"; Hamm, *Arming the Two Koreas*, 91–100.

187 Regarding the US reduction of military grant to the ROK, see "Memorandum from the President's Assistant for National Security Affairs (Kissinger) to President Ford, Washington."

188 Kukpangbu, *Yulgok Saŏp*, 27–28 and 31.

189 Ch'oe Chongch'ŏl, "Han'guk ŭi chaju kukpang," 193; Kukpangbu, *Kukpangsa*, 4:398; O W., "Yulgok Saŏp ch'ulpal," 480.

190 Kukpangbu, *Yulgok Saŏp*, 26; "Pangwise," Kukka Kirogwŏn, Feb. 20, 2014.

191 O W., "Yulgok Saŏp ch'ulpal," 481. See also O, *Korea Story*, 30.

192 Kukpangbu, *Yulgok Saŏp*, 31.

193 Hyŏn, *Han'guk ŭi pangwibi*, 102–3.

194 See H. Kim, *Korea's Development*, 190; O W., "25-cho wŏn Yulgok," 419–24.

195 Kim Kwangmo, interview, April 22, 2013; O W., "25-cho wŏn Yulgok," 422.

196 See, for example, PS, "Sohyŏng kosokchŏng kŏnjo rŭl wihan pangwi sŏnggŭm sayong," Sept. 10, 1974, EA0004808, PA (Seongnam).

197 *HGKK*, 5:235.

198 O W., "25-cho wŏn Yulgok," 420.

199 *HGKK*, 5:235, 240–41.

200 Park Chung Hee's distrust of the military leadership, along with the MND's disinclination toward Park's efforts to establish an independent defense industry, are discussed in chapter 2.

201 O, *Korea Story*, 29–30. Kim Chŏngnyŏm, Park's chief of staff at the time, concurrently held the title of the First Senior Presidential Secretary for the Economy.

202 In May 1976, for example, Park issued a direct order to expedite and scale up the production of the Vulcan cannon. See PS, "Palk'anp'o ryangsan kyehoek," May 3, 1976, EA0004874, PA (Seongnam). See also Kim Kwangmo, interview, April 22, 2013.

203 *HGKK*, 5:239–40. See also H. Kim, *Korea's Development*, 189–90.

204 O W., "25-cho wŏn Yulgok," 423.

205 Shaw, "South Korean Foreign Military Sales," 8. The restructured authorization process under the Military Procurement Law was designed to address past financial scandals among military officers who had distorted weapons deals through illegal commissions. See Han'guk Pangwi Sanŏp Chinhŭnghoe, *Pangjinhoesa*, 285, 293.

206 Shaw, "South Korean Foreign Military Sales," 8.

207 *Tonga Ilbo*, Oct. 20, 1977.

208 Newspapers also reported cases in which the government had punished local authorities for not reporting collected defense donations and for using the funds for personal gain or taking bribes. See, for example, *Kyŏnghyang Sinmun*, Nov. 16, 1976; *Kyŏnghyang Sinmun*, June 8, 1976; *Tonga Ilbo*, Sept. 27, 1976.

209 PS, "Pangwi sŏnggŭm ch'wigŭpsang ŭi munjejŏm e kwanhan pogo," July 26, 1977, EA0008039, PA (Seongnam).

210 *Tonga Ilbo*, June 8, 1993; *Kyŏnghyang Sinmun*, June 7, 1993.

211 The FIP component of the Yulgok Operation continued under different programs, such as the Defense Capability Improvement Program (1997–98), the Acquisition Program (1999–2001), the Force Investment Program (2002–5), and the Defense Improvement Program (2006–20). See Boo, "North Korea's Nuclear Reality"; Kukpangbu Kunsa P'yŏnch'an Yŏn'guso, *Kukpang chŏngch'aek pyŏnch'ŏnsa 1988–2003*, 163. For more on Yulgok corruption, see Sŏ U., Sin, and Chang, *Pangwi sanŏp*, 158–64.

212 H. Kim, *Korea's Development*, 191–92. However, numerous stories and allegations have been made regarding Park's secret personal wealth and political slush funds. These include a 1977 testimony by former KCIA director Kim Hyŏnguk to the Fraser committee in the United States, related to the "Koreagate" scandal of 1976, as well as more recent investigative reporting by Korean news outlets. See, for example, *JTBC News*, Dec. 12, 2018, https://news.jtbc.joins.com/article/article.aspx?news_id=NB11741514; *YTN*, Jan. 3, 2017, https://www.ytn.co.kr/_ln/0103_201701032152016811.

213 *Tonga Ilbo*, June 28, 1975; *Kyŏnghyang Sinmun*, June 30, 1975.

214 The New Democratic Party also opposed subsequent increases in the NDT rate. See *Kyŏnghyang Sinmun*, Nov. 23, 1976.

215 Legislators and the opposition party had fought to ensure that the NDT would be a progressive tax. See *Maeil Kyŏngje*, July 7, 1975; *Chosŏn Ilbo*, July 9, 1975; *Kyŏnghyang Sinmun*, July 3, 1975. In addition to imposing new taxes, such as an imported goods tax (at a rate of 2.5 percent), a tax on farm- and forest lands (0.2 percent), and an advertising tax (20 percent), the NDT added surtax rates to various existing taxes on income and consumer goods. With the revisions of the National Defense Tax Law in the late 1970s, those surtax rates were also revised. PS, "Pangwisebŏp," July 16, 1975, EA0012310, PA (Seongnam); "Pangwisebŏp," Kukka Pŏmnyŏng Chŏngbo Sent'ŏ, https://www.law.go.kr/LSW/lsInfoP.do?lsiSeq=5183#0000; Kim Chŏngnyŏm, *Ch'oebin'guk*, 437.

216 The nation's income and property tax rates, especially for those in lower income brackets, were relatively modest compared with average rates in other developing countries. See OECD, "Tax on Personal Income" (search "South Korea") and "Tax on Property" (search "South Korea"), OECD Data, www.oecd.org/statistics. See also Hamm, *Arming the Two Koreas*, 153–54.

217 *Chungang Ilbo*, June 28, 1975.

218 Anonymous, email interview with the author, Nov. 26, 2021.

219 *Maeil Kyŏngje*, March 24, 1974.

220 *Maeil Kyŏngje*, June 5, 1976.

221 The sense of alarm with regard to US troop withdrawals was shared by leaders in both the ruling party and the opposition. Following the 1970 US announcement of its plan to withdraw troops, Yu Chinsan, chair of the New Democratic Party, the main opposition party, agreed to Park's request for full cooperation from him and his party on national security. Likewise, after President Carter's announcement of his plan to withdraw US ground forces in 1977, Park was joined in his effort to persuade Carter to go against the plan by Yi Ch'ŏlsŭng, the new chair of the New Democratic Party, who wrote letters to both Carter and Vice President Walter Mondale in 1977, pleading for the reversal of the withdrawals. See "Letter, from Lee Chul Seung to Walter F. Mondale," June 7, 1977, and "Letter for President Jimmy Carter from Lee Chul Seung," May 25, 1977, CO82-2, 7/1/77–8/31/78, Box CO-41, White House Central File, Subject File: Countries, Jimmy Carter Presidential Library; Yang, Pak, and Chang, *Pak Chŏnghŭi*, 5:215–16. See also Kim Chŏngnyŏm, *A Pak Chŏnghŭi*, 203; O, *Korea Story*, 406; "Memorandum of Conversation," May 8, 1975, Gerald R. Ford Presidential Library and Museum, https://www.fordlibrarymuseum.gov/library/document/0314/1553068.pdf.

222 *Chosŏn Ilbo*, May 30, 1976; *Kyŏnghyang Sinmun*, Jan. 14, 1975.

223 *Tonga Ilbo*, Jan. 21, 1975.

224 Christian churches in South Korea at this time were generally divided between conservative denominations that supported the Park regime's anticommunism and liberal activist churches that opposed Park's repressive human rights policies.

225 *Tonga Ilbo*, April 28, 1975.

226 *Tonga Ilbo*, May 6, 1975; *Kyŏnghyang Sinmun*, April 30, 1975; *Kyŏnghyang Sinmun*, May 1, 1975.

227 M. Park, "*Chaeya*," 391.

228 For examples, see *Kyŏnghyang Sinmun*, March 29, 1974; *Tonga Ilbo*, Oct. 8, 1974; *Tonga Ilbo*, Nov. 2, 1974; *Tonga Ilbo*, May 29, 1975; *Maeil Kyŏngje*, June 2, 1975; *Kyŏnghyang Sinmun*, Aug. 28, 1976; *Maeil Kyŏngje*, June 18, 1979.

229 Sangseok Moon, "Mechanism of Mass Mobilization," 59.

230 In July and August 2015 (in Los Angeles), June 2019 (in Seoul), September 2020 to June 2021 (online and in person), November 2021 to January 2022 (online), and May to June 2022 (in Seoul), I surveyed a combined total of 313 Korean respondents who had lived in South Korea under the Park regime. I conducted the first survey (2015) at the Koreatown Senior and Community Center in Los Angeles; those 100 participants, born in 1955 and before, were age sixty and older in 2015. Participants in the rest of my survey groups (213 individuals) were born in 1960 and earlier. Although the surveys in South Korea were conducted in Seoul, most participants had lived in other regions of the country in the 1970s. I asked all participants the same yes/no and open-ended questions about their experiences with the NDT and NDD, and asked them to characterize their perspective at the time on Park's national security policy.

231 Most interviewees were drawn from the group of survey participants; I conducted separate interviews with them during my in-person research in Los Angeles and Seoul. I also conducted some interviews separately.

232 Kim (full name withheld), interview with the author, July 20, 2015, Los Angeles.

233 Paek (full name withheld), interview with the author, July 20, 2015, Los Angeles.

234 Pak (full name withheld), interview with the author, July 8, 2013, Seoul.

235 Kwŏn (full name withheld), interview with the author, July 23, 2015, Los Angeles. The National Security Law was enacted in 1948 by the Rhee Syngman regime to suppress domestic communism and political opposition to Rhee's rule, and it was similarly employed by Park.

236 See Im C. and Kim, *Taejung tokchae*, vol. 1.

237 Corner and Lim, introduction, xxiii.

238 Corner and Lim, introduction, xxiv.

239 J. Lim, "Historiographical Perspectives," 326–27. See also Corner and Lim, introduction, xxiii.

240 Antonio Gramsci defines the state as the sum of coercion and civil consent; when coercion becomes reasonable and justifiable to the popular base, consensus expands. See Gramsci, *Prison Notebooks*, 1:153; Gramsci, *Gramsci Reader*, 192–96; and Morera, *Gramsci's Historicism*, 164. See also Hamm, *Arming the Two Koreas*, 7 and 164.

241 Inglehart, *Cultural Shift in Advanced Industrial Society*, 371.

242 Following Park, the succeeding Chun administration extended the NDT twice, first from 1979 to 1985 and again from 1985 to 1990.

243 *Chungang Ilbo*, Oct. 19, 1988.

244 *Kyŏnghyang Sinmun*, July 23, 1993; *Chosŏn Ilbo*, Feb. 26, 1994; *Tonga Ilbo*, Sept. 26, 1994; *Han'gyŏrye*, March 5, 1994; *Tonga Ilbo*, Oct. 18, 1996; *Maeil Kyŏngje*, July 22, 1998.

245 For recent examples of defense donations, see *Ŭisa Sinmun*, June 9, 2022, http://www.doctorstimes.com/news/articleView.html?idxno=219078; *Ŭihak Sinmun*, Feb. 23, 2019, http://www.bosa.co.kr/news/articleView.html?idxno=2099984; *ChosunBiz*, Oct. 12, 2022, https://biz.chosun.com/distribution/food/2022/10/12/H5CT6YQJW5FULFPBF2A6BOKL7M/.

246 On public donations to aid the families and to boost national security in response to *Cheonan*, see *Taehan Min'guk Chŏngch'aek Pŭrip'ing*, April 19, 2010, https://www.korea.kr/news/policyNewsView.do?newsId=148692595#policyNews; *Chosŏn Ilbo*, July 7, 2010, https://www.chosun.com/site/data/html_dir/2010/07/07/2010070701096.html; *KBS News*, June 15, 2010, https://news.kbs.co.kr/news/view.do?ncd=2112963; *Tonga Ilbo*, Aug. 12, 2021, https://www.donga.com/news/People/article/all/20210811/108512131/1.

247 The Cheonan Ship Foundation, created in 2010, collected donations to support the families of *Cheonan* victims. The foundation still exists today. See "Chaedan pŏbin ch'ŏnanham chaedan," http://cheonanham.org/.

248 *Tonga Ilbo*, May 26, 2010, https://www.donga.com/news/Opinion/article/all/20100526/28629439/9. For more about Kim's donation, see *Sŏul Kyŏngje*, Aug. 22, 2016, https://www.sedaily.com/NewsVIew/1L08PQKCJQ.

249 Under the former Moon Jae-in administration, which was widely perceived to prioritize its pro–North Korea policies and criticized for its silence on the *Cheonan* incident, citizens in 2020 took the initiative to organize a memorial concert, commemorating the tenth anniversary of the incident and raising funds for the victims' families. However, due to the government's COVID-19 regulations, the event was canceled. See *Wŏlgan Chosŏn*, Feb. 16, 2020, https://monthly.chosun.com/client/mdaily/daily_view.asp?Idx=8853&Newsnumb=2020028853.

250 I distinguish this age group from those born in or after 1960, who form what is now known as the 386 generation of South Koreans—members of which led democratic protests following Park's era. The name "386" refers to South Koreans who were in their thirties (the "3") during Roh Moo-hyun's presidency (2003–8), attended college in the 1980s (the "8") under Chun Doo-hwan's military regime and Roh Tae-woo's government, and were born in the 1960s (the "6"). Many of them became activists in the democracy movements against Chun and vocal critics of the previous Park regime for its authoritarianism and hard-line policies on national security.

251 *Mŏnit'udei*, Oct. 13, 2013, https://news.mt.co.kr/mtview.php?no=2013101309531271186.

252 An, Kim, and Cho, *Taehan Min'guk ch'oech'o ŭi chidaeji*, 316.

253 Chŏng Chaegyŏng, *Pak Chŏnghŭi silgi*, 634–35.

254 O, *Korea Story*, 419.

255 For example, during the Chosŏn dynasty (1392–1897), the central government relied on local administrations in each district to collect national tax. Local *yangban* (elite scholar-officials during the dynasty) wielded significant authority over local affairs at the village level. Led by these people, rural villages maintained considerable social and cultural autonomy from the central rule. See Sun Joo Kim, "Taxes, the Local Elites," 1007 and 1011.

256 S. Jones, *Antonio Gramsci*, 41. See also Gramsci, *Prison Notebooks*, 1:21 and 137. For Gramsci, hegemony, understood as "government with permanently organized consent" (Morera, *Gramsci's Historicism*, 164), is a dynamic process in which society's consent to be governed must be won and then continually renewed.

257 Antitax attitudes and tax evasion were prevalent in South Korea until Park instituted comprehensive tax reforms and centralized tax collection in the late 1960s. See Prasad and Nickow, "Mechanisms," 1621–22.

Conclusion

1 The phrase "cultural superstructure" is connected to Antonio Gramsci's interpretation of the relationship between infrastructure (economic base) and superstructure, which he described as "dialectical" or "reflexive" (S. Jones, *Antonio Gramsci*, 34). According to Gramsci, the superstructure consists of cultural, political, and ideological elements that arise from the economic base and reciprocally influence it. For more discussion of the Park state-society relations using the Gramscian framework, refer to chapter 5.

2 In overplaying the patron-client relationship without sufficiently analyzing uniquely Korean motives and inputs, the literature has long overstated the central dominance of US military, economic, and technical aid in the trajectory of the ROK's military modernization.

3 Korean historiography on the Park era tends to attribute national industrialization to the actions of a few elite technocrats (or a particular elite agency), to view bureaucracies only through their leaders, and to equate state administration with Park himself.

4 In Gramsci's view, a hegemonic state must form and maintain a broad base of support among the people to hold power. Popular ideas spread by the cultural leadership—the state and its ruling class—work to consolidate an "ideological bloc" among the people and thus maintain their consent to be governed. See Gramsci, *Prison Notebooks*; Morera, *Gramsci's Historicism*, 164; S. Jones, *Antonio Gramsci*, 3.

5 B. Hwang, "Ruling Discourse and Mass Politics," 12 (italics added).

6 Richard Bitzinger observes that, among East Asian nations, independent arms production has been driven by a strong sense of techno-nationalism, "which views autarky (self-sufficiency in armaments) [as] serving not only national defense needs, but also as maximizing national political, strategic, and economic autonomy" ("Defense Industries in Asia," 453).

7 Sang-Hyun Kim, "Science, Technology, and the Imaginaries," 334–35.

8 Kwon, "Mars and Manna," 38.

9 Sang-Hyun Kim, "Science, Technology, and the Imaginaries," 334.

10 S. Yoo, "Innovation in Practice," 390–91.

11 After Chun cut ADD funding for weapons programs, scientists and engineers who had worked in the ADD went into private industry and spread its R & D practices in the commercial sector. See D. Hwang, "Role of Defense Industry," 158–59, 165. See also Min S., *Kisul chugwŏn hoebok ŭi chuyŏk*, 96–97.

12 Sang-Hyun Kim, "Science, Technology, and the Imaginaries," 334; Y. Lim, *Technology and Productivity*, 97–98; Seungsook Moon, *Militarized Modernity*, 61. Altogether, about two million skilled workers were trained during the regimes of Park and Chun. See *Mirae Han'guk*, Nov. 17, 2016, http://www.futurekorea.co.kr/news/articleView.html?idxno=33829.

13 C. Moon and Lee, "Revolution in Military Affairs," 121.

14 Hahm and Plein, "Institutions and Technological Development," 63–64.

15 Sang-Hyun Kim, "Science and Technology," 94. Given the limited natural resources of South Korea such as oil, nuclear power was considered crucial to the country's energy independence, and the political doctrine of self-reliance only reinforced this notion. As a result, subsequent administrations maintained heavy investment in nuclear power. See Ahn and Han, "Korean Experience in Self-Reliance," 200–201.

16 Ministry of National Defense (MND), *2006 Defense White Paper*, 92–95; C. Moon and Lee, "Revolution in Military Affairs," 121–23.

17 C. Moon and Paek, "Defense Innovation," 4.

18 C. Moon and Lee, "Revolution in Military Affairs," 122 and 129.

19 S. Nathan Park, "Why South Korea's Liberals Are Defense Hawks."

20 Boo, "North Korea's Nuclear Reality"; Paek, "Analysis of 2021 ROK Defense Budget," 1.

21 *Korea Herald*, Nov. 18, 2020, http://www.koreaherald.com/view.php?ud=20201118000541; *Han'gyŏre*, Aug. 28, 2017, http://www.hani.co.kr/arti/politics/defense/808676.html.

22 "Defense Budget," Defense Policy, Ministry of National Defense, accessed Aug. 17, 2022, https://www.mnd.go.kr/mbshome/mbs/mndEN/subview.jsp?id=mndEN_030900000000; L. Kim, "A Hawkish Dove?"

23 Paek, "Analysis of 2021 ROK Defense Budget," 4 and 6; Sheen, "South Korea's Overdue Defence Reforms"; *Yonhap News Agency*, May 13, 2019, https://en.yna.co.kr/view/AEN20190513004100320.

24 *Korea Times*, March 30, 2019, https://www.koreatimes.co.kr/www/nation/2019/03/113_265465.html.

25 "Buying a Big Stick," Reuters, Sept. 10, 2019; Kwon, "South Korea's Ongoing Quest." In 2006, through his Defense Reform Plan 2020, Roh took major steps to accelerate South Korea's military modernization. He also established a timeline for transferring wartime OPCON from the United States Forces Korea to the ROK military. However, the process was delayed under the two administrations that followed (2008–17). Moon's Defense Reform 2.0 plan, widely seen as an upgrade of Defense Reform 2020, revived Roh's effort for independent military modernization and the transfer of wartime OPCON. By demonstrating South Korea's advanced defense capabilities, both Roh and Moon sought to persuade Washington to transfer wartime OPCON to Seoul. See Chun, "Korean Defense Reform"; Nick Simeone, "Hager Details U.S., South Korean Wartime Control Agreement," *DoD News*, Oct. 23, 2014, https://www.defense.gov/News/News-Stories/Article/Article/603502/.

26 See L. Kim, "A Hawkish Dove?"; Sheen, "South Korea's Overdue Defence Reforms."

27 L. Kim, "A Hawkish Dove?"

28 *VOA*, April 7, 2022, https://www.voakorea.com/a/6518866.html; *Japan Times*, Aug. 31, 2022. https://www.japantimes.co.jp/news/2022/08/31/asia-pacific/seoul-hike-defense-spending-2023/.

29 White House, "Washington Declaration." This declaration reaffirmed the US and ROK commitment to their combined defense posture under the 1953 US-ROK Mutual Defense Treaty and included plans to expand joint response measures to counteract North Korea's nuclear threats.

30 See, for example, a published interview with Chung-in Moon, a political scientist and special adviser to former president Moon, in which he stated: "If South Korea sides with the US . . . it would become harder to guarantee peace and prosperity on the Korean Peninsula, including [with] North Korea" (*Hankyoreh*, April 21, 2021, http://english.hani.co.kr/arti/english_edition/e_international/990682.html). Chung-in Moon and many other liberals also see South Korea's alliance with the United States as hindering their efforts to build a close economic partnership with China.

31 *Korea JoongAng Daily*, June 1, 2023, https://koreajoongangdaily.joins.com/2023/06/01/national/politics/Korea-bio-cluster-Boston-biotech-hub/20230601164508457.html?fbclid=IwAR3F-_Jotx3nEbfeL-t4IiLTlZe5905XZAArNZzuliPwIA1cDbNB1ImXtuQ.

32 *Yŏnhap inp'omaeksŭ*, July 28, 2022, https://news.einfomax.co.kr/news/articleView.html?idxno=4226278.

33 *News1*, July 26, 2022, https://www.news1.kr/articles/?4753555; *Taehan Min'guk Chŏngch'aek Pŭrip'ing*, Aug. 10, 2022, https://www.korea.kr/news/pressReleaseView.do?newsId=156520388.

34 Bitzinger and Kim, "Why Do Small States Produce Arms?," 187.

35 Defense spending's share of the gross domestic product began to decrease in the early 1980s, and from 2000 to 2021 it remained at around 2.5 percent. "South Korea Military Spending/Defense Budget 1960–2021," *Macrotrends*, https://www.macrotrends.net/countries/KOR/south-korea/military-spending-defense-budget. It can be argued that the ROK diverged from Park's defense industry model during Chun's tenure, as Chun prioritized the import of US weapons instead of indigenous production. Similarly, Kim Young-sam's emphasis on purging military authorities from politics and the lower priority he placed on military advancement contributed to a decline in the overall strength of the military sector.

36 Eunwoo Lee, "President Moon's Legacy," *Diplomat*, March 23, 2022, https://thediplomat.com/2022/03/president-moons-legacy-boosted-arms-exports-for-south-korea/.

37 *Yŏnhap Inp'omaeksŭ*, July 28, 2022, https://news.einfomax.co.kr/news/articleView.html?idxno=4226278; *Straits Times*, Oct. 17, 2017, https://www.straitstimes.com/asia/east-asia/south-korean-leader-calls-for-export-oriented-arms-development-enhanced-defence; MND, *2010 Defense White Paper*, 228; Joyce Lee and Tony Munroe, "South Korea Wants to Turn Its Arms Industry into an Export Powerhouse," *Business Insider*, April 22, 2015, http://www.businessinsider.com/r-south-korea-seeks-bigger-role-in-global-arms-bazaar-2015-4.

38 "Top List TIV Tables." According to the Stockholm International Peace Research Institute Arms Transfers Database, South Korea was ranked tenth among the largest arms exporters in 2022, a remarkable rise from thirty-first on the same list back in 2000 ("Top List TIV Tables"); *Korea Times*, July 24, 2022, https://m.koreatimes.co.kr/pages/article.asp?newsIdx=333257&fs=e&s=cl.

39 *Japan Times*, July 28, 2022, https://www.japantimes.co.jp/news/2022/07/28/asia-pacific/south-korea-weapons-exports-2/; *Korea Times*, July 24, 2022, https://m.koreatimes.co.kr/pages/article.asp?newsIdx=333257&fs=e&s=cl.

40 International Trade Administration, "South Korea Country"; Trading Economics, "South Korea Exports."

41 See, for example, *Yŏnhap inp'omaeksŭ*, July 28, 2022, https://news.einfomax.co.kr/news/articleView.html?idxno=4226278.

42 *Newspim*, June 17, 2022, https://www.newspim.com/news/view/20220617000570.

43 "President Yoon Wants South Korea to Become One of World's Top Weapons Suppliers," *CNN*, Aug. 17, 2022, https://www.cnn.com/2022/08/17/asia/south-korea-arms-exports-yoon-intl-hnk-ml.

44 *KoreaPro*, Dec. 16, 2022, https://www.nknews.org/koreapro/2022/12/big-year-for-south-korean-arms-sales-masks-vulnerabilities-in-national-defense/; J. Cho and Lee, "South Korea Exporting Arms"; *Korea Economic Daily*, May 3, 2023, https://amp.kedglobal.com/newsAmp/ked202305030023. In September 2022, South Korea's landmark arms agreement with Poland, a key NATO member, included the latter's purchase of an assortment of advanced Korean weaponry including K2 tanks, K9 self-propelled howitzers, and FA-50 light combat

aircraft. See "Poland Buys 48 Light Combat Aircraft from South Korea," Reuters, Sept. 16, 2022, https://www.reuters.com/business/aerospace-defense/poland-buys-48-light-combat-aircraft-south-korea-2022-09-16/; *Korea JoongAng Daily*, June 12, 2023, https://koreajoongangdaily.joins.com/2023/06/12/business/industry/defense-export-KoreaPoland-K2/20230612101500642.html.

45 *Korea Times*, June 9, 2023, https://www.koreatimes.co.kr/www/nation/2023/06/113_352669.html.

46 *Bemil*, June 16, 2018, http://bemil.chosun.com/nbrd/bbs/view.html?b_bbs_id=10067&num=1101.

47 Bitzinger, "China's Defense Technology," 432.

48 Pak Ch'anggyu, interview with the author, Oct. 29, 2012, Taejŏn.

49 MND, *2014 Defense White Paper*, 187–88; Rim and Lee, "Effects," 3; MND, *2020 Defense White Paper*, 144–45.

50 Korea Aerospace Industries (commonly known as KAI), the primary aerospace manufacturer in South Korea, was established in 1999 as a joint venture of Samsung Aerospace, Daewoo's aerospace division, and Hyundai Space and Aircraft Company. With state support, KAI subsequently evolved into an independent company. The leading defense manufactures LIG Nex1 and Daewoo Shipbuilding and Marine Engineering originated from LG and Daewoo respectively, both of which operated as chaebol under Park. Samsung, once a prominent defense producer, exited the defense sector following Hanwha's acquisition of Samsung Techwin in 2015.

51 "Insight: Inside South Korea's Race to Become One of the World's Biggest Arms Dealers," Reuters, May 29, 2023, https://www.reuters.com/business/aerospace-defense/inside-south-koreas-race-become-one-worlds-biggest-arms-dealers-2023-05-29/.

52 See, for example, P. Lee, "Economic Crisis and Chaebol Reform."

53 C. Moon, "Military Self-Reliance," 208.

54 Ch'ae, *Hwanggŭmal ŭl nannŭn*, 21–23; *ChosunBiz*, Nov. 12, 2019, https://biz.chosun.com/site/data/html_dir/2019/11/12/2019111200175.html; *Han'guk Kyŏngje*, Dec. 14, 2018, https://www.hankyung.com/economy/article/2018121492161; *Han'gyŏng Sanŏp*, Aug. 30, 2022, https://www.hankyung.com/economy/article/202205066938i; "Pangsan ŏpch'e kyŏngyŏng silt'ae."

55 *Kŭllobŏ Tip'ensŭ Nyusŭ*, April 20, 2016, http://www.gdnews.kr/news/article.html?no=3482; "Samsung Electronics Profit Margin (Quarterly)," *YCharts*, https://ycharts.com/companies/SSNGY/profit_margin.

56 See Pak H., *Pangwi sanŏp piri (pangsan piri) pŏmjoe ŭi ch'ŏbŏl.*

57 According to An Tongman, DAPA's involvement in defense production resulted in excessive regulation of weapons R & D by bureaucrats who are not weapon specialists and a significant loss of authority for the ADD (interview with the author, July 23, 2021, Taejŏn).

58 See, for example, *Chugan Han'guk*, June 3, 2017, http://weekly.hankooki.com/news/articleView.html?idxno=6437398.; *Han'gyŏrye*, July 19, 2015, https://www.hani.co.kr/arti/politics/defense/700890.html.

59 Kim Kyegwan, interview with the author, Aug 5, 2021, Ch'angwŏn.

60 An, interview.

61 *Segye Ilbo*, Jan. 20, 2021, http://m.segye.com/view/20210119512838.

62 An, interview.

63 In South Korea, politicians of all stripes (both liberals and conservatives), business leaders, and other public figures unanimously voice support for self-reliant national defense; virtually no one opposes it, at least publicly. Despite the poor outcomes of former president Moon's "income-led" policies, including the high unemployment rate, and his unsuccessful attempts to persuade the DPRK to de-nuclearize, his push for self-reliant national defense was widely embraced by the South Korean populace. The salience and significance of self-reliant national defense in Korean popular culture is evident through the presence of many YouTube channels and TV programs dedicated to national defense and military affairs. Media outlets such as Kukpang TV (National Defense TV), Kukpang FM (National Defense FM, a radio station), and the newspaper *Kukpang Ilbo* (Defense daily) further highlight the salience of this topic. Yu Yongwŏn's *World of the Military* (https://bemil.chosun.com/) is a popular website and online forum dedicated to issues related to the Korean defense industry and military affairs. The popularity of military-themed TV dramas and reality shows, such as *Descendants of the Sun* (2016), *Real Man* (2013–16), *Steel Troops* 1–3 (2021–23), *The Soldiers* (2021), *Hell Week* (2021), and *Toy Soldiers: Fake Men* 2 (2021), also points to the significance of the military and national defense in the public consciousness. These cultural references serve as further evidence of the subject's importance and resonance within South Korean society.

64 Prior to the Park administration's initiatives for the defense industry, large gaps in knowledge and experience had separated the military from commercial industry. Businesses, driven by profit and the private market, had no experience with defense industry requirements for weapons and quality control. The two sectors also differed in their management methods, budgeting decisions, responses to supply and demand, and work cultures. See O W., "25-cho wŏn Yulgok," 421.

65 Since the United States' display of technological prowess during the Gulf War in the 1990s, the phrase "revolution in military affairs" has been widely used to refer to rapid advances in technology and military organization in response to cyber warfare, unmanned aerial vehicles, drones, and other emerging technologies that are transforming warfare (Hundley, *Past Revolutions*, 8). See also Neuman and Kurç, "Defence Industries," 219; C. Moon and Lee, "Revolution in Military Affairs," 118.

66 Israel and South Korea are similar in the extent to which both merged national defense with national technological development and exports, and both were driven by defense needs.

Bibliography

Newspapers, Periodicals, and Online News Sources

ABC News
Bemil
Business Insider
Chosŏn Ilbo
ChosunBiz
Chugan Han'guk
Chungang Ilbo
Chungchung Today
CNN
Defense News
Diplomat
DoD News
Han'guk Kyŏngje
Han'gyŏng Sanŏp
Han'gyŏrye
Hankyŏng nyusŭ
Hankyoreh (English outlet of *Han'gyŏrye*)
Herŏldŭ Kyŏngje
Japan Times
Japan Times & Mail
JTBC News
KBS News
KCNA Watch
Korea Economic Daily
Korea Herald (English outlet of *Herŏldŭ Kyŏngje*)
Korea JoongAng Daily (English outlet of *Chungang Ilbo*)
KoreaPro
Korea Times
Kukpang Ilbo
Kŭllobŏ Tip'ensŭ Nyusŭ

Kyŏnghyang Sinmun
Maeil Kyŏngje
Mirae Han'guk
Mŏnit'udei
News1
Newspim
New York Times
P'enaendŭmaik'ŭ
Pulse
Pusan Ilbo
Reuters
Science Times
Segye Ilbo
Shindonga
Sŏul Kyŏngje
Straits Times
Taehan Min'guk Chŏngch'aek Pŭrip'ing
Tonga Ilbo
Tonga Saiŏnsŭ
Ŭihak Sinmun
Ŭisa Sinmun
U.S. News & World Report
VOA
Washington Post
Wŏlgan Chosŏn
Yŏnhap Inp'omaeksŭ
Yonhap News Agency
YTN

Korean Archives

Kukka Kirogwŏn [National Archives of Korea], Taejŏn
Selected archival documents are available online at the official website, at https://theme.archives.go.kr/next/koreaOfRecord/viewMain.do.
Kukpangbu Kunsa P'yŏnch'an Yŏn'guso [Institute for Military History, Ministry of National Defense (MND)], Yongsan
The archival room located in the institute provided access to official MND and other military publications cited in this volume, some which are not available to the public.
Naver News Library, https://newslibrary.naver.com/search/searchByDate.naver.
Oegyo Saryogwan [Diplomatic Archives], Ministry of Foreign Affairs, Seoul

Taehan Min'guk Sinmun Ak'aibŭ [Newspaper Archives of the Republic of Korea, National Library of Korea], https://nl.go.kr/newspaper/.

Taet'ongnyŏng Kirokkwan [Presidential Archives (PA)] (in Seongnam City, 2008–16; Sejong City, 2016–present)

Please note that the cited documents acquired in Seongnam prior to the relocation of the Presidential Archives to Sejong City in 2016 include the label "(Seongnam)," whereas the documents acquired at Sejong after 2016 include the label "(Sejong)."

Includes documents of the Presidential Secretariat (PS). Selected archival documents are available online at the official website, https://www.pa.go.kr/research/contents/open/index.jsp. I obtained copies of some presidential archival documents from archival collections at the Institute of State Governance Studies at Yonsei University (https://devcms.yonsei.ac.kr/isgsen/index.do).

Government and Corporate Sources in Korean

Han P'ilsun. *Suryut'an esŏ wŏnjaro kkaji* [From grenade to nuclear reactor]. Taejŏn: Kukpang Kwahak Yŏn'guso, 2000.

Hangnok Ryu Ch'anu Hoejang Ch'umo Wiwŏnhoe [Memorial Committee of Chairman Hangok Ryu Ch'anu]. *Hak, San ŭl kkum kkuda* [A crane that dreams of the mountain]. N.p.: Poongsan, 2009.

Han'guk Kwahak Kisul Yŏn'guwŏn [Korea Institute of Science and Technology]. *KIST 30-yŏnsa: Ch'angjojŏk wŏnch'ŏn kisul eŭi tojŏn* [Thirty-year history of KIST: The challenges of achieving creative core technologies]. Seoul: KIST, 1998.

Han'guk Pangwi Sanŏp Chinhŭnghoe [Korea Defense Industry Association]. *Pangjinhoesa* [The history of Korean defense businesses]. Seoul: Han'guk Pangwi Sanŏp Chinhŭnghoe, 1988.

———. *Pangwi sanŏp kaeron* [An introduction to the defense industry]. Vol. 1. Seoul: Han'guk Pangwi Sanŏp Chinhŭnghoe, 2012.

Hanwha Inch'ŏn Kongjang 50-yŏn P'yŏnch'an Wiwŏn [Compilation Committee on the Fifty Years of the Hanwha Inch'ŏn Factory]. *Hanwha Inch'ŏn Kongjang 50-yŏn (HIK)* [Fifty years of Hanwha Inch'ŏn factory]. Seoul: Hanwha, 2005.

Hanwha Kinyŏmgwan [Hanwha Historical Museum]. *Sajin ŭro tasi ponŭn Hanwha Inch'ŏn Kongjang 50-yŏn* [Fifty years of Hanwha Inch'ŏn factory through photos]. Inch'ŏn: Hanwha Kinyŏmgwan, 2011.

Hanwha Kŭrup 50-yŏnsa P'yŏnch'an Wiwŏn [Compilation Committee of the Fifty-Year History of Hanwha Group]. *Hŭimang ŭro ŭi yŏjŏng: Hanwha 50-yŏn* [A journey of hope: Fifty years of Hanwha]. 2 vols. Seoul: Hanwha Kŭrup, 2002.

Kia Chunggongŏp [Kia Heavy Industries]. *Kia Chunggongŏp 20-yŏnsa* [The twenty-year history of Kia Heavy Industries]. Ch'angwŏn: Kia, 1999.

Kim Ilsŏng. *Nam Chosŏn hyŏngmyŏng kwa choguk t'ongil e taehayŏ* [Regarding the revolution in South Korea and unification of the fatherland]. Pyongyang: Chosŏn Nodongdang Ch'ulp'ansa. 1969.

Kukka Pŏmnyŏng Chŏngbo Sent'ŏ [Korean Law Information Center]. https://law.go.kr/LSW/main.html.

Kukpang Kwahak Yŏn'guso [The Agency for Defense Development]. *Kukpang Kwahak Yŏn'guso 50-yŏnsa* [The fifty-year history of the Agency for Defense Development]. Taejŏn: Kukpang Kwahak Yŏn'guso, 2020.

———. *Kukpang Kwahak Yŏn'gusosa* (*KKYS*) [The history of the Agency for Defense Development]. 3 vols. Taejŏn: Kukpang Kwahak Yŏn'guso, 1989–2007. The first two volumes of this multivolume work were initially published under the title *Kukpang Kwahak Yŏn'guso yaksa*.

———. *Kukpang ŭi ch'osŏk 40-yŏn, 1970–2010* [Cornerstone of the national defense: Forty years, 1970–2010]. Taejŏn: Kukpang Kwahak Yŏn'guso, 2010.

———. *Ŏttŏk'e haegyŏl haetchi? Kukpang Kwahak Yŏn'guso kyohun saryejip* [How did we solve this? Collection of lessons from the Agency for Defense Development]. Taejŏn: Kukpang Kwahak Yŏn'guso, 2020.

Kukpangbu [ROK Ministry of National Defense]. *Kukpang Paeksŏ* [Defense white paper]. Seoul: Kukpangbu, 1967, 1968, 1988, 2008, 2009, 2010, 2012, 2014, 2020, 2022.

———. *Kukpangsa*. Vol. 4: *1972.1–1981.12* [The history of national defense, vol. 4: January 1972–December 1981]. Seoul: Kukpangbu Kunsa P'yŏnch'an Yŏn'guso, 2002.

———. *Yulgok Saŏp ŭi ŏje wa onŭl kŭrigo naeil* [The past, present, and future of the Yulgok Operation]. Seoul: Kukpangbu, 1994.

Kukpangbu Kukpang Kunsa Yŏn'guso [Institute for Defense and Military History Research, MND]. *Kŏn'gun 50-yŏnsa* [The fifty-year history of the ROK military]. Seoul: Sŏul Inswae Kongŏp Hyŏptong Chohap, 1998.

———. *Tae pijŏnggyujŏnsa II, 1961–1980* [A record of countermeasures against unconventional warfare, vol. 2, 1961–1980]. Seoul: Kukpang Kunsa Yŏn'guso, 1998.

Kukpangbu Kunsa P'yŏnch'an Wiwŏnhoe [Compilation Committee of Military History, MND]. *Kukpang choyakchip, 1945–1980* [The treaties of the national defense, 1945–1980]. Vol. 1. Seoul: Kukpangbu, 1981.

Kukpangbu Kunsa P'yŏnch'an Yŏn'guso [Institute for Military History, MND]. *Kukpang chŏngch'aek pyŏnch'ŏnsa 1988–2003* [History of defense policy transformation, 1988–2003]. Seoul: Kukpangbu Kunsa P'yŏnch'an Yŏn'guso, 2016.

———. *Kukpang sagŏnsa* [A record of national security incidents]. Vol. 1. Seoul: Kukpangbu Kunsa P'yŏnch'an Yŏn'guso, 2012.

Kwahak Kisulch'ŏ [Ministry of Science and Technology]. *Kwahak kisulgye illyŏk chawŏn chosa* [A survey on the scientific and technical manpower]. Seoul: Illyŏk Kaebal Yŏn'guso, 1973.

Kyŏngje 2 [Second Economic Secretariat (SES)]. *Chunghwahak kongŏphwa chŏngch'aek sŏnŏn e ttarŭn kongŏp kujo kaep'yŏnnon* [*Kaep'yŏnnon*] [Theory on the restructuring of industrial organization in accordance with the heavy and chemical industrialization promulgation]. January 30, 1973.

Mun'gyobu [Ministry of Education]. *Anbo kyoyuk mit Saemaŭl kyoyuk: Mobŏm saryejip* [Education on national security and Saemaŭl: Collection of model examples]. Seoul: Mun'gyobu, 1972.

———. *Sasang kyoyuk chido charyojip* [Material for ideological training]. Vols. 1–2. Seoul: Mun'gyobu, 1975.

Pak Chŏnghŭi. "1968-yŏn chejŏng toen kungmin kyoyuk hŏnjang" [The 1968 National Charter on Education]. Kuksa P'yŏnch'an Wiwŏnhoe [National Institute of Korean History], December 5, 1968. http://contents.history.go.kr/front/hm/view.do?treeId=010804&tabId=01&levelId=hm_163_0060.

———. *Han'guk kungmin ege koham* [My call to the Korean people]. Seoul: Tongsŏ Munhwasa, 2005.

———. *Kukka wa hyŏngmyŏng kwa na* [The country, the revolution, and I]. Seoul: Tosŏch'ulp'an Chiguch'on, 1997. Reprint version.

———. *Nara ka wigŭp hal ttae ŏtchi moksum ŭl akkiri* [How could I spare my life when my nation is in danger]. Seoul: Tongsŏ Munhwasa, 2005.

———. *Uri minjok ŭi nagal kil* [Our nation's path]. Seoul: Tonga Ch'ulp'ansa, 1962.

Pak Hangmo. *Pangwi sanŏp piri (pangsan piri) pŏmjoe ŭi ch'ŏbŏl kanghwa mit ŏche pangan* [Research on preventing defense industry corruption and strengthening its criminal punishments]. Seoul: Han'guk Hyŏngsa Chŏngch'aek Yŏn'guwŏn, 2016.

Pak Yŏnggu, and Kim Namil. *Kukka Kirogwŏn sojang chuyo chŏngch'aek kirok haesŏl chip*. Vol. 2: *Sanŏp p'yŏn* [Collection of commentary on major policy records held by the National Archives, vol. 2: Industry]. Taejŏn: Kukka Kirogwŏn, 2015.

"Pangsan ŏpch'e kyŏngyŏng silt'ae" [Operational Status of Defense Industry Companies]. *e-nara chip'yo*, January 26, 2023. https://www.index.go.kr/unity/potal/main/EachDtlPageDetail.do?idx_cd=1703.

"Pangwise" [National defense tax]. Kukka Kirogwŏn [National Archives of Korea]. February 20, 2014. https://www.archives.go.kr/next/search/listSubjectDescription.do?id=006405&pageFlag=&sitePage=1-2-1.

P'ohang Chonghap Chech'ŏl Chusik Hoesa [Pohang Iron and Steel Company]. *P'ohang Chech'ŏl 10-yŏnsa: Pyŏlch'aek purok* [Ten-year history of Pohang Iron and Steel Company: Supplementary book]. Pohang: P'ohang Chech'ŏl, 1979.

Taehan Min'guk Yŏksa Pangmulgwan [National Museum of Korean Contemporary History]. *Kukpang kwahak kisul palchŏn ŭl ikkŭn chuyŏktŭl kusulch'aerok saŏp ch'oejong kyŏlgwa pogosŏ* [Final report on the oral records of the leaders who led the development of science and technology for national defense]. Seoul: Taehan Min'guk Yŏksa Pangmulgwan, December 5, 2015.

Taet'ongnyŏng Pisŏsil [Presidential Secretariat]. *Pak Chŏnghŭi Taet'ongnyŏng yŏnsŏl munjip* [President Park Chung-Hee's speeches collection (*PPCHS*)]. Vols. 1–14. Seoul: Tonga Ch'ulp'ansa, 1965–77.

———. *Pak Chŏnghŭi Taet'ongnyŏng yŏnsŏl munjip* [President Park Chung-Hee's speeches collection (*PPCHS*)]. Vols. 15–16. Seoul: Koryŏ Sŏjŏk, 1979.

Yŏnsŏl kirok [Records of presidential speeches]. Taet'ongnyŏng Kirokkwan [Presidential Archives]. https://www.pa.go.kr/research/contents/speech/index.jsp.

Yukkun Ponbu [Army headquarters]. *Taech'imt'u chakchŏnsa: 1971–1980* [A record of counter-infiltration operations, 1971–1980]. Kyeryong: Yukkun Ponbu, 2011.

Yukkun Taehak [Army Staff College]. *Kukpangbi wa kunwŏn* [National defense budget and military aid]. September 1, 1967. Instructional textbook for the Army officers.

Secondary Sources in Korean

An Tongman, Kim Pyŏnggyo, and Cho T'aehwan. *Taehan Min'guk ch'oech'o ŭi chidaeji misail kaebal iyagi: Paekkom, tojŏn kwa sŭngni ŭi kirok* [The story of the development of South Korea's first surface-to-surface missile: The record of challenge and victory of Polar Bear]. Seoul: P'ŭllaenit Midiŏ, 2016.

Ch'ae Usŏk. *Hwanggŭmal ŭl nannŭn ch'oech'ŏmdan pangwi sanŏp Samsung ŭn wae p'ogi haenna* [Why did Samsung give up on the cutting-edge defense industry, the goose that lays the golden eggs?]. Seoul: Winwinmidiŏ, 2018.

Chang Yongun. "Pet'ŭnam Chŏnjaeng i Han'guk kun e mich'in yŏnghyang" [The impact of the Vietnam War on the ROK military]. *Kukpang chŏngch'aek yŏn'gu* 26, no. 4 (Winter 2010): 209–45.

Chi Hyokŭn. "1970-yŏndae Han'guk ŭi chaju kukpang chŏngch'aek" [The ROK's self-reliant national defense policy in the 1970s]. *Kunsa nondan* 43 (Fall 2005): 169–90.

Cho Ch'ŏlho. "1970-yŏndae ch'oban Pak Chŏnghŭi ŭi tokchajŏk haek mugi kaebal kwa Han-Mi kwan'gye" [Park Chung Hee's independent nuclear arms development and ROK-US relations in the early 1970s]. *P'yŏnghwa yŏn'gu*, no. 9 (December 2000): 189–207.

———. "Pak Chŏnghŭi haek oegyo wa Han-Mi kwan'gye pyŏnhwa" [Park Chung Hee's nuclear diplomacy and changes in ROK-US relations]. PhD diss., Korea University, 2000.

———. "Pak Chŏnghŭi ŭi chaju kukpang kwa haek kaebal." [Park Chung Hee's self-reliant national defense and nuclear development]. *Yŏksa pip'yŏng* 80 (August 2007): 356–73.

Cho Hŭiyŏn. "Pak Chŏnghŭi ch'eje ŭi pokhapsŏng kwa mosunsŏng: Im Chihyŏn tŭng ŭi pallon e taehan chaeballon" [A study of the complex and contradictory character of the Park Chung Hee regime: A reply to the responses of Im Chihyŏn et al.]. *Yŏksa pip'yŏng*, no. 70 (February 2005): 388–426.

———. "Pak Chŏnghŭi sidae ŭi kangap kwa tongŭi: Chibae, chŏnt'ong, kangap kwa tongŭi ŭi kwan'gye rŭl tasi saenggak handa" [The coercion and consent of the Park Chung Hee era: Rethinking the relationship among rule, tradition, coercion, and consent]. In *Taejung tokchae*, edited by Im Chihyŏn and Kim Yongu, 2:401–75. Seoul: Ch'aek Sesang, 2005.

Cho Ije and Carter Eckert, eds. *Han'guk kŭndaehwa, kijŏk ŭi kwajŏng* [The modernization of the Republic of Korea: A miraculous process]. Seoul: Wŏlgan Chosŏnsa, 2005.

Cho Yŏnggap. "Han'guk kukpang chŏngch'aek ŭi yŏksajŏk pyŏnch'ŏn kwa t'ŭkching chŏngnip e kwanhan yŏn'gu" [A study of the historical transformation and characteristics of the ROK's defense policies]. *Kunsa*, no. 64 (August 2007): 257–96.

Ch'oe Changjip. *Han'guk ŭi nodong undong kwa kukka* [The Korean labor movement and the nation]. Seoul: Nanam, 1997.

Ch'oe Chongch'ŏl. "Han'guk ŭi chaju kukpang t'aese hwangnip: 1970-yŏndae ŭi kukpangsajŏk ŭiŭi" [The establishment of the ROK's self-reliant national defense posture: Its historical significance to the national defense in the 1970s]. *Han'guk chŏngch'aek hakhoe*, no. 6 (July 1998): 181–208.

Ch'oe Hyŏngsŏp. *Ch'oe Hyŏngsŏp hoegorok: Pul i kkŏjiji annŭn yŏn'guso* [Memoirs of Ch'oe Hyŏngsŏp: A research institute where the light was never turned off]. Seoul: Han'guk Kwahak Kisul Yŏn'guwŏn, 2011.

Ch'oe Hyŏngsŏp and Im Chaeyun. "Ch'oe Hyŏngsŏp kwa 'Han'gukhyŏng palchŏn model' ŭi kiwŏn" [Ch'oe Hyŏngsŏp and the origins of the "Korean-style development model"]. *Yŏksa pip'yŏng* 118 (February 2017): 169–93.

Ch'oe Sŏngbin, Ko Pyŏngsŏng, and Yi Hosŏk. "Han'guk pangwi sanŏp ŭi 40-yŏn palchŏn kwajŏng kwa sŏnggwa" [The progress and achievements of the Korean defense industry over forty years]. *Kukpang chŏngch'aek yŏn'gu* 26, no. 1 (2010): 74–117.
Ch'oe Tongju. "Han'guk ŭi Pet'ŭnam Chŏnjaeng ch'amjŏn tongŭi e kwanhan chaegoch'al" [A reexamination of South Korea's agreement to participate in the Vietnam War]. *Han'guk chŏngch'ihak hoebo* 30, no. 2 (1996): 267–87.
———. "Pet'ŭnam p'abyŏng i Han'guk kyŏngje ŭi sŏngjang kwajŏng e mich'in yŏnghyang." [The influence of the dispatch of ROK forces to Vietnam on the Korean economy's growth]. *Tongnam Asia yŏn'gu* 11 (January 2001): 205–44.
Ch'oe Yongho. "Han'guk kun Pet'ŭnam p'abyŏng kwa Pak Chŏnghŭi" [Park Chung Hee and the dispatch of the ROK military to Vietnam]. In *Pak Chŏnghŭi sidae yŏn'gu ŭi chaengjŏm kwa kwaje,* edited by Chŏng Sŏnghwa, 355–403. Seoul: Sŏnin, 2005.
Chŏn Hohwŏn. "Miguk ŭi tae-Han kunwŏn chŏngch'aek (1976–1980) yŏn'gu: K'atŏ haengjŏngbu ŭi t'ŭkchingjŏk in chŏngch'aek naeyong ŭl chungsim ŭro" [A study of US military aid policy to the ROK, 1976–1980: With a focus on the distinct aspects of the Carter administration's policy]. *Kunsa*, no. 66 (April 2008): 225–56.
Chŏn Pŏmsŏng. *Kim Chonghŭi ŭi kiŏpka chŏngsin* [Kim Chonghŭi's entrepreneurial spirit]. Seoul: WMidiŏ, 2010.
Chŏn Sanggŭn. *Han'guk ŭi kwahak kisul kaebal* [South Korea's development of scientific and technical skills]. Seoul: Sam kwa Kkum, 2010.
———. "Pak Chŏnghŭi Taet'ongnyŏng ŭi kisul kaebal chimnyŏm: Han chŏngch'aek ibanja ŭi chŭngŏn" [President Park Chung Hee's will for technical development: A policy planner's testimony]. In *Kwahak taet'ongnyŏng Pak Chŏnghŭi wa ridŏsip*, edited by Kim Yŏngsŏp et al., 120–163. Seoul: MSD Midiŏ, 2010.
Chŏng Chaegyŏng. *Pak Chŏnghŭi silgi: Haengjŏk ch'orok* [Park Chung Hee records: Administrative summaries]. Seoul: Chimmundang, 1994.
Chŏng China. "Che-1 Konghwakukki (1948–1960) Yi Sŭngman chŏnggwŏn ŭi kyŏngje chŏngch'aengnon yŏn'gu" [A study on the economic policy of the Syngman Rhee regime's First Republic, 1948–1960]. PhD diss., Yonsei University, 2007.
———. "Yi Sŭngman chŏnggwŏn'gi kyŏngje kaebal 3-kaenyŏn kyehoek ŭi naeyong kwa sŏnggyŏk" [The contents and character of the three-year economic plan of the Syngman Rhee regime]. *Han'guk hak yŏn'gu* 31 (November 2009): 353–86.
Chŏng Ilchun. "Yusin ch'eje ŭi mosun kwa Han-Mi kaldŭng: Minjujuŭi ŏmnŭn kukka anbo" [The Yusin system's contradictions and US-ROK

conflicts: National security without democracy]. *Sahoe wa yŏksa* 70 (2006): 149–78.

Chŏng Kwangmin. *Kim Ilsŏng kwa Pak Chŏnghŭi ŭi kyŏngje chŏnjaeng* [The economic war between Kim Il Sung and Park Chung Hee]. Seoul: Kkorea, 2012.

Chŏng Sŏnghwa, ed. *Pak Chŏnghŭi sidae wa Han'guk hyŏndaesa* [The Park Chung Hee era and contemporary Korean history]. Seoul: Sŏnin, 2006.

———. *Pak Chŏnghŭi sidae yŏn'gu ŭi chaengjŏm kwa kwaje* [The controversies and tasks of studies on the Park Chung Hee era]. Seoul: Sŏnin, 2005.

Chŏng Sŏnghwa and Kang Kyuhyŏng, eds. *Pak Chŏnghŭi sidae wa Han'guk hyŏndaesa: Yŏn'guja wa ch'ehŏmja ŭi taehwa* [The Park Chung Hee era and contemporary Korean history: Conversations between researchers and living witnesses]. Seoul: Sŏnin, 2007.

Chŏng Yonguk et al. *Kusul ro pon Han'guk hyŏndaesa wa kun* [Contemporary Korean history and the military as viewed through oral testimony]. Seoul: Sŏnin, 2020.

Chungang Ilbo T'ŭkpyŏl Ch'wijaet'im [Chungang Daily Special Report Team]. *Sillok Pak Chŏnghŭi* [A true record of Park Chung Hee]. Seoul: Chungang M&B, 1998.

Han Honggu. *Ojik han saram ŭl wihan sidae: Yusin* [An era for only one person: Yusin]. Seoul: Han'gyŏre Ch'ulp'an, 2014.

Han Sŏkchŏng. *Manju modŏn: 60-yŏndae Han'guk kaebal ch'eje ŭi kiwŏn* [Manchuria modern: The origins of South Korea's developmental system in the 1960s]. Seoul: Munhak kwa Chisŏngsa, 2016.

Han Yongsŏp. "Han'guk ŭi chaju kukpang kwa Han-Mi tongmaeng: Yŏksajŏk koch'al kwa yangnip kanŭngsŏng e kwanhan yŏn'gu" [South Korea's self-reliant national defense and the US-ROK alliance: A study on the historical investigation and possibility for compatibility]. In *Kunsasa yŏn'gu ch'ongsŏ*, 4:1–68. Seoul: Kukpangbu Kunsa P'yŏnch'an Yŏn'guso, 2004.

Han'gukhak Chungang Yŏn'guwŏn [The Academy of Korean Studies], ed. *Pak Chŏnghŭi sidae Han-Mi kwan'gye* [ROK-US relations during the Park Chung Hee Era]. Seoul: Paeksan Sŏdang, 2009.

Hong Chaehak. "Kukpang Kwahak Yŏn'guso wa Pak Chŏnghŭi Taet'ongnyŏng" [The Agency for Defense Development and President Park Chung Hee]. In *Kwahak taet'ongnyŏng Pak Chŏnghŭi wa ridŏsip*, edited by Kim Yŏngsŏp et al., 472–520. Seoul: MSD Midiŏ, 2010.

Hong Kyudŏk. "Pak Ch'ŏnghŭi Pet'ŭnamjŏn ch'amjŏn kyŏljŏng kwa Han-Mi tongmaeng ŭi pyŏnhwa" [Park Chung Hee's decision to dispatch troops to Vietnam War and the changes in the ROK-US alliance]. In *Pak Chŏnghŭi sidae yŏn'gu ŭi chaengjŏm kwa kwaje*, edited by Chŏng Sŏnghwa, 295–328. Seoul: Sŏnin, 2005.

Hong Sŏnggŏl. "Pak Chŏnghŭi ŭi haek kaebal kwa Han-Mi kwan'gye" [Park Chung Hee's nuclear weapons development and ROK-US relations]. In *Pak Chŏnghŭi sidae yon'gu ŭi chaengjŏm kwa kwaje*, edited by Chŏng Sŏnghwa, 257–93. Seoul: Sŏnin, 2005.

Hong Sŏngnyul. "1960-yŏndae Han-Mi kwan'gye wa Pak Ch'ŏnghŭi kunsa chŏnggwŏn" [ROK-US relations in the 1960s and the military regime of Park Chung Hee]. *Yŏksa wa hyŏnsil*, no. 56 (2005): 269–302.

———. "Pak Chŏnghŭi chŏngbugi Nambuk taehwa wa Miguk" [The North-South Korea talks and the United States during the Park Chung Hee regime]. In *Pak Chŏnghŭi sidae Han-Mi kwan'gye*, edited by Han'gukhak Chungang Yŏn'guwŏn, 299–371. Seoul: Paeksan Sŏdang, 2009.

Hong Ŭnju and Yi Ŭnhyŏng. *K'orian mirak'ŭl*. Vol. 3: *Sumŭn kijŏktŭl: Chunghwahak kongŏp, chich'uk ŭl hŭndŭlda* [Korean miracle, vol. 3: Hidden miracles: Heavy and chemical industries are shaking the world]. P'aju: Nanam, 2015.

Hwang Pyŏngju. "Pak Ch'ŏnghŭi sidae ŭi kukka wa 'minjung'" [The state and "the people" in the Park Chung Hee era]. *Tangdae pip'yŏng* 12 (2000): 46–68.

———. "Pak Chŏnghŭi wa kŭndaehwa ŭi kkum" [Park Chung Hee and the dreams of modernization]. *Tangdae pip'yŏng* 28 (2004): 89–102.

Hwang Pyŏngt'ae. *Pak Ch'ŏnghŭi p'aerŏdaim* [The Park Chung Hee paradigm]. Seoul: Chosŏn News Press, 2011.

Hwang Tongjun. "Miguk ŭi tae-Han anbo chiwŏn chŏngch'aek kwa Han'guk ŭi pangwi sanŏp" [US policy on ROK security and the Korean defense industry]. *Han'guk kwa Miguk* (1988): 57–78. https://kiss.kstudy.com/Detail/Ar?key=15636.

———. "Sŏnjin'guk ilsurok pangwi sanŏp e t'uja" [Advanced nations invest more in defense industry]. *Han'guk nondan* 50, no. 1 (September 1993): 93–102.

Hwang Tongjun, Han Namsŏng, and Yi Sanguk. *Miguk ŭi tae-Han anbo chiwŏn p'yŏngga wa Han-Mi pangwi hyŏmnyŏk chŏnmang* [An evaluation of the US policy on military aid to the ROK and the prospect of ROK-US defense cooperation]. Seoul: Minyŏngsang, 1990.

Hyŏn Int'aek. *Han'guk ŭi pangwibi* [South Korea's defense costs]. Seoul: Hanul, 1991.

Im Chihyŏn. "Taejung tokchae ŭi chihyŏngdo kŭrigi" [Drawing up a map of mass dictatorship]. In *Taejung tokchae*, edited by Im Chihyŏn and Kim Yongu, 1:17–51. Seoul: Ch'aek Sesang, 2004.

Im Chihyŏn and Kim Yongu, eds. *Taejung tokchae*. 2 vols. Seoul: Ch'aek sesang, 2004–5.

Im Chihyŏn and Yi Sangnok. "'Taejung tokchae' wa 'posŭt'ŭ-p'asijŭm': Cho Hŭiyŏn kyosu ŭi pip'an e puch'ŏ" [Mass dictatorship and post-fascism: A response to Professor Cho Hŭiyŏn's criticism]. In *Taejung tokchae*, edited by Im Chihyŏn and Kim Yongu, 2:476–518. Seoul: Ch'aek sesang, 2005.

Im Hyŏkpaek. "Yusin ŭi yŏksajŏk kiwŏn: Pak Chŏnghŭi ŭi mak'iabellijŏk in sigan" [The historical origins of Yusin: The Machiavellian hour of Park Chung Hee]. *Han'guk chŏngchi yŏn'gu*, 14, no. 1 (2005): 115–46.

Im Tongwŏn. *P'isŭmeik'ŏ* [Peacemaker]. Seoul: Chungang Books, 2008.

Kim Chin'gi. "Han'guk pangwi sanŏp ŭi palchŏn chŏllyak e taehan yŏn'gu: Pak Chŏnghŭi sidae ŭi pangwi sanŏp ŭl chungshim ŭro" [A study of the ROK's developmental strategy for the defense industry: With a focus on the Park Chung Hee era's developmental strategy for the defense industry]. *Kukka chŏllyak* 14, no. 1 (2008): 95–121.

———. "Pak Chŏnghŭi wa Han'guk ŭi mugi, pangwi sanŏp" [Park Chung Hee and the South Korean weapons, defense industry]. In *Pak Ch'ŏnghŭi sidae rŭl hoego hada*, edited by Yi Chisu, 163–211. Seoul: Sŏnin, 2010.

Kim Chŏngnyŏm. *A Pak Chŏnghŭi* [Ah, Park Chung Hee]. Seoul: Chungang M&B, 1997.

———. *Ch'oebin'guk esŏ sŏnjin'guk munt'ŏk kkaji* [From the poorest nation to the threshold of a developed nation]. Seoul: Random House Chungang, 2006.

Kim Chongp'il. *Kim Chongp'il chŭngŏnnok* [The testimony of Kim Chongp'il]. Vols. 1–2. Seoul: Waijŭberi, 2016.

Kim Hyŏnggyun. "T'allaengjŏn'gi Han'guk kunsu sanŏp ŭi hwan'gyŏng kwa saeroun mosaek" [The environment and the new attempt of the South Korean military industry in the post–Cold War era]. *Sahoe chosa yŏn'gu* 10, no. 1 (1995): 83–104.

Kim, Hyung-A, and Ryu Sŏkch'un. "1970-yŏndae kinŭnggong yangsŏng kwa Asan Chŏng Chuyŏng" [Asan Chŏng Chuyŏng and the development of skill workers in the 1970s]. In *Asan Chŏng Chuyŏng kwa Han'guk kyŏngje palchŏn model*, edited by Asan Sahoe Pokchi Chaedan, 99–146. Seoul: Chimmundang, 2011. http://sclew.yonsei.ac.kr/thesis/t238/t238.pdf.

Kim Insu. "Kwahak kisul chinhŭng kwa kyŏngje palchŏn" [Science and technology promotion and economic development]. In *Han'guk kŭndaehwa kijŏk ŭi kwajŏng*, edited by Cho Ije and Carter Eckert, 343–66. Seoul: Wŏlgan Chosŏnsa, 2005.

Kim Kisŏk. "Uri nara chobyŏng kisul palchŏnsa (3): Kukkwayŏn ŭi t'ansaeng kwa ch'och'anggi hwaltong" [The history of the development of the arms manufacturing technology of our country, part 3: The birth of the Agency for Defense Development and its early activities]. *Kukpang kwa kisul* 4, no. 134 (1990): 46–57.

Kim Kwangmo. *Ch'ŏngwadae pisŏgwan ŭi Pak Chŏnghŭi Taet'ongnyŏng chunghwahak kongŏp hoesang* [A Blue House secretary's recollection of

President Park Chung Hee's heavy and chemical industrialization policy]. Seoul: Pak Chŏnghŭi Taet'ongnyŏng Kinyŏm Chaedan, 2018.
———. *Chunghwahak kongŏp e Pak Chŏnghŭi ŭi hon i saraitta* [Park Chung Hee's soul lives in the heavy and chemical industries]. Seoul: Kip'arang, 2015.
———. *Han'guk ŭi sanŏp palchŏn kwa chunghwahak kongŏphwa chŏngch'aek* [South Korea's industrial development and heavy and chemical industrialization policy]. Seoul: Chigu Munhwasa, 1988.
———. "Pak Chŏnghŭi Taet'ongnyŏng i pobae ro yangsŏng han kisul illyŏk i ŏpsŏttamyŏn Han'guk ŭi kongŏphwa nŭn pulganŭng haetta" [South Korea's industrialization would have been impossible without President Park Chung Hee's development of skilled labor]. *Pak Chŏnghŭi*, no. 39 (April 2014): 42–50.
———. "Pak Chŏnghŭi Taet'ongnyŏng ŭn pangwi sanŏp yuksŏng e kugun ŭl kŏrŏtta" [President Park Chung Hee wagered the national destiny on the development of the defense industry]. *Pak Chŏnghŭi*, no. 35 (April 2013): 34–48.
———. "Pak Chŏnghŭi ŭi chunghwahak yuksŏng: Kongŏp ipkuk p'ilsu yoso yuksŏng susun" [Park Chung Hee's cultivation of heavy and chemical industries: The sequence of fostering the necessary elements for national industrialization]. *Kyŏngje p'ungwŏl*, no. 211 (March 2017): 232–35.
———. "Such'ul 100-ŏkpul mokp'yo rŭl chogi talsŏng han chunghwahak kongŏphwa chŏngch'aek" [Heavy and chemical industrialization policy, which expedited the achievement of Korea's $10 billion export goal]. *Pak Chŏnghŭi*, no. 33 (October 2012): 42–57.
Kim Kwangmo, Ryu Sŏkch'un, Pak Kiju, and Chu Taehwan. "Pak Chŏnghŭi Taet'ongnyŏng ŭi chunghwahak kongŏp ŏttŏk'e pol kŏt in'ga?" [How should we view President Park Chung Hee's heavy and chemical industrialization?]. *Pak Chŏnghŭi chŏngsin* 4 (July–August 2017): 30–79.
Kim Sŏngŭn. *Na ŭi chan i nŏmch'i naida* [My cup overflows]. Seoul: Ait'emp'ŭl K'oria, 2008.
Kim T'aeho, ed., *"Kwahak taet'ongnyŏng Pak Chŏnghŭi" sinhwa rŭl nŏmŏ: Kwahak kwa kwŏllyŏk, kŭrigo kukka* [Overcoming the myth of the "Science President Park Chung Hee": Science, power, and the state]. Seoul: Yŏksa Pip'yŏngsa, 2018.
Kim Yonghwan. *Imja, chanega saryŏnggwan anin'ga* [Are you not the commander?]. Seoul: Maegyŏng Ch'ulp'an, 2006.
———. *Kaebal nyŏndae wa IMF wigi si ŭi chaejŏng, kŭmyung chŏngch'aek pisa* [The hidden history of fiscal policies during the development and IMF eras]. Seoul: Maegyŏng Ch'ulp'an, 2006.
Kim Yŏngsŏp et al. *Kwahak taet'ongnyŏng Pak Chŏnghŭi wa ridŏsip* [The Science President Park Chung Hee and his leadership]. Seoul: MSD Midiŏ, 2010.
Ku Sanghoe. *Han'guk ŭi pangwi sanŏp* [South Korea's defense industry]. Seongnam: Sejong Yŏn'guso, 1998.

———. “Ku Sanghoe Paksa ŭi Han’guk misail kaebal e taehan hoego” [Dr. Ku Sanghoe’s recollection of South Korea’s missile development]. *Shindonga*, February 1999. http://www.donga.com/docs/magazine/new_donga/9902/nd99020340.html. In author’s possession.

Kwŏn Insuk. *Taehan Min’guk ŭn kundaeda: Yŏsŏnghakchŏk sigak esŏ pon p’yŏnghwa, kunsajuŭi, namsŏngsŏng* [The Republic of Korea is an army: Peace, militarism, and masculinity viewed from a feminist perspective]. Seoul: Ch’ŏngnyŏnsa, 2005.

Kwŏn T’aeyŏng. “Wuri ŭi chaju kukpang noryŏk kwa 21-segi sŏnjin kukpang panghyang” [Our efforts for self-reliant national defense and the twenty-first century movement toward an advanced national security]. *Kunsa nondan* 12 (Fall 1997): 35–61.

Ma Sangyun. “Pak Chŏnghŭi wa Nambuk taehwa” [Park Chung Hee and the North-South Korean dialogue]. In *Pak Ch’ŏnghŭi sidae rŭl hoego hada*, edited by Yi Chigu, 133–51. Seoul: Sŏnin, 2010.

———. “Tet’angt’ŭ ŭi wihŏm kwa kihoe: 1970-yŏndae ch’o Pak Chŏnghŭi wa Kim Taejung ŭi anbo insik kwa nolli” [Danger and opportunity of détente: Park Chung Hee and Kim Dae-jung’s understanding and rationale on the national security in the early 1970s]. *Segye chŏngch’i* 14 (2011): 103–234.

Min Pyŏngman. *Han’guk ŭi hwayak yŏksa*. [A history of explosives in Korea]. Seoul: Iworkbook, 2009.

Min Sŏnggi. *Kisul chugwŏn hoebok ŭi chuyŏk Han’guk pangwi sanŏp* [The key player in restoring technological sovereignty: South Korea’s defense industry]. Seoul: Munwŏn, 1996.

Mun Chŏngin. “Han’guk ŭi pangwi sanŏp palchŏn ŭl wihan cheŏn: Anbo hwan’gyŏng kwa mugi ch’egye” [Proposals to improve the Korean defense industry: The security environment and weapons system]. *Kukpang kwa kisul* 188 (October 1994): 10–31.

Mun Manyong. “‘Chŏn kungmin ŭi kwahakhwa undong’: Kwahak kisulcha rŭl wihan kwahak kisulcha ŭi kwahak undong” [The scientization movement of the entire nation: The science movement of scientists for scientists]. In *“Kwahak taet’ongnyŏng Pak Chŏnghŭi” sinhwa rŭl nŏmŏ: Kwahak kwa kwŏllyŏk, kŭrigo kukka*, edited by Kim T’aeho, 162–98. Seoul: Yŏksa Pip’yŏngsa, 2018.

———. *Han’guk kwahak kisul yŏn’gu ch’eje ŭi chinhwa* [Evolution of science and technology research systems in South Korea]. Seoul: Tŭllyŏk, 2017.

———. *Han’guk ŭi hyŏndaejŏk yŏn’gu ch’eje ŭi hyŏngsŏng* [The formation of Korea’s modern research system]. Seoul: Sŏnin, 2010.

———. “KIST esŏ Taedŏk Yŏn’gu Tanji kkaji, chŏngbu ch’uryŏn yŏn’guso ŭi t’ansaeng kwa chaesaengsan” [From Tedŏk Science Town to KIST: The birth and reproduction of the government-funded research institutes]. In *“Kwahak taet’ongnyŏng Pak Chŏnghŭi” sinhwa rŭl nŏmŏ: Kwahak kwa kwŏllyŏk, kŭrigo kukka*, edited by Kim Taeho, 75–108. Seoul: Yŏksa pip'yŏngsa, 2018.

Mun Manyong and Kang Mihwa. "Pak Chŏnghŭi sidae kwahak kisul 'chedo kuch'ukcha': Ch'oe Hyŏngsŏp kwa O Wŏnch'ŏl" [The builders of the science and technology policies during the Park Chung Hee Era: Ch'oe Hyŏngsŏp and O Wŏnch'ŏl]. *Han'guk kwahaksa hakhoeji* 35, no. 1 (2013): 225–44.

Na Inho. "Nach'i tokchae ŭi chŏngch'i chonggyo wa chŏnch'ejuŭijŏk taejung mandŭlgi" [The Nazi dictatorship's political religion and making of the totalitarian mass]. In *Taejung tokchae*, edited by Im Chihyŏn and Kim Yongu, 1:208–32. Seoul: Ch'aek Sesang, 2004.

Nam Aeri. "Taehan Min'guk ŭi sumŭn chŏllyŏk" [South Korea's hidden power]. Kukka Kirogwŏn [National Archives of Korea]. Accessed June 17, 2023. https://theme.archives.go.kr/next/koreaOfRecord/reservist.do.

Nishino Junya. "Han'guk ŭi sanŏp chŏngch'aek pyŏnhwa wa Ilbon ŭro put'ŏ ŭi haksŭp, 1960–1970-yŏndae rŭl chungsim ŭro" [Changes in South Korean industrial policy and lessons from Japan: With a focus on the 1960s and 1970s]. PhD diss., Yonsei University, 2005.

———. "Ilbon model esŏ Han'gukchŏk hyŏksin ŭro: 1970-yŏndae chunghwahak kongŏphwa rŭl tullŏssan chŏngch'aek kwajŏng" [Korean-style innovation on the Japanese model: Policy formation surrounding the 1970s heavy and chemical industrialization]. *Segye chŏngch'i* 14, no. 1 (2011): 167–206.

O Tongnyong. "1972-yŏn O Wŏnch'ŏl Kyŏngje Susŏk i chaksŏng, pogo han haek mugi kaebal ŭi masŭt'ŏ p'ŭllaen; 1980-yŏndae ch'o, kosundo p'ŭllut'onyum t'an ŭl wansŏng handa" [The master plan for nuclear arms development, drafted and reported by Presidential Economic Secretary O Wŏnch'ŏl in 1972; we will make high-purity plutonium warheads by the early 1980s]. *Chugan chosŏn*, August 2003, 190–99. http://monthly.chosun.com/client/news/viw.asp?nNewsNumb=200308100032.

O Wŏnch'ŏl. "25-cho wŏn Yulgok Saŏp chinsil: Kungmin ton, han p'un to pujŏng ŭn andwae" [Out of the people's money, not even one cent of corruption can be tolerated]. *Shindonga*, April 1995, 410–25.

———. *Han'gukhyŏng kyŏngje kŏnsŏl: Enjiniŏring ŏp'ŭroch'I* (*HGKK*) [The South Korean model of economic development: Engineering Approach]. Vols. 1–5. Seoul: Kia Kyŏngje Yŏn'guso, 1995–96.

———. *Han'gukhyŏng kyŏngje kŏnsŏl: Enŏji chŏngch'aek kwa chungdong chinch'ul* (*HGKK*) [The South Korean model of economic development: Energy policy and advancement into Middle East]. Vol. 6. Seoul: Kia Kyŏngje Yŏn'guso, 1997.

———. *Han'gukhyŏng kyŏngje kŏnsŏl: Nae ka chŏnjaeng ŭl haja nŭn kŏt to aniji annŭnya* (*HGKK*) [The South Korean model of economic development: I'm not saying to start a war]. Vol. 7. Seoul: Kia Kyŏngje Yŏn'guso, 1999.

———. "Pak Chŏnghŭi chŏnggwŏn Yulgok Saŏp ch'ong ch'aegimja O Wŏnch'ŏl chŭngŏn: Kalp'ang chilp'ang hanggong sanŏp chŏngch'aek chaebŏl muhan kyŏngjaeng pullŏtta" [A testimony by O Wŏnch'ŏl, the person in charge of the Park Chung Hee regime's Yulgok Operation: Wishy-washy policy on aviation industry led to limitless competition among conglomerates]. *Shindonga*, April 1996, 368–88.

———. *Pak Chŏnghŭi nŭn ŏttŏtk'e kyŏngje kangguk mandŭrŏnna* [How did Park Chung Hee establish South Korea as an advanced economic nation?]. Seoul: Tongsŏ Munhwasa, 2006.

———. "Yulgok Saŏp ch'ulpal: Pak Chŏnghŭi, Kim Ilsŏng ogi ssaum" [The start of the Yulgok Operation: Park Chung Hee and Kim Il Sung's battle of pride]. *Shindonga*, June 1995, 468–93.

Ŏm Chŏngsik. "K'at'ŏ haengjŏngbu ŭi tae-Han mugi ijŏn chŏngch'aek ŭi pyŏnyong" [The shift in the Carter administration's arms transfer policy on South Korea]. PhD diss., Seoul National University, 2012.

———. "Miguk mugi ijŏn chŏngch'aek ŭi Han'guk chŏgyong" [The application of the US arms transfer policies in South Korea]. *Kunsa*, no. 82 (March 2012): 275–303.

———. "Pak Chŏnghŭi chŏngbu ŭi chaju kukpang chŏngch'aek kwa Han-Mi kwan'gye: Chajujŏk mugi kaebal mit mugi toip tabyŏnhwa chŏllyak" [The Park Chung Hee administration's self-reliant national defense policy and US-ROK relations: Independent weapon development and the diversification of strategy for weapon procurement]. *Taet'ongnyŏng kirongmul usu yŏn'gu nonmun* 2 (2012): 9–35.

Pae Chinyŏng. "Taet'ongnyŏng pisŏsiljanggye ŭi 'sara innŭn chŏnsŏl' Kim Chŏngnyŏm" [Kim Chŏngnyŏm, the "living legend" of presidential secretaries]. *Wŏlgan Chosŏn Newsroom*, December 2009. http://monthly.chosun.com/client/news/viw.asp?ctcd=E&nNewsNumb=200912100041.

Paek Hwan'gi. "Han'guk pangwi sanŏp ŭi yuksŏng panghyang, kibon kusang ŭl chungsim ŭro" [On the direction and basic plans for the development of South Korean defense industry]. *Kukpang yŏn'gu* 30 (1971): 71–91.

———. *Pangwi sanŏp kwa kwahak kisul* [Defense industry and scientific technology]. Seoul: Han'guk Pangsan Hakhoe, 1979.

Paek Kwangil. "Han'guk ŭi mugi such'ul kwa Miguk ŭi t'ongje e kwanhan yŏn'gu" [A study of South Korea's weapon exports and US restrictions]. *Han'guk chŏngch'ihak hoebo* 19 (1985): 419–36.

Pak Chinhwan. *Pak Chŏnghŭi Taet'ongnyŏng ŭi Han'guk kyŏngje kŭndaehwa wa Saemaŭl Undong* [President Park Chung Hee's modernization of the Korean economy and the New Village Movement]. Seoul: Pak Chŏnghŭi Taet'ongnyŏng Kinyŏm Saŏphoe, 2005.

Pak Chŏnghŭi Taet'ongnyŏng Yuk Yŏngsu Yŏsa Kinyŏm Saŏphoe [President Park Chung Hee and Madame Yuk Yŏngsu Memorial Foundation]. *Kyŏre ŭi chidoja: Pak Chŏnghŭi Taet'ongnyŏng ŭi ch'ijŏk ŭl chungsim ŭro han Han'guk hyŏndaesa* [The leader of our countrymen: A contemporary history of Korea centered around President Park Chung Hee's administrative achievements]. Seoul: Yugyŏng Chaedan, 1990.

Pak Chunbok. *Han'guk misail 40-yŏn ŭi sinhwa: Chaju kukpang kŭrigo kkum ŭl irun saramdŭl* [The forty-year legend of South Korean missiles: Self-reliant national defense and the people who achieved their dream]. Seoul: Iljogak, 2011.

Pak Ilsŏng. "Chaju kukpang chŏngch'aek ŭi ch'ujin kwa kun ŭi hyŏndaehwa, 1970–1997" [Self-reliant national defense policy and military modernization, 1970–1997]. *Kunsa*, no. 68 (August 2008): 93–130.

Pak Kŭnho. *Pak Chŏnghŭi kyŏngje sinhwa haebu chŏngch'aek ŏmnŭn kodo sŏngjang* [Dissecting Park Chung Hee's economy myth: Rapid growth without policy]. Seoul: Hoehwa Namu, 2017.

Pak Pongsu. "1970-yŏndae Han'guk chaju kukpang chŏngch'aek yŏn'gu: Taet'ongnyŏng Kirokkwan kukpang, anbo kwallyŏn pogo munsŏ rŭl chungsim ŭro" [A study of South Korea's self-reliant national defense in the 1970s based on the national security documents in the Presidential Archives]. *Kunsa*, no. 78 (March 2011): 169–203.

Pak T'aegyun. "8.3 choch'i wa sanŏp hamnihwa chŏngch'aek" [The 8.3 measure and the rationalization policy for businesses]. *Yŏksa wa hyŏnsil*, no. 88 (June 2013): 87–144.

———. "1960-yŏndae chungban anbo wigi wa che-2 kyŏngjeron" [The security crisis in the mid-1960s and the concept of second economy]. In *Pak Chŏnghŭi sidae yŏn'gu ŭi chaengjŏm kwa kwaje*, edited by Chŏng Sŏnghwa, 117–53. Seoul: Sŏnin, 2005.

———. "Chaebŏl t'ansaeng ŭi kiwŏn ŭn Pak Chŏnghŭi chŏnggwŏn 8.3 choch'i" [The birth of chaebŏl is attributed to the Park Chung Hee regime's 8.3 measure]. *Naver News*, June 24, 2013. https://n.news.naver.com/mnews/article/001/0006331684?sid=103.

———. "Pak Chŏnghŭi Taet'ongnyŏng sigi kukpang kwallyŏn munsŏ haeje" [Declassified documents related to defense during Park Chung Hee's presidency]. Taet'ongnyŏng Kirokkwan. Accessed July 30, 2021. https://www.pa.go.kr/research/contents/open/index_list03.jsp.

———. *Wŏnhyŏng kwa pyŏnyong: Han'guk kyŏngje kaebal kyehoek ŭi kiwŏn* [Archetype and metamorphosis: The origins of Korea's economic development plans]. Seoul: Sŏul Taehakkyo Ch'ulp'anbu, 2007.

Pak Yŏnggu. "4 Taehaek Kongjang Saŏp ŭi kwajŏng kwa sŏnggyŏk, 1969.11–1971.11" [The process and character of the Four Core Factories project, November 1969–November 1971]. *Kyŏngje sahakhoe* 44 (2008): 81–107.

———. *Han'guk chunghwahak kongŏphwa yŏn'gu ch'ongsŏl* [Survey of research on Korea's heavy and chemical industrialization]. Seoul: Haenam, 2008.

———. *Han'guk ŭi chunghwahak kongŏphwa kongŏppyŏl yŏn'gu: Chosŏn kongŏp* [Studies about Korea's heavy and chemical industrialization classified by industry: Shipbuilding industry]. Seoul: Haenam, 2018.

———. *Han'guk ŭi chunghwahak kongŏphwa kongŏppyŏl yŏn'gu: Kigye kongŏp* [Studies about Korea's heavy and chemical industrialization classified by industry: Machine industry]. Seoul: Haenam, 2015.

———. *Han'guk ŭi chunghwahak kongŏphwa: Kwajŏng kwa naeyong* [South Korea's heavy and chemical industrialization: Process and its contents]. 3 vols. Seoul: Haenam, 2012.

Ryu Kiljae. "1960-yŏndae mal Pukhan ŭi tobal kwa Han-Mi kwan'gye ŭi kyunyŏl" [North Korea's provocations in the late 1960s and a rupture in ROK-US relations]. In *Pak Chŏnghŭi sidae Han-Mi kwan'gye*, edited by Han'gukhak Chungang Yŏn'guwŏn, 185–242. Seoul: Paeksan Sŏdang, 2009.

———. "1960-yŏndae Pukhan ŭi sukch'ŏng kwa sult'anijŭm ŭi tŭngjang" [Purges in the 1960s and the rise of sultanism in North Korea]. *Kukche kwan'gye yŏn'gu* 9, no. 1 (March 2004): 77–110.

Ryu Sangyŏng. "Pak Chŏnghŭi ŭi chunghwahak kwa pangwi sanŏp chŏngch'aek: Kujo haengwija model esŏ pon cheyak toen sŏnt'aek" [Heavy and chemical industrialization and defense industry under the Park Chung Hee regime: A constrained choice from the structure-agency model]. *Segye chŏngch'i* 14, no. 1 (2011): 137–66.

Sin Chongdae. "Han'guk chŏngch'i ŭi Pukhan yoin yŏn'gu: 1961–72-yŏn ŭl chungsim ŭro" [A study of the North Korea factor in South Korean politics: With a focus on the 1961–72 period]. PhD diss., Sŏgang University, 2002.

———. "Yusin ch'eje ch'ulbŏm kwa Han-Mi kwan'gye" [The emergence of the Yusin system and ROK-US relations]. In *Pak Chŏnghŭi sidae Han-Mi kwan'gye*, edited by Han'gukhak Chungang Yŏn'guwŏn, 243–982. Seoul: Paeksan Sŏdang, 2009.

Sin Inho. *Munaemi enŭn kijŏk i ŏpta: Kukpang Kwahak Yŏn'guso wa han'gukhyŏng sin mugi kaebal* [There are no miracles in Munaemi: The Agency for Defense Development and Korean-style development of new weapons]. Seoul: Ch'aegŭro Mannanŭn Sesang, 2003.

Sin Ukhŭi. *Sunŭng kwa chŏhang ŭl nŏmŏsŏ: Yi Sŭngman kwa Pak Chŏnghŭi ŭi tae-Mi chŏngch'aek* [Beyond accommodation and resistance: Rhee Syngman and Park Chung Hee's policies toward the United States]. Seoul: Sŏul Taehakkyo Ch'ulp'an Munhwawŏn, 2010.

———. "Tet'angt'ŭ sigi ŭi Han-Mi kaldŭng" [ROK-US conflict during the détente era]. In *Pak Chŏnghŭi sidae yŏn'gu ŭi chaengjŏm kwa kwaje*, edited by Chŏng Sŏnghwa, 329–53. Seoul: Sŏnin, 2005.

Sin Ukhŭi and Cho Tongjun, eds. *Kowi kwallyodŭl, Puk haek wigi rŭl marhada* [Highly ranked government officials discuss North Korea's nuclear threats]. Kwach'ŏn: Kuksa P'yŏnch'an Wiwŏnhoe, 2009.

Sŏ Munsŏk. "Hyŏnam Kim Chonghŭi ŭi ch'angŏp kwa Hanwha kŭrup ŭi hyŏngsŏng" [Hyŏnam Kim Chonghŭi's start-up business and formation of the Hanwha Group]. *Kyŏngyŏng sahak* 24, no. 4 (December 2009): 307–33.

Sŏ Udŏk, Sin Inho, and Chang Samyŏl. *Pangwi sanŏp 40-yŏn: Kkŭt ŏmnŭn tojŏn ŭi yŏksa* [Forty years of the defense industry: A history of endless challenges]. Seoul: P'ŭllaenit Midiŏ, 2015.

Song Hŭijun. "Han'guk ŭi kukpang kisul kwa kyŏngje palchŏn e taehan yŏn'gu" [A study of the correlation between South Korea's national defense technology and economic development]. *Han'guk chŏngch'aekhak hoebo* 4, no. 2 (1995): 58–80.

Song Munhong. "Kukpang Kwahak Yŏn'guso kukpang yesan nangbi ŭi chuyŏk in'ga" [Is the ADD the main culprit behind the waste in defense spending?]. *Shindonga*, March 1995, 404–19.

Surdej, Éric. *Han'gugin ŭn mich'yŏtta* [These Koreans are crazy]. Translated by Kwŏn Chihyŏn. Seoul: Pukhausŭ, 2015 (originally published in French as *Ils sont fous ces Coréens! Dix ans chez les forcenés de l'efficacité* [These Koreans are crazy: Ten years among fanatics of efficiency]. Paris: Calmann-Lévy, 2015).

Yamamoto, Sintaro. "Han'guk chunghwahak kongŏp kwa pangwi sanŏp ŭi pyŏngjin chŏngch'aek" [South Korea's parallel policy of heavy and chemical industrialization and the defense industry]. MA thesis, Yonsei University, 1997.

Yang Sŭngham, Pak Myŏngnim, and Chang Hun'gak. *Pak Chŏnghŭi.* Vol. 5: *Chuhan Migun ch'ŏlsu* [Park Chung Hee, vol. 5: The withdrawal of United States Forces Korea]. Seoul: Yŏnse Taehakkyo Kukka Kwalli Yŏn'guwŏn, 2010.

Yang Sŭngham, Pak Myŏngnim, and Chi Chuhyŏng. *Pak Chŏnghŭi.* Vol. 4: *Yusin ch'eje hyŏngsŏng* [Park Chung Hee, vol. 4: The formation of the Yusin system]. Seoul: Yŏnse Taehakkyo Kukka Kwalli Yŏn'guwŏn, 2010.

Yang Sŭngham, Pak Myŏngnim, and Cho Suhyŏn. *Pak Chŏnghŭi.* Vol. 1: *Sanŏphwa wa taeoe chawŏn tongwŏn* [Park Chung Hee, vol. 1: Industrialization and utilization of foreign aid]. Seoul: Yŏnse Taehakkyo Kukka Kwalli Yŏn'guwŏn, 2010.

Yang Sŭngham, Pak Myŏngnim, and Pak Yongsu. *Pak Chŏnghŭi.* Vol. 3: *Pet'ŭnam p'abyŏng.* [Park Chung Hee, vol. 3: The dispatch of troops to Vietnam]. Seoul: Yŏnse Taehakkyo Kukka Kwalli Yŏn'guwŏn, 2010.

Yang Sŭngham, Pak Myŏngnim, and Yun Minjae. *Pak Chŏnghŭi.* Vol. 2: *P'uebŭllo ho sagŏn* [Park Chung Hee, vol. 2: The Pueblo incident]. Seoul: Yŏnse Taehakkyo Kukka Kwalli Yŏn'guwŏn, 2010.

Yi Chaehak. "Pak Chŏnghŭi chŏngbu ŭi kukpang oegyo e taehan yŏn'gu" [A study on the Park Chung Hee administration's defense diplomacy]. *Kunsa*, no. 78 (2011): 205–234.

Yi Chisu, ed. *Pak Ch'ŏnghŭi sidae rŭl hoego hada* [Recollections of the Park Chung Hee era]. Seoul: Sŏnin, 2010.

Yi Kyejae. "Pak Chŏnghŭi chŏngbu ŭi pangwi sanŏp chongch'aek yŏn'gu" [A study on the Park Chung Hee government's defense industry policy]. M.A. thesis, Seoul: Yonsei University, 2001.

Yi Kyŏngsŏ, *Pak Chŏnghŭi ŭi chaju kukpang* [Park Chung Hee and Self-Reliant National Defense]. Seoul: Irŭn ach'im, 2023.

Yi Minhyŏng. "Chŏngbu ch'uryŏn yŏn'guso 50-yŏn t'ŭkchip: Ch'uryŏn yŏn'gu kigwan yŏksajŏk pyŏnhwa kwajŏng kwa mirae palchŏn pangyang" [A special feature article for the 50th anniversary of government-funded research institutes: Historical changes in government-funded research institutions and directions for future progress]. *Kwahak kisul chŏngch'aek*, no. 213 (April 2016): 18–25.

Yi P'iljung and Kim Yonghwi. "Chuhan Migun ŭi kunsaryŏk pyŏnhwa wa Han'guk ŭi kunsaryŏk kŏnsŏl sai ŭi sanggwan kwan'gye" [Correlation between changes in the military strength of United States Forces Korea and building of Korea's military power]. *Kunsa*, no. 62 (April 2007): 273–311.

Yi Pyŏngch'ŏn, ed. *Kaebal tokchae wa Pak Chŏnghŭi sidae: Uri sidae ŭi chŏngch'i kyŏngjejŏk kiwŏn* [Developmental authoritarianism and the Park Chung Hee era: The political-economic origins of our times]. Seoul: Ch'angbi, 2003.

———. "Pak Chŏnghŭi chŏnggwŏn kwa palchŏn kukka mohyŏng ŭi hyŏngsŏng: 1960-yŏndae ch'ojungyŏp ŭi chŏngch'aek chŏnhwan ŭl chungsim ŭro" [Park Chung Hee's regime and the formation of a developmental state model: With a focus on the policy change in the early and mid-1960s]. *Kyŏngje palchŏn yŏn'gu* 5, no. 2 (1999): 141–87.

Yi Seho. *Han kil ro sŏmgyŏttŏn nae choguk* [My fatherland, the only path on which I served]. Seoul: Taeyang Midiŏ, 2009.

Yi Tongwŏn. "Yi Sŭngman chŏnggwŏn'gi Miguk ŭi tae-Han kunsa wŏnjo yŏn'gu" [A study of American military aid to Korea during the Rhee Syngman regime]. PhD diss., Seoul National University, 2019.

Yi Ŭnyŏng. "ADD mugi kaebal 3 ch'ongsa ŭi haek misail kaebal pihwa" [A secret account of the three ADD scientists who were involved in nuclear missile development]. *Shindonga*, December 13, 2006. https://shindonga.donga.com/3/all/13/105990/.

Yi Yongsu. "Chaju kukpang kwa Han'guk Pangwi Sanŏp Chinhŭnghoe" [Self-reliant national defense and the Korean Defense Industry Association]. *Kukpang kwa kisul*, no. 254 (April 2000): 6–11.

Yu Chaehŭng. *Kyŏktong ŭi sewŏl* [An era of turbulence]. Seoul: Ŭlryu Munhwasa, 1994.

Yu Hansik. "Onŭl sŏnjin kongŏphwa rŭl irun kŏt ŭn Pak Taet'ongnyŏng ŭi pangwi sanŏp" [It was President Park's defense industry development that helped South Korea achieve today's advanced industrialization]. *Pak Chŏnghŭi*, no. 4 (July 2005): 16–19.

Yu Pyŏngt'ae. "Han'guk ŭi pangwi sanŏp ŭi hyŏnhwang kwa chŏn'gae" [The evolution and present state of the defense industry in South Korea]. *Kunsu sanŏp* 43, no. 1 (June 2000): 119–42.

Yu Sangwŏn. "Kukka yŏn'gu kaebal saŏp ŭi kunsajŏk kiwŏn" [The military origin of national R&D programs in South Korea]. *Han'guk kwahaksa hakhoeji* 42, no. 1 (2020): 163–85.

Yun Ch'ungno, *Pet'ŭnam Chŏnjaeng ŭi Han'guk sahoesa: Ich'in chŏnjaeng, orae toen hyŏnjae* [A social history of Korea in the Vietnam War: Forgotten war, distant present]. Seoul: P'urŭn Yŏksa, 2015.

US Archives

American Presidency Project, University of California, Santa Barbara, http://www.presidency.ucsb.edu/index.php

Central Intelligence Agency (CIA), Freedom of Information Act Electronic Reading Room, https://www.cia.gov/readingroom/. All information cited was released to the CIA's Freedom of Information Act Electronic Reading Room or the Nautilus Institute under the FOIA.

History and Public Policy Program (HPPP), Wilson Center Digital Archive, Woodrow Wilson Center for International Scholars, Washington, DC, http://digitalarchive.wilsoncenter.org/

Jimmy Carter Presidential Library, Atlanta, GA

Gerald R. Ford Presidential Library and Museum, Ann Arbor, MI, Digital Library, https://www.fordlibrarymuseum.gov/

Lyndon B. Johnson Presidential Library, Austin, TX, Digital Library, https://www.discoverlbj.org/

National Security Archive, George Washington University, Washington, DC, Virtual Reading Room, https://nsarchive.gwu.edu/virtual-reading-room

US National Archives and Records Administration, College Park, MD, https://www.archives.gov/

US Department of State, *Foreign Relations of the United States* (*FRUS*), Washington, DC, https://history.state.gov/historicaldocuments

Official Sources in English

Central Intelligence Agency (CIA). "2 Carter Backers Challenge Korea Troop Plan." Dec. 20, 1977. https://www.cia.gov/readingroom/docs/CIA-RDP99-00498R000100120012-8.pdf.

———. *Arms Sales to the Third World, 1976*. https://www.cia.gov/readingroom/docs/CIA-RDP79B00457A000700110001-4.pdf.
———. "Confrontation in Korea." Special National Intelligence Estimate No. 14.2-69. January 30, 1969. https://www.cia.gov/readingroom/docs/DOC_0001218149.pdf.
———. "Kim Il Sung's New Military Adventurism." Intelligence Report, November 26, 1968. https://www.cia.gov/readingroom/docs/esau-39.pdf.
———. "The Military Balance." November 17, 1976. https://www.cia.gov/readingroom/docs/CIA-RDP81T00700R000100050009-0.pdf.
———. "North Korea: Foreign Trade as a Force for Industrialization." Intelligence Memorandum, July 1971. https://www.cia.gov/readingroom/docs/CIA-RDP85T00875R001700010071-1.pdf.
———. "North Korean Intentions and Capabilities with Respect to South Korea." Special National Intelligence Estimate No. 14.2-67, September 21, 1967. https://www.cia.gov/readingroom/docs/DOC_0001218147.pdf.
———. "Sale of Korean Manufactured M-16 Rifles to a Third Country." August 15, 1974. https://www.cia.gov/readingroom/docs/CIA-RDP80R01731R002400170032-7.pdf.
———. "Sale of Korean Manufactured M-16 Rifles to Morocco." August 1974. https://www.cia.gov/readingroom/docs/CIA-RDP80R01731R002400170031-8.pdf.
———. "South Korea: Nuclear Developments and Strategic Decisionmaking." June 1978. Released to the Nautilus Institute under the FOIA. https://nautilus.org/wp-content/uploads/2011/09/CIA_ROK_Nuclear_DecisionMaking.pdf.
———. "Task for the CIA from PRM on Korea." April 28, 1977. https://www.cia.gov/readingroom/docs/CIA-RDP79R00603A002500020022-2.pdf.
Daggett, Stephen. "Costs of Major U.S. Wars." Congressional Research Service, June 29, 2010. https://fas.org/sgp/crs/natsec/RS22926.pdf.
Economic Planning Board (EPB). *Economic Survey of the 1973 Korean Economy*. Seoul: EPB, 1974.
Federal Research Division, Library of Congress. *South Korea: A Country Study*. Edited by Andrea Matles Savada and William Shaw. 4th ed. Washington, DC: LOC, 1992.
Heavy and Chemical Industry Promotion Council Planning Office (HCI Promotion Council). *Heavy and Chemical Industry*. Seoul: Government of the Republic of Korea, 1976.
———. *Heavy and Chemical Industry Development Plan*. Seoul: Government of the Republic of Korea, June 1973.
International Institute for Strategic Studies (IISS). *The Military Balance 1979–1980*. London: Adlard and Son, 1979.
Jack, Bryan, Marcella Agmon, Steven Head, David McGarvey, Beverley Rowen, Henry S. Rowen. *Regional Rivalries and Nuclear Responses*. Vol. 2:

The South Korean Case: A Nuclear Weapons Program Embedded in an Environment of Great Power Concerns. Berkeley, CA: Nautilus Institute for Security and Sustainability, 1978.

Kim Il Sung Works. Vol. 20: *November 1965–December 1966*. Pyongyang: Foreign Languages Publishing House, 1984. https://www.marxists.org/archive/kim-il-sung/cw/20.pdf.

Korea Institute of Science and Technology (KIST). *Plan for Development of Korean Mechanical Engineering Industry*. N.p.: KIST, 1970.

Manyin, Mark E., Mary Beth Nikitin, Emma Chanlett-Avery, Ian E. Rinehart, and William H. Cooper. "U.S.–South Korea Relations." Congressional Research Service, February 5, 2013. https://www.ncnk.org/sites/default/files/content/resources/publications/US_ROK_Relations.pdf.

Ministry of National Defense (MND). *Defense White Paper* (various years; English version). Seoul: MND, 2006–20. (Most of the ROK's recent defense white papers are published in both Korean and English, which is why they are listed in both the Korean and English sources sections.)

O, Wonchol. "Opportunities to Participate in Heavy and Chemical Industries in Korea." May 1973. Park Chung Hee Memorial Museum and Library.

Park, Chung Hee. *The Country, the Revolution and I*. Seoul: Hollym Corporation Publishers, 1970.

———. *Our Nation's Path: Ideology of Social Reconstruction*. 2nd ed. Seoul: Dong-a Publishing Company, 1964.

———. *To Build a Nation*. Washington, DC: Acropolis Books, 1971.

Rich, Robert G. "U.S. Ground Force Withdrawal from Korea: A Case Study in National Security Decision Making." US Department of State, June 1982. https://nautilus.org/wp-content/uploads/2012/09/U.S.-Ground-Force-Withdrawal-from-Korea-A-Case-Study-in-National-Security-Decision-Making.pdf.

Schlesinger, James R. *Annual Defense Department Report, FY 1975*. Report of the secretary of defense to Congress. Washington, DC: Government Printing Office, March 4, 1974.

Simpson, James M. "Wartime Interoperability Problems Posed by Differences in South Korea and United States Army Tactics." MA thesis, US Army Command and General Staff College, 1980. https://apps.dtic.mil/sti/pdfs/ADA094211.pdf.

Stockholm International Peace Research Institute (SIPRI). *SIPRI Yearbook 2011: Armaments, Disarmament and International Security*. New York: Oxford University Press, 2011.

———. "Top List TIV Tables." https://armstrade.sipri.org/armstrade/page/toplist.php.

———. *World Armaments and Disarmament: SIPRI Yearbook 1983*. New York: Taylor and Francis, 1983.

US Arms Control and Disarmament Agency. *World Military Expenditures and Arms Transfers, 1968–1977.* US Arms Control and Disarmament Agency, October 1979. https://2009-2017.state.gov/documents/organization/185665.pdf.

US Congress, House Committee on International Relations. *Investigation of Korean-American Relations: Report of the Subcommittee on International Relations, U.S. House of Representatives.* 95th Cong., 2nd sess. Washington, DC: Government Printing Office, 1978.

US Congress, Office of Technology Assessment. *Arming Our Allies: Cooperation and Competition in Defense Technology.* OTA-ISC-449. Washington, DC: Government Printing Office, May 1990.

US Congress, Senate Committee on Foreign Relations. *Implications of President Carter's Conventional Arms Transfer Policy.* 95th Cong., 1st sess. Washington, DC: Government Printing Office, December 1977.

———. *United States Security Agreements and Commitments Abroad: Hearings before the Subcommittee on United States Security Agreements and Commitments Abroad*, vol. 2, parts 5–11. 91st Cong., 2nd sess. Washington, DC: Government Printing Office, 1970.

US Department of Defense. *Military Standard Gage Inspection.* Washington, DC: Government Printing Office, 1951.

US Department of Defense, Defense Security Cooperation Agency. "Foreign Military Sales FAQ." Accessed January 28, 2023. https://www.dsca.mil/foreign-military-sales-faq.

US Department of State. *Foreign Relations of the United States* (*FRUS*). *1964–1968.* Vol. 6: *Vietnam, January–August 1968.* Edited by Kent Sieg. Washington, DC: Government Printing Office, 2002. https://history.state.gov/historicaldocuments/frus1964-68v06.

———. *FRUS. 1964–1968.* Vol. 29, part 1: *Korea.* Edited by Karen L. Gatz. Washington, DC: Government Printing Office, 2000. https://history.state.gov/historicaldocuments/frus1964-68v29p1.

———. *FRUS. 1964–1968.* Vol. 30: *China.* Edited by Harriet Schwar. Washington, DC: Government Printing Office, 1998. https://history.state.gov/historicaldocuments/frus1964-68v30.

———. *FRUS. 1969–1976.* Vol. 1: *Foundations of Foreign Policy, 1969–1972.* Edited by Louis J. Smith and David H. Herschler. Washington, DC: Government Printing Office, 2003. https://history.state.gov/historicaldocuments/frus1969-76v01.

———. *FRUS. 1969–1976.* Vol. 19, part 1: *Korea, 1969–1972.* Edited by Daniel J. Lawler and Erin R. Mahan. Washington, DC: Government Printing Office, 2009. https://history.state.gov/historicaldocuments/frus1969-76v19p1.

———. *FRUS. 1969–1976*. Vol. E-12: *Documents on East and Southeast Asia, 1973–1976*. Edited by Edward Keefer. Washington, DC: Government Printing Office, 2010. https://history.state.gov/historicaldocuments/frus1969-76ve12.

———. "United States Air Force Pacific Bases in the 70's." Foreign Service Institute, Washington, DC, April 1971. NAPSNet FOIA Document Special Reports, October 2, 2012. Released to the Nautilus Institute under the FOIA. https://nautilus.org/wp-content/uploads/2012/10/728-William-L.-Roche.pdf.

White House. "Washington Declaration." April 26, 2023. https://www.whitehouse.gov/briefing-room/statements-releases/2023/04/26/washington-declaration-2/.

Woolf, Amy F., and Emma Chanlett-Avery. "Redeploying U.S. Nuclear Weapons to South Korea: Background and Implications in Brief." Congressional Research Service, September 14, 2017. https://fas.org/sgp/crs/nuke/R44950.pdf.

Secondary Sources in English

Ahn, J. H., and K. I. Han, "Korean Experience in Self-Reliance for Nuclear Power Technology." International Nuclear Information System (INIS) repository, IAEA. https://inis.iaea.org/collection/NCLCollectionStore/_Public/31/060/31060504.pdf.

Amsden, Alice H. *Asia's Next Giant: South Korea and Late Industrialization*. New York: Oxford University Press, 1989.

Baldwin, Frank. "America's Rented Troops: South Koreans in Vietnam." *Bulletin of Concerned Asian Scholars* 7, no. 4 (1975): 33–40.

Bandow, Doug. "Free Rider: South Korea's Dual Dependence on America." *Cato Policy Analysis*, no. 308 (May 19, 1998): 1–28. https://www.cato.org/policy-analysis/free-rider-south-koreas-dual-dependence-america.

Baradaran, Sharon S. "The Transformation of the South Korean Defense Industries." PhD diss., University of Southern California, 1999.

Barnhart, Michael A. *Japan Prepares for Total War: The Search for Economic Security, 1919–1941*. Ithaca, NY: Cornell University Press, 1987.

Benoit, Emile. *Defense and Economic Growth in Developing Countries*. Lexington, MA: Lexington Books, 1973.

Bitzinger, Richard A. "China's Defense Technology and Industrial Base in a Regional Context: Arms Manufacturing in Asia." *Journal of Strategic Studies* 34, no. 3 (June 2011): 425–50.

———. "Defense Industries in Asia and the Technonationalist Impulse." *Contemporary Security Policy* 36, no. 3 (January 2015): 453–72.

———. *Towards a Brave New Arms Industry?* Oxford: Oxford University Press, 2003.

Bitzinger, Richard A., and Mikyoung Kim. "Why Do Small States Produce Arms? The Case of South Korea." *Korean Journal of Defense Analysis* 17, no. 2 (Fall 2005): 183–205.

Bolger, Daniel P. *Scenes from an Unfinished War: Low-Intensity Conflict in Korea, 1966–1969*. Leavenworth, KS: Combat Studies Institute, 1991.

Boo, Seung-chan. "North Korea's Nuclear Reality, South Korea's Arms Anxiety." *GlobalAsia* 13, no. 1 (March 2018). https://globalasia.org/v13no1/cover/north-koreas-nuclear-reality-south-koreas-arms-anxiety_seung-chan-boo.

Brazinsky, Gregg. *Nation Building in South Korea*. Chapel Hill: University of North Carolina Press, 2007.

Bruno, Lars, and Stig Tenold. "The Basis for South Korea's Ascent in the Shipbuilding Industry, 1970–1990." *Mariner's Mirror* 97, no. 3 (August 2011): 201–17.

Burr, William, ed. *Stopping Korea from Going Nuclear, Part I*. Washington, DC: National Security Archive, George Washington University, March 22, 2017. https://nsarchive.gwu.edu/briefing-book/henry-kissinger-nuclear-vault/2017-03-22/stopping-korea-going-nuclear-part-i.

Carney, Christopher. "International Patron-Client Relationships: A Conceptual Framework." *Studies in Comparative International Development* 24, no. 2 (1989): 42–55.

Cha, Victor. "Strategic Culture and Military Modernization of South Korea." *Armed Forces & Society* 28, no. 1 (Fall 2001): 99–127.

Cheon, Sehun, and Joonsoo Park. "Is South Korea's Booming Defence Industry Here to Stay?" *East Asia Forum*, December 14, 2022. https://www.eastasiaforum.org/2022/12/14/is-south-koreas-booming-defence-industry-here-to-stay/.

Chibber, Vivek. "Building a Developmental State: The Korean Case Reconsidered." *Politics and Society* 27, no. 3 (September 1999): 309–46.

———. "The Developmental State in Retrospect and Prospect: Lessons from India and South Korea." In *The End of the Developmental State*, edited by Michelle Williams, 30–54. New York: Routledge, 2014.

Cho, Joohee, and Hakyung Kate Lee. "South Korea Exporting Arms to Poland amid Controversy over Lethal Aid to Ukraine." *ABC News*, April 20, 2023. https://abcnews.go.com/International/south-korea-exporting-arms-poland-amid-controversy-lethal/story?id=98718452.

Cho, Soon Sung. "North and South Korea: Stepped-Up Aggression and the Search for New Security." *Asian Survey* 9, no. 1 (January 1969): 29–39.

Choi, Dai-Seok. "The Limits of State Strength in South Korea: The Case of the Heavy and Chemical Industrialization Plan." *Korea Observer* 26, no. 1 (Spring 1995): 63–95.

Choi, Hee Jung, and Ga Young Chung. "Divergent Paths toward Militarized Citizenship: The 'Unending' Cold War, Transnational Space of Citizenship, and International Korean Male Students." *Korea Journal* 58, no. 3 (Autumn 2018): 76–101. https://accesson.kr/kj/assets/pdf/8458/journal-58-3-76.pdf.

Choi, Hyungsub. "Manufacturing Knowledge in Transit: Technical Practice, Organizational Change, and the Rise of the Semiconductor Industry in the United States and Japan, 1948–1960." PhD diss., Johns Hopkins University, 2007.

Choi, Lyong. "The First Nuclear Crisis in the Korean Peninsula, 1975–76." *Cold War History* 14, no. 1 (2014): 71–90.

Chun, In-Bum. "Korean Defense Reform: History and Challenges." Brookings Institution, October 31, 2017. https://www.brookings.edu/research/korean-defense-reform-history-and-challenges/.

Chung, Ju-young. *Born of This Land: My Life Story*. Seoul: Asan Academy, 2019.

Chung, Oknim. "The US-ROK Private Sector Role in Peace and Security on the Korean Peninsula." *Korean Journal of Defense Analysis* 6, no. 1 (Summer 1999): 101–26.

Chung, Patrick. "From Ham Radio to Microchips: Kang Ki Dong, the U.S. Military, and the Rise of Global High Tech." Paper presented at the Association for Asian Studies Conference, Seattle, WA, March 22, 2022.

———. "From Korea to Vietnam: Local Labor, Multinational Capital, and the Evolution of US Military Logistics, 1950–1997." *Radical History Review* 133 (2019): 31–55.

Corner, Paul, and Jie-Hyun Lim. Introduction to *The Palgrave Handbook of Mass Dictatorship*, edited by Paul Corner and Jie-Hyun Lim, xix–xxx. London: Palgrave Macmillan, 2016.

———, eds. *The Palgrave Handbook of Mass Dictatorship*. London: Palgrave Macmillan, 2016.

Cumings, Bruce. "Power and Plenty in Northeast Asia: The Evolution of US Policy." *World Policy Journal* 5, no. 1 (Winter 1987): 79–106.

Dallin, David. *Soviet Foreign Policy after Stalin*. Philadelphia, PA: J. B. Lippincott, 1961.

Deyo, Frederic. *Beneath the Miracle: Labor Subordination in the New Asian Industrialization*. Berkeley: University of California Press, 1989.

DiMoia, John. "Han-Mi Hyŏpcho (Korean-American Cooperation) and the Origins of South Korean State Science (1945–1975)." PhD diss., Princeton University, 2007.

———. "Reconfiguring Transport Infrastructure in Post-War Asia: Mapping South Korean Container Ports, 1952–1978." *History and Technology* 36, nos. 3–4 (2020): 382–99.

Downs, Chuck. *Over the Line: North Korea's Negotiating Strategy.* Washington, DC: AEI Press, 1999.

Eckert, Carter. "Economic Development in Historical Perspective, 1945–1990." In *Korea, Old and New: A History*, by Carter Eckert, Ki-Baik Lee, Young Ick Lew, Michael Robinson, and Edward W. Wagner, 389–418. Seoul: Ilchogak, 1990.

———. *Offspring of Empire: The Koch'ang Kims and the Colonial Origins of Korean Capitalism 1876–1945.* Seattle: University of Washington Press, 1991.

———. *Park Chung Hee and Modern Korea: The Roots of Militarism, 1866–1945.* Cambridge, MA: Belknap Press of Harvard University Press, 2016.

———. "Total War, Industrialization and Social Change in Late Colonial Korea." In *The Japanese Wartime Empire, 1931–1945*, edited by Peter Duus, Ramon H. Myers, and Mark R. Peattie, 3–39. Princeton, NJ: Princeton University Press, 1996.

Eckert, Carter, Ki-Baik Lee, Young Ick Lew, Michael Robinson, and Edward W. Wagner. *Korea, Old and New: A History.* Seoul: Ilchogak, 1990.

"Eisenhower's Farewell Address to the Nation." National Archives, January 17, 1961. https://www.archives.gov/milestone-documents/president-dwight-d-eisenhowers-farewell-address.

Evans, Peter. *Embedded Autonomy: States and Industrial Transformation.* Princeton, NJ: Princeton University Press, 1995.

French, Paul. *North Korea: The Paranoid Peninsula—A Modern History.* 2nd ed. London: Zed Books, 2007.

Gansler, Jacques S. *The Defense Industry.* Cambridge, MA: MIT Press, 1982.

Glassman, Jim. *Drums of War, Drums of Development: The Formation of a Pacific Ruling Class and Industrial Transformation in East and Southeast Asia, 1945–1980.* Chicago: Haymarket Books, 2019.

Glassman, Jim, and Young-jin Choi. "The *Chaebol* and the US Military-Industrial Complex: Cold War Geopolitical Economy and South Korean Industrialization." *Environment and Planning A* 46, no. 5 (2014): 1160–80.

———. "A Geopolitical Economy of Heavy Industrialization and Second-Tier City Growth in South Korea: Evidence from the 'Four Core Plants Plan.'" *Critical Sociology* 44, no. 3 (2017): 405–20.

GlobalFirePower.com. "2023 Military Strength Ranking." 2023. https://www.globalfirepower.com/countries-listing.php.

———. "Active Military Manpower by Country (2023)." 2023. https://www.globalfirepower.com/active-military-manpower.php.

Gordon, Andrew. *The Evolution of Labor Relations in Japan: Heavy Industries, 1853–1955.* Cambridge, MA: Harvard University Press, 1988.

Gramsci, Antonio. *The Gramsci Reader: Selected Writings 1916–1935.* Edited by David Forgacs. New York: New York University Press, 2000.

———. *Prison Notebooks*. Edited by Joseph A. Buttigieg. Translated by Joseph A. Buttigieg and Antonio Callari. Vol. 1. New York: Columbia University Press, 1992.

Green, Michael J. *Arming Japan*. Columbia University Press, 1995.

Gulati, Umesh C. "The Foundations of Rapid Economic Growth: The Case of the Four Tigers." *American Journal of Economics and Sociology* 51, no. 2 (April 1992): 161–72.

Hahm, Sung Deuk, and L. Christopher Plein. "Institutions and Technological Development in Korea: The Role of the Presidency." *Comparatives Politics* 28, no. 1 (October 1995): 55–76.

Hamm, Taik-young. *Arming the Two Koreas: State, Capital and Military Power.* London: Routledge, 1999.

Han, Kyonghee, and Gary Lee Downey. *Engineers for Korea*. San Rafael, CA: Morgan and Claypool, 2013.

Hartley, Keith, and Jean Belin, eds. *The Economics of the Global Defence Industry.* London: Routledge, 2020.

Hayes, Peter, and Chung-in Moon. "Park Chung Hee, the CIA, and the Bomb." *Global Asia* 6, no. 3 (Fall 2011): 46–58.

Hedinger, Daniel. "Introduction: Militarization and Dictatorship in the Age of Total War." In *The Palgrave Handbook of Mass Dictatorship*, edited by Paul Corner and Jie-Hyun Lim, 287–92. London: Palgrave Macmillan, 2016.

Henry, Todd A. "Ch'anggyŏng Garden as Neocolonial Space: Spectacles of Anticommunist Militarism and Industrial Development in Early South(ern) Korea." *Journal of Korean Studies* 21, no. 1 (Spring 2016): 7–43.

Heo, Uk, and Karl DeRouen Jr. "Military Expenditures, Technological Change, and Economic Growth in the East Asian NICs." *Journal of Politics* 60, no. 3 (August 1998): 830–46.

Hogan, Michael H. *A Cross of Iron: Harry S Truman and the Origins of the National Security State, 1945–1954*. Cambridge: Cambridge University Press, 1998.

Hong, Sung Gul. "The Search for Deterrence: Park's Nuclear Option." In *The Park Chung Hee Era: The Transformation of South Korea*, edited by Byung-Kook Kim and Ezra F. Vogel, 483–510. Cambridge, MA: Harvard University Press, 2011.

Horikane, Yumi. "The Political Economy of Heavy Industrialization: The Heavy and Chemical Industry (HCI) Push in South Korea in the 1970s." *Modern Asian Studies* 39, no. 2 (May 2009): 369–97.

Hundley, Richard O. *Past Revolutions, Future Transformations: What Can the History of Revolutions in Military Affairs Tell Us about Transforming the U.S. Military?* Santa Monica, CA: RAND, 1999.

Hundt, David, and Jitendra Uttam, eds. *Varieties of Capitalism in Asia: Beyond the Developmental State*. London: Palgrave Macmillan, 2017.

Hwang, Byeong-ju. "The Ruling Discourse and Mass Politics of the Park Chung Hee Regime." *Review of Korean Studies* 12, no. 3 (September 2009): 11–40.

Hwang, Dong Joon. "The Role of Defense Industry in Innovation and the Development of Dual-Use Technology." *Korean Journal of Defense Analysis* 8, no. 1 (Summer 1996): 153–76.

Ienaga, Saburo. *The Pacific War, 1931–1945: A Critical Perspective on Japan's Role in World War II*. New York: Pantheon Books, 1978.

Inglehart, Ronald. *Culture Shift in Advanced Industrial Society*. Princeton, NJ: Princeton University Press, 1989.

International Trade Administration. "South Korea Country—Commercial Guide." August 2, 2022. https://www.trade.gov/country-commercial-guides/south-korea-defense-industry-equipment.

Jasanoff, Sheila. "Future Imperfect: Science, Technology, and the Imaginations of Modernity." In *Dreamscapes of Modernity: Sociotechnical Imaginaries and the Fabrication of Power*, edited by Sheila Jasanoff and Sang-Hyun Kim, 1–33. Chicago: University of Chicago Press, 2015.

Johnson, Chalmers. "The Developmental State: Odyssey of a Concept." In *The Developmental State*, edited by Meredith Woo-Cumings, 32–59. Ithaca, NY: Cornell University Press, 1999.

———. *MITI and the Japanese Miracle: The Growth of Industrial Policy, 1925–1975*. Stanford, CA: Stanford University Press, 1982.

———. "Political Institutions and Economic Performance: The Government-Business Relationship in Japan, South Korea, and Taiwan." In *The Political Economy of the New Asian Industrialism*, edited by Frederic C. Deyo, 136–64. Ithaca, NY: Cornell University Press, 1987.

Jones, Leroy P., and Il Sakong. *Government, Business, and Entrepreneurship in Economic Development: The Korean Case*. Cambridge, MA: Harvard University Asia Center, 1980.

Jones, Steve. *Antonio Gramsci*. London: Routledge, 2006.

Jung, Jiwon, and Jai S. Mah. "R&D Policies of Korea and Their Implications for Developing Countries." *Science, Technology and Society* 18, no. 2 (2013): 165–88.

Kang, David, and Jiun Bang. "The Pursuit of Autonomy and South Korea's Atypical Strategic Culture." In *Strategic Asia 2016–2017: Understanding Strategic Cultures in the Asia Pacific*, edited by Michael Wills, Ashley J. Tellis, and Alison Szalwinski, 113–40. Seattle, WA: National Bureau of Asian Research, 2016.

Kim, Byung-Kook, and Ezra F. Vogel, eds. *The Park Chung Hee Era: The Transformation of South Korea*. Cambridge, MA: Harvard University Press, 2011.

Kim, Choong Soon. *The Culture of Korean Industry: An Ethnography of Poongsan Corporation*. Tucson: University of Arizona Press, 1996.

———. *A Korean Nationalist Entrepreneur: A Life History of Kim Songsu, 1891–1955*. Albany: State University of New York Press, 1998.

Kim, Chung-yum. *From Despair to Hope: Economic Policymaking in Korea, 1945–1979*. Seoul: Korea Development Institute, 2011.

Kim, Dong-Won. "Transfer of 'Engineer's Mind': Kim Choong–Ki and the Semiconductor Industry in South Korea." *Engineering Studies* 11, no. 2 (2019): 83–108.

Kim, Eun Mee. *Big Business, Strong State: Collusion and Conflict in South Korean Development, 1960–1990*. Albany: State University of New York Press, 1997.

Kim, Eun Mee, and Nancy Kim. "Chaebŏl and the Political Economy of South Korean Development, 1945–Present." In *Routledge Handbook of Contemporary South Korea*, edited by Sojin Lim and Niki J. P. Alsford, 99–135. Abingdon, UK: 2021.

Kim, Eun Mee, and Gil-Sung Park. "The *Chaebol*." In *The Park Chung Hee Era: The Transformation of South Korea*, edited by Byung-Kook Kim and Ezra F. Vogel, 265–94. Cambridge, MA: Harvard University Press, 2011.

Kim, Geun Bae. "The Political Power–Mediated Expansion of Science and Technology under the Park Chung Hee Regime." *Korea Journal* 58, no. 4 (Winter 2018): 114–142.

Kim, Hyung-A. "Heavy and Chemical Industrialization, 1973–1979: South Korea's Homeland Security Measures." In *Reassessing the Park Chung Hee Era, 1961–1979: Development, Political Thought, Democracy, and Cultural Influence*, edited by Hyung-A Kim and Clark W. Sorensen, 19–43. Seattle: University of Washington Press, 2011.

———. "Industrial Warriors: South Korea's First Generation of Industrial Workers in Post-Developmental South Korea." *Asian Studies Review* 37, no. 4 (October 2013): 577–595.

———. *Korean Skilled Workers: Toward a Labor Aristocracy*. Seattle: University of Washington Press, 2020.

———. *Korea's Development under Park Chung Hee: Rapid Industrialization, 1961–1979*. New York: RoutledgeCurzon, 2004.

Kim, Hyung-A, and Clark W. Sorensen, eds. *Reassessing the Park Chung Hee Era, 1961–1979: Development, Political Thought, Democracy, and Cultural Influence*. Seattle: University of Washington Press, 2011.

Kim, Jiyul. "Crisis and Ideology: Culture, Diplomacy and Mobilization in South Korea's Quest for 'National Restoration,' 1968–1972." Dissertation prospectus, Harvard University, June 2005. https://www.academia.edu/28794990/Crisis_and_Ideology_Culture_Diplomacy_and_Mobilization_in_South_Koreas_Quest_for_National_Restoration_1968_1972_Jun_2005_Dissertation_prospectus.

———. "Strategic Culture of the Republic of Korea." *Contemporary Security Policy* 35, no. 2 (2014): 270–89.

———. "War, Diplomacy, Mobilization, and Nation Building in South Korea." Paper for a seminar on modern Korean history, Harvard University, May 2004. https://www.academia.edu/28794943/War_Diplomacy_Mobilization_and_Nation_Building_in_South_Korea_1968_May_2004.

Kim, Joo-Hong. "The Armed Forces." In *The Park Chung Hee Era: The Transformation of South Korea*, edited by Byung-Kook Kim and Ezra F. Vogel, 168–99. Cambridge, MA: Harvard University Press, 2011.

Kim, Kwangmo. *The Odyssey of Korean Heavy and Chemical Industrialization*. Seoul: RH Korea, 2017.

Kim, Lami. "A Hawkish Dove? President Moon Jae-in and South Korea's Military Buildup." *War on the Rocks*, September 15, 2021. https://warontherocks.com/2021/09/a-hawkish-dove-president-moon-jae-in-and-south-koreas-military-buildup/.

Kim, Michael. "The Aesthetics of Total Mobilisation in the Visual Culture of Late Colonial Korea." *Totalitarian Movements and Political Religions* 8, nos. 3–4 (September–December 2007): 483–502.

———. "The Brassware Industry and the Salvage Campaigns of Wartime Colonial Korea (1937–1945)." *Business History* 64, no. 5 (2022): 923–45.

———. "Industrial Warriors: Labour Heroes and Everyday Life in Wartime Colonial Korea, 1937–1945." In *Mass Dictatorship: Collusion and Evasion in Everyday Life*, edited by Alf Lüdtke, 126–46. London: Palgrave Macmillan, 2016.

Kim, Monica. *The Interrogation Rooms of the Korean War: The Untold History*. Princeton, NJ: Princeton University Press, 2019.

Kim, Sang-Hyun. "Science and Technology: National Identity, Self-Reliance, Technocracy and Biopolitics." In *The Palgrave Handbook of Mass Dictatorship*, edited by Paul Corner and Jie-Hyun Lim, 81–97. London: Palgrave Macmillan, 2016.

———. "Science, Technology, and the Imaginaries of Development in South Korea." *Development and Society* 46, no. 2 (September 2017): 317–47.

Kim, Sonja M., and Robert Ji-Song Ku, eds. *Future Yet to Come: Sociotechnical Imaginaries in Modern Korea*. Honolulu: University of Hawai'i Press, 2021.

Kim, Sun Joo. "Taxes, the Local Elite, and the Rural Populace in the Chinju Uprising of 1862." *Journal of Asian Studies* 66, no. 4 (November 2007): 993–1027.

Kim, Taekyoon. "History of the Developmental State: The Case of South Korea." In *Routledge Handbook of Contemporary South Korea*, edited by Sojin Lim and Niki J. P. Alsford, 85–98. Abingdon, UK: 2021.

Kim, Young Jak. "Park Chung Hee's Governing Ideas: Impact on National Consciousness and Identity." In *Reassessing the Park Chung Hee Era, 1961–1979: Development, Political Thought, Democracy, and Cultural Influence*, edited by Hyung-A Kim and Clark W. Sorensen, 95–106. Seattle: University of Washington Press, 2011.

Koh, B. C. "The Pueblo Incident in Perspective." *Asian Survey* 9, no. 4 (April 1969): 264–80.

Koketsu, Atsushi. "Total War and Japan: Reality and Limitations of the Establishment of the Japanese Total War System." *History of Global Arms Transfers* 6 (2018): 61–72. http://www.isc.meiji.ac.jp/~transfer/paper/pdf/06/05_Koketsu.pdf.

Koo, Hagen. *Korean Workers: The Culture and Politics of Class Formation*. Ithaca, NY: Cornell University Press, 2001.

———. "Labor Policy and Labor Relations during the Park Chung Hee Era." In *Reassessing the Park Chung Hee Era, 1961–1979: Development, Political Thought, Democracy, and Cultural Influence*, edited by Hyung-A Kim and Clark W. Sorensen, 122–44. Seattle: University of Washington Press, 2011.

Kwak, Tae Yang. "Anvil of War: The Legacies of Korean Participation in the Vietnam War." PhD diss., Harvard University, 2006.

Kwon, Peter Banseok. "The Anatomy of *Chaju Kukpang*: Military-Civilian Convergence in the Development of the Defense Industry under Park Chung Hee, 1968–1979." PhD diss., Harvard University, 2016.

———. "Beyond Patron and Client: Historicizing the Dialectics of US-ROK Relations amid Park Chung Hee's Independent Defense Industry Development in South Korea, 1968–1979." *Seoul Journal of Korean Studies* 30, no. 2 (December 2017): 185–216.

———. "Building Bombs, Building a Nation: The State, *Chaebŏl*, and the Militarized Industrialization of South Korea, 1973–1979." *Journal of Asian Studies* 79, no. 1 (February 2020): 51–75.

———. "Defender of the Nation, Champion of Science: The Agency for Defense Development as a Nexus for the Technological Transformation of South Korea." *Journal of Korean Studies* 28, no. 1 (March 2023): 59–90.

———. "Mars and Manna: Defense Industry and the Economic Transformation of Korea under Park Chung Hee." In "Legacies of Militarism in the Korean Peninsula in the 21st Century." Special issue, *Korea Journal* 58, no. 3 (Autumn 2018): 15–46.

———. "South Korea's Ongoing Quest for Security Independence." *East Asia Forum*, January 20, 2021. https://www.eastasiaforum.org/2021/01/20/south-koreas-ongoing-quest-for-security-independence/.

Lee, Chong-Sik. *The Korean Workers' Party: A Short History*. Stanford, CA: Hoover Institution Press, 1978.

Lee, Grace. "The Political Philosophy of *Juche*." *Stanford Journal of East Asian Affairs* 3, no. 1 (Spring 2003): 105–12.

Lee, Namhee. "The Theory of Mass Dictatorship: A Re-examination of the Park Chung Hee Period." *Review of Korean Studies* 12, no. 3 (September 2009): 41–69.

Lee, Phil-Sang. "Economic Crisis and Chaebol Reform in Korea." Columbia Business School Discussion Paper No. 14, October 2000. https://business.columbia.edu/sites/default/files-efs/imce-uploads/PFS/APEC_New/PSLee.PDF.

Lee, Rachel M. "Kim Jong Un's Tortuous Path to Economic Reform." *War on the Rocks*, June 9, 2022. https://warontherocks.com/2022/06/kim-jong-uns-tortuous-path-to-economic-reform/.

Lerner, Mitchell B. "'Mostly Propaganda in Nature': Kim Il Sung, the Juche Ideology, and the Second Korean War." Wilson Center, December 2010. https://www.wilsoncenter.org/publication/mostly-propaganda-nature-kim-il-sung-the-juche-ideology-and-the-second-korean-war.

———. *The Pueblo Incident: A Spy Ship and the Failure of American Foreign Policy*. Lawrence: University of Press of Kansas, 2002.

———. "The Second Korean War." Wilson Center. Accessed April 3, 2023. https://digitalarchive.wilsoncenter.org/essays/second-korean-war.

Lerner, Mitchell B., and Jong-Dae Shin. "New Romanian Evidence on the Blue House Raid and the USS Pueblo Incident." Wilson Center. Accessed January 18, 2023. https://www.wilsoncenter.org/publication/new-romanian-evidence-the-blue-house-raid-and-the-uss-pueblo-incident.

Lew, Seok-Choon, ed. *The Korean Economic Developmental Path: Confucian Tradition, Affective Network*. New York: Palgrave Macmillan, 2013.

Lew, Seok-Choon, and Hye Suk Wang. "Generalized Reciprocity between Strong State and Strong Society." In *The Korean Economic Developmental Path: Confucian Tradition, Affective Network*, edited by Seok Choon Lew, 119–40. New York: Palgrave Macmillan, 2013.

Lim, Jie-Hyun. "Conference Report: Coercion and Consent: A Comparative Study of 'Mass Dictatorship.'" *Contemporary European History* 13, no. 2 (May 2004): 249–52.

———. "Historiographical Perspectives on 'Mass Dictatorship.'" *Totalitarian Movements and Political Religions* 6, no. 3 (December 2005): 325–31.

Lim, Youngil. *Technology and Productivity: The Korean Way of Learning and Catching Up*. Cambridge, MA: MIT Press, 1999.

Martin, Bradley. *Under the Loving Care of the Fatherly Leader*. New York: St. Martin's, 2007.

Michishita, Narushige. *North Korea's Military-Diplomatic Campaigns, 1966–2008*. London: Routledge, 2010.

Migdal, Joel S. *Strong Societies and Weak States: State-Society Relations and State Capabilities in the Third World*. Princeton, NJ: Princeton University Press, 1988.

Mills, C. Wright. *The Power Elites*. Oxford: Oxford University Press, 1956.

Mizuno, Hiromi. *Science for the Empire: Scientific Nationalism in Modern Japan*. Stanford, CA: Stanford University Press, 2009.

Mizuno, Hiromi, Aaron S. Moore, and John DiMoia, eds. *Engineering Asia: Technology, Colonial Development, and the Cold War Order*. New York: Bloomsbury Press, 2018.

Moon, Chung-in. "Military Self-Reliance, the Big Push, and the Growth of the Defense Industry: Lessons and Implications." In *Korea and the World: Contemporary History and Its Implications*, edited by Myung Jae Moon and Stephan Haggard, 205–38. Seoul: National Museum of Korean Contemporary History, 2015.

———. "The Political Economy of Defense Industrialization in South Korea: Constraints, Opportunities, and Prospects." *Journal of East Asian Affairs* 5, no. 2 (Summer–Fall 1991): 438–65.

———. "U.S. Third Country Arms Sales Regulation and the South Korean Defense Industry: Supplier Control and Recipient Dilemma." In *Alliance under Tension: The Evolution of South Korean–US Relations*, edited by Manwoo Lee, Ronald D. McLaurin, and Chung-in Moon, 79–102. Boulder, CO: Westview Press, 1988.

Moon, Chung-in, and Byung-joon Jun. "Modernization Strategy: Ideas and Influences." In *The Park Chung Hee Era: The Transformation of South Korea*, edited by Byung-Kook Kim and Ezra F. Vogel, 115–39. Cambridge, MA: Harvard University Press, 2011.

Moon, Chung-in, and Jin-Young Lee. "The Revolution in Military Affairs and the Defence Industry in South Korea." *Security Challenges* 4, no. 4 (Summer 2008): 117–34.

Moon, Chung-in, and Sangkeun Lee. "Military Spending and the Arms Race on the Korean Peninsula." *Asia-Pacific Journal: Japan Focus* 8, issue 13, no. 2 (March 2010): 1–18. https://apjjf.org/-Sangkeun-Lee--Chung-in-Moon/3333/article.pdf.

Moon, Chung-in, and Jae-Ok Paek. "Defense Innovation and Industrialization in South Korea." Institute on Global Conflict and Cooperation, Policy Brief no. 14. September 2010. https://escholarship.org/uc/item/29n4c3jv.

Moon, Manyong. "Postcolonial Desire and the Tripartite Alliance in East Asia: The Hybrid Origins of a Modern Scientific and Technological System in South Korea." In *Engineering Asia: Technology, Colonial Development, and the Cold War Order*, edited by Hiromi Mizuno, Aaron S. Moore, and John DiMoia, 165–88. New York: Bloomsbury Press, 2018.

Moon, Sangseok. "Mechanism of Mass Mobilization and Creating State Citizens during the Economic Development Period: A Case of South Korea." PhD diss., University of Texas, 2008.

Moon, Seungsook. "The Cultural Politics of Remembering Park Chung Hee." *Asia-Pacific Journal: Japan Focus* 7, issue 19, no. 5 (May 2009): 1–33.

———. "Legacies of Militarism in the Korean Peninsula in the Twenty-First Century." *Korea Journal* 58, no. 3 (Autumn 2018): 5–14.

———. *Militarized Modernity and Gendered Citizenship in South Korea*. Durham, NC: Duke University Press, 2005.

Moore, Aaron. *Constructing East Asia: Technology, Ideology, and Empire in Japan's Wartime Era, 1931–1945*. Stanford, CA: Stanford University Press, 2015.

Morera, Esteve. *Gramsci's Historicism: A Realist Interpretation*. London: Routledge, 1990.

Morris-Suzuki, Tessa. *The Technological Transformation of Japan*. Cambridge: Cambridge University Press, 1994.

Nam, Hwasook. *Building Ships, Building a Nation*. Seattle: University of Washington Press, 2009.

Narita, Ryuichi. "Women's Total War: Gender and Wartime Mobilization in the Japanese Empire, 1931–1945." In *The Palgrave Handbook of Mass Dictatorship*, edited by Paul Corner and Jie-Hyun Lim, 337–49. London: Palgrave Macmillan, 2016.

Neuman, Stephanie G. "Arms Transfers, Military Assistance, and Defense Industries: Socioeconomic Burden or Opportunity?" *Annals of the American Academy of Political and Social Science* 535 (September 1994): 91–109.

Neuman, Stephanie G., and Çağlar Kurç. "Defence Industries in the 21st Century: A Comparative Analysis." *Defence Studies* 17, no. 3 (2017): 219–27.

Nixon, Richard. "Informal Remarks in Guam with Newsmen." American Presidency Project. Accessed January 18, 2023. https://www.presidency.ucsb.edu/node/239667.

Nolan, Janne E. *Military Industry in Taiwan and South Korea*. London: Macmillan, 1986.

O, Won-chol. *The Korea Story: President Park Jung-hee's Leadership and the Korean Industrial Revolution*. Seoul: Wisdom Tree, 2009.

O'Mara, Margaret. *The Code: Silicon Valley and the Remaking of America*. New York: Penguin Press, 2019.

Paek, Jae Ok. "Analysis of 2021 ROK Defense Budget and Its Policy Implications." *ROK Angle: Korea's Defense Policy*, no. 232 (February 10, 2021): 1–7.

Palmer, Brandon. *Fighting for the Enemy: Koreans in Japan's War, 1937–1945*. Seattle: University of Washington Press, 2013.

Park, Myung-lim. "The 'American Boundary,' Provocation, and the Outbreak of the Korean War." *Social Science Japan Journal* 1, no. 1 (April 1998): 31–56.

———. "The *Chaeya*." In *The Park Chung Hee Era: The Transformation of South Korea*, edited by Byung-Kook Kim and Ezra F. Vogel, 373–400. Cambridge, MA: Harvard University Press, 2011.

Park, S. Nathan. "Why South Korea's Liberals Are Defense Hawks." *Foreign Policy*, October 22, 2021. https://foreignpolicy.com/2021/10/22/south-korea-slbm-liberals-defense-hawks/.

Park, Tae Gyun. *An Ally and Empire: Two Myths of South Korea–United States Relations, 1945–1980*. Translated by Ilsoo David Cho. Seongnam: Academy of Korean Studies Press, 2012.

———. "Beyond the Myth: Reassessing the Security Crisis on the Korean Peninsula during the mid-1960s." *Pacific Affairs* 82, no. 1 (Spring 2009): 93–110.

———. "The Roles of the United States and Japan in the Development of South Korea's Science and Technology during the Cold War." *Korea Journal* 52, no. 1 (March 2012): 206–31.

Paupe, William. "The Korea Institute of Science and Technology (KIST)." November 17, 1981. US Agency for International Development. http://pdf.usaid.gov/pdf_docs/PNAAP798.pdf.

POSCO. "History of POSCO." Accessed June 22, 2023. https://www.posco.co.kr/homepage/docs/eng6/jsp/company/posco/s91a1000012c.jsp.

Prasad, Monica, and Andre Nickow. "Mechanisms of the 'Aid Curse': Lessons from South Korea and Pakistan." *Journal of Development Studies* 52, no. 11 (2016): 1612–27.

Prentice, Michael. *Supercorporate: Distinction and Participation in Post-Hierarchy South Korea*. Stanford, CA: Stanford University Press, 2022.

Radchenko, Sergey S. "The Soviet Union and the North Korean Seizure of the USS Pueblo: Evidence from the Russian Archives." Washington, DC: Woodrow Wilson International Center for Scholars, 2005.

Rees, David. *Korea: The Limited War*. Baltimore, MD: Penguin, 1964.

Rhyu, Sang-young. "Institutionalizing Property Rights in Korean Capitalism: A Case Study on the Listing of Samsung Life." In *The Rule of Law in South Korea*, edited by Jongryn Mo and David W. Brady, 159–88. Stanford, CA: Hoover Institution Press, 2010.

———. "Stirring Up Debate on a Korean Caesar." *Global Asia* 11, no. 4 (Winter 2016): 126–28.

Rhyu, Sang-young, and Seok-jin Lew. "Pohang Iron & Steel Company." In *The Park Chung Hee Era: The Transformation of South Korea*, edited by Byung-Kook Kim and Ezra F. Vogel, 322–44. Cambridge, MA: Harvard University Press, 2011.

Rim, Chicue, and Hoonyoung Lee. "The Effects of Korean Government's Defense Industry Fostering Policy on the Performance of Defense Industry Enterprises." International Public Procurement Conference. http://www.ippa.org/IPPC4/Proceedings/19Others/Paper19-3.pdf.

Robinson, Michael. *Cultural Nationalism in Colonial Korea, 1920–1925*. Seattle: University of Washington Press, 1988.

Samuels, Richard. *Rich Nation, Strong Army: National Security and the Technological Transformation of Japan*. Ithaca, NY: Cornell University Press, 1996.

Sanders, Ralph. *Arms Industries: New Suppliers and Regional Security*. Washington, DC: National Defense University Press, 1990.

Sarantakes, Nicholas Evan. "The Quiet War: Combat Operations along the Korean Demilitarized Zone, 1966–1969." *Journal of Military History* 64, no. 2 (April 2000): 439–57.

Scalapino, Robert A., and Chong-Sik Lee. *Communism in Korea*. 2 vols. Berkeley: University of California Press, 1972.

Schaefer, Bernd. "North Korean 'Adventurism' and China's Long Shadow, 1966–1972." Working Paper 44, Cold War International History Project. Washington, DC: Woodrow Wilson International Center for Scholars, 2004.

Seltzer, Nicholas. "Baekgom: The Development of South Korea's First Ballistic Missile." *Nonproliferation Review* 26, nos. 3–4 (2019): 289–327.

Shaw, William. "South Korean Foreign Military Sales (FMS) Program." Federal Research Division, Library of Congress, September 1984. https://apps.dtic.mil/sti/pdfs/ADA323767.pdf.

Sheen, Seong-ho. "South Korea's Overdue Defence Reforms." *East Asia Forum*, May 29, 2019. https://www.eastasiaforum.org/2019/05/29/south-koreas-overdue-defence-reforms/.

Shin, Eunjung, and Eric Welch. "Korean Science and Technology Policies." In *Routledge Handbook of Korean Politics and Public Administration*, edited by Chung-in Moon and M. Jae Moon, 466–83. London: Routledge, 2020.

Shin, Gi-Wook. *Ethnic Nationalism in Korea: Genealogy, Politics, and Legacy*. Stanford, CA: Stanford University Press, 2006.

Shin, Wookhee. *Dynamics of Patron-Client State Relations: The United States and Korean Political Economy in the Cold War*. Seoul: American Studies Institute of Seoul National University, 1993.

Slusser, Robert. "Soviet Far Eastern Policy, 1945–1950: Stalin's Goals in Korea." In *The Origins of the Cold War in Asia*, edited by Yonosuke Nagai and Akira Iriye, 123–46. Tokyo: University of Tokyo Press, 1977.

Stern, Joseph, Ji-hong Kim, Dwight Perkins, and Jung-ho Yoo. *Industrialization and the State: The Korean Heavy and Chemical Industry Drive*. Cambridge, MA: Harvard University Press, 1995.

Stubbs, Richard. "War and Economic Development: Export-Oriented Industrialization in East and Southeast Asia." *Comparative Politics* 31, no. 3 (April 1999): 337–55.

Suh, Dae-Sook. *Kim Il Sung: The North Korean Leader*. New York: Columbia University Press, 1988.

———. *Korean Communism, 1945–1980: A Reference Guide to the Political System*. Honolulu: University Press of Hawai'i, 1981.

Suh, Dae-Sook, Wam Bom Lee, and Seung Hyun Lee, eds. *North Korean Modern History: A Sourcebook*. 2 vols. Seongnam: Academy of Korean Studies Press, 2018.

Szalontai, Balázs. "In the Shadow of Vietnam: A New Look at North Korea's Militant Strategy, 1962–1970." *Journal of Cold War Studies* 14, no. 4 (Fall 2012): 122–66.

———. *Kim Il Sung in the Khrushchev Era: Soviet-DPRK Relations and the Roots of North Korean Despotism, 1953–1964*. Stanford, CA: Stanford University Press, 2005.

Szalontai, Balázs, and Sergey Radchenko. "North Korea's Efforts to Acquire Nuclear Technology and Nuclear Weapons: Evidence from Russian and Hungarian Archives." Washington, DC: Woodrow Wilson Center for International Scholars, 2006.

Tenold, Stig, J. Y. Kang, Song Kim, and Hugh Murphy. "International Transfer of Tacit Knowledge: The Transmission of Shipbuilding Skills from Scotland to South Korea in the Early 1970s." *Enterprise & Society* 22, no. 2 (June 2021): 335–67.

Tikhonov, Vladimir. "Militarism and Anti-Militarism in South Korea: 'Militarized Masculinity' and the Conscientious Objector Movement." *Asia-Pacific Journal: Japan Focus* 7, issue 12, no. 1 (2009): 1–35.

"Top 100 for 2022." *Defense News*. Accessed January 24, 2023. https://people.defensenews.com/top-100/.

Trading Economics. "South Korea Exports of Arms and Ammunition, Parts and Accessories to Saudi Arabia." Accessed June 7, 2023. https://tradingeconomics.com/south-korea/exports/saudi-arabia/arms-ammunition-parts-accessories.

Tsurumi, E. Patricia. "Colonial Education in Korea and Taiwan." In *The Japanese Colonial Empire, 1895–1945*, edited by Ramon H. Myers and Mark R. Peattie, 294–311. Princeton, NJ: Princeton University Press, 1984.

Uchiyama, Benjamin. "The Munitions Worker as Trickster in Wartime Japan." *Journal of Asian Studies* 76, no. 3 (August 2017): 655–74.

Vogel, Ezra. *The Four Little Dragons: The Spread of Industrialization in East Asia*. Cambridge, MA: Harvard University Press, 1991.

Wade, Robert. *Governing the Market: Economic Theory and the Role of Government in Taiwan's Industrialization*. Princeton, NJ: Princeton University Press, 1990.

Weathersby, Kathryn. "Dependence and Mistrust: North Korea's Relations with Moscow and the Evolution of Juche." US-Korea Institute Working Paper Series, WP 08-08, December 2008. https://www.jstor.org/stable/resrep11127.

Weiss, Linda. *America Inc.? Innovation and Enterprise in the National Security State*. Ithaca, NY: Cornell University Press, 2014.

Wolf, Charles, Jr., Donald P. Henry, K. C. Yeh, James H. Hayes, John Schank, and Richard L. Sneider. "The Changing Balance: South Korea and North Korean Capabilities for Long-Term Military Competition." Santa Monica, CA: RAND, December 1985. https://www.rand.org/content/dam/rand/pubs/reports/2007/R3305.1.pdf.

Woo, Jung-en. *Race to the Swift: State and Finance in Korean Industrialization*. New York: Columbia University Press, 1991.

Woo-Cumings, Meredith, ed. *The Developmental State*. Ithaca, NY: Cornell University Press, 1999.

Work, Clint. "The Long History of South Korea's OPCON Debate." *Diplomat*, November 1, 2017. https://thediplomat.com/2017/11/the-long-history-of-south-koreas-opcon-debate/.

World Bank. *The East Asian Miracle: Economic Growth and Public Policy*. Oxford: Oxford University Press, 1993.

Yang, Jae-jin. *The Political Economy of the Small Welfare State in South Korea*. New York: Cambridge University Press, 2017.

Yim, Yong Soon. "The Dynamics of North Korean Military Doctrine." In *The Two Koreas in World Politics*, edited by Tae-hwan Kwak with Wayne Patterson and Edward A. Olsen, 103–28. Seoul: Institute for Far Eastern Studies, Kyungnam University, 1983.

Yoo, Ilho. "Experience with Tax Reform in the Republic of Korea." *Asia-Pacific Development Journal* 7, no. 2 (December 2000): 75–104.

Yoo, Sangwoon. "Innovation in Practice: The 'Technology Drive Policy' and the 4Mb DRAM R&D Consortium in South Korea in the 1980s and 1990s." *Technology and Culture* 61, no. 2 (2020): 385–415.

Yoon, Hyun-Kun. "National Security: Defense, Development and Self-Reliance through Defense Industrialization: The Case of South Korea." PhD diss., University of Maryland, 1991.

Young, Louise. *Japan's Total Empire: Manchuria and the Culture of Wartime Imperialism*. Berkeley: University of California Press, 1998.

Media Clips, Films, and Television Shows

Ch'ŏmdan kukka ŭi ch'osŏk pangwi sanŏp [The defense industry, cornerstone of a scientifically advanced nation]. Television series. *Kukpang TV.* YouTube, posted 2015–21. https://www.youtube.com/playlist?list=PLMVkaEHUCNifGUe2cvYoJWUxdWUKEooaA.

———. Episode 6: "Pangwi sanŏp i ingt'ae han chunghwahak kongŏp" [Heavy and chemical industry conceived by the defense industry]. March 4, 2015. https://www.youtube.com/watch?v=53DiRLdcApA&list=PLMVkaEHUCNifGUe2cvYoJWUxdWUKEooaA&index=307.

———. Episode 29: "Puguk kangbyŏng ŭi pul kkot ŭl irŭk'ida: Hanwha" [Launching the flame for rich nation, strong army: Hanwha]. September 4, 2015. https://www.youtube.com/watch?v=zqbDcI4sza8&list=PLMVkaEHUCNifGUe2cvYoJWUxdWUKEooaA&index=284.

Kungnip Yŏnghwa Chejakso [National Film Production Center]. "Chikchang yebigun kyedo (Han'guk Hwayak kwa Taehan Sŏgyu Kongsa yebigun hullyŏn sanghwang)" [A record of the workplace reserve forces (reserve forces' training situation at Korea Explosives and the Korean National Oil Corporation)]. 1968. Video clip. File no. CEN0003299. Kukka Kirogwŏn [National Archives of Korea].

———. "Mangjŏn p'irwi" [Disaster avoidance strategy]. 1978. Video clip. File no. CEN0005398. Kukka Kirogwŏn [National Archives of Korea]. https://theme.archives.go.kr/next/movie/viewMovieDetail.do?archiveEvntId=0052374276.

Kwak, Chŏnghyŏn. Recorded testimony, oral histories, Saemaul Undong Archives (online). http://archives.saemaul.com:81/oralrecord/video/93/0.

Taehan Min'guk Yŏksa Pangmulgwan [National Museum of Korean Contemporary History]. "Rise of the Defense Industry in the 1970s: Building the Foundation for Independent National Defense." Accessed February 3, 2023. https://www.much.go.kr/en/contents.do?fid=03&cid=03_10.

Yi Kyuyŏn ŭi sŭp'ot'ŭrait'ŭ [Yi Kyuyŏn's spotlight]. Episode 152, "Yi Kyŏngsŏ Paksa ŭi chŭngŏn: Haek kip'ok changch'i kaebal hago issŏtta" [Testimony of Dr. Yi Kyŏngsŏ: They were developing a nuclear detonator]. *T'ŭkpyŏl ch'wijae! Hanbando 'haek samgukchi'* [Special coverage! The Korean peninsula's "nuclear three kingdoms"]. Aired June 21, 2018, on JBTC. Accessed April 1, 2021. https://vod.jtbc.co.kr/player/clip/v010232379. As of 2022, this episode was no longer available for viewing on this website.

Index

Harvard East Asian Monographs

(most recent titles)

421. James McMullen, *The Worship of Confucius in Japan*
422. Nobuko Toyosawa, *Imaginative Mapping: Landscape and Japanese Identity in the Tokugawa and Meiji Eras*
423. Pierre Fuller, *Famine Relief in Warlord China*
424. Diane Wei Lewis, *Powers of the Real: Cinema, Gender, and Emotion in Interwar Japan*
425. Maram Epstein, *Orthodox Passions: Narrating Filial Love during the High Qing*
426. Margaret Wan, *Regional Literature and the Transmission of Culture: Chinese Drum Ballads, 1800–1937*
427. Takeshi Watanabe, *Flowering Tales: Women Exorcising History in Heian Japan*
428. Jürgen P. Melzer, *Wings for the Rising Sun: A Transnational History of Japanese Aviation*
429. Edith Sarra, *Unreal Houses: Character, Gender, and Genealogy in the* Tale of Genji
430. Yi Gu, *Chinese Ways of Seeing and Open-Air Painting*
431. Robert Cliver, *Red Silk: Class, Gender, and Revolution in China's Yangzi Delta Silk Industry*
432. Kenneth J. Ruoff, *Japan's Imperial House in the Postwar Era, 1945–2019*
433. Erin L. Brightwell, *Reflecting the Past: Place, Language, and Principle in Japan's Medieval Mirror Genre*
434. Janet Borland, *Earthquake Children: Building Resilience from the Ruins of Tokyo*
435. Susan Blakely Klein, *Dancing the Dharma: Religious and Political Allegory in Japanese Noh Theater*
436. Yukyung Yeo, *Varieties of State Regulation: How China Regulates Its Socialist Market Economy*
437. Robert Goree, *Printing Landmarks: Popular Geography and* Meisho Zue *in Late Tokugawa Japan*
438. Lawrence C. Reardon, *A Third Way: The Origins of China's Current Economic Development Strategy*
439. Eyck Freymann, *One Belt One Road: Chinese Power Meets the World*
440. Yung Chul Park, Joon Kyung Kim, and Hail Park, *Financial Liberalization and Economic Development in Korea, 1980–2020*
441. Steven B. Miles, *Opportunity in Crisis: Cantonese Migrants and the State in Late Qing China*

442. Grace C. Huang, *Chiang Kai-shek's Politics of Shame: Leadership, Legacy, and National Identity in China*
443. Adam J. Lyons, *Karma and Punishment: Prison Chaplaincy in Japan*
444. Craig A. Smith, *Chinese Asianism, 1894–1945*
445. Sachiko Kawai, *Uncertain Powers: Sen'yōmon-in and Landownership by Royal Women in Early Medieval Japan*
446. Juliane Noth, *Transmedial Landscapes and Modern Chinese Painting*
447. Susan Westhafer Furukawa, *The Afterlife of Toyotomi Hideyoshi: Historical Fiction and Popular Culture in Japan*
448. Nongji Zhang, *Legal Scholars and Scholarship in the People's Republic of China: The First Generation (1949–1992)*
449. Han Sang Kim, *Cine-Mobility: Twentieth-Century Transformations in Korea's Film and Transportation*
450. Brian Hurley, *Confluence and Conflict: Reading Transwar Japanese Literature and Thought*
451. Simon Avenell, *Asia and Postwar Japan: Deimperialization, Civic Activism, and National Identity*
452. Maura Dykstra, *Uncertainty in the Empire of Routine: The Administrative Revolution of the Eighteenth-Century Qing State*
453. Marnie S. Anderson, *In Close Association: Local Activist Networks in the Making of Japanese Modernity, 1868–1920*
454. John D. Wong, *Hong Kong Takes Flight: Commercial Aviation and the Making of a Global Hub, 1930s–1998*
455. Martin K. Whyte and Mary C. Brinton, compilers, *Remembering Ezra Vogel*
456. Lawrence Zhang, *Power for a Price: The Purchase of Appointments in Qing China*
457. J. Megan Greene, *Building a Nation at War: Transnational Knowledge Networks and the Development of China during and after World War II*
458. Miya Qiong Xie, *Territorializing Manchuria: The Transnational Frontier and Literatures of East Asia*
459. Dal Yong Jin, *Understanding Korean Webtoon Culture: Transmedia Storytelling, Digital Platforms, and Genres*
460. Takahiro Yamamoto, *Demarcating Japan: Imperialism, Islanders, and Mobility, 1855–1884*
461. Elad Alyagon, *Inked: Tattooed Soldiers and the Song Empire's Penal-Military Complex*
462. Börje Ljunggren and Dwight H. Perkins, eds., *Vietnam: Navigating a Rapidly Changing Economy, Society, and Political Order*
463. En Li, *Betting on the Civil Service Examinations: The Lottery in Late Qing China*
464. Matthieu Felt, *Meanings of Antiquity: Myth Interpretation in Premodern Japan*
465. William D. Fleming, *Strange Tales from Edo: Rewriting Chinese Fiction in Early Modern China*
466. Mark Baker, *Pivot of China: Spatial Politics and Inequality in Modern Zhengzhou*
467. Peter Banseok Kwon, *Cornerstone of the Nation: The Defense Industry and the Building of Modern Korea under Park Chung Hee*